State, Society,
and the Elementary School
in Imperial Germany

State, Society, and the Elementary School in Imperial Germany

Marjorie Lamberti

New York   Oxford
Oxford University Press
1989

Oxford University Press

Oxford   New York   Toronto
Delhi   Bombay   Calcutta   Madras   Karachi
Petaling Jaya   Singapore   Hong Kong   Tokyo
Nairobi   Dar es Salaam   Cape Town
Melbourne   Auckland

and associated companies in
Berlin   Ibadan

Copyright © 1989 by Oxford University Press, Inc.

Published by Oxford University Press, Inc.,
200 Madison Avenue, New York, New York 10016

Oxford is a registered trademark of Oxford University Press

Library of Congress Cataloging-in-Publication Data
Lamberti, Marjorie, 1937–
State, society, and the elementary school
in imperial Germany
Marjorie Lamberti.
p.   cm.
Bibliography: p.
Includes index.
ISBN 0-19-505611-6
1. Education, Elementary—Germany—History—19th century.
2. Education, Elementary—Germany—History—20th century.
3. Education and state—Germany—History—19th century.
4. Education and state—Germany—History—20th century   I. Title.
LA723.L36 1989   88-30283
372.943—dc 19

9 8 7 6 5 4 3 2 1

Printed in the United States of America
on acid-free paper

for my brother Jim

Acknowledgements

For the happiness I enjoyed during the years of my research for this book, I wish to thank the archivists and librarians at the institutions where I worked. The completion of my book owes much to their generous help and willingness to fulfill my numerous requests with utmost courtesy and efficiency. The Hessisches Staatsarchiv in Marburg proved to be an ideal place to begin my research; it prepared me well for my subsequent investigations in the Geheimes Staatsarchiv in Berlin-Dahlem and the Zentrales Staatsarchiv in Merseburg in 1979, and in the Hauptstaatsarchiv in Düsseldorf and the Landeshauptarchiv in Koblenz in 1982. In the Staatsbibliothek preussischer Kulturbesitz in Berlin, the Universitätsbibliothek in Düsseldorf, and the Stadtbibliothek in Mönchengladbach, I was deeply moved by the kindness shown to a visiting scholar from another country. The Sterling Memorial Library at Yale University has had a special place in my life for many years, as a youth growing up in New Haven, as a graduate student, and as a scholar. At the Starr Library at Middlebury College, Fleur Laslocky, Mark Proctor, and Hans Raum were supportive and friendly when I requested interlibrary loan material and facilities in the microfilm reading room.

Generous financial assistance made it possible for me to travel and live abroad. I received a research fellowship from the National Endowment for the Humanities in 1981–1982, and many grants from the Middlebury College Faculty Research Fund. One grant covered the expenses of typing my manuscript with a word processor, which my neighbor Helene Rieff did with cheerfulness and patience.

When I needed constructive criticism, encouragement, and hope, I had the good fortune to find support in fellow scholars. I wish to express my gratitude to Margaret Anderson, Kenneth Barkin, Peter Demetz, Geoff Eley, Peter Gay, Konrad Jarausch, and Vernon Lidtke. Vernon Lidtke and Kenneth Barkin commented on papers that I presented at the annual meetings of the American Historical Association (1984) and the German Studies Association (1986). Konrad Jarausch read one of the papers after the meeting and was kind enough to send me a lengthy commentary with much sound advice. Geoff Eley read my manuscript and offered many good suggestions for its revision. His critical comments made the task of revising my manuscript an experience of great intellectual pleasure. The advice of Paul Schlotthauer, associate editor at Oxford University Press, and the queries of Stewart Perkins, who copyedited my manuscript, helped me to make further improvements.

Contents

Chronology

*The dates for the terms of office of the ministers of education are taken from Reinhard Lüdicke, *Die preussischen Kultusminister und ihre Beamten* (Stuttgart, 1918), Appendix II.

1854   The introduction of Ferdinand Stiehl's *Regulative* of October 1, 2, and 3, on the curriculums of the Protestant elementary schools and the teachers' seminaries

1858   The appointment of Moritz August von Bethmann Hollweg as the minister of education (November 6, 1858–March 12, 1862)

1862   The appointment of Heinrich von Mühler as the minister of education (March 19, 1862–January 17, 1872)

1869   Mühler's failure to obtain the passage of the school bills of 1868 and 1869 in the Prussian House of Deputies

1872   The appointment of Adalbert Falk as the minister of education (January 22, 1872–July 14, 1879)

            The enactment of the Prussian School Supervision Law of March 11, 1872

            The removal of Polish Catholic priests from school inspection offices

            The introduction of the General Regulations of October 15 on the organization and curriculum of the Prussian elementary schools

1873   The directives of the provincial governors of Posen and East and West Prussia on the use of German as the language of instruction for Polish schoolchildren

1874   The secularization of the county school inspectorate for the Catholic schools in the Rhineland

1874–1876   The removal of a large number of parish priests in the Rhineland from their offices as local school inspectors and from the direction of religious instruction in the schools

1875–1876   Massive Catholic demonstrations in the Rhineland against the *Kulturkampf* in the school system

1876   Falk's decree of February 18 on Catholic religious instruction in the elementary schools

            The founding of the Union for the Preservation of the Evangelical Elementary Schools on September 6

1879   The appointment of Robert von Puttkamer as the minister of education (July 13, 1879–June 17, 1881)

            Puttkamer's announcement of September 8, promising to reinstate Catholic priests in local school inspection offices

            The minister's instructions of November 5 on readmitting Catholic priests to the schools to direct religious education

1881   The appointment of Gustav von Gossler as the minister of education (June 17, 1881–March 12, 1891)

1886   The enactment of the Law of July 15 on the Appointment of School Teachers in the Region of the Provinces of Posen and West Prussia

1887   The enactment of the fiscally conservative Law of May 26 on Setting Requirements for the Elementary Schools

1889   Emperor William's Cabinet Order of May 1 on the use of the elementary schools to counteract the spread of socialist ideas

1890–1891   The political conflict over Gossler's school bill from December 1890 until the government's withdrawal of the bill on May 4, 1891

1891   The appointment of Robert von Zedlitz-Trützschler as the minister of education (March 12, 1891–March 23, 1892)

1892   The political conflict over Zedlitz's school bill from January until the government's withdrawal of the bill on April 28

            The appointment of Robert von Bosse as the minister of education (March 23, 1892–September 2, 1899)

1894   The minister's edict of March 16, reintroducing the instruction of Polish reading and writing on a limited scale in the schools in the province of Posen

1899   The appointment of Konrad Studt as the minister of education (September 2, 1899–June 24, 1907)

1904   The school compromise of the Conservative, Free Conservative, and National Liberal parties in the Prussian House of Deputies on May 13

1906   The enactment of the Prussian Law of July 28 on the Maintenance of the Public Elementary Schools

1906–1907   The school strikes of Polish children in the provinces of Posen and West Prussia

1907   The appointment of Ludwig Holle as the minister of education (June 24, 1907–July 14, 1909)

1909   The appointment of August von Trott zu Solz as the minister of education (July 14, 1909–July 14, 1917)

State, Society,
and the Elementary School
in Imperial Germany

Introduction

This study of the elementary school in Prussia began with the question of why the largest state in the German Empire, which had a government that was preoccupied with social and national integration and a political culture that was deeply affected by the ideology of nationalism, had a public elementary school system that served to reinforce religious particularism through its confessionally divided organization and its confessionally oriented textbooks and instruction. Confessional schooling remained the predominant form of elementary education for Catholics and Protestants in the Prussian state throughout the nineteenth century despite the changes that came in the wake of national unification, industrialization, and urbanization. Neither the secular school nor the interconfessional school providing a common educational experience for all children without distinction as to church affiliation ever took hold. The interconfessional school (the so-called *Simultanschule*), in which the Catholic, Jewish, and Protestant religions were taught to the pupils of each faith in separate classes as one subject in an otherwise religiously neutral curriculum, was the pedagogic ideal of a large number of schoolteachers in Prussia. They saw it as a means of diminishing church influence in the schools as well as promoting tolerance and social harmony in a confessionally segmented nation. When a school law was enacted in 1906 after more than fifty years of political controversy over the school question and abortive school bills, it categorized the interconfessional school as the exception to the rule. A legal seal was put on the prevailing practice of having children and teachers of one and the same faith in a school.

Although the confessional public school under the supervision of school inspectors who were clergy by vocation appeared to the schoolteachers to be an anachronism in a modern society, it survived the

3

revolution of 1918 and the efforts of the Socialists to abolish the instruction of religion in the schools. In the Weimar Republic the Social Democrats did not succeed in establishing a secular school system for the entire nation, and no more successful were the German Democrats who sought to make the interconfessional school the only legally valid norm. Under a compromise negotiated by the Center, German Democratic, and Social Democratic parties and embodied in Article 146 of the constitution of August 11, 1919, the interconfessional "community school" was to be designated as the rule in the school law for the Reich, and under certain conditions confessional and secular schools could also exist. In the 1920s Center politicians, yielding to the intransigent views of the Catholic episcopacy, altered their understanding of the "Weimar school compromise," and the interpretation of the school articles of the constitution was now passionately disputed by the political parties. Because Article 174 prohibited the federal states from changing the existing organization of their school systems until the enactment of the Reich school law, the stalemate produced by the failure of repeated attempts to pass school legislation in the Reichstag enabled confessional schooling to thrive. Throughout the era of the Weimar Republic the confessional school retained its ascendancy in Prussia. While nonconfessional school systems prevailed in the states of Baden, Hesse, Saxony, and Thuringia and in the city-states of Bremen and Hamburg, about 4 percent of the schools in Prussia were nonconfessional by 1931. Attending schools of their own confession were 92 percent of the Catholic schoolchildren and 95 percent of the Protestant schoolchildren in Prussia.[1]

The first stage of my research was concentrated on the Wilhelminian era—a period I knew well from my earlier study of the Jewish experience of discrimination in the Prussian elementary school system and the lobbying activity of Jewish interest groups in school politics. My studies generated more questions than explanations, and I soon discovered that the answers that I sought had to be found by moving back in time, first to the years before 1870 when the state and the church were close partners in the administration of the schools, and then to the *Kulturkampf* era when the Ministry of Education under Adalbert Falk adopted the program of school reforms championed by the liberal parties throughout the 1860s.

In the course of my research, I learned that the *Kulturkampf* had a tremendous if somewhat uneven impact on the elementary school system in Prussia; yet historians in the past have hardly examined how this struggle intruded into the school system in the Catholic Rhineland and in the Polish-speaking areas of the Prussian state. Erich Schmidt-Volkmar and other scholars who have written studies of the *Kulturkampf* in

Prussia do not discuss the fight that the state waged against the Catholic church in the schools beyond the enactment of the School Supervision Law of 1872.[2] The sole major biography of Falk written by Erich Foerster in the 1920s offers a superficial and uncritical account of school politics during his years in office, without any analysis of how the school reforms were carried out, how the Catholic and Protestant clergy and laity reacted, and why Falk failed as a school reformer.[3]

Furthermore, I found that historical research on the making of the school law from 1850 to 1906 was meager and that the government activity and party politics that finally produced the Elementary School Maintenance Law of July 28, 1906, had not been the subject of historical investigation at all. The promise contained in the Prussian constitution of 1850 that the organization and administration of the schools would be regulated by law rather than by the will of the school bureaucracy was not fulfilled until 1906. During this long interval every minister of education with two exceptions tried to enact a school law without success.

In contrast to the politically successful and yet historically neglected school bill of 1905–1906, the abortive school bills of the early 1890s have long found a place in the historical scholarship of imperial Germany. These fragmentary accounts of the political battle over the school law have generally taken two directions. J. Alden Nichols and J.C.G. Röhl discuss the school bills of the early 1890s in the context of the political strategy of the imperial chancellor, who sought to secure the support of the Center party for government bills in the Reichstag with the concession of a school law.[4] Folkert Meyer and Hartmut Titze depict the school bill of 1892 as a kind of *Kampfgesetz* (legal offensive) against Social Democracy, arguing that the Prussian state government in the imperial era put the school in the service of combatting socialism.[5] Both interpretations rest on the mistaken assumption that it was state officials who took the initiative. As a result, they do not illuminate the actual problems that led groups in society and in the House of Deputies to put pressure on the government to introduce a school bill. The second interpretation suffers from the graver flaw of making the fear of socialism the leitmotif of school politics in Prussia during the imperial era. The contention that the state used the school as "an instrument in the class struggle from above" and that opposition to Social Democracy united the National Liberals and the Conservatives—parties that had not agreed on the school question since the 1860s—to pass a reactionary school bill in 1906 offers no more than an attenuated and crude explanation of what actually happened.[6]

Since 1970, historians have studied the relations between the school, society, and political power in nineteenth-century Prussia with a more critical appreciation of how the social policies of the state government and the class structure affected the educational system. This research has deepened our understanding of the socialization function that the state assigned to the school and has subjected to critical scrutiny commonplace assumptions connecting schooling with social mobility and economic modernization, but it has not always done justice to the diversity of influences in society that shaped the history of the elementary school. Many problems of interpretation arise from the inadequacy and lack of subtlety of the organizing concepts used to reconstruct the past.[7]

The thesis that the General Civil Code of 1794 began the *Verstaatlichung* (nationalization) of the school, a process in which the state removed the church from the province of the school and took exclusive possession of the school for its own political and social purposes, fosters a tunnel vision of the history of the Prussian elementary school focusing on the expanding controls and interventions of the state.[8] This view produces misleading impressions about the intent and implementation of the School Supervision Law of 1872. The *Staatsschule* (state school) was not the outcome of the law. Substantial collaboration between the state and the church characterized the school administration in Prussia until the end of the monarchy in 1918. A more profound understanding of school policy and the administration of the schools in Prussia can only be acquired when historians address the question of why the concept of the school as a state institution was not rigorously applied except in the eastern districts, where the government used the school to germanize the Polish population.

This historical approach minimizes as well how much the progress of the school system depended on the local community, which bore the responsibility for school maintenance. The state's investment in elementary education was paltry up to 1870 and thereafter quite modest. Grave deficiencies prevailed in the rural schools in the provinces east of the Elbe River. School conditions never matched the high reputation that the Prussian *Volksschule* (elementary school) enjoyed abroad. Hindering the improvement of school facilities was an inefficient and unjust system of school maintenance based on obsolete regulations in the General Civil Code of 1794. In most parts of East Elbia the manorial lords were not counted among the householders who were obliged to pay the school tax. In the provinces of East and West Prussia where the school regulation of 1845 abolished the school tax exemption of the landed nobility, the estate owners who had little interest in the education of peasant children kept school expenditures down to a bare minimum. The question of who should pay for school maintenance became an issue of judicial litigation and public strife. Rather than accepting the principle of equality before the law and assuming responsibility for school maintenance, the Conservative agrarians preferred to exploit their political influence to obtain state subsidies that relieved rural school districts of much of the burden of school costs. During his long term in office Bismarck blocked the attempts to reform the policies on school maintenance, and after his resignation the seat of resistance shifted to the Ministry of Finance.

The concept of the school as an instrument of social control to train the lower classes to be obedient and loyal to the state authorities, and industrious and contented in their humble occupations, has been a belabored theme in recent historical literature on education.[9] Historians have used this concept to describe the achievement of social integration in imperial Germany as well as to explain the survival of confessional schooling and the failure of school reform in Prussia. Meyer and Titze argue that beginning in 1890 the Prussian state adopted a new policy for fighting Social Democracy, renouncing repression in favor of a strategy of immunizing the lower classes against socialist agitation by the indoctrination of the youth in the schools. In Meyer's view, the state's struggle against socialism had a retarding effect on the modernization of the school system. The government preserved the confessional character of the schools and expected the instruction of religion together with history to provide the pupils with an ideological shield against socialism. Although demographic mobility increased the confessional mixture of the population in many localities, the school authorities gave preference to the opening of one-classroom schools for Catholic and Protestant minorities over the organization of interconfessional schools.[10] The evidence for this interpretation stems from the Cabinet Order of May 1, 1889, which expressed Emperor William's wish to "make the elementary schools useful in counteracting the spread of Socialist and Communist ideas," and the rhetoric of the politicians of the Center and Conservative parties who defended the confessional school and the traditional relationship between the church and the school with allusions to the threat of revolutionary socialism.

The Cabinet Order of May 1, 1889, is probably the most frequently cited statement of government policy in the historical documentation for the elementary school in imperial Germany. From the point of view of its execution, however, it is one of the least known policies of the Prussian school administration. Many historians have attributed immense significance to the language of the emperor's decree without examining how school officials and teachers implemented it. Given the dearth of evidence, Geoff Eley's skeptical approach toward the imperial decree and the measures taken by the school administration to ensure ideological conformity and national integration was well warranted.[11] Wolfgang Kopitzsch's recent investigation of the implementation of the imperial order in Schleswig-Holstein points to the conclusion that many earlier works have grossly overstated the practical effects of William's words.[12]

The Ministry of Education did not act swiftly to carry out the king's wish. Only after a delay of eighteen months did the minister issue a directive to the provincial administration. No sense of urgency was felt in the ministry because officials there did not think that William had uncovered any real deficiency in the patriotic content of the history books already in use in the schools.[13] In Schleswig-Holstein, as Kopitzsch's research shows, the imperial order did not produce any substantial changes in the curriculum of the teachers' seminaries and in the examinations for the teacher's certificate. The fight against Social Democracy did not become a central concern of the clerical officials who supervised the schools. The school inspectors continued to regard the instruction of religion as the best means of fortifying the hearts of the youth against the appeals of socialist propaganda. Very seldom did the teachers adopt a pedagogic strategy of combatting Social Democracy directly. Instead, they continued to instill in their pupils a loyalty to the fatherland and a respect for the established political system by extolling the heroism and benevolence of the rulers of Prussia in the traditional manner of teaching history. The history lessons could hardly cover more than royal biography. After 1889 the time devoted to the instruction of history was still only two hours per week, and in overcrowded schools with half-day sessions barely one hour was available for the subject.[14]

The Cabinet Order of 1889 did not bring about an intense politicization of school instruction, as some historians claim. More than a decade later, Albert Grimpen, an ultranationalist pedagogue, began to agitate for an antisocialist orientation in the teaching of history and for an increase in the time allotted for the history lessons. He deplored the priority still given to religious instruction and the preparation of the schoolchildren for church life and contended that the expectation of state officials that Social Democracy could be repelled in this manner would meet with disappointment.[15]

Besides presenting an overblown description of the politicization of elementary education, the thesis that the Prussian state used the schools as a *Herrschaftsinstrument* (instrument of social control) in its struggle against Social Democracy does not provide a sound conceptual framework for understanding the persistence of anachronistic features in the school system and the making of school policy in the imperial era. By emphasizing political manipulation and control from above, it underestimates the significance of the opinions and preferences of the clients served by the schools and the social and cultural determinants of school policy. By focusing on antisocialism, it obscures the government's use of the schools to suppress the Polish nationality and the political conflicts that arose from Polish resistance to the policy of germanizing the school-children. Despite the strategies devised by the state government to achieve social integration, Prussia remained a segmented society with confessional and ethnic divisions that ran as deep as the class antagonisms. The intensity of confessional identity and solidarity in Prussian society, the lively consciousness of the historical hostilities and doctrinal differences separating the Catholics and the Protestants, and the anti-Catholicism of Protestant churchmen and the National Liberal bourgeoisie, had a greater effect on the organization of the school system than historians have hitherto recognized.

Far from being a specialized and isolated section of historical inquiry, the study of the Prussian *Volksschule* in society and politics does make a major contribution to the reexamination of the history of the *Kaiserreich* (empire) that has been underway since the 1970s. The politics of school reform during the *Kulturkampf* provides a new perspective for understanding the nature and meaning of the political campaign against the Catholic church and the seemingly "unliberal" politics of the German liberals, divided after 1867 into the National Liberal party and the Progressive party further to the Left. The political conflicts over the schools that broke out in the cities of the Rhineland show that the *Kulturkampf* was more than a clash between the Bismarckian state and the church. Historical accounts of this battle that dwell on Bismarck's political calculation and manipulatory strategies relate a small part of the story and miss altogether the resonance that the *Kulturkampf* had for the liberal bourgeoisie.[16] The agitation for school reform conducted by the liberals in the Prussian parliament and in urban politics, at first as an opposition party in the 1860s and then in an alignment with Bismarck's government in the 1870s, puts in sharp focus the active participation of the liberals in the opening and the implementation of the *Kulturkampf*.

School politics gives a concreteness to the clash that is seldom found in analyses that trace the antagonism between the liberals and the Catholics to different concepts of the state. It is essential to restore to the history of the *Kulturkampf* the political passion and moral fervor with which the liberals fought and the Catholics resisted. Only with such a view can we discern its profound effect on popular politics. Those areas deeply affected by the *Kulturkampf* in the schools also witnessed the transformation of the party of notables to the party of mass membership.[17]

Probably better than any other aspect of liberal politics during the 1870s, the school reform movement reveals what the *Kulturkampf* essentially meant to the liberals and what their fundamental concerns and objectives were. The evaluation of the political behavior of the National Liberals during these years has been generally negative in historical scholarship. Their anticlerical ideology and their support of the coercion employed by the state government against the Catholics have led historians to criticize them for squandering their political and moral energies in a struggle against political Catholicism when they should have been striving to advance the development of constitutional government and liberties in the new empire. These interpretations, which present the politics of the National Liberals exclusively in terms of their assertion of the supremacy of the state's authority and chastise them for abandoning the principles of freedom that an earlier generation had defended in 1848–1850, do not explain adequately their purposes for attacking the social and cultural power of the church.[18] The propaganda for school reform brings out clearly the idealistic political ethos of the liberals, and the lack of popular consent to their reform program indicates why they were maneuvered into a repressive campaign against the Catholic clergy. The *Kulturkampf* reflected not only their views on the sovereignty of the state in the administration of education but also their hopes for social progress, civic emancipation, and a tolerant society released from the shackles of religious superstition.[19]

The *Kulturkampf* was, as the propaganda for school reform demonstrates so well, related to the constructive functions of nation-state building. For the liberals educational reform was the logical accompaniment of political unification. Their fight against a confessionally divided school system under clerical supervision was waged with the intention of using education to break down religious particularism, to foster cultural integration, to establish the primacy of the citizen's loyalty to the nation-state, and to nationalize the consciousness of the German people.[20]

The school conflicts of the 1870s also open up a promising line of historical inquiry into the political mobilization of the Catholic population and the initial expansion of the Center party's constituency. Recent studies of the *Kulturkampf* have put a greater emphasis on the structural differences of the Protestant liberal bourgeoisie and the rural and petty bourgeois Catholic population, and have argued that the Catholic opposition was generated by hostility to laissez-faire liberalism, large-scale capitalism, and urban interests.[21] Although this research has added a valuable socioeconomic dimension to the historiography of the *Kulturkampf*, such interpretations run the risk of underestimating the importance of religious and cultural influences in Catholic behavior. As Josef Becker contends in his monumental history of the *Kulturkampf* in Baden, socioeconomic tensions provided the Catholic movement with a social substratum and a political potential, but this potential would not have been activated without the *Kulturkampf.*[22] His contention that the school question was the catalyst in the emergence of Catholicism's opposition to liberalism applies to Prussia as well. Popular politics in the Rhineland was heavily influenced by the hotly contested school issue. Here the 1870s witnessed the appearance of well-organized local party clubs with a mass membership.[23]

School politics and the debates over the school law from 1890 to 1906 offer a new perspective for examining the place of the Center party in Wilhelminian politics. After much of the antichurch legislation was dismantled at the end of the 1880s, the Center party began to move out of political isolation and to become a governmental party. When the number of Conservatives and National Liberals in the Reichstag declined, the stable block of votes from the Center party became indispensable for the passage of military, tariff, and fiscal bills. The alignment of the Center party with the Conservatives rather than the Progressives and the Social Democrats was of crucial importance for the democratization of Germany. Its participation in a "reform block" was essential if the parties of the Left were to achieve parliamentary control of the government.

In discussing the reasons for the Center's refusal to ally with the Left, David Blackbourn points out that the material interests of its rural and small-town constituency and the grievances nurtured by a "backward" Catholic subculture separated the Center from the Progressives and the Social Democrats. The new generation of Center leaders, he adds, were socially ambitious laymen who wanted the Catholics to gain respectability and public influence, and who cultivated the goodwill of high state officials. This argument, valid as it is, has some drawbacks. In overstating the "declericalization" of the leadership of the Center party and its new secular concern with economic issues, he reduces the party essentially to "a vehicle of the economic interests" of its supporters.[24]

After the *Kulturkampf*, religious and cultural issues were not pushed to the sidelines by the Center's involvement in legislation concerning economic and military matters. Its opposition to the legacy of the *Kulturkampf* in the schools and defense of confessional schooling and clerical supervision of the schools remained constant and lively. On these issues a wide chasm separated the Catholics from the Progressives and the Socialists. The Catholics' uncompromising commitment to confessional schooling was a key determinant for the Center party in the decision to select the Conservatives as an ally.[25] The Catholics' dependence on the support of Protestant Conservatives during the school conflicts of the 1870s continued in the debates over the school law in the Wilhelminian era.

The passionate involvement of the political parties in school issues underscores the need to modify the widely held picture of political life in imperial Germany with economic pressure groups and demagogic nationalistic leagues in the foreground. Cultural goals and religious loyalties determined political behavior as much as material interests.[26] The school conflicts in the Catholic Rhineland and the Polish-speaking areas in the eastern provinces show a political landscape with more diversity than is conveyed by the image of Prussia associated with the heartland of Protestant culture and Junker ascendancy east of the Elbe River. Solidarities based on religion and nationality and reinforced by geographic segregation were a salient feature of the society and public life of nineteenth-century Prussia.

1

The School System before 1870

Through most of the nineteenth century the public elementary school in Prussia was de jure an institution of the state but de facto an institution of the church through the clergy's virtual monopoly of school inspection offices and the precedence given to confessional religious instruction in the curriculum. So extensive was church influence in the public school system that Catholic Bishop Wilhelm von Ketteler of Mainz was moved to praise the Protestant monarchy in the north. In 1867 he wrote that a peaceful solution of the school question, which had kindled a bitter conflict between the state and the Catholic church in Baden, was already present in Prussia, in the practices of the school administration and in the constitution of 1850.[1] The bishop's depiction of the Prussian school administration as a model for the other German states to emulate is a poignant reminder of a point that has not always been fully appreciated in modern historical scholarship. The *Volksschule* in Prussia was not an affair of the state alone. The traditional partnership of the church and the state in the supervision of the schools was put on a secure and enduring foundation when the constitution recognized the church, the local community, and the state as social entities with legitimate interests and formal rights in the public schools.

The Partnership of Church and State

The General Civil Code of 1794 defined the *Volksschule* as an institution of the state but did not consistently carry out this principle. While the civil code proclaimed that the schools were under the supervision of the state authorities, it also recognized the church's historical ties to the schools and entrusted school supervision to the superintendents of the church dioceses and the parish clergy. The local pastors or priests inspected the schools, watched the work and personal conduct of the schoolmasters, and reported any deficiency or disorder to the civil and church authorities.[2] Adding to the ambiguity of the school's institutional nature was the continuation of the *Küsterschule* in which the teacher served also as the church organist and sexton. In many villages the school remained an extension of the parish church. The parish and civic community held in common school property and endowments and negotiated over the contributions to be made for the teacher's salary. The connection of school and church offices made the teacher a servant of the pastor or priest and the parishioners. Besides playing the organ at liturgical services, he kept the church in good repair, cleaned the pews, and rang the tower bells. In the course of the nineteenth century this practice faded away slowly, and as late as 1901 nearly 20 percent of the male teachers were still in offices that required them to fulfill the duties of a church organist.[3]

When State Chancellor Karl von Hardenberg established the Ministry of Education and Religious Affairs in 1817, he merged the two departments for church and school affairs housed in the Ministry of the Interior. In effect, he acknowledged that in Prussia a clear bureaucratic separation between the functions of education and religious life could not be made. His choice for the new office was Karl von Altenstein, a moderate reformer who prevented the forces of reaction from taking over the school administration completely during the *Vormärz*. During his years in office from 1817 to 1840, reforms in teacher training and the certification of teachers were introduced. The reforms were brought to a halt by his successor, Friedrich von Eichhorn, who discerned in the professionalization of elementary teaching a potential threat to the social status quo. A conservative with a pietistic outlook, Eichhorn shielded the historical bond between the school and the church against the challenge of modern pedagogic and political thinking in the 1840s, a time of social unrest among the teachers.[4]

The execution of the minister's school policies and orders and the supervision of the schools were responsibilities assigned to the district governors and school officials in the twenty-five provincial districts. The advent of a school bureaucracy did not displace clerical influence in the schools because many *Schulräte* (school officials) had studied theology and were ordained. Nor did the creation of a school bureaucracy lead to a highly centralized administration. No school law for the entire kingdom was promulgated during the first half of the century. Because school ordinances were issued by the district governments, regulations concerning the appointment of schoolteachers and other matters varied from one provincial district to another.

The supervision of the schools on the county level was entrusted to the superintendents of the Protestant Territorial church and the archdeacons of the Catholic church. Although the Catholic Elementary School Regulation of 1801 in Silesia stated that the school inspectorate should not be regarded as an *officium perpetuum* of the archdeacons and that the two offices could be separated, this clause was never applied.[5] The bishop of Breslau enjoyed the prerogative of selecting the county inspectors for the Catholic schools in Silesia. Altenstein tightened the link between the two offices in 1823 when he announced that the release of church superintendents from the duties of school inspection was "an exception to the rule" that could be permitted only if old age and frail health made it necessary to lighten their work.[6] The church superintendents and archdeacons did not have sufficient time to make frequent or thorough visitations to the village schools scattered across their deaneries. When the county inspector did visit a school, he examined the pupils in order to evaluate their achievement and the effectiveness of the teachers' instruction. His judgment of the classroom performance and moral behavior of the teachers was recorded in an annual report to the district government.

In comparison, the parish pastor in the office of local school inspector was a more visible figure in school life. He was responsible for seeing that school facilities were in sound condition, and brought deficiencies to the notice of the local school board. As the local agent for the enforcement of compulsory schooling, he had to examine the teacher's attendance roll to make certain that children entered school at the age of six and attended school regularly. His close supervision of the teachers covered not only their methods of instruction, observance of the lesson plan, and enforcement of obedience in the classroom, but also their moral conduct in private life.[7]

School supervision by the clergy had many inadequacies. The concerns of the clerical school inspectors were quite narrow, confined to the instruction of religion and the teachers' moral character. They gave little attention to the problem of truancy and granted dispensations too readily when parents requested the release of their children from obligatory schooling before the age of fourteen. Fearful of incurring the wrath of their parishioners by proposing costly school innovations, they did not strive to improve school facilities. And yet the appointment of clergy as school inspectors seemed appropriate and expedient to the Ministry of Education. The perspective from which officials in the ministry viewed this practice was the conviction that the church was an indispensable influence of social order and political stability in the state and that the purposes that the state and the church sought to accomplish in the schools could not be considered as different.[8] The government was unwilling to allocate funds to appoint laymen as salaried, full-time school inspectors. It was financially advantageous to have clergy serve as an arm of the school authorities.

By the 1840s the ministry could no longer ignore the shortcomings of the clerical inspectors. The *Lehrerseminare*, the normal schools that had been established for training teachers during the previous two decades, had produced a generation of professionals. Young teachers with pedagogic training questioned the credentials of churchmen to judge their work. Rather than reforming the system and recruiting secular educators, Eichhorn took steps to strengthen the qualifications of the clergy. A ministerial decree in 1842 conceded that the clergy were "behind the teachers in matters of pedagogy." Candidates for clerical office were required to demonstrate their skill to teach religion and to possess a knowledge of instructional methods for the other subjects in the school curriculum. Two years later the minister added the requirement that they should attend a normal school as an auditor for six to eight weeks.[9]

Karl von Altenstein made a momentous decision for the history of the *Volksschule* when he adopted the policy of organizing elementary education along confessional lines. The rationale for this decision given in his decree of April 27, 1822 reveals that officials in the ministry had grave misgivings about the social and political effects of interconfessional schools in a society in which confessional differences were intensely felt:

> Experience has taught us that in the interconfessional schools the principal element of education, religion, is not properly fostered, and it lies in the nature of these schools that this can not happen. The aim of promoting greater tolerance among diverse religious believers through such schools is seldom or never achieved; rather any tension which breaks out among the teachers and the parents of the schoolchildren degenerates too easily into religious dissension, which often tears an entire community apart.

He declared that the interconfessional schools "cannot be the rule," and laid down for the exceptional cases conditions that were essentially obstacles.[10]

State officials in the provinces of Posen* and West Prussia, where the Polish nationality had been under Prussian rule since the partition of Poland in the late eighteenth century, saw financial and political advantages in an interconfessional school system. On two occasions, Provincial Governor Eduard von Flottwell of Posen urged the minister to repeal the decree of 1822. He wrote that the decree undermined his efforts to plant loyalty to the Prussian monarchy in Posen because the confessional schools accentuated ethnic and religious differences.[11] Altenstein adhered to the policy that children and teachers in a school should be of one and the same faith. His directive of July 20, 1834, outlined long and complicated procedures for establishing interconfessional schools so that they would never be more than "an exception."

Altenstein's directive of 1834 provoked much opposition in West Prussia, where the communes feared that the separation of Catholic and Protestant schoolchildren would add to the costs of school maintenance. In the Marienwerder district more than 50 percent of the schools had a confessionally mixed enrollment. When the provincial diet appealed to the king for permission to continue these schools in 1837, Provincial Governor Theodor von Schön supported the petition. He pointed out that "the order to separate the confessions in the elementary schools cannot be carried out without imposing on the school districts increased expenses beyond their means." Furthermore, he contended that the policy of confessional schooling was "an unfortunate regression for the culture of the province because the schools that unite the youth without distinction in respect to religion have happily served to tie more firmly the bonds of love and harmony among diverse believers of the Christian faith, to enliven tolerance and mutual trust, and to ensure that these salutary fruits of education are carried over later into civic life."[12] Altenstein made no concession to the communes in West Prussia, nor did his successors relax his policy.

Expansion of the School System

What prevented the school system from expanding at a pace that matched the rapid growth of the population in Prussia during the nine-

---

*For the sake of consistency and simplicity geographical places in the Polish-speaking areas of the Prussian monarchy are called by the German names used by state officials rather than by their Polish names. Thus, the province appears in this book as Posen rather than Poznań.

teenth century was an antiquated system of school maintenance and the lack of finances. Under the General Civil Code of 1794, the householders who lived in the town or the neighboring villages that formed a school district, known collectively as the *Schulsozietät*, were responsible for maintaining the schools. The communes were not obliged to provide for school expenses through their tax revenues. In confessionally mixed localities where more than one school was established, householders contributed only for the maintenance of the school belonging to their religious group. The civil code distinguished the manorial lords from the householders and placed upon them only the responsibility to supply lumber from their forestlands for the construction of the school. Thus, the *Gutsherren* (manorial lords) in the provinces under the civil code— east of the Elbe River—were exempted from the payment of school taxes (*Schulbeiträge*). Disputes broke out over the liability of the estate owners to pay school taxes insofar as they represented their workers or owned properties apart from their manors. Eichhorn's arbitration in 1842 served the interests of the landowning elite more than the rural school districts. He ruled that the exemption of the manorial lords from school taxation was not altered when they acquired other properties. Their sole obligation was to assist the laborers on their estates in paying school fees.[13]

School funds were woefully inadequate. The *Schulsozietäten* kept the assessment of school rates low and relied heavily on the fees paid by the parents to cover as much as 25 percent of the school costs. The frugality of the householders reflected their indifference and hostility toward an institution that had gained public status because of meddling state laws. School fees were a heavy burden for lower-class families, and even those parents who were not in poverty resented compulsory schooling and expected their children to contribute to the family economy.[14] Moreover, the financial resources of rural *Schulsozietäten* were weak, and the state government gave little financial help for school maintenance. In 1861 state subsidies amounted to an average of 4 percent of all the funds spent for the public elementary schools throughout Prussia.[15]

Although the Ministry of Education did not conduct the first comprehensive statistical inquiry until 1886, the surveys published by the Royal Bureau of Statistics and the ministry's own reports provide enough information to chart the development of the school system. Between 1816 and 1846 the school system expanded rapidly with a 40 percent increase in the number of teachers. The rise of school enrollments by more than 1 million children reflected the spread of schooling as well as the tremendous growth of the population. The extent to which compulsory schooling was enforced with greater effectiveness can be gauged from the increase in school attendance by 108.4 percent in comparison with the 44.7 percent rate of growth in the school-aged population. By the year 1849, 81 percent of the school-aged children in Prussia were attending school, a proportion that was far greater than the school enrollments in England or France.[16]

During the next two decades, the expansion of the school system at a slower rate did not keep pace with the growth of the population. Between 1849 and 1864 the number of schoolchildren rose by more than 500,000. The school system descended into a crisis that lasted for over a decade. Extremely overcrowded conditions in 1861 existed in the rural schools of Silesia and Westphalia where the average number of pupils per teacher was 96 and 103, respectively. In the urban schools of the Rhine Province the average class size was 91 children per teacher. Many children who had attained the age of six could not enter school because of the lack of classroom space. In Berlin the practice of admitting children to school at an older age grew to such an extent that the proportion of school-aged children not attending school leaped from 13 to 21.5 percent from 1858 to 1864.[17]

The problem of overcrowded schools was aggravated by a desperate shortage of teachers. In the 1850s the number of youths entering the *Lehrerseminare* dropped sharply. State officials did not have to look far for the reason. Schoolteachers sent petitions to the Ministry of Education and the House of Deputies complaining about their pay, because from 1850 to 1860 the 10 percent increase in teachers' salaries fell far below the more than 30 percent rise in the cost of living. Teachers earned salaries that were substantially less than the wages paid to skilled workers and subaltern civil servants. Because teachers' incomes rose faster in the cities than in the countryside, highly qualified teachers quickly fled the village schools.[18]

The ministry's reports in the 1860s do not provide a true picture of the school crisis. Minister Heinrich von Mühler authorized the publication of an 1864 statistical inquiry in a form that avoided any politically damaging disclosures. Fearful of criticism from the liberal opposition, he withheld from publication the results of the inquiry for 1865–1867 and a large part of the inquiry for 1869–1871. The quality of education suffered from the measures that the school administration took to cope with the emergency of vacant teaching offices. School officials resorted to the expedients of introducing half-day sessions and appointing teachers who had no license and little pedagogic training. The extent of these practices can be judged from the first report concerning the shortage of teachers that the ministry released for publication. Of the vacant offices for licensed teachers in 1873, 1,230 were filled by introducing half-day sessions, 1,421 were occupied by *Präparanden* who had not completed their training, and 129 remained unoccupied. Although more than 3,000 women filled teaching offices in 1873, the school administration in Prussia was loath to find a solution for the shortage of teachers with a feminization of the profession.[19]

A distinctive character of elementary education in Prussia was the predominance of public over private schools. In 1861 private schools provided instruction for 2.7 percent of all schoolchildren, and of these private schools most were located in cities and were founded as a result of the stratification of urban society or the presence of a religious minority. In comparison with France, where the liberty of teaching was incorporated in the school laws of 1833 and 1852 and where Catholic religious orders made extensive use of the freedom to open private schools, the Prussian state never lost its monopoly in elementary education. During the last quarter of the century, the proportion of schoolchildren taught in private schools dwindled to a fraction of 1 percent.[20] By adapting the municipal school systems to the class structure of urban society and by adhering consistently to a policy of confessional schooling, the school administration in effect prevented the development of a competitive system of private or parochial schools.

Whereas the one-classroom school (*Volksschule*) was the norm in the countryside, elementary education was highly differentiated in the cities. The municipal authorities took into account the social aspirations and exclusiveness of middle-class parents who desired the separation of their children from those of the working class. In the cities, there were free schools for the poor and other public *Volksschulen* in which the scale of fees automatically segregated the pupils by social class. The *Bürgerschulen* to which bourgeois families sent their children set higher educational goals and offered in the curriculum, besides the three R's, a foreign language, history, geography, geometry, and natural science. The *Vorschulen*, or elementary classes, attached to the elitist secondary schools following a classical curriculum catered to the educated bourgeoisie.

The policy of confessional schooling was carried out with astonishing success for both the Protestants, who formed two thirds of the population, and the Catholic minority. In 1861, 99 percent of the Protestant pupils and 97 percent of the Catholic pupils attended schools of their own confession. Only in six of the twenty-five provincial districts—Breslau, Bromberg, Danzig, Marienwerder, Oppeln, and Posen—did the number of Catholic and Protestant children enrolled in schools of another confession altogether exceed 3,000. The small Jewish community did not fare so well. The proportion of Jewish children attending public schools of their own confession was very low, 50 percent in the cities and 5 percent in the countryside. The majority of Jewish children were instructed in Protestant schools with separate classes for the subject of religion.[21]

The geographic distribution of the Catholic and Protestant populations facilitated the organization of the school system along confessional lines. Both religious communities tended to settle in regionally concentrated masses. Protestants constituted more than 90 percent of the population in the provinces of Pomerania and Saxony and more than 85 percent in Brandenburg and East Prussia; conversely, Catholics formed a majority in Posen and the Rhine Province. In Silesia the population was solidly Protestant in the Liegnitz district and Catholic in the Oppeln district, and a sizeable Catholic minority lived in the predominantly Protestant Breslau district. Only in Westphalia and West Prussia was the population almost equally divided between Catholics and Protestants.[22] Whereas the two confessions dwelled in close proximity in West Prussia, they intermingled in the towns and villages of Westphalia so slightly that fewer than 1,000 Catholic and Protestant pupils attended schools of another confession in 1861.

School Attendance and Instruction

The curriculum reflected the functions that a nonconstitutional monarchy and the Christian churches expected the *Volksschule* to fulfill. The idea of a unitary school system providing a humanistic education for children of all social classes, which Wilhelm von Humboldt and Johann Wilhelm Süvern had proposed during the Reform Era, was rejected by the conservative bureaucrats who entered the Ministry of Education and Religious Affairs after 1820. They feared that the same basic education for all schoolchildren would foster illusions of social equality, produce friction between the classes, and stimulate aspirations for social mobility that the established order could not satisfy.[23] The ministry adopted a policy of maintaining qualitative differences between various types of public elementary schools in the interests of preserving political stability and the social hierarchy. Karl von Altenstein limited the educational goals of the *Volksschule* and confined its instruction to religion, reading, writing, and arithmetic. In 1822 he expressed his disapproval of a curriculum encompassing the subjects of history, geography, and science, and declared that "an education for piety, reverence of God, and Christian humility" was the prime task of the school.[24]

Despite the advances of industrialism in nineteenth-century Prussia, the school curriculum remained geared to the standards of a premodern society. The ministry's policy of reducing elementary education to the skills of literacy and of giving precedence to an education for Christian piety over utilitarian and intellectual goals was embodied in the *Regulativ* of October 3, 1854, the standardized curriculum that Ferdinand Stiehl wrote for the Protestant schools. The son of a Lutheran pastor, Stiehl thought that the task of the public *Volksschule* was "to provide through instruction, practice, and orderliness the foundations of an education required for life in the state and in the church."[25] His skeptical opinion about "impractical" modern theories of pedagogy, which strove to develop the intellectual faculties of the child and to cultivate individual initiative and moral self-responsibility, hardened into outright opposition when he witnessed the social and political disorders of 1848. Elected to the *Landtag* (diet) in 1849, he stood close to a faction of neopietistic conservatives who fought liberal constitutionalism. In the aftermath of the revolution, he was convinced that the state and the church had to work together to restore a moral standard to public life.[26]

With morning prayers opening each school day, religion formed the core of Stiehl's curriculum. The lesson in religion, assigned to the first hour, was expected to "have through hymn singing, prayers, the recitation of Bible verses, and the entire conduct of the teachers and pupils a devotional character besides the instructional purpose." Every Saturday, after covering Bible history and the Lutheran catechism, the teacher explained the Epistle and Gospel lessons appointed for the Sunday church services. The pupils were required to recite by memory the catechism and to memorize gradually the Sunday readings from the Scripture. The music lessons continued the preparation for church life, and the children learned church hymns and liturgical chants as well as folk melodies and patriotic songs. Whereas the *Regulativ* made six hours of weekly instruction mandatory for religion and three hours for music, it merely recommended three hours for history and the natural world. In these lessons the teacher was expected to show how divine providence revealed itself in the history of Prussia's rulers and "to fill the hearts and minds of the pupils with love for the king and respect for the laws and institutions of the fatherland."[27]

Prussia was far ahead of England and France in making school attendance compulsory in the late eighteenth century. The district governments set the age of six to fourteen as the years of school attendance and relied on the local school inspectors to enforce the law. The inspectors admonished the parents who failed to send their children to school, and if the warnings were not heeded, the law empowered the police to fine them as a penalty.[28] At the same time, the district governments took into account the needs of peasant farms and the interests of large-scale agriculture and applied the rule of compulsory schooling with considerable flexibility. They issued regulations permitting the local school boards to reduce school hours from Easter to the end of September and to suspend school instruction during the weeks of the wheat and potato harvests.[29]

Because most of the population in Prussia was engaged in agriculture and the industrial working class was still quite small, the employment of children in factories did not have as disadvantageous an effect on schooling as it did in England. Working in factories in 1849 were 29,149 children under the age of fourteen, a figure that amounted to 1 percent of all children between the ages of nine and thirteen. Child labor was confined to a few industrial areas, and its impact on school attendance was more harmful in some cities than in others. In Berlin, where many children entered school at seven years old and started to work at eleven, 69 percent of the children attended school in 1849. However, Berlin was hardly typical of other urban areas. In the Düsseldorf district, which included the manufacturing towns of Duisburg and Krefeld, the children who worked in factories were only 7 percent of the school-aged population in 1849.[30]

Concern for the health of future army recruits and the moral dissolution of unschooled factory workers led the Prussian government to issue the first legal measure restricting child labor in Germany. The regulation of March 9, 1839 prohibited the employment of children in factories and mines before the age of nine, restricted juvenile labor to a maximum of ten hours daily, and required the young workers to attend school five hours daily. Although this inadequate law could not curb the exploitation of child labor, the increasing mechanization of industries in the late 1840s and the 1850s was excluding school-aged children from factory production. By the time that Prussia's second and stricter child protection labor law went into full effect in 1855, fewer than 20,000 children under fourteen were working in factories. The law of May 16, 1853 raised the age of employment to twelve years, reduced the working day for children to six hours, and required them to receive three hours of school instruction daily until the age of fourteen. Factory inspectors were now appointed to enforce a strict observance of the law. Protective legislation and technological innovations in industries caused a rapid decline in the employment of children. Factory owners learned that highly mechanized industrial production required workers with better mental skills than the abilities of untrained children. By 1875 the number of children under fourteen working in factories decreased to 5,667.[31]

Because the child labor legislation was not extended beyond factories and mines, the employment of children in agriculture and handicraft workshops remained widespread. The extent of this labor cannot be analyzed because state officials did not gather statistical data on school-aged children working in the countryside. In the provinces of East and West Prussia, Pomerania, and Posen, as the reports of school inspectors and official visitors indicate, a large number of children skipped school during the summer and early autumn. The enforcement of regular school attendance was undermined by the indifferent or hostile attitude of the parents toward schooling as well as by the resistance of the estate owners who had an economic interest in the supply of cheap labor. Big and small landowners hired children as young as the age of ten to tend cattle and to harvest potatoes and other crops. During the summer months these children received practically no school instruction. In the rural districts, where the school boards reduced the hours of instruction, children who did farm work from six to ten o'clock came to school physically exhausted—a condition that made them listless and phlegmatic and diminished their capacity to learn. Of little use were the regulations of the provincial bureaucracy, which restricted the practice of hiring children as shepherds and provided penalties for the estate owners responsible for a youth's truancy. The schoolteachers were loath to make public complaints or to report cases of truancy to the school authorities because their appointment and income depended on the goodwill of the manorial lords, whose prerogatives included school patronage and the chairmanship of the local school board.[32]

After 1860 the school bureaucracy tried to restrict the dispensations that permitted children to leave school before the age of fourteen to "especially urgent cases caused by the poverty of the parents and other unavoidable circumstances."[33] Already by 1864 the proportion of school-aged children who did not attend school had declined to 7 percent. The observance of compulsory schooling was very high in Brandenburg, the Rhine Province, Saxony, and Westphalia.[34] In these provinces the belief in the utility of schooling seems to have gained ground. Although it is difficult with the available sources to trace the gradual change in the attitudes of the parents toward schooling, it is likely that the rise in school attendance reflected the higher value that all social classes placed on school instruction.[35]

Because the sources describing the experiences of the children in school and verifying the skills and values that they acquired through schooling in nineteenth-century Prussia are so scanty,[36] social historians have tended to evaluate the impact of the *Volksschule* by examining the state's objectives in laying down rules for the curriculum. Writing in the name of a critical, emancipatory history, the "revisionists" deplore the low educational goals set for the elementary schools and describe how the training socialized the children into an authoritarian political order and drilled into them the attitudes and habits appropriate for the social discipline of the laboring class in an industrial capitalist system.[37] More impressed by "the new and the essential" than the inadequacies of the schools measured "by the ideals of that time and later standards," sophisticated neohistoricists highlight the astounding effects of the schooling revolution, including the expansion of the school system, the enforcement of compulsory schooling and the growth in school enrollments, and the decline in illiteracy. Noting the resistance of the local citizenry to these innovations, they emphasize the role of the state as "the promoter of this profound modernization."[38] While it is true that the radical "revisionists" overexaggerate the extent to which the school functioned as a mechanism of social control and integration, some of their critics make the mistake of ignoring the obstacles and deficiencies that circumscribed the achievements of the schooling revolution.

The schools imparted to the pupils only a minimal knowledge of religion, reading and writing skills, and a smattering of arithmetic. The progress of the schoolchildren was hindered by the irregularity of school attendance. The large size of the classes and the prevalence of small rural schoolhouses without separate classrooms for each grade posed other obstacles to effective teaching. Children employed in agriculture left school as semiliterates, knowing how to read but unable to spell correctly or to write German grammatically. The curriculum had to be simplified in the one-classroom school (*Volksschule*), which meant that history, geography, and natural science were not taught. Much of the school day was devoted to religion. In working-class autobiographies whatever fragmentary recollections of school life that the authors had were mostly of the hours of reciting biblical passages and the catechism. The schools did not provide a level of education requisite to comprehend political issues and to participate in civic life.[39]

The inadequacies of the instruction should not obscure the foremost achievement of the *Volksschule*, namely the diffusion of the skills of reading and writing. The first comprehensive inquiry about literacy conducted at the time of the 1871 census revealed that a substantial part of the population had been taught to read and write. Of that segment of the total population born before 1861, 89.1 percent of the men and 83.5 percent of the women were able to read and write, 1.3 percent of the men and 1.6 percent of the women were classified as having "doubtful" reading and writing abilities; 9.5 percent of the men and 14.7 percent of the women could not read and write. Because literacy was measured by the use of the German language, the percentage of illiterates recorded for the Polish-speaking areas was very high, 31.8 percent for the men and 41 percent for the women in the province of Posen.[40] The success of the *Volksschule* in bringing literacy to the lower classes must be qualified on two counts. It did not hasten the assimilation of the Prussian Polish population into German society. Judging from the low circulation figures of provincial newspapers, neither did it cultivate in its pupils firm reading habits.[41]

The School Question and the Revolution of 1848

School officials who witnessed the revolution of 1848 saw the upheaval as a turning point for the school system in Prussia. What they observed with apprehension and gloom was the intrusion of party politics into school affairs. Ludwig Wiese, who was a councillor in the Ministry of Education, compared the school system before and after the 1840s with a nostalgic longing to return to the time when school policy was a matter of administrative decision rather than politics:

> In the state government under Frederick William III and just as much in the school administration, public agitation had no significant effect on the decisions of officials. Minister von Altenstein could still reign over the whole system like a grand seigneur. . . . Beginning in 1840 all this changed; the political movements in public life did not go without a noticeable effect on the school system. The time of its peaceful development was past. Following the civil code's conception of the school as an institution of the state, there came next the political parties with their claims to the school; it has remained since then an arena of conflict between various and often conflicting principles and interests.[42]

The radical political activism of the schoolteachers in 1848 was the culmination of nearly a decade of discontent. The reforms of the Altenstein era improved the training of the teaching profession but did not fulfill the expectations of the younger generation. In 1806 the government began to elevate the training of teachers to a pedagogic discipline with the establishment of *Lehrerseminare*. The professionalization of schoolteaching advanced further when the ministry introduced formal examinations for the certification of teachers in 1826. These reforms were, as Anthony La Vopa points out, a controlled experiment.[43] It was not the ministry's intention that the sons of artisans and peasants who attended the normal schools should acquire the intellectual pretensions and social aspirations of university students. The *Lehrerseminare* were not granted the status of an academic institution, and the curriculum was confined to the subjects taught in the elementary schools.

By the 1840s, the majority of younger teachers had acquired a professional consciousness but had not yet attained the social status and financial rewards of a respected profession. In the press and in the clubs that they organized, young teachers vented their grievances and called for the emancipation of the school from the church. They demanded the separation of school offices from the demeaning chores of the church sexton and the abolition of school inspection by the local priest or pastor, whose surveillance and moral conduct reports offended their professional self-esteem. They advocated the reform of school supervision so that professional educators would replace the clergy in the county school inspectorate. Although they embraced the political ideals of liberalism, they had an ambivalent attitude toward local self-government and pinned their hopes on a centralized state school system to obtain civil service status, secure salaries, and pension benefits.[44]

Immediately after the insurrection in March 1848, the teachers' associations mobilized their members for political action, and reformers in the teaching profession published programs for the reorganization of the school system. At a massive convention in Berlin on April 26, more than 500 teachers endorsed a set of principles for a future school law and addressed a petition to the Prussian National Assembly. The teachers proposed the appointment of secular school inspectors, the reorganization of the elementary schools with the state assuming complete responsibility for school maintenance and the appointment of teachers, the integration of schools at all levels of learning into a single system with the comprehensive school as the foundation of the system (*allgemeine Schule*) educating the youth of all social classes, and the elevation of the *Lehrerseminare* to a branch of the university with the same admission requirements.[45] The innovations proposed by the teachers spelled a radical reconstruction of the educational system. The *Staatsschule* standing directly under the Ministry of Education would replace the *Gemein-*

deschule with its ties to the parish church. The comprehensive school would eliminate the existing social stratification in elementary education and widen access to the institutions of higher learning.

The liberties that the government allowed the teachers to exercise since March were withdrawn when a counterrevolution was launched. Adalbert von Ladenberg, who now headed the ministry, rebuked those members of the teaching profession who "propagate views at variance with the existing state system among the immature youth." On December 20 he ordered the district governments to act with severity against any misuse of the teaching office and to fire the offenders. In July 1849 he suppressed the political rights of the teachers more decisively and instructed the district governments to dismiss teachers who "violate the obligation of loyalty" and "are guilty of taking a hostile partisan position against the state government."[46]

The brief period of unfettered political activity allowed the teachers to bring the school question into the nation's new parliamentary forum. By the time the National Assembly began its work of transforming Prussia's authoritarian regime into a constitutional government, school reform programs had circulated widely. The National Assembly decided that the constitution should contain fundamental principles for subsequent school legislation and turned over to the constitution committee the task of drafting an entire section relating to the schools. Democrats on the committee proposed two articles declaring that the *Volksschule* was an institution of the state and had to be maintained by state funds, and that the schools stood "under the supervision of their own authorities" and were "free of any church supervision."[47] The public was left in no doubt about the meaning of both articles when the democratic deputies issued a manifesto on July 21, calling for the education of children of all faiths in nondenominational schools and the exclusion of confessional religious instruction from the curriculum.[48]

During the summer months a sharp division of opinion on the school question emerged within the nation. Coming mainly from Catholic areas in the Rhine Province and Westphalia, 600 petitions sent to the National Assembly assailed the school reform programs and warned of the dire consequences of abandoning Christian principles in the education of the youth. The petitions were the work of priests who condemned secular schools from the pulpit and urged their parishioners to sign. Catholic parents threatened to open private schools if the church was deprived of its right to participate in the supervision of the public schools. In one of the petitions addressed to the minister of education, two priests warned that "the inevitable outcome" of the reforms proposed by the teachers "would be the sad experience that, like the example of Belgium, we would see confessional parochial schools established independently beside the state schools and such a host of problems arising."[49]

The Catholics in the National Assembly's constitution committee argued that the school should not be the exclusive domain of the state. Opposing a state monopoly in education, they sought protection in the right of citizens to establish private schools and the responsibility of the communes to maintain the public schools. They defended the appointment of churchmen as school inspectors by contending that the task of the *Volksschule* could not be accomplished without religion. Clerical inspectors provided a guarantee that the school's task would not be reduced to the mere instruction of practical skills but would remain first and foremost the education of the youth in the spiritual and moral teachings of Christianity.[50]

Before the deliberations on the constitution were completed, the government dissolved the National Assembly and promulgated a constitution by royal edict on December 5. Once the success of the counterrevolution was assured, the government placed the constitution before a new legislature for revision and ratification. The elections in February 1849 produced a parliamentary majority that was moderately conservative. With the support of conservative Protestants, the Catholics were now in a better position to influence the wording of the articles on education than they had been in the National Assembly. In March Cardinal Johannes Geissel of Cologne summoned the bishops in Prussia to a conference to discuss the constitution, and in the following months he communicated frequently with Peter Reichensperger, a deputy from Cologne.[51]

During the deliberations on the revision of the constitution, Adalbert von Ladenberg relied heavily on two councillors in the Ministry of Education, Heinrich von Mühler and Ferdinand Stiehl, whose memorandums on the school question written in August 1848 had made a profound impression on him. Mühler and Stiehl were convinced that the state's interests in the education of its citizens were too vital to permit an unrestricted liberty for private instruction. They doubted the wisdom of conceding to any citizen the freedom to open institutions of learning as a basic right because private schools offered no guarantee that the state's educational goals would be fulfilled. Although they affirmed the state's supreme supervision over the schools, they acknowledged the necessity of granting some participation to the church as long as religious instruction remained a part of the school curriculum. They foresaw dangerous consequences in the removal of religious instruction from the public schools and warned that such an innovation would provoke a conflict with the

Catholic church and the rise of a competitive system of private schools independent of the state.[52]

Ladenberg agreed that it was in the state's best interests to make accommodations to church claims. The Catholic opposition to the school reform program of the democrats in 1848 impressed him deeply and convinced him that secular schools would not be accepted by the people. He thought that the secularization of the schools would constitute a grave danger for the state, and his view of the outcome of such a reform was disquieting:

> Then conflict would arise in the school system as the church would exert all its efforts to establish its own confessional schools in competition against the religiously neutral communal schools. Even if the communal school is regarded as the norm, so freedom of teaching could not be logically denied. One is compelled to fear that this confessional school, against whose power of religious conviction the school without religious instruction would have no similar inner power to match, would carry away the victory in the embittered conflict breaking out in families and communes, and that a system of church schools would be organized independently of the state and would get in its control the instruction of the people to an overwhelming extent. This danger, which threatens to prevent a unified development of the school system and to remove a large part of popular education from the influence of the state, would make the plan to exclude religious instruction from the school appear inexpedient and questionable even if other reasons did not speak against it.[53]

To prevent such conflicts, he was willing to concede to the church the right to direct religious instruction in the schools. But he refused to surrender his fundamental principles and insisted that "the *Oberaufsichtsrecht* of the state over the schools cannot be limited or made insecure by the church's supervision of religious instruction."

The revised Constitution of January 31, 1850 made generous concessions to the Catholic and Protestant churches. Several amendments proposed by Theodor Brüggemann, a Catholic councillor in the Ministry of Education who had been elected to the *Landtag*, were adopted. The wording of Article 23 on the state's supervision of the schools was altered so that it would not be construed to mean the exclusion of clergymen from the office of school inspector. The revision of Article 24, which granted the churches the right to direct religious instruction in the schools, was a significant victory for the Catholic bishops who had contended that the vague language used in the constitution of 1848 did not guarantee them a decisive form of authority. A new clause in Article 24 placed the confessional *Volksschule* on a more secure foundation by stipulating that "confessional conditions are to be considered as much as possible in the organization of the public elementary schools."[54]

To carry out the provision for a school law in Article 26, Ladenberg commissioned Stiehl to draft a bill. When the Catholic bishops requested an opportunity to express their views before the school bill was introduced in the *Landtag*, Ladenberg reluctantly granted their wish. In his reply on September 28, he underscored the wide scope of influence conceded to the church in the school bill. Officials in the ministry who drafted it proceeded from the premise that "the school and the teacher should serve the purposes which the state and the church had to achieve through the schools and that the purposes of both should and cannot be considered as different from, hindering, or excluding each other."[55]

Ladenberg's school bill provided solid guarantees for the confessional organization of the school system. It obliged the communes to establish and maintain at public expense confessional schools for children of the same faith if they numbered at least sixty in any school district. The school administration had to consult church officials in setting the curriculum and selecting the school textbooks. The church authorities were entitled to attend the examinations for the teacher's license and to certify the qualifications of the candidates to teach religion.[56]

On the other side, the state's supreme authority over the schools was upheld. The draft law empowered the district governments to appoint school inspectors, who were to exercise their office "in the commission of and according to the instruction of the government." The state reserved to itself the freedom to name churchmen or laymen to the office. In his letter to the bishops, Ladenberg contended that because school inspectors were designated as state officials by the constitution, the school law could not allow the church authorities to exercise any formal right in their appointment. He wrote that "school inspection must no longer be seen, as it was customary and legal in many districts up till now, as an attribute of the office of the deanery superintendents, for which not the slightest influence is granted to the government in the selection of the appropriate persons."[57]

Whereas the royal appointees on the Protestant High Church Council acknowledged those parts of the draft law that were sympathetic to church interests, the Catholic bishops expressed their dissatisfaction bluntly. They objected that the school bill did not grant to the church any formal right to participate in the appointment of county school inspectors. They demanded that Catholic teachers giving religious instruction should obtain a special commission from the bishop of their diocese, the *missio canonica*, and be subject to his discipline.[58] Dismayed at their opposition, Ladenberg decided not to introduce the school bill and resigned on December 19, 1850. No other course seemed acceptable to him. He thought that the draft law had gone "up to the limits" of what the rights of the state permitted in determining the extent of the church's influence in the schools. He had no desire to provoke a dispute with the Catholic hierarchy at a time when the state and the church had to work together to uphold the foundations of society that were so badly shaken by the revolution.[59]

Karl von Raumer, who succeeded Adalbert von Ladenberg, did not believe that the constitutional provision for a school law had to be carried out immediately. When the liberal faction in the House of Deputies raised this issue in 1851, he noted how "difficult it is to make a law of such importance and to preserve at the same time the rights of the state and the church."[60] The liberals continued to put pressure on the government and introduced in 1852 a motion demanding the introduction of a school bill. In the debate on this motion, Raumer questioned the necessity for enacting a school law and said that "even if it had to be issued now, it could not say anything other than that the existing regulations remain in effect."[61]

Raumer's decision to shelve the school bill grew out of his own disposition as well as attitudes within the higher bureaucracy in the aftermath of the revolution. Raumer saw no need to change the status quo. He was not inclined to assert boldly the state's sovereignty in the realm of elementary education and thought that the *Volksschule* was the joint responsibility of the church and the state.[62] A bureaucrat in the old Prussian style, he was intent on shielding the school administration from party politics. The experience of officials in the Ministry of Education during 1848 reinforced their distrust of and contempt for parliamentary institutions. They dismissed as "vulgar liberalism" the demand for legislation that would define formal rights and obligations, and thought that administrators should have the authority to act at their discretion.[63]

Liberals and the Cause of School Reform

Expectations of a new era were awakened in 1858 when Prince William, in his capacity as regent, dismissed Raumer and the rest of the reactionary cabinet. Moritz von Bethmann Hollweg entered the office of minister of education with a reputation for liberalism, which he had acquired from his opposition to the government during the reaction after 1848. Very quickly he annulled Raumer's decree that prohibited teachers in

Prussia from participating in the annual convention of the German Teachers' Association, a rallying point for teachers of progressive pedagogic views, and revived the teaching profession from nearly a decade of silence and stagnation. In the newly elected House of Deputies his announcement that a school bill would be introduced in the next session was greeted by the liberal majority.

Economic grievances and the minister's promise spurred the teachers to mobilize for political action. During the early 1860s, teachers' associations sent petitions to the House of Deputies stating the principles on which they thought the school law should be based. Their petitions gave the Progressives in the education committee of the House of Deputies two occasions for discussing at length the reforms proposed by liberals in the teaching profession. In 1863 the House of Deputies adopted a resolution calling for the enactment of a school law. The Progressives endorsed the teacher's demands for the abolition of school supervision by the local clergy, the appointment of experienced educators as county school inspectors, the separation of schoolteaching from the duties of the church sexton, and the reform of the intellectually narrow and confessionally oriented curriculum for teachers' training that Ferdinand Stiehl had introduced in 1854. In declaring that the school law should apply the principle of communal self-government in lieu of bureaucratic centralization and grant the communes the full right of appointing the teachers, the Progressives were also expressing the new mood of skepticism in the teaching profession about the advantages of a school system directly under the state. After their experiences in the reactionary 1850s, the teachers were more interested in restraining the interference of the state bureaucracy in school life and strengthening the rights of local government than they had been in 1848.[64]

Pedagogic reformers found a sympathetic hearing in the Progressive party, whose program for the development of a modern society and constitutional state entailed not only the removal of anachronistic constraints but also the transformation of politically passive subjects into patriotic citizens. The Progressives were convinced that school reform was the precondition for the emancipation of society from the forces of obscurantism and intolerance that hindered progress, and that an enlightened public would emerge only after the church's influence in the school came to an end. Their commitment to this cause corresponded to their self-image as a party whose victory would ensure the triumph of enlightenment and freedom. This self-image evolved naturally in a party whose national leadership was drawn from the educated elites within the middle strata of society. Judicial officials, lawyers, professors, and physicians constituted a large percentage of the Progressive *Fraktion*, the party's delegation in the House of Deputies. The right-wing liberals who seceded from the Progressive ranks and organized the National Liberal party in 1867 came from the same social strata. Commerical cities with large Protestant populations were the backbone of liberalism's political strength.[65]

The National Liberals and the Progressives conceived of the Prussian *Volksschule* as an institution of a confessionally neutral state and thought that the church was not entitled to any rights in the school system. Rudolf Gneist, liberalism's foremost publicist in the 1860s, argued, "Under the name of religious instruction the *ecclesia militans* should not enter the schools in order to reproach and fight other religious believers who are compelled by the state to send their children to these institutions and to maintain them out of their own funds."[66] Religion should be given a place in the curriculum that was consistent with the nonsectarian character of the state, the whole community's responsibility to maintain the schools, and the rule of compulsory schooling. For the liberals the interconfessional school was the corollary of these three principles.

Gneist crystallized liberalism's argument against the confessional school in a tract published in 1869. A confessional school system violated the autonomy of learning and "subordinated all subjects [of instruction] to the distinctive doctrines and partisan views of the church." Teachers were robbed of professional integrity in an educational system in which the judgment of the church authorities carried more weight than pedagogic standards. Clerical influence conspired to prevent the introduction of a modern curriculum, which would reduce the hours of instruction devoted to religion and require the instruction of history and natural science.[67]

Gneist prophesied that in the coming years confessional schools would create political trouble. Observing that the mobility of the population was intermixing the confessions and producing sizeable minorities in the cities, he warned that parents who were compelled to send their children to schools of another confession would protest loudly and that one or the other religious group would complain that it had fewer schools than what it was entitled to have according to its proportion of the population. "The more lively protests of this kind become, the more they succeed in stamping on the schools a politico-ecclesiastical character," he said.[68]

The conflict that broke out in 1862 between the government and the Progressive party in the House of Deputies over a bill to reorganize and expand the army produced a political atmosphere that made the enactment of a school law impossible. However, the prospects for the introduction of Moritz von Bethmann Hollweg's school bill were poor even before Bismarck's appointment as minister-president and the embitterment of the Progressives opposed to his unconstitutional measures. When the cabinet discussed the draft law in March 1861, the ministers made the repeal of the last clause of Article 25 on free instruction in the elementary schools a precondition for their approval. They were worried about the financial burden that would fall on the manorial lords if the school law made the estate villages (*Gutsbezirke*) and communes responsible for school maintenance and prohibited school fees at the same time.[69]

Within the Ministry of Education itself grave doubts about the wisdom of making a law based on Articles 22–25 of the constitution could be heard. A memorandum written for the cabinet in 1860 concluced that it would be "trial and experimentation," not justified by necessity, to carry out "abstract axioms and principles which upon closer examination would be harmful to the progress of the school system and a source of unavoidable conflicts between state, church, and commune in the areas of the school system where their fundamental differences cannot be ignored."[70] Officials in the ministry were reluctant to bring into effect the freedom of teaching proclaimed in Article 22. They thought that the state was so deeply affected by the ideas and values taught to the youth that the public school had to be the norm. Disturbing them more profoundly was the unresolved dualism in Articles 23 and 24, which recognized the state and the church as powers with an interest in the schools and with legitimate claims to the direction of school affairs. They feared that "the dualism" created by the constitution "could make the schools an arena of recurring and irresolvable conflicts if it is not mediated by the law to produce a unity in the supervision and direction of the schools."[71]

In the course of 1861 Moritz von Bethmann Hollweg's relations with the conservatives in the ministry grew cool. They had no regret when he resigned in March 1862. Heinrich von Mühler, who replaced him, decided not to present a school bill to the *Landtag* in the midst of the political conflict over the army bill. The presence of a large Progressive majority in the House of Deputies made further action on school legislation seem inadvisable to him. The conservatives in the ministry applauded this decision. Ludwig Wiese queried, "Is it realistic to expect that large legislative bodies are able and qualified by virtue for their composition to solve the kinds of technical questions whereby the most divergent views on the church, the state, and the school strive to vindicate themselves."[72]

It was not until 1868 that Mühler took steps to enact a school law. The establishment of the North German Confederation in 1867 and the need to apply the principles of Prussian administration to the recently annexed states made the introduction of a school bill politically opportune in 1868. Apart from the territorial expansion of Prussia, Mühler was under pressure to act because economic and social changes since 1850 had made the existing system of school maintenance obsolete and impractical. He admitted in the *Motive* appended to the draft law that the regulations in the civil code of 1794 were the prime obstacle to the improvement of teachers' salaries and school facilities. Many city officials, recognizing the anachronism of the civil code, had already put school expenses on the municipal budget. In the Rhine Province, which was not under the jurisdiction of the civil code, the Communal Ordinance of 1845 required the communes to maintain the schools through their tax revenues. In most areas east to the Elbe River, the civil code still regulated school maintenance "all the more detrimentally, the more the actual conditions upon which it was based have been eliminated or have changed substantially."[73] Between 1820 and 1860 peasant land ownership in the eastern provinces had diminished as agrarian capitalists bought peasant farms and absorbed them into big estates cultivated by a propertyless proletariat. By the 1860s rural society consisted of fewer peasant farmers, and the *Schulsozietäten* composed of a declining number of householders became less viable financially.

The provisions of the civil code provoked resentment and stubborn resistance among those legally obliged to pay school rates. The Ministry of Education concluded from the litigation in the courts that the defiance was due less to the disinclination of the householders to fulfill their legal duty than to the unfairness of the regulations.[74] The exemption of the manorial lords from the school tax seemed all the more unjust because this privilege did not prevail in all the eastern provinces. The School Regulation of 1845 for the Province of East and West Prussia made the communes and *Gutsbezirke* responsible for school maintenance.

When Mühler introduced a school bill in the *Landtag* in 1868, he encountered irate opposition from the National Liberal and Progressive parties. The draft law ignored their proposals for school reform; it safeguarded the confessional organization of the school system and left intact the clergy's traditional monopoly of school inspection offices.[75] A companion bill provided for the repeal of the clause in Article 25 on free elementary school instruction. Estate owners in the House of Lords who opposed the abolition of school fees demanded that this issue be settled before the enactment of a school law.[76] The fate of the school bill was decided when the liberal coalition defeated the repeal bill after a heated debate in the House of Deputies on February 9 and 10, 1869.

A second school bill was introduced in November 1869 only after Mühler circumvented Bismarck's disapproval with the help of the cabinet. In the House of Deputies, Mühler aroused the wrath of his liberal critics by declaring that the state could not adopt an adversary position to the church in the province of the school and that "any attempt to dissolve the intimate relationship between education and religion, the school and the church, in our nation would be an impossibility." He reminded the National Liberals and the Progressives that popular opposition to their school reform program remained as strong as it had been in 1848. He defended the school bill by invoking those provisions of the constitution that "regard religion as an integral part of the entire school instruction [and] guarantee to the church authorities the influence due to them."[77] His opponents were fuming and wanted to defeat the school bill immediately. Once again, as in February, they called for Mühler's resignation. The majority was finally persuaded to send the bill to a committee for revision. The legislative session ended before the committee completed its work, and Mühler's school bill died.

Early in the nineteenth century the state and the church forged an intimate partnership in elementary education that was to characterize school life in Prussia right to the end of the monarchy in 1918. The principle of the *Volksschule* as an institution of the state, which the General Civil Code of 1794 enunciated, did not have as great an effect on school administration and teaching before 1870 as historians have generally assumed. The conservative officials in the Ministry of Education from the long Altenstein era to Mühler's years in office acknowledged unambiguously that the Catholic and Protestant churches had formal rights and legitimate interests in the schools. The church's extensive influence in elementary education was sustained by the customary appointment of clergy to the office of school inspector, the confessional character of the schools, and the central place assigned to religion in the instruction of the schoolchildren. When the schools became a political issue in public life during the revolution of 1848 and again in the 1860s, the reformers defined the school question primarily as the emancipation of the school from the church.

The radical changes proposed by political activists in the teaching profession and democrats in the Prussian National Assembly in 1848 quickly produced a deep division of opinion on the school question. School reform came under fire from the countermobilization of Catholics and neopietistic conservatives who were aroused to defend the Christian-confessional school. Catholics in the National Assembly countered the threat to the church's influence in the schools by denouncing theories that supported the supremacy of the state's power and the state's monopoly of education and by linking the defense of the church's prerogatives with the rights of the parents to decide what kind of education their children should have. The same strategy guided those parish priests who drafted petitions and exhorted their flock to sign. A flood of petitions warned the state authorities that the Catholics would open private schools if their church was stripped of its traditional rights in the schools.

The popular responses to the emancipation movement made a deep impression in the Ministry of Education and showed that the scale of agitation of the teachers' associations was out of proportion to their support in the nation. Although Adalbert von Ladenberg believed that the state's sovereignty over the schools should not be limited by the church's special custody for religious instruction, he was not tempted to exploit the emancipation movement to expand the state's control. He foresaw grave dangers to the state arising from the establishment of a nonconfessional school system and feared that such an innovation would antagonize the Catholic church and incite it to create a competitive system of private schools. To preserve the state's monopoly of education as much as to prevent political strife, he was willing to accept the concessions that Article 24 of the revised constitution of 1850 made to the church. The debate over the school question during the revolution ended with a constitution that guaranteed the church's supervision of religious instruction and the organization of the school system along confessional lines.

In the 1860s liberal parliamentary majorities, elected on the basis of an unequal franchise, demanded the emancipation of the school from the church in Baden and Prussia. In the two states the school administration took a different course. In Baden, where a Protestant dynasty ruled a population that was two-thirds Catholic, a *Kulturkampf* broke out when the government collaborated with a Protestant liberal coalition and carried out reforms with the underlying objective to assert the state's exclusive control over elementary education and to push back the influence of the Catholic clergy in the schools.[78]

In Prussia the orthodox Protestant officials in the Ministry of Education thought that supervision over the schools belonged unconditionally to the state, but they had a conciliatory attitude toward the Catholic church and never underestimated the potential for a church–state conflict over the schools. From the central place of religion in the school curriculum and from the church's constitutional right to direct the instruction of this subject, they recognized as "the necessary consequence" an extensive *Mitwirkungsrecht* (right to participate) for the church—a role in planning the curriculum for religious instruction in the elementary and normal schools, a right to attend the examinations for the teacher's license and to certify the qualifications of the candidates to give religious instruction, and the power to disqualify from appointment any teacher against whom objections of a religious nature were raised. They rejected the idea of the *Staatsschule* and thought that the school administration should adhere to the policy that "one and the same school and one and the same teacher should serve the purposes which the state and the church had to achieve through the school."[79]

2

The Politics of School Reform
and the *Kulturkampf*

Bismarck's struggle against political Catholicism and dissatisfaction with
the supervision of the schools in the Polish-speaking areas of Prussia
propelled the school administration on to a new course after 1870. His
choice of Adalbert Falk brought to the head of the Ministry of Education
on January 22, 1872 a judicial official who was philosophically close to
the National Liberal party. During his seven years in office, Falk broke
with the practices followed by his predecessors and introduced measures
to dissolve the traditional bonds between the church and the school. The
objectives of the school reforms were to professionalize school supervision by the appointment of full-time school inspectors in place of the
clergy, to weaken the church's influence in the school system by curtailing
its right to direct the instruction of religion, and to merge Catholic and
Protestant public schools into interconfessional schools, providing an
education that would dissolve religious particularism and cultivate German national consciousness and patriotic feeling. These innovations
thrust school politics into the foreground of the *Kulturkampf* in Prussia.

Catholic School Inspectors and
the Opening of the *Kulturkampf*

School affairs became a matter of high politics for Bismarck when
groups whom he regarded as enemies of the German Empire coalesced

into a Catholic political party in 1870. Opposition in the Catholic Rhineland to Prussia's aggressive war against Austria in 1866 led him to question the political loyalty of the Catholics, and the political behavior of the Catholics after the founding of the North German Confederation confirmed his suspicion. While the Polish faction in the Reichstag of 1867 protested the absorption of Polish Prussia into a German confederation, other Catholic deputies took up the defense of federalism and criticized those articles in Bismarck's draft of the constitution that created too strong a central government. In the final vote the Catholics formed part of the minority that rejected the constitution. This act reinforced his image of political Catholicism as an intransigent and unpatriotic opposition.[1]

The organization of the Center party was a defensive response to the vulnerable position of the Catholic minority in the new empire, which had a political climate of liberal anticlericalism and Protestant nationalist euphoria that seemed to threaten the rights and interests of the Catholic church. The Catholics campaigned under the banner of the Center party for the first time in the Reichstag election of March 1871. Many priests served as campaign agents and urged their parishioners to vote for Center party candidates. Twelve of the priests running for election won seats in the Reichstag. Showing a lapse of cool reason, Bismarck failed to see the insecurity and anxiety of the Catholics and, with a nervous sense of the fragility of the empire, exaggerated the role that Bavarian and Hanoverian particularists played in the party. He resolved to break up this party of malcontented Catholics and to strike at the root of its power—the Catholic church.[2]

The Vatican Council's proclamation of the doctrine of papal infallibility in 1870 struck Bismarck as a challenge to the sovereignty of the national state. Controversies arising from the refusal of university and high school teachers to accept the dogma and the bishops' threats to revoke the *missio canonica* granted to them strained the relations between the church hierarchy and the state authorities.[3] In July 1871 Bismarck wrote to an aide of Emperor William that "recent events in the church sphere make it seem inadvisable for the Ministry of Education to appoint Catholic priests as *Schulräte*." At Bismarck's urging, the emperor ordered Mühler to cease recruiting Catholic clergymen for the school bureaucracy and asked him to consider the advisability of removing those churchmen who were presently in such offices.[4]

Bismarck lost confidence in Mühler when he told the cabinet on October 9 that he considered "an aggressive action by the state against the church as unjustified." He declined to dismiss Catholic clergymen en bloc from the school administration and declared that such a step would be warranted only if the doctrine of papal infallibility influenced a clerical school official to behave in a politically unreliable manner. Proceeding on the basis of individual cases was not only "a requirement of justice but also advisable" because the ministry "would have great difficulties in finding an appropriate substitute for these men."[5]

Bismarck easily marshaled the National Liberal and Progressive parties into the battle against the Center party. In the 1860s political liberals and the Catholics in Germany took opposing sides on the question of national unity. An ideologically tinged anti-Catholicism fused with nationalism as the Protestant liberals increasingly equated Catholicism with particularism and the Protestant culture of northern Germany with the idea of freedom in the nation-state. The wars of national unification and the founding of the German Empire swelled Protestant cultural nationalism to a floodtide, and an anti-Catholic tone permeated triumphant accounts of the wars. At the same time, the proclamation of the doctrine of papal infallibility seemed to the Protestant liberals to be further proof of the Catholics' supranational allegiances and weak national identity. National Liberals such as Heinrich von Sybel thought that "political Catholicism and national loyalty in the sense of an unlimited cultural and political bond with the German nation" were "irreconcilable values."[6]

More alarming to Bismarck than Bavarian particularism was the appearance of Polish associations in Posen and West Prussia that strove to increase the national consciousness of the masses. In 1870 he read reports from the provincial bureaucracy about the spread of Polish nationalist agitation and the poor progress made by Polish schoolchildren in the mastery of the German language. The governor of the Danzig provincial district wrote that "among the Polish population a synthetic agitation is constantly fueled by a seditious party insofar as it describes efforts to improve the instruction of the schoolchildren in the German language as [measures] directed against the Catholic church." He criticized the local Catholic clergy for striving "to preserve among the people the deplorable identification of Catholicism and Polish nationality."[7] When the reports were discussed at a cabinet meeting, Bismarck lamented that the use of the Polish language was gaining ground in West Prussia at the expense of German and that regulations on the instruction of Polish schoolchildren in German were "unavailing in the face of the resistance of Polish Catholic pastors functioning as local school inspectors."[8]

After the war of 1870, Bismarck turned his attention once again to the "Polonizing influence" exercised by the Catholic clergy in the schools. At a cabinet meeting in October 1871 he reproached the Ministry of Education for allowing the instruction of German to be neglected. He thought that Mühler had not acted vigorously against Polish school inspectors who were sabotaging the government's policy of assimilation. He was convinced that the state had to take measures to eliminate clerical influence in the schools and to make more effective use of the *Volksschule* to germanize the Polish population.[9]

Enactment of the School Supervision Law

Under pressure from Bismarck, Heinrich von Mühler hastily drafted a bill that placed school supervision under the exclusive jurisdiction of the state and clarified the status of school inspectors as state officials. The government's power to dismiss clerical school inspectors "at any time" was affirmed.[10] On November 1 the cabinet debated at length whether the law should apply to the entire state or be confined to the eastern provinces. The ministers of commerce and the interior warned that extending the jurisdiction of the law would provoke opposition from the Conservative party. The minister of justice and Mühler contended that the law had to be worded to apply to all parts of the kingdom because it was a matter of implementing a constitutional principle. Bismarck adopted this position with another motive in mind. Foreseeing the possibility that the political activity of Catholic priests in Westphalia might give cause for the dismissal of clerical school inspectors there, he declared that "the fear of the law's application will have a beneficial effect."[11]

Neither Bismarck nor any of the other ministers expected the law to be the first step in a reform of the school system. The emancipation of the school from the church and the professionalization of school supervision did not enter into the cabinet's discussion. Minister of Finance Ludwig Camphausen opposed the appointment of secular school inspectors throughout the state and consented to appropriate money only for the application of the law in districts where Polish priests were school inspectors.[12] When Bismarck requested the emperor's permission to introduce the bill, the reasons he cited were totally political. He explained that "in the Polish Catholic areas of the monarchy the germanization task of the elementary schools is pushed into the background." He added that "ultramontane purposes" were promoted in the schools in other areas populated by the Catholics, and "thereby conditions arise which together with the current innovations in the dogma of the Catholic church assume the nature of a danger to the state."[13]

By the time the Prussian parliament began its deliberations of the School Supervision Bill, changes in the Ministry of Education aroused the National Liberals' expectations of reform. Bismarck's intrigues finally brought about the resignation of Heinrich von Mühler in January 1872. Bismarck chose Adalbert Falk for the vacant office because Falk seemed well qualified for the task that he wanted the new minister to accomplish, namely to strengthen the state's authority vis-à-vis the church's traditional rights. He admired Falk's undogmatic Protestantism, strong consciousness of national and state interests, and immense energy and resolute will.[14] Falk brought into the ministry a new team of councillors, bureaucrats whom he had known in the Ministry of Justice and whose outlook was close to the views of the National Liberal party. He appointed Karl Schneider, a progressive pedagogue who was the director of the *Lehrerseminar* in Berlin, to head the department for elementary school affairs when Ferdinand Stiehl resigned in protest of the new minister's decision to reform the school curriculum.[15]

The School Supervision Bill aroused the most widespread popular protest of all the *Kulturkampf* laws. Over 19,000 petitions bearing more than 326,000 signatures were sent to the House of Deputies.[16] Especially painful for Emperor William and Bismarck was the opposition of the Conservative party and Protestant churchmen.[17] The loose wording of the bill and uncertainty about the government's intentions led the Conservatives to join the Catholic opposition.

During the debates in the House of Deputies from February 8 to 13, 1872, the Center party questioned the constitutionality of the bill. Catholic deputies pointed out that the bill did not define the extent of the state's authority or make clear how this power was limited by the constitutional rights of the churches and the communes to participate in the administration of the schools. Ludwig Windthorst, the leader of the Center *Fraktion*, reproached the National Liberals and the Progressives for abandoning their tradition of defending communal self-government. Declaring that they were indulging in self-deception, he warned the House of Deputies that once Bismarck obtained his objective, he would feel no political pressure or moral obligation to enact a comprehensive school law that would affirm the rights of the communes.[18]

The Center's criticism stung the left-wing liberals in the Progressive party, and their discomfort was clearly apparent in Rudolf Virchow's announcement that his party decided to support the bill "not without very grave misgivings." He conceded that the bill was "very incomplete" and "one-sided," and regretted that it did not provide any counterweight to the power of the state by making the rights of the communes secure.

The Progressives were willing to "make allowance for the deficiencies of the law" because they saw a glimmer of hope in the possibility that it might be the first step in breaking the church's control over elementary education and in reforming the supervision of the schools.[19]

The consciences of the members of the National Liberal party were less troubled by the contention that a school law had to bring into effect all of the provisions on education in the constitution. Their experience with Mühler's school bills taught them that the constitution of 1850 did not lay the foundation for a liberal school law. Rudolf Gneist criticized the ambiguity of the language of Article 24, which he knew was a stumbling block in the path of school reform.[20] In their defense of the bill the National Liberals resorted to demagogic tactics. Attacks on the Catholics for opposing national unification and the founding of the German Empire enabled them to evade the criticism of the bill by the Center party. Charging that Catholic churchmen had taken a hostile position to the Prussian government during the war of 1870, anticlerical deputies demanded the removal of priests from school inspection offices. "The German nationality is harmed when the education of the youth is influenced by the clergy," remarked Wilhelm Löwe.[21]

After the enactment of the School Supervision Law of March 11, 1872, the government was confronted with the possibility that some clergymen would refuse to serve as school inspectors, because school inspection was now defined as a state office under a commission that the government could revoke at any time. Acting firmly to quell any protest, the Protestant High Church Council notified the consistories under its jurisdiction that clergymen could not resign from their school offices without the consent of the church authorities.[22] In the province of Hanover the consistory declined to restrict the freedom of the clergy, and the response of the pastors there revealed the indignation that swept throughout the church. At a church conference in the city of Hanover on March 19, some clergymen called for a mass resignation in protest of the new law. The majority decided instead to remain in office and to declare formally that the performance of this duty signified no approval of the new law and that the state's commission would be handed back if they were ordered to act contrary to their consciences. By the summer of 1872, twenty pastors resigned and five were dismissed after declaring defiantly that they inspected the schools under a church commission.[23]

The Catholic bishops were very circumspect in their reaction to the law. After the House of Deputies passed the bill, Archbishop Heinrich Foerster of Breslau summoned the bishops to take a resolute stand against it. He was the first bishop to contemplate a boycott of the school administration because the law affected him more than any other bishop in Prussia. The traditional prerogatives of the bishop of Breslau included the appointment of county school inspectors. In the other dioceses the bishops exercised only the right to approve the individuals selected by the district governments before they were installed in office. The other bishops were not tempted to challenge the power of the state and preferred to wait and see how the government applied the law. "If the previous state of affairs is essentially preserved," replied the bishop of Fulda, "I would never provoke a conflict." The bishops thought that a mass exodus of Catholic clergymen from school inspection offices would only propel the government to appoint laymen in their place.[24]

While the bishops watched the changes in the Ministry of Education with uncertainty in the spring of 1872, the predominantly Protestant membership of the recently organized Elementary Schoolteachers' Association of Prussia greeted the arrival of Adalbert Falk with excited expectations of reform. In April the new minister granted an audience to the association's executive board, who pleaded for the improvement of teachers' salaries and the professionalization of school supervision. Perhaps the clearest signal to the teachers that a new era was dawning was his decision in June to summon a conference in Berlin to discuss the reorganization of the schools and the reform of the curriculum.

In July the leaders of the Elementary Schoolteachers' Association published a set of proposals that they hoped would guide Falk in drafting a school law. Standing in opposition to confessional schooling and to the social stratification of elementary education, they advocated the formation of large interconfessional schools with classrooms for each age group and the abolition of the *Vorschule*, which prepared a privileged minority of children for admission to the socially prestigious *Gymnasium*. They demanded the reform of school supervision with the appointment of experienced teachers as full-time county school inspectors. Disregarding Article 24 of the constitution, they contended that a separate supervision for the subject of religion need not be instituted because the churches could be informed about it without interfering in the teacher's instruction.[25] With this program the association took a position in school politics that placed it in the same camp with the liberal *Kulturkämpfer*. As one moderate pedagogic reformer sadly observed in 1881, it was the "unfortunate fate" of the teachers in the 1870s that their agitation for reforms in the interests of the schools and their professional status gave an impression of hostility to the church and exposed them to misinterpretation.[26]

Impact of the *Kulturkampf* on the School System

The impact of the *Kulturkampf* on the school system varied from one province to another. In its struggle against the Catholic church, the state allowed the district governments in the provinces a wide scope of discretionary action. The execution of measures diminishing the church's influence in the schools ranged from mildness in the province of Hesse–Nassau to severity in Posen and the Rhine Province.[27] The dean of the cathedral chapter in Fulda made precisely this point when he wrote to Archbishop Paulus Melchers in December 1874 that "the lamentable conditions in the archdiocese of Cologne have not yet occurred in the diocese of Fulda."[28] He reported that only two priests had been dismissed from local school inspection offices and that the archdeacons were still functioning as county school inspectors.

A combination of circumstances made the Rhine Province that area in Prussia where the *Kulturkampf* led to the most extensive school reforms carried out in the nineteenth century. At the head of the provincial administration were men who had an intense hostility to political Catholicism. In the vanguard of the conflict were Provincial Governor Moritz von Bardeleben and District Governor August vom Ende of Düsseldorf. Answerable to Ende in the chain of command in the Düsseldorf district government was *Regierungsrat* (government councillor) Albert von Juncker, the director of the *Abteilung des Innern* (Department of the Interior), whose authoritarian and high-handed administration of school affairs made him the most unpopular state official in the province. At the same time, the district governments were staffed by a corps of school officials who had strong professional integrity and a dedication to educational reform. The *Kulturkampf* created the circumstances that made it possible to alter the historical relations between the school and the church, and they readily seized this opportunity. But they were not captive to doctrinaire anticlericalism. The desire to improve elementary education motivated them to redress the deficiencies of school supervision. Their aspirations were very different from the political viewpoint of those administrators who supported the secularization of the Catholic school inspectorate as part of the government's struggle against ultramontanism.

From the start of the *Kulturkampf*, District Governor August vom Ende showed a marked tendency to behave combatively. Soon after the enactment of the School Supervision Law, he devised a scheme to harass Catholic churchmen in county school inspection offices. In 1850 Raumer allowed the clergy to add to their oath of loyalty to the king—required of all state officeholders by the new constitution—the reservation that obedience was pledged as long as nothing contrary to the commands of God and their consciences was demanded of them. On March 25, 1873 Falk prohibited this practice for Catholic priests who assumed state offices.[29] With the exception of Ende, the district governors in the Rhine Province thought that the minister's confidential order had no application to clerical school inspectors. Throughout the province clergymen who inspected the schools on a part-time basis and without salary had never been required to perform the oath like other civil servants. In a letter to the district governors on April 8, Ende contended that under the School Supervision Law clerical school inspectors should take the oath, and inquired whether they intended to demand an unconditional oath from Catholic priests in the future.

The other district governors preferred a milder execution of the law to avoid conflicts with the church. District Governor Emil von Bernuth in Cologne expressed the apprehension that "the performance of the oath could easily lead to very distasteful conflicts if reservations should be preferred by the clergy." He thought that the power of the state to revoke the commission at any time was a sufficient safeguard. District Governor Arthur von Wolff in Trier also foresaw resistance and predicted that 90 percent of the school inspectors in his district would resign if they were required to take an unconditional oath. "Since such an eventuality would be undesirable, and since neither the necessary personnel for replacements nor the necessary money for another organization of school inspection is available," he did not intend to alter the present practice.[30]

The replies of the district governors indicate that state officials in the Rhine Province did not expect a sweeping reform of school supervision in the spring of 1873. Neither did Falk. When the state budget for 1873 was prepared, the ministry requested an appropriation for fifty county school inspectors. It increased the number to sixty in the budget for 1874. This modest budget was intended to cover salaries for school inspectors in the provincial districts with large Polish populations. When the National Liberals in the House of Deputies wanted to increase the appropriation to 100 full-time offices, the spokesman for the minister advised the budget committee against such a change.[31]

And yet by June 1875, 373 Catholic and 19 Protestant clergymen in the state had been removed from county school inspection offices alone. The number of churchmen dismissed from county and local school inspection offices was especially high in certain provincial districts in the Rhineland and the Polish-speaking areas, amounting to 341 in Oppeln, 242 in Düsseldorf, 235 in Posen, 137 in Trier, 116 in Marienwerder, 108 in

Aachen, 89 in Koblenz, 78 in Cologne, 76 in Münster, and 67 in Arnsberg. In the county school inspectorate 119 laymen replaced clergymen, with 34 in the Rhine Province, 27 in Silesia, 23 in Posen, 16 in East and West Prussia, and 16 in Westphalia.[32]

The swiftness of the change in the Rhine Province was not anticipated by officials in Berlin. An examination of how the secularization of the school inspectorate started reveals that the minister of education was far from being the initiator of the change or having a well-conceived plan. The *Kulturkampf* and the school bureaucrats in the province were the driving forces behind it. In the reform process Falk responded to political circumstances and initiatives in the province. He was overtaken by the pace of events in the Düsseldorf district and admitted in the House of Deputies on January 31, 1874, that had the budget for 1874 been prepared on that day, an appropriation for a larger number of full-time school inspectors would have been requested.[33]

Following Falk's orders for the execution of the School Supervision Law, the Düsseldorf district government requested the county councillors to file reports on school inspectors whose dismissal "should seem necessary or desirable in the interests of the schools." Their reports, submitted in May and June 1872, noted that some inspectors gave little attention to the schools because of old age or the heavy burden of pastoral work, but no recommendations for their removal were made. The county councillor in Moers wrote that "a forceful dismissal of the local school inspectors from their office, given the newness of the law, would only arouse hostility and discontent." After reporting that Father Lelotte belonged to a political club, the county councillor in München-Gladbach expressed "misgivings about the announcement of his removal at the present time on the basis of this circumstance alone."[34]

A year later the county councillor in München-Gladbach provided the first case for the appointment of a secular school inspector. He reported to Juncker in March 1873 that "the vehemently active ultramontane movement patronized by all priests in the county hindered the execution of new school regulations" and recommended the dismissal of Lelotte and Schrötteler. The misdemeanors of the two priests were not recorded. On May 4 Juncker forwarded to Falk a report containing vague and undocumented charges about the participation of the clergy in ultramontane political clubs in München-Gladbach county. He proposed that the inspection districts of Lelotte and Schrötteler be merged into one and entrusted to a layman appointed to a full-time office. Without an investigation Falk approved the change.[35]

Success in driving Catholic clergymen out of school inspection offices in one county emboldened the Düsseldorf district government to appoint secular inspectors for Catholic schools elsewhere. Juncker reported to Falk on July 14 that the Catholic schools in all counties on the left bank of the Rhine were "exposed to the same dangers" as those in München-Gladbach. He noted that in Geldern county many priests belonged to the *Mainzer Verein deutscher Katholiken* (Mainz Union of German Catholics). This association, founded in 1872 to defend the independence and rights of the church, was eyed by state officials with distrust. Juncker recommended the appointment of a secular school inspector because the government could place confidence in none of the Catholic clergymen in the county.[36]

The movement to secularize the school inspectorate gained momentum as opposition to the May Laws of 1873 provoked an increasing number of priests into political activity. Under the new legislation candidates for the priesthood were required to study only at diocesan seminaries placed under the authority of the state. The provincial governors were empowered to veto out of political considerations the appointment of any priest to a parish within thirty days of the bishop's notification. The church resisted these incursions. None of the bishops applied for state accreditation for the seminary in his diocese or fulfilled the legal obligation to register clerical appointments with the provincial governors for approval. Prosecuted by the government, many priests were sentenced to prison and five bishops were deposed from their episcopal offices. Archbishop Melchers was confined to a Cologne penitentiary in 1874.[37]

In the election campaign for the House of Deputies in October 1873, clergymen worked long hours to deliver the Catholic vote to the Center party, which increased its seats from 58 in 1870 to 88.[38] Throughout October and November the county councillors filed reports on the activity of priests who campaigned for Center party candidates in the *Mainzer Katholiken-Vereine* and in other parish clubs. When the Cologne district government asked *Landrat* (county councillor) von Sandt in Bonn to present evidence for his report on a priest, he replied that it was "an impossible task since Father Minnartz, although known to the masses as a leading and tireless agitator, does not lack cleverness and moves mostly on a boundary which precludes the application of criminal law." The lack of proof did not prevent the district governor from requesting and receiving authorization from Falk to oust Minnartz from his school office.[39]

August vom Ende in Düsseldorf exceeded the other district governors in the severity of his disciplinary actions after the election. On November 26 he informed the school officials in the *Abteilung des Innern* that Falk had assigned him the special task of directing "with utmost decisiveness" the dismissal of school inspectors who had participated in the agitation of the ultramontane party. He instructed Juncker "to settle cases still pending with as much haste as possible and to act firmly so that the minister's orders are carried out unrelentingly."[40]

When school officials in Düsseldorf submitted to Falk on December 5 a proposal for the appointment of more laymen to county school inspection offices, the minister and his chief advisers discussed whether it would not be more expedient to reorganize school supervision systematically throughout the Rhine Province rather than to handle it case by case. Falk decided to set aside the Protestant schools for the time being and to appoint secular inspectors for the Catholic schools in the entire province. In his guidelines for the recruitment of the new inspectors, he recommended that the district governors select *Gymnasium* and *Lehrerseminar* teachers and give particular attention to applicants of the Catholic faith without being bound to any confessional requirement. On December 15 Provincial Governor Moritz von Bardeleben informed the district governors of Falk's decision and ordered them to set the boundaries of school inspection districts and to nominate candidates for the new offices.[41]

School officials in the district governments began this undertaking eagerly and with the conviction that the appointment of professional educators as school inspectors was "the first prerequisite for the improvement of the schools."[42] The proposals that they sent to Provincial Governor Moritz von Bardeleben criticized the traditional system of school inspection without reference to the rhetoric of the anticlerical *Kulturkämpfer*. They noted that the clergy "with their wide range of pastoral work in heavily populated parishes lack the time and energy to devote themselves to school supervision with all its demands."[43] Because extensive travel and robust health were required of the county school inspectors, supervision was deficient wherever the pastors or priests in the office were old and ill. They were optimistic in their expectations of the benefits that would come from the change. The secular inspectors would rectify poor instruction in German grammar, the history and geography of the fatherland, and natural science, provide expert pedagogic direction in schools staffed with teachers without a certificate because of the shortage of *Lehrerseminar* graduates, and enforce rigorously school attendance in localities where truancy was high because of the employment of school-aged children in sugar beet refining and other industries.

The school officials did not conceal their profound disappointment with Falk's decision to confine the reform to the Catholic schools. In their reports to the provincial governor they expressed "the urgent wish and expectation" that a similar system of school supervision would be extended to the Protestant schools. *Schulräte* Bernhard Henrich and Ferdinand Stiehl in Koblenz wrote that the restricted implementation of the reform "would discriminate and harm Protestant schools and create discontent among the Catholic population, who would easily see an insult in the elimination of only Catholic clerical county school inspectors." *Schulräte* Albert Florschütz and Franz Linnig in Cologne argued that because the school inspector's work was technical, professional qualifications rather than confessional considerations should determine the appointment. A dual system would be a constant source of Catholic grievance and an obstacle in providing a national education for school children of all religious faiths. They appealed to Falk to revise his policy:

> From the standpoint of peace among the confessions, we must consider it opportune to extend secular school inspection to all schools without differences in respect to religion because the equal treatment of the confessions would take away from each one the grounds for complaint. We consider this measure desirable and timely in another respect as well, because through it the first successful step would be taken to the goal toward which modern culture constantly strives: to emancipate the school more and more from confessional and church influence and to claim for the school, on the basis of the peaceful equality [of the confessions], the character of a purely cultural and educational institution for the entire nation without distinction in respect to confession.[44]

In his report to Berlin on January 28, 1874, Bardeleben did not communicate to Falk the grave concerns expressed by school officials in Cologne and Koblenz. He mentioned briefly their wish to extend the advantages of school supervision by full-time professionals to the Protestant schools and omitted altogether the arguments that they had made for treating the Catholics and the Protestants alike. He advised Falk to begin the reorganization of school inspection with the Catholic schools and "to await the practical results before the reforming hand is placed on all county school inspection offices." The extension of the reform to the Protestant schools was postponed for political reasons. The financial cost of implementing a comprehensive change was not weighed. What concerned Bardeleben instead were the political repercussions of removing Protestant church superintendents from the school inspectorate, namely the protests of clergymen throughout the state and the opposition of the Conservatives in the *Landtag*. Falk's reply of February 12 confirmed his decision to exclude the Protestant schools from the reform "for the time being."[45]

The disparity in the treatment of the Catholic and Protestant clergy was Falk's first serious blunder in the execution of the reform of school supervision. Another mistake was his insensitive response to the question of whether members of the Old Catholic sect, who had seceded from the Roman church after the proclamation of the dogma of papal infallibility, should be selected for the new school inspection offices. District Governor August vom Ende thought that they were *staatsfreundlich* (well-disposed toward the state government) and more reliable politically than the ultramontanes. But he knew that the appointment of members of the Old Catholic sect, whom the Roman church regarded as excommunicated, would be provocative, and he turned to Bardeleben for advice on February 7. Ten days later the provincial governor announced Falk's decision that the Old Catholics should not be disqualified.[46] The district governors selected altogether eight members of the sect. The appointment of these dissenters gave the millions of Catholics loyal to the Vatican one more reason to reject the reform.

Extension of the Reform to the Protestant Schools

The reform of Protestant school supervision was not delayed for long. Already in the summer of 1875 school officials in the Düsseldorf and Koblenz districts, which included a sizeable Protestant minority, were making plans to organize school supervision more efficiently in counties where the population was confessionally mixed and to put both Catholic and Protestant schools under the jurisdiction of the same inspector. Falk approved of the concept of nonconfessional inspection districts but made the establishment of new full-time school inspection offices dependent on the availability of funds in the budget of 1876.[47]

A hasty implementation of the reform in the Düsseldorf district caused Falk considerable political embarrassment in Berlin. On December 14 the district government removed Protestant clergymen from school inspection offices in five counties and, then forming nonconfessional inspection districts, transferred the Protestant schools to secular inspectors of the Catholic faith. These events came to the notice of Emperor William when the *Neue Preussische Zeitung*, the prestigious organ of Prussian conservatism, published a critical report on the dismissal of Pastors Schürmann and Zillessen from their school inspection offices in Moers county. William was upset when he read the article and demanded an explanation from Falk. Quickly Falk retreated and ordered the district governor to restore the two churchmen to their offices promptly.[48]

Falk did not cancel the changes introduced by the district government in the other four counties because there were very few Protestant schools, but his political intervention in Moers county undermined the efforts of the school bureaucracy to carry out an equitable reform of school supervision. Falk's special concession to the Protestants offended the Catholic citizens in the county. *Landrat* von Hochwächter observed that Catholic liberals were now murmuring that the state government was partial to the Protestants and discriminated against the Catholics. He thought that Falk's annulment of the order that transferred the Protestant schools to the supervision of a secular inspector of the Catholic faith had "caused much more bad blood than the issue of the order itself." If the state carried out a consistent policy and applied the same principles to both confessions, progressive-minded Catholics would not object to the reform of school supervision.[49]

In April 1876, Falk granted the Düsseldorf and Koblenz district governments the funds to establish full-time inspection offices for the Protestant schools and instructed them to consider the confessional character of the majority of schools in a county as much as possible in the selection of the inspectors.[50] Politics once again interfered in the implementation of the reform in Moers county. The Catholics constituted a little more than half of the population, but the Protestants had the advantage of having a few more schools. To be conciliatory and fair to both groups, *Schulräte* Johann Giebe and Franz Wittig had proposed in March that the Catholic schools in Moers county be assigned to the Catholic inspector in Cleve county and that the Protestant schools there be put under the supervision of a Protestant in Moers county. Falk rejected this compromise.[51]

In June rumors of the imminent appointment of a Protestant inspector for all schools in Moers county aroused the indignation of the local Catholic community. The county councillor reported to the district governor that Catholic liberals would transfer their support to the Center party in the upcoming election of the House of Deputies if a Protestant school inspector was installed in office. After consulting the leadership of the National Liberal party in Moers, the district governor concluded that the reelection of the party's candidate would indeed be in jeopardy, and he advised Falk to delay the appointment until after the autumn election. Assessing the situation from this own political perspective, Falk declined. He thought that any compromise or postponement of the reform in Moers county would bring down on him the wrath of the National Liberals and the Progressives in the House of Deputies who were beginning to express impatience with the slow pace of the school reforms. He was determined to appoint secular school inspectors for the Protestant schools in the province as quickly as possible in order to fulfill the expectations that his remarks in the House of Deputies had raised.[52]

Falk's speech in the House of Deputies on March 15 was his strongest public statement in support of the secularization of the school inspectorate since taking office and revealed how much the reform initiatives of the school bureaucracy in the Rhineland had influenced his thinking. He praised the district governments that had seen the advantages of school supervision by professional educators and were now proposing full-time county inspectors for the Protestant schools. He concurred with their viewpoint that it was not practical or efficient to form school inspection districts along confessional lines. He pointed out that the new inspectors in the Rhineland had been selected with great care, and he emphasized their qualifications as former school principals and teachers in *Lehrerseminare*. After admitting that *Gymnasium* teachers were not the most suitable candidates for the office, he held out the hope that more elementary schoolteachers would be recruited once the level of their professional training was raised.[53]

Supervision of Religious Instruction

The secularization of the school inspectorate did create problems for the supervision of religious instruction, as earlier generations in the Ministry of Education had foreseen. A mediation of the dualism between the state's supervision of the schools and the church's constitutional right to direct the instruction of religion was made all the more difficult because hundreds of Catholic priests were dismissed from local school inspection offices. Instead of waiting for the *Landtag* to pass a school law and without consulting the bishops, Falk issued a regulation on Catholic religious instruction on February 18, 1876. This decree became one of the most contested school measures of the imperial era. Among the Catholics the decree acquired the notoriety of being "the ultimate blow of the *Kulturkampf* in school affairs."[54] During Falk's administration 2,848 priests were prohibited from giving and directing religious instruction in the schools.[55] An examination of the circumstances in which the decree was issued shows that Falk was, in fact, redressing abuses of power in the provincial administration.

Unlike the Protestant schools in which the instruction of religion was given entirely by the teachers, the responsibility for teaching the subject in the Catholic schools was divided between the parish priest and the lay teacher. With the intensification of the *Kulturkampf* in 1874 and 1875, the Ministry of Education allowed the district governments a wide scope of discretionary power in banning the Catholic clergy from the schools. Parish priests who were charged with antigovernment political activity and dismissed from local school inspection offices were also forbidden to direct religious instruction. They were warned that the state government would prosecute them if they entered the schools. Similar disciplinary action was taken to combat the passive resistance of the clergy. Some priests contested the right of the secular school inspectors to supervise religious instruction by refusing to teach in their presence and found excuses to be absent from school during the inspector's visit. Other priests refused to comply with the ministry's command to remove from the Catholic schools a biblical history book that had been used for three decades with the approval of the archbishop of Cologne. They protested that Falk's order had violated the right of the church authorities to select the books used for religious instruction in the schools.[56]

The Düsseldorf district government exceeded the other provincial administrators in the severity with which it conducted a campaign to expel the Catholic clergy from the schools. Even the staff of Provincial Governor Moritz von Bardeleben was moved to question the grounds for the arbitrary action taken in the case of Father Driessen in August 1874. After *Landrat* Devens reported that the priest had declined to ring the church bells on the national holiday celebrating the victory of the Prussian Army at Sedan, he and the curates assisting him in the parish were forbidden to teach religion in the schools. *Regierungsrat* von Juncker authorized the county councillor to proceed along these lines promptly "if similar cases should arise in which the instruction of religion in school by the clergy could lead to inconveniences or could raise any kind of doubt."[57]

The campaign to banish the Catholic clergy from the schools in the Düsseldorf district culminated in two radical decrees in 1875. The first regulation on February 3 excluded all priests from the instruction of religion in the schools. Not yet satisfied, the *Kulturkämpfer* in the district government suspected that antigovernment priests would strive to regain influence over the youth by giving parallel religion lessons after school hours. On February 11 Juncker issued another regulation that denied the Catholic clergy the use of school facilities for religious instruction and required them to obtain special permission from the city councils for the use of the classrooms to prepare the children for Holy Communion and confirmation.[58]

Catholic priests who were prohibited from teaching religion in the schools protested that the district governments had violated Article 24 of the constitution. In their petitions to Falk and the provincial governor, they complained that the secular inspectors who extended their supervision to the instruction of religion were encroaching on the rights of the church. In response to these remonstrances, Falk formulated a new interpretation lessening the significance of Article 24. He stated that it was not yet a formal law and that the direction of religious instruction promised to the church did not encompass the authority to teach and to supervise.[59]

Falk's position was strengthened by a decision of the High Judicial Court in Berlin in the case of a priest who had been prosecuted for giving religious instruction in school without government authorization. The defendant contended that he was teaching religion under a commission from his bishop and as a priestly duty. The court ruled that the state had complete jurisdiction over the schools, including the instruction of religion, and that the activity of the clergy in the schools represented a commission granted by the state. Article 24 belonged to those provisions of the constitution that had been "suspended in their application until the enactment of a comprehensive school law." In the meantime it had "only the importance of a guiding principle for legislators."[60]

Catholic opposition and the dubious legality of the actions taken by the district governments forced Falk to open an inquiry on October 6, 1875. The investigation showed a wide diversity of administrative practices and convinced the minister of the necessity to regulate Catholic religious instruction according to common principles and "to moderate in important and essential points the edicts of the district governments that went too far."[61] Falk had a second motive: he knew that Article 24 posed difficulties for the enactment of the school law that was being drafted by his appointees in the ministry. At a time when the Catholic church was vulnerable, he saw the political expedience of specifying what the direction of religious instruction entailed so that the legal rights granted to the church would be minimal.[62]

The decree of February 18, 1876, laid down the fundamental principle that religious instruction in the schools was under the state's supervision and was given by teachers who were required to have only a state license. The instruction of religion was assigned to the lay teachers. But wherever it was customary for the parish clergy to teach the catechism in the schools, the decree allowed this practice to "continue under the condition that the pastor [or priest] arouses no misgivings in respect to his attitude toward the state within the school administration and follows obediently all [its] ordinances." The parish priest was permitted to exercise the church's direction of religious instruction in the schools "only as long as he does not endanger by his conduct those purposes which the state pursues in the education of the youth through the schools." In such a case the district governments were empowered to withdraw this prerogative from him. He was entitled to attend the religion lesson in order "to find out" whether the instruction was given properly and to present complaints to the state authorities, which alone had the power to censure and discipline the teachers.[63]

Catholics in the *Landtag* assailed Falk's decree and "the state's monopolization of religious instruction." Peter Reichensperger and Ludwig Windthorst charged that Falk had usurped the legislature's responsibility to determine the intent of the provisions of the constitution. They objected to the decree's treatment of religious instruction as a state function and argued that the government had neither the right nor the competence to appoint religion teachers and to decide what was authentic Catholic doctrine. Johann Alois Dauzenberg, a priest who had been discharged from his school inspection office when he campaigned as a Center candidate, criticized the elastic wording of the decree, which gave the district governments an extraordinary latitude for arbitrary behavior. He feared that the decree could "be interpreted and applied in a *kulturkämpferisch* manner."[64]

In 1876 the leaders of the Center party in the *Landtag* informed the government that the decree was so unacceptable to the church that "[the Catholics] would consider it better to banish religious instruction from the school so that the state could then leave it up to the churches alone." Baron Ignaz von Landsberg-Steinfurt and Ludwig Windthorst hinted that once the public schools were secularized, the Catholics would open private schools. A year later Reichensperger introduced a motion that requested the state government to revoke the decree, and warned that "the Catholics would be forced to demand the complete removal of religious instruction from the schools" if the subject was not taught under the supervision of the church.[65]

Although members of the National Liberal and Progressive parties defended Falk's policy and succeeded in tabling Reichensperger's motion, they did not conceal their disappointment in Falk. They were hoping that his administration would separate the school and the church, and regretted that this break had not been carried out completely.[66] To their chagrin he did not include Article 24 in the law of June 18, 1875, that repealed Articles 15, 16, and 18 of the constitution guaranteeing the church's independence in regulating its own affairs. Eduard Windthorst, a Progressive who belonged to the Old Catholic community in Bielefeld, lamented that the minister had lost an opportunity to "prepare the only possible free path for the school law." He exclaimed, "We have repeatedly expressed our fear that this article would pose very grave and insurmountable difficulties for the future enactment of the school law."[67]

Falk's Interconfessional School Policy

By 1876 Falk's school policies stood in the foreground of national politics. Besides the Catholic outcry, there was now a highly vocal Protestant opposition to the opening of interconfessional schools in the Rhine Province. For the public at large this innovation was the most unsettling educational reform of the 1870s. Unlike earlier ministers, Falk did not interpret Article 24 to mean that the confessional school had to be the norm in Prussia. He could not accept the view that the consideration of confessional conditions should take precedence over state interests in the organization of the public schools. The phrase "as much as possible" in Article 24, he contended, contained two reservations: first insofar as the claims that the state made on the schools permitted confessional issues to be considered, and second insofar as the number of pupils made it practical to take their religion into account.[68]

Falk revealed his sympathy for the concept of the interconfessional school shortly after he entered office. To generate public support for his plans to modernize the curriculum and structure of the *Volksschule*, he summoned a conference held in Berlin from June 11 to 29, 1872. Hardly more than five out of the twenty-eight participants were partisans of school reform. Two of the reformers spoke in favor of eliminating the differences of confessional doctrine in the instruction of the Christian religion, but none of the twenty-eight participants supported a completely secular school. They argued instead for the creation of interconfessional schools with three or more classrooms so that the instruction could be tailored to the learning ability of the pupils grouped by age. They wanted to set higher educational goals for the elementary school in order to prepare the youth for life in a modern industrial society. The Center and Conservative party notables, Hermann von Mallinckrodt and Hans von Kleist, as well as Ferdinand Stiehl defended the continuation of the one-classroom school as the means of ensuring that children of the same confession would be instructed by a teacher of that religious faith. When Stiehl claimed that the constitution required the confessional school to be the rule, Falk stepped into the heated debate and disputed his interpretation of Article 24.[69]

The new instructions for the school curriculum drafted by Karl Schneider after the conference represented a modest victory for the reformers. The General Regulations of October 15, 1872, encouraged the communes to merge one-classroom schools and made the school with at least three classrooms the norm to be attained in every school district.[70] Stiehl could not acquiesce in Falk's policy and resigned on October 14. Karl Schneider, who succeeded him as the minister's chief councillor for elementary school affairs, was convinced of the educational benefits of interconfessional schools in areas with a confessionally mixed population. He supported the reform without being dogmatic.[71]

The Ministry of Education encouraged the city councils in municipalities where the schools were maintained through communal taxes to merge small confessional schools so that the pupils could be taught in classrooms designated for each grade. Local officials had to submit their plans for reorganizing the schools to the district government for approval. Two directives issued by the Ministry of Education in 1873 and 1874 enjoined the district government not to reject as a matter of principle the opening of the interconfessional schools. Falk stated that the organization of interconfessional schools "deserves preference" over the establishment or continuation of small schools, which could not achieve high educational goals or provide a national education free of narrow opinions and prejudices.[72]

Falk never issued a general regulation ordering at one stroke the formation of interconfessional schools throughout the state. His policy was to introduce the reform cautiously and gradually. The Ministry of Education ordered the district governments "not to handle the matter uniformly according to general principles but to make a decision in each particular case after examining the circumstances." They were authorized to "give an impetus to the merger of confessional schools only if the deficiencies" of the existing arrangements "hinder the fulfillment of the tasks of the school and cannot be eliminated in any other way." Should the city councils wish to organize interconfessional schools, their proposals were to be approved under "the condition" that "the school system experiences a substantial improvement." Falk's strategy was to encourage and rely on local initiatives. He assumed that public apprehensions would vanish once the parents understood that the interconfessional schools did make adequate provisions for the instruction of religion according to the doctrines of the churches to which the pupils belonged.

Falk's strategy of gradual reform guided Franz Foerster and other officials in the ministry when they began to draft a school law in 1874. The draft of the school law, which Falk presented in a final form to the cabinet in June 1877, clarifies how he intended to achieve his goal. Exclusive legal sanction was given to neither the confessional school nor the interconfessional school; instead, the draft law fixed as the norm the school with three classrooms and set the school with three to six classrooms as a desirable goal for school districts with more than 5,000 inhabitants. Falk and his staff proceeded on the assumption that residential conditions would produce interconfessional schools as a matter of course wherever Catholics and Protestants lived together. More moderate than the politicians in the liberal parties, they eschewed ideological and categorical pronouncements on the interconfessional school. The *Motive* appended to the draft law declared that there was "little reason to require generally the interconfessional school and to make a decision in a question whose pedagogic aspect has not yet found agreement among educators and in which many political points of view come into consideration."[73]

The provisions in Falk's draft law aimed at a gradual elimination of small confessional schools. Existing confessional schools were allowed to continue, but the establishment of new ones was restricted by the condition that they had to have at least three classrooms to receive government approval. If the merging of confessional schools would "produce an improvement in the school system," the state authorities had to order the reorganization when the city council and the school board agreed and also in those instances when the school board balked at the reform voted by the city council.[74]

The organization of interconfessional schools provoked widespread Catholic and Protestant resistance. Protestant opposition on this issue contributed substantially to Falk's political decline from 1876 until his resignation in July 1879. The hostility astonished Falk and Schneider because the ministry's support for the reform was motivated by pedagogic rather than political considerations.[75] The scale of the opposition seemed to them to be out of proportion to the modest change that took place. A statistical report prepared shortly after Falk left office recorded 446 schools with both Catholic and Protestant teachers and 71 schools with Christian and Jewish teachers. The interconfessional schools were concentrated in a few provinces, including 200 in West Prussia, 76 in Posen, and 68 in the Rhine Province.[76] Most of the 78 interconfessional schools in Hesse–Nassau were founded under the School Edict of 1817 before the Prussian annexation of the duchy.[77]

Falk thought that Catholic and orthodox Protestant agitators had misled the public by characterizing the interconfessional school as the first stage in the elimination of Christian influence from the *Volksschule*.

Actually Falk was hurt less by his opponents in the Center and Conservative parties than by his National Liberal party supporters. His interconfessional school policy failed because of the manner in which it was carried out on the local level. The introduction of the interconfessional schools in the Rhineland from 1874 to 1879 is essentially a story of how and why the reform went astray.

The Opening of Interconfessional Schools

In the Rhineland political pressure for the organization of interconfessional schools came from a coalition of liberals who formed the *Gesellschaft für Verbreitung von Volksbildung* (Society for the Dissemination of Public Instruction) with local chapters or *Bildungsvereine* in Bonn, Cologne, Düsseldorf, Krefeld, and other cities. Jürgen Bona Meyer, a professor at the university in Bonn, and Ludwig Friedrich Seyffardt, a silk manufacturer in Krefeld and a member of the National Liberal party in the House of Deputies, were the foremost leaders and publicists of this advocacy group.[78] Its membership roll listed many other liberal politicians, including Max Duncker, Johannes Miquel, and Hermann Schulze-Delitzsch.

The *Bildungsvereine* did not advocate the secularization of the elementary schools. Few liberals thought, as Max Duncker did, that the only honest solution to the school question was to eliminate religion from the curriculum and to leave the instruction ultimately to the churches entirely.[79] Miquel, Seyffardt, and other members of the National Liberal party did not champion this cause because they wanted to maintain the state's monopoly in the field of education and to extend it to the instruction of religion. Teaching religion as a required subject in the public schools guaranteed that the instruction would be given in the state's interests and under the state's supervision.

Moreover, members of the National Liberal party feared that if the public schools were secularized, the Catholic church would invoke the right to teach and open private schools. This anxiety about the church's use of *Unterrichtsfreiheit* (freedom of teaching) made them reluctant to see education as a matter falling within the province of individual rights. In the sphere of education, they thought, only through the limitation of individual rights could the state protect its own interests as well as genuine freedom and modern culture against any attempt by the church to establish a parochial system of popular education. Seyffardt argued that the state must make public school attendance obligatory and that "this control should not be relinquished for the sake of a philosophical theory of tolerance." If the state "permits private schools freely in order to satisfy special confessional interests, then it is only serving the ambitions of the clergy to dominate [education], as the example of Belgium proves."[80]

Much of the ideological fervor with which the liberals fought for the organization of interconfessional schools sprang from an idealistic political ethos. They were convinced that the separation of Catholic and Protestant schoolchildren bred intolerance and a deep alienation of one segment of the nation from the other. They argued that the civic consciousness of German society could not be nationalized by preserving in sharp extremity the differences of religion and politics that divided citizens into hostile camps. Through a national education they hoped to diminish confessional particularism, to cultivate patriotism and shared political loyalties, and to establish the primacy of the relationship of the citizen to the state. In the aftermath of political unification, an interconfessional school system seemed to the liberals to be a panacea for a segmented society that had not yet attained cultural and national integration.[81]

In the propaganda of the *Bildungsvereine*, anticlericalism seeped in through the cracks between the reformers' lofty educational goals of tolerance, moral self-responsibility, and patriotism. The anticlericalism of the Protestant liberals in the Rhineland arose not only out of their hostility to political Catholicism but also out of their elitist disdain for Catholic piety, which had a resurgence after 1850. In the enhanced authority of a more ultramontane clergy, in the increased cult of the Virgin Mary and the Sacred Heart of Jesus, and in the growing number of pilgrimages to sites associated with apparitions of the Virgin and healing miracles, they saw a religion of superstition and obscurantism that posed a threat to the moral and cultural progress of human society.[82]

The propagandists of the *Bildungsvereine* depicted the Catholic school as a cradle of religious fanaticism, cutting the pupils off from all emotional ties to the fatherland and instilling in them complete devotion to the church and subordination to the church hierarchy. The confessional bias that penetrated the instruction heightened the children's awareness of the historical hostilities of the Catholics and the Protestants and gave them a distorted view of the epochs of the Reformation and the Thirty Years' War. The arguments of the liberals frequently lapsed into a polemic against the Catholic clergy and teaching nuns. In a tract published in 1876, Seyffardt blamed the poor learning achievement of Catholic schoolchildren in the Rhineland on the priests in school inspection offices to whom "it seemed much easier for the preservation of their clerical domination not to bring the children beyond the minimum of school education which is needed or required for communion and confirmation instruction." He censured teachers belonging to Catholic religious orders for reducing the education of the girls to the memorization of prayers.[83]

The members of the *Bildungsvereine* fought to introduce interconfessional schools wherever they were elected to the city councils. Cologne was the first big city in the Rhineland where liberal-oriented politicians attempted to carry out a sweeping reform. Their opportunity for dissolving the confessional schools came when *Schulrat* Franz Linnig proposed a plan for the reorganization of the city's fragmented system of school supervision. A Catholic and a former *Gymnasium* teacher, Linnig was the most dedicated reformer in the school bureaucracy in the province in the 1870s. In 1874 he proposed the abolition of the city's nineteen parish school boards, the appointment of a secular school inspector for the entire city, and the expansion of the size of the schools to six classrooms. Through these changes he intended to eliminate the domination of the parish clergy over the schools and to provide the pupils with a broader curriculum in schools with six grades.[84]

Linnig did not recommend the organization of an interconfessional school system. A pragmatic and moderate reformer, he wrote to Mayor Alexander Bachem that merging the Catholic and Protestant schools in the city in one stroke was not feasible. The most efficient way to carry out the reforms was "to take a middle road which proceeds from the existing conditions and adheres to them as much as possible."[85] The liberal politicians in the city council were disappointed and named a special committee to revise his reform plan under the chairmanship of Johann Hamspohn, a member of the Old Catholic sect and the leader of the *Bildungsverein* in Cologne.

On April 29, 1875, the city council voted to open interconfessional schools and to assign teachers to the schools without regard to their religious faith. The vote of the city councilmembers, who were elected under an unequal franchise based on the payment of taxes, did not reflect the sentiments of the Catholic population well. Mayor Bachem, one of the Catholic dissenters, argued that it would be presumptuous to establish interconfessional schools before a school law laid down the norms for implementing Article 24 of the constitution. He warned that the "experiment" would offend both Catholic and Protestant parents.[86]

The actions of the city council angered Linnig. He feared that the city council's decision would disrupt the implementation of his own proposals. In the district government's report to Falk on May 15, *Schulräte* Florschütz and Linnig contended that while the establishment of inter-confessional schools was in principle a suitable means to promote reli-gious tolerance, during the present church–state conflict it would not be prudent to introduce the reform in Cologne. They warned that the opening of interconfessional schools would "offer welcomed nourishment to the ultramontane agitation and lend it the appearance of justification in the eyes of a large mass." They pointed out, furthermore, that a multitude of problems would beset such a reorganization of the school system because of the shortage of Protestant teachers and because "a large part of the present teaching personnel as a result of their pro-nounced confessional training may lack that pedagogic tact which is required for working in interconfessional schools."[87]

A petition sent to Falk by the presbytery of the Protestant congrega-tion of Cologne reinforced the argument made by Florschütz and Linnig. Claiming to speak for the interests of the Protestants who lived in a Catholic population that was eight times greater in number, the presby-tery contested the city council's decision and itemized the disadvantages of an interconfessional school system for the Protestant children. Be-cause the Catholic teachers outnumbered the Protestant teachers by seven to one, the Protestant pupils would be taught mostly by Catholics. The preconditions for interconfessional school instruction were missing in the Rhineland because all Catholic teachers had been trained in confessional *Lehrerseminare* and were exposed to the confessional bias of the Catholic clergy.[88]

The Cologne case revealed to Adalbert Falk the difficulties of introduc-ing the interconfessional school. The Catholics were not alone in their opposition. Resistance would come also from the Protestants especially in areas where they were a small minority and fearful that Protestant life would be submerged by the cultural environment of the Catholic major-ity. This anxiety was expressed in the presbytery's petition. In his reply to the district government on August 16, 1875, Falk agreed that the im-provement of the school system in Cologne should be carried out "with as much respect for the existing conditions as possible." He cited the short-age of Protestant teachers when he rejected the city council's proposal as unfeasible. His optimistic expectations of the pace of eliminating confes-sional schools up to now had been tempered, and his policy took a moderate course:

Consideration of the practical need and pedagogic advantage alone must be decisive in making decisions on the confessional character that is to be given to the schools. Announcing the interconfessionalization of the schools all at once as a matter of policy, as the city council proposes, is to be done as seldom as the rejection of the interconfessional school in all cases.[89]

Johann Hamspohn and other politically liberal city councilmembers who sat on the municipal school board continued their fight for the interconfessional school. A plan adopted by the school board in February 1877 proposed the dissolution of the four Protestant schools in the city and the creation of eight interconfessional schools.[90] After the district government refused to approve it, Mayor Hermann Becker, a Progressive party politician who had been elected to the office in 1875, appealed to Falk to override this decision, and a delegation of city councilmembers went to Berlin to meet with him.

The disadvantages of interconfessional schooling for the Protestant minority in Cologne once again determined Falk's response. Florschütz and Linnig enclosed in their report to the minister a petition from the presbytery protesting the action of the school board. The presbytery contended that no practical or pedagogic need warranted so disruptive a measure as the dissolution of the Protestant schools. After hinting that the school board was motivated by political considerations, the presbytery stated flatly that it would not let the Protestant community of Cologne become a victim of liberal partisan politics.[91] Falk turned down the mayor's appeal on the grounds that the proposed change would not affect the Catholics and the Protestants equally. When he read the district government's report, what struck him was that all Protestant pupils would attend interconfessional schools while some 11,000 Catholics would continue to receive instruction in confessional schools.[92]

In the 1870s the residents of the Rhineland frequently compared the political battles over the schools in Cologne and Krefeld. Unknown to the public were the reasons for the school system becoming interconfessional in Krefeld but not in Cologne or Düsseldorf. In the House of Deputies in 1877, Julius Bachem, a young lawyer from Cologne, remarked that the Catholic population in the industrial city of Krefeld—being less educated and affluent than the Catholics in Cologne—had not fought the change as vigorously.[93] His explanation overestimated the impact of the Catholic opposition in Cologne and did not do justice to the tenacity with which the Catholics in Krefeld had defended their schools. In the Cologne conflict the arguments of the school officials and the opposition of the Protestant presbytery weighed heavily in the ministry's deliberations. In Krefeld the National Liberals fought the school bureaucrats stubbornly and were successful in applying political pressure on Falk in the House of Deputies.

In September 1875 the city council in Krefeld adopted an interconfessional school policy and a plan to implement the change in stages.[94] The National Liberal majority in the city council that voted for the reform represented the city's Protestant bourgeois elite. The Catholics constituted a big majority of the population, but as taxpayers they fell mainly in the third electoral class and were underrepresented in the city council, elected on the basis of an unequal suffrage.[95] Mayor Christian Roos encountered an unexpected obstacle when he requested authorization from the Düsseldorf district government to carry out the reform. *Schulräte* Giebe and Wittig applied the policy set by Falk in the Cologne case on August 16, and stated that the city council had to justify the reorganization of each school "with reasons of practical need and pedagogic expediency."[96]

The National Liberals in Krefeld were determined to open interconfessional schools and submitted a second plan to the district government in January 1876. Mayor Roos made no attempt to disguise the political reasons that motivated the city council. The new challenge of a strong Center party in Krefeld roused the National Liberals to fight the Clericals in the school domain. The mayor wrote that the Center party had captured the Reichstag seat in the last election and that a National Liberal party defeat in the upcoming *Landtag* election could also happen. Although only one candidate of the Center party won in the last city council election, he explained that the exclusion of the Catholic majority from the city's government had been achieved "only artificially by a tax qualification for the vote, which would not have been set so high under other circumstances. This is a situation which must produce only constant mistrust, hatred, and bitterness among the citizens," he bewailed.

Mayor Roos argued that the mentality of the Catholic population had to be changed before they could be granted a voice in the city council. In the confessional schools the Catholic youth were imbued with a sharp distrust toward citizens of another faith. While complete devotion to the church and unconditional subordination to the authority of the church hierarchy were taught, "the precept of duty to the state and the civic community retires to the background." The nature of the mayor's interest in school reform was fully exposed in the conclusion of his argument:

> It is a matter of reforming gradually the fundamental spirit of this population and preparing for a future time when the Catholics will be seen again as fully qualified citizens of the community, . . . when the Catholic citizen

does not deny a worthy Protestant candidate his vote for the Reichstag and
the House of Deputies, [and] when the label 'Clerical' will have here only an
historical importance. These results will be achieved slowly but all the more
securely and permanently if the intellectual preparation is done through the
interconfessional schools.[97]

The district government continued to adhere scrupulously to the policy
set by Falk in the Cologne case and declined to approve the reorganization of the entire school system in Krefeld. With similar firmness, the
district government blocked the execution of a plan to make the school
system interconfessional in the city of Düsseldorf, which a liberal majority in the city council adopted in the fall of 1875. The liberals resented
these decisions and chided the school officials for interpreting errone-
ously the minister's directive of August 16, 1875.[98]

Early in 1876 the National Liberals began to show signs of impatience
with Falk. Friedrich Seyffardt thought that the directive issued in the
Cologne case had been contrived "to avoid embarrassing demands by
creating artificial obstacles."[99] He was disappointed in Falk's unwillingness to take a stand on the school question in principle and reproached
him for showing a lack of consistency and resolution. He detected in
Falk's behavior "a timidity which makes concessions to the objections
raised by the orthodox Protestants."[100]

The National Liberals and the Progressives put pressure on Falk in the
House of Deputies. On February 23 they confronted him with an interpellation to find out when he intended to introduce a school bill. The
legislative session was approaching an end without the enactment of a
school law, and they were worried because the reforms that had been
carried out did not rest on the enduring foundation of a school law and
could be canceled by any minister in the future. Eduard Windthorst
acknowledged the difficulties created by Article 24 of the constitution
and assured Falk that after showing their willingness to repeal Articles
15, 16, and 18, the two liberal parties would "not hesitate to create for the
minister a free path so that he can carry out his reform ideas unob-
structed and give the country a liberal school law."[101] Without going into
details, Falk communicated to the House of Deputies his desire to have
more practical experience with the innovation of interconfessional
schools before setting general legal norms:

> The danger which lies here is that the most important questions are
> decided, or the tendency arises to decide them, simply according to abstract
> principles and without examining the actual conditions. Therefore, it is

necessary to show by the creation of certain institutions how they operate in practical life so that a more correct decision is made than if it was done a priori.[102]

Under the pressure of restless and discontented supporters in the House of Deputies, Falk responded to an appeal from Mayor Roos on March 8. In his letter the mayor related the efforts of the city council to open interconfessional schools and accused the school bureaucrats in Düsseldorf of employing obstructionist tactics. He referred to the political circumstances in Krefeld and complained that the district government had "ignored the political and national point of view." Urging Falk to intervene and settle the dispute, he wrote that "the creation of interconfessional schools should be promoted especially where political and national considerations make a change of the existing conditions necessary and expedient."[103]

On March 27 Falk ordered District Governor Karl von Bitter—who came to Düsseldorf when August vom Ende was promoted to the provincial governorship of Hesse–Nassau—to conduct an inquiry. Several days later he instructed Bitter to negotiate a settlement in Krefeld personally because Mayor Roos had no confidence in *Schulrat* Wittig.[104] He took this step to conciliate the National Liberal party in Krefeld after a private discussion with Roos in Berlin. Bitter conceded to the mayor's wishes when they met on April 10 and recommended to Falk the opening of six interconfessional schools in the city.[105]

From 1876 on, Krefeld was torn apart by the most vehement political battle over the schools fought in the Rhineland. Local Center party politicians and the editor of the *Niederrheinische Volkszeitung* were untiring in their agitation against the interconfessional schools, and the issue dominated the election campaigns for the city council and the House of Deputies.[106] In March 1877 the city council adopted another plan to reorganize school instruction and to make eight more schools interconfessional. The Catholics staged a massive protest rally, and the local clergy appealed to the district government to reject the proposal of the city council. For over three months the district government made no decision. Before Karl von Bitter left the district to assume a new office in Berlin, he yielded to the strong-willed mayor and granted approval for the opening of the interconfessional schools.[107]

The school conflicts in Cologne and Krefeld were not isolated instances of disagreement between the school bureaucrats in the provincial districts and the political liberals in city government whose zeal for educational reform was kindled by the *Kulturkampf* and party politics. The attempt of the mayor and the city council in Kirn to merge the Catholic and Protestant schools also encountered resistance from the Koblenz district government. Like the events in Krefeld, the school conflict in Kirn shows how politics took over the cause of educational reform during Falk's administration and how the interconfessional school became discredited as a *Kulturkampf* institution throughout the Rhineland.

Kirn had two confessional schools with overcrowded classrooms, which led each school board to request the appointment of a new teacher. In June 1874 the city council voted instead for a plan devised by Mayor Rau to save money by merging the two schools and adding only one classroom. The Koblenz district government declined to authorize the consolidation of the two confessional schools and ordered the appointment of an additional teacher for each school. This decision was made with the advice of the county councillor, who warned the district government that the approval of the proposal of the city council would have far-reaching consequences for the entire county whose population was confessionally mixed. Many communes with a Protestant majority would imitate Kirn and "in all cases the Catholic population will be deeply offended." He reported that in Kirn the two Catholics in the city council had voted against the merger and the Catholic school board had voiced its opposition.[108]

In an appeal to the minister, Mayor Rau criticized the district government for ignoring "the national side of the question," which had led the city council to make its decision:

> To be exact, the national education of the youth has been neglected in the Catholic schools. How else does one explain the fact that Catholic subjects appear as enemies of the state government in questions which do not affect religion. It is without a doubt that a decisive improvement will come if Catholic and Protestant children are instructed in the history of the fatherland alike and if they are educated to be devoted to the fatherland and its princes. The entire education must be changed, and clerical influence must be pushed back with a better education. Then the state will no longer find itself in the situation of having to fight among its own subjects enemies who are led by clerical influence to recognize not the princes of their country but the bishops as their rulers.[109]

Falk responded to this crude anticlerical argument by ordering District Governor Karl von Konopacki to submit a report.

The district governor ordered *Schulrat* Henrich and the county school inspector to report on school conditions in Kirn and requested the two school boards to express their views. Henrich sent the school boards a copy of the mayor's letter, apparently with the intention of disgracing him. The mayor's letter wounded the Catholic citizens of Kirn and intensified their opposition to the opening of an interconfessional school. In a protocol sent to the district government, the Catholic school board rebuked Mayor Rau for resorting to "the now very popular platitudes of the '*Kulturkampf*'" to prop up the interconfessional school cause. The school board served notice that if nonconfessional schools were "introduced by force and without reason," political strife would bring to an end the peaceful coexistence of both confessions in Kirn.[110]

In his report to Falk on March 30, 1875, District Governor von Konopacki wrote that when his staff first discussed the issue in 1874, both supporters and opponents of the interconfessional school agreed that it was not advisable to introduce the reform in the Koblenz district at the present time because it would only inflame political strife and heighten the consciousness of confessional divisions within the nation. The district government had already ordered, in accordance with the General Regulations of 1872, the consolidation of confessional schools with one classroom in three villages. Konopacki referred to these experiences and told Falk that the opening of interconfessional schools was bitterly contested by both Catholic and Protestant parents. Taking issue with the mayor, he contended that the establishment of interconfessional schools was not required for the cultivation of national consciousness and patriotism because the state already had control over the school curriculum and the training of teachers.[111]

The arguments made by *Schulräte* Henrich and Stiehl in the district governor's report made little impression in the ministry. In his reply, Falk silently passed over their advice about the untimeliness of the reform and their observations about public sentiments. Little weight was given to their objections because the vocal opposition in Kirn, as Falk took care to point out, came only from the Catholics. The Protestant school board to which the mayor belonged supported the merging of the two schools by a margin of one vote. Declaring that "better attention" was "given to national education in the interconfessional school," Falk granted his approval of the proposal to the city council.[112] He was personally sympathetic to the mayor's argument. A year later in a debate on the interconfessional school in the House of Lords, he hinted that had the political point of view been the sole decisive consideration, the school administration would have promoted the merging of confessional schools on a wider scale.[113]

In the Koblenz district, interconfessional schools were opened in small towns and villages where Protestant majorities in the communal councils voted to merge the confessional schools. Their deliberations were heavily influenced by financial considerations; they sought to avoid the expenditures of appointing an additional teacher or building a new schoolhouse. Everywhere the Catholic parishes protested the decision to the state authorities, and in some localities the Protestant presbytery joined the opposition. In four cases in 1874 and 1875, the new schools were organized after Falk intervened and annulled the negative decision made earlier by the district government.[114]

The different decisions made by the school officials in the Düsseldorf and Koblenz districts and the Ministry of Education in Berlin bring to light Falk's inconsistency and susceptibility to liberal political pressure and the profound reservations about interconfessional schooling that prevailed within the school bureaucracy. In a detailed report in 1878, Henrich and Stiehl described the interconfessional schools as "defective institutions" for the instruction of history and religion. Unity and continuity in the instruction of history were sacrificed because the teachers excluded those centuries that were subject to confessionally different interpretations. The subject of the Reformation was added to the lessons for biblical history. For the instruction of religion, the children belonging to the minority in various grades left their classrooms and were taught by another teacher of their own faith. Any reference to the religion lesson in the instruction of the other subjects was prohibited. Under these conditions, concluded Henrich and Stiehl, "it is obvious that the intensive influence of religious instruction must suffer." A teacher who did not give religious instruction to all pupils in his class and who could talk about religious behavior and motivation in the other lessons "only with great caution and reserve on account of religious differences and distrust cannot exercise an effective educational influence."[115]

Catholic Opposition

Public reaction in the Rhineland to the school reforms was overwhelmingly hostile. The liberals in the *Bildungsvereine* never countered the Catholic opposition by employing the same tactics of mass demonstrations and petition campaigns. Support for their school reform program was confined to a segment of the Protestant laity, and they had no other option than to rely on the powerful state machine.[116] Although the

Catholic movement had a stronger popular base and drew crowds of more than 1,000 supporters to mass rallies, it was the outcry of the Protestant church that proved to be more effective politically. The grievances of the Protestants in the Rhineland found a hearing in the highest official circles in Berlin, from Emperor William to the High Church Council and the Conservative party in the *Landtag*.

Parish priests played an instrumental role in the Catholic opposition movement. Clergymen became bold and intransigent opponents of Falk's administration because of their experience of injustice and persecution during the *Kulturkampf*. The circumstances in which they were discharged from local school inspection offices and prohibited from giving and directing religious instruction in the schools embittered them. The district governments took disciplinary action against many priests following reports from local informers. The allegations were made by mayors affiliated with the liberal parties and by teachers who had personal grudges and/or legitimate grievances. For example, the teacher who denounced Father Marx had been reprimanded by him for drunkenness and neglect of school duties, and the teacher who testified against Father Berrisch resented the public censure of his brother, an Old Catholic, in a Sunday sermon. Priests were accused of being "ultramontane agitators" and "enemies of the state" because they had joined a pilgrimage of condolence to visit the imprisoned archbishop of Cologne or had declined to hoist the national flag on the church tower and to participate in the festivities on Sedan Day.[117]

The mayors who notified the school inspectors of their dismissal did not inform them of the grounds for the government's action. The government's conduct seemed all the more arbitrary to the clergymen because they were denied the right to hear the charges and to respond. The parishioners stood faithfully by their priests, and the district governments could seldom find educated Catholic laymen who were willing to fill the vacant offices. They had no other choice than to commission mayors and village magistrates to serve as local school inspectors.[118]

Many priests who suspected foul play submitted petitions demanding to know the reasons for their dismissal. The government's replies were a cold rebuff. Father Berrisch, who had served as an army chaplain during the recent wars, stubbornly took his appeal to the minister of education. His petition led to an inquiry that exposed the high-handed manner in which the state bureaucracy in the Rhineland executed the School Supervision Law of 1872. State officials in Cologne thought that it would not be consistent with the authority of the school administration to inform Berrisch and other priests of the reasons for their dismissal or to present them beforehand with a formal list of charges. Local school inspection was a commission granted by the state, and the revocation of the commission was "not bound to any judicial procedure with an investigation and judgment." They claimed that "the harmful influence of a priest on the school is self-evident even though it cannot be traced back to specific individual and proven actions."[119]

Beginning with a rally in Münster on October 19, 1875, the Center party organized a mass protest movement against the *Kulturkampf* in the school system. At this meeting two members of the House of Deputies and Father Franz Schulte spoke to a crowd of nearly 3,000. In the early months of 1876 big demonstrations took place in other cities in the Rhineland.[120] As Norbert Schlossmacher's study of Catholic grassroots politics in the city and rural county of Düsseldorf suggests, the school question played a central role in the political mobilization of the Catholic populace in the Rhineland.[121] The emotions of Catholic citizens were aroused more quickly by the issues of confessional schooling and religious instruction in the schools than by any other measures of the *Kulturkampf*. The local leaders of the Center party built up a mass political movement in the 1870s by focusing much of their agitation on the *Kulturkampf* in the schools and by exploiting Catholic antipathy to exaggerated claims about the sovereign power of the state and the school monopoly of the state. At club meetings and popular rallies Catholic priests and local politicians drove home the message that the conflict was precipitated by a state that claimed the school as its exclusive domain and deprived the parents of their rights in respect to the education of their children. They inveighed against "the liberalism of our times" whose tendency was "to remove the children from the sphere of parental rights and to declare them to be more or less state property."[122]

Catholic dissidence grew bolder after Falk issued the decree of February 18, 1876. The clergy were so alienated by the state's attempt to control the instruction of religion in the schools that many priests employed the tactic of threatening the government with resistance. One petition signed by nearly 500 priests in the dioceses of Münster and Paderborn admonished Falk that religion could be an obligatory subject of school instruction only with the cooperation of the church. If the state acted without the participation or against the will of the church authorities, "the church would have to consider immediately whether it should forbid the teachers to give the instruction and the faithful to attend the state's instruction of religion."[123] In September 1877 the *Katholikentag* threatened the government again with the possibility of a test of strength between the church and the state. This annual gathering of German

Catholics, a popular forum for Center party politicians, adopted a resolution declaring that the instruction of religion without any church supervision could not be recognized as Catholic instruction and that Catholic parents were "obliged and entitled to keep their children from [it]."[124]

Reaction of the Protestant Clergy

The Protestant clergymen who protested Falk's school policies acted within the unique traditions of Rhineland Protestantism. Behind them was a heritage of defending the church's autonomy and resisting state control. After the province was incorporated into the Prussian monarchy in 1815, the Protestants fought for nearly twenty years to preserve their presbyteries and synods, composed of clergymen and elected lay elders, as the only governing bodies for the church. The dispute ended with a compromise. The Rhenish-Westphalian Church Regulation of 1835 placed church administration in the hands of a provincial consistory appointed by the king and also allowed the county and provincial synods to continue. The synods remained thereafter a vital part of the church's life, and a highly educated and economically prosperous laity represented in equal number with the clergy lent them strength and influence.[125]

The Protestant clergy's response to the school reforms was deeply affected by the circumstances of living amid a Catholic majority. According to the census of 1871, the Düsseldorf and Koblenz districts alone had a sizeable Protestant community of around one third of the population. The Protestants were a smaller fraction of the population in the other three provincial districts.[126] Protestant churchmen were too conscious of the historical hostility dividing the two confessions to believe that they could live together on the grounds of mutual respect and tolerance. In an address at the Duisburg synod in 1876, Pastor Hermann Graeber challenged the optimistic assumptions of the liberal school reformers: "The powerful historical differences of many centuries cannot be blown away with the pipe of the interconfessional schools. Whoever thinks that he can do so knows neither the inner power of true religion nor that of superstition and fanaticism."[127]

Protestant churchmen had deep apprehensions that Protestant culture would be swamped by the Catholic environment of the Rhineland. When they opposed the merging of confessional schools in communes with a small Protestant parish, their views of Protestant interests were skewed by fear of the Catholic church. Graeber told the Duisburg synod: "These small parishes, which have to defend themselves against the superior power of Rome constantly pressing upon them, lose with their schools their strongest support and an essential condition for existence."[128] Impressed by the powerful resources available to the Catholic church—the confessional, a sensual liturgy, processions and pilgrimages, and the authority of the priesthood—Protestant clergymen contended that it did not need the confessional schools to the same extent as the Protestant church.[129]

Protestant churchmen manifested signs of discontent with Falk's administration as early as the provincial synod of 1874, where one after another lamented the radical change in the relationship between the church and the school brought about by the School Supervision Law. A passionate debate arose over the appointment of clerical school inspectors on the basis of a state commission that could be revoked at any time. The pastors called it an offense to their dignity, and a few went so far as to argue that honor obliged the clergy to decline the office under the new law. The presiding church superintendent implored them not to resign school inspection offices except for well-founded reasons and expressed the hope that the law would be revised when the *Kulturkampf* ended.[130]

The discontent, smoldering for more than a year, was aflame in 1876. Protestant churchmen suspected that Falk intended to appoint secular school inspectors for all Protestant schools in the province. Because he had authorized the opening of interconfessional schools in several towns, they mistrustfully concluded that he was introducing a radical reform quietly and that the school law being drafted in the ministry would place elementary education on a nonconfessional foundation. Furthermore, they began to fear that the rights and interests of their own church would be sacrificed in the state's struggle to break the power of ultramontanism. Their attitude toward the *Kulturkampf* became ambivalent. Graeber criticized the tendency of the liberal *Kulturkämpfer* to extend the power of the state:

> The task of true liberalism is to oppose the omnipotence of the state and to recognize the rights of the family and the commune in the schools. . . . But the *Kulturkampf* seems at the present time to blind many eyes and to lead intelligent men to measures which they would otherwise disavow in principle.[131]

A committee formed by Pastors Engelbert in Duisburg and Zillessen in Orsoy called upon devout Protestants to attend a public demonstration in Düsseldorf set for March 15. The protest meeting with about 300 participants took a more moderate course than the organizers had expected. General Superintendent Friedrich Nieden from Koblenz, who had recently returned from a visit to Berlin, assured them that "in the highest government circles significant misgivings against interconfessional schools exist and are expressed." He dissuaded them from launching a mass petitioning movement and advised them to protest to the state authorities in specific cases.[132] The assembly decided to issue a declaration to the press, rejecting "the interconfessionalization of the *Volksschule* [as] an unlawful encroachment on the religious liberty of the people" and demanding that the government take the rights of the family into account in any reorganization of the school system.[133]

District Governor Karl von Bitter was astonished at the independent spirit of the Rhineland clergy and reacted vigorously to quell the opposition. He issued an order to the Protestant school inspectors on March 14 not to engage in dissident political activity in the future, and reprimanded Engelbert and Graeber for agitating against the school authorities. He appealed to the provincial consistory to pronounce the establishment of interconfessional schools a matter falling outside the jurisdiction of the synods. The consistory's ruling that the Rhenish-Westphalian Church Regulation of 1835 granted the synods the right to discuss school affairs exposed the clumsiness of his efforts to silence the opposition.[134]

The opposition of the Protestant clergy in the Rhine Province led Protestants elsewhere in Prussia to fasten their attention on the *Kulturkampf* in the schools and to anticipate its consequences for Protestant life. The grievances from the people of the Rhineland were aired in the House of Lords on June 17, 1876 when the Conservatives contested Falk's school policies by means of an interpellation. Referring to recent events in the province, Hans von Kleist reproached the school administration for discounting confessional circumstances when school inspectors were appointed and when the boundaries of the inspection districts were fixed. He mentioned that the district governor of Düsseldorf had threatened to dismiss Protestant pastors from their school inspection offices for speaking out against the establishment of interconfessional schools. He disputed the pedagogic wisdom of putting "the principle of learning more" above the confessional character of the schools and declared that an education for nurturing religious faith and moral character was "more important than a higher degree of knowledge." He complained that the General Regulations of 1872 had reduced the weekly hours for religious instruction to four and had relegated religion to the status of a mere subject in the curriculum.[135]

Although Falk had discussed with a member of the *Landtag* from the Düsseldorf district in March the Protestant opposition to the interconfessional school, he did not address the grievances of the clergymen until he was confronted with the interpellation bearing the signatures of Kleist and other Conservatives in the House of Lords.[136] In a letter to the provincial consistory dated June 16, Falk attempted to allay the apprehensions of the churchmen by emphasizing the moderateness of his interconfessional school policy. His letter had the opposite effect and confirmed their suspicions. One statement left them with the impression that he favored interconfessional schools and did not place a high value on the preservation of confessional schools. The authorization for the opening of interconfessional schools, he wrote, could "not be denied" by the government in cases in which the schools were maintained by municipal tax revenues and where the city council voted for the change as a means of improving the instruction.[137] The provincial synod took issue with him and declared that the organization of interconfessional schools should be "permitted on an exceptional basis in circumstances of extreme necessity" and should "not be left to the discretion of the municipal authorities."[138]

At an assembly in Düsseldorf on September 6, activist clergymen founded the *Verein zur Erhaltung der evangelischen Volksschule* (Union for the Preservation of Evangelical Elementary Schools).[139] They were resolved to fight the introduction of interconfessional schools by city council decisions against the will of the parents and to prevent the enactment of a liberal school law. In the election of the House of Deputies in the autumn of 1876, the association circulated leaflets that criticized the National Liberal party for steering the nation toward a nonconfessional school system. After the election campaign it continued its propaganda battle against the National Liberals and tried to disengage devout Protestants from the *Kulturkampf*. It lamented that "the fight against ultramontanism has so confused minds" in Prussia that "one considers the sacrifice of the Protestant *Volksschule* as indispensable in order to fight and conquer the spirit of the Roman hierarchy."[140] Friedrich Seyffardt and other political liberals were described as disciples of modern secularism whose ultimate goal was to remove traditional Christianity and religious instruction from the schools.[141]

A delegation of clergymen met with Emperor William when he came to the Rhineland to observe the army's maneuvers in the autumn of 1877. The meeting apparently made a strong impression on him, and early in 1878 he sent an inquiry about the interconfessional schools in Krefeld to the Ministry of Education. The report that District Governor Robert von Hagemeister sent to Falk confirmed many of the misgivings of the Protestant churchmen. The Catholic confession was preponderant in the city's thirteen interconfessional schools. In none of the schools did the Protestant pupils reach 50 percent of the enrollment, and the imbalance between the two confessions was great in three schools. The district governor stated that although the Catholic clergy had lost their official relationship to the schools, "the great influence that they had exercised on the teachers has not diminished." All Catholic teachers in Krefeld, with two exceptions, were "subject to clerical and extreme ultramontane influence now as before."[142]

The provincial consistory, which had admonished the clergy not to agitate against the school administration in the spring of 1876, had come to agree with the opposition by 1878. Two years of experience uncovered the problems of teaching history and religion in the interconfessional schools. In a report to the Protestant High Church Council in Berlin on January 18, the consistory stated that the interconfessional school created difficulties for the educational function of the school and was detrimental to the vitality of parish life.[143] A month later its views were brought to Hagemeister's notice when General Superintendent Nieden interceded on behalf of the Protestants in Kaldenkirchen. The city council there decided to merge a Protestant school with an overcrowded Catholic school in order to avoid the expenses of building a new schoolhouse. Nieden implored him to prevent the execution of this plan and discussed at length how the interconfessional school posed a threat to the future of Protestant life in the Rhineland:

> It lies without a doubt in the interests of the Prussian state to preserve the small Protestant congregations in predominantly Catholic areas as hotbeds of patriotism and to prevent them from languishing and declining. By introducing interconfessional schools in place of schools with a Protestant character, these congregations would be cut off from a source of sustaining life and would be deprived of the main means of cultivating Protestant Christian life. Every interconfessional school among a predominantly Catholic population assumes more or less the character of a Catholic school and prevents thereby the maintenance and cultivation of Protestant consciousness in the Protestant children even if provision is made for their religious instruction.[144]

Hagemeister had no sympathy for the interconfessional school cause. He authorized the organization of an interconfessional school in Kaldenkirchen solely because the small schoolhouse for Catholic children had reached a desperate condition of overcrowdedness. In Düsseldorf, on the other hand, he turned down the proposal of the city council to expand and make a Protestant school interconfessional. In a confidential letter to Falk in April 1879, he criticized the political judgment of the mayor and

the liberal majority of the city council that saw "in the interconfessionalization of the schools a way of reconciling the presently intensified confessional differences or performing a service to the cause of the state in the
politico-ecclesiastical conflict." He observed that "the highest value is
placed on the preservation of the confessional character of the school in
all devout circles of both churches" and thought that "the interconfessionalization of the schools may be undertaken only with great caution
and only in such cases where the purposes of the school require it
urgently."[145]

By 1878 the experiences of the Rhine Province led many members of
the Protestant High Church Council to join the opposition to Falk's
school policies. The councillors, who were royal appointees and mostly
distinguished church superintendents and theologians, expressed their
dissent in a declaration issued on August 12, 1879, in preparation for the
forthcoming meeting of the General Synod. The council stated that the
social benefits expected from the interconfessional schools were exaggerated and that the disadvantages for the education of the youth, especially
in the instruction of history and religion, outweighed the desirability of
multiple classrooms in a school. It contended that "the Protestant church
suffers all the more because the school, especially in the diaspora, is its
most effective means of keeping the people in close relationship with the
church constantly." It deplored the opening of interconfessional schools
against the will of the parents and the local pastors. A proposal made by
the city council and "based on money-saving considerations or political
motives" had sufficed to secure the government's approval for an innovation that was "not required by necessity."[146]

In the circumstances surrounding Falk's resignation on July 14, 1879,
historians have focused on Bismarck's decision to shift from a free-trade
to a protectionist economic policy and to end the government's parliamentary alliance with the National Liberal party. Seeking a parliamentary majority for this new policy, Bismarck met on March 31 with
Ludwig Windthorst, who tied the willingness of the Center party to
support a tariff bill to the demand for Falk's removal.[147] Falk's departure
in the same month that the tariff bill was passed by the Reichstag led
many National Liberals and Catholics to conclude that it was part of a
bargain negotiated by Bismarck and Windthorst. Even without Bismarck's change of course in 1879, Falk's dismissal was bound to come
because of Protestant opposition to his school policies. Falk knew how
formidable this opposition was when he announced to the cabinet on
October 6, 1877 that he had decided not to introduce the school bill in the
coming session of the *Landtag*.[148] Since 1876, Emperor William had

become increasingly unhappy over Falk's school policies because of their impact on the Protestant church. Had William not been seriously wounded in the second of two assassination attempts and unable to conduct government business for months, he would have cashiered Falk in 1878.

The New Secular School Inspectorate

The political circumstances concerning the secularization of the school inspectorate prevented the Catholic community from viewing the reform dispassionately. Many Catholics regarded the new school inspectors as ambitious careerists and political opportunists. In 1877 a Catholic deputy from the Rhineland charged that "the newly appointed school inspectors have plunged themselves into the *Kulturkampf* and have seen their task essentially in the exercise of their authority in the service of a certain partisan line."[149]

The performance of the new school inspectors depended to a large extent on the political circumstances in the areas where they worked. In Posen a large proportion of the inspectors for the Catholic schools were German Protestant outsiders with little knowledge of the language and culture of the Polish-speaking people. As Chapter 4 shows, they became entangled in the nationality conflict by enforcing the government's regulations on school instruction in the German language. Upon them fell all of the resentment that the Polish people felt toward the Prussian state authorities. In the Rhineland the school inspectors belonging to the Old Catholic sect also encountered many difficulties and, as the school bureaucracy recognized by the early 1880s, they "never attained the confidence and respect necessary for a successful performance in the office." They had to contend with the ill will of the Catholic clergy and the unending attacks of the Center party's press.[150]

The results of the reform of school supervision in the Rhine Province were more beneficial than Catholic critics acknowledged. Appointed as county school inspectors were secondary schoolteachers, school principals, and instructors in *Lehrerseminare*. Carefully screening the applications, school officials in the provincial districts looked for candidates who were recommended for their pedagogic abilities, conscientious performance of duties, tolerance, circumspect judgment, and personal courtesy. The successful candidates were generally Catholics who were reserved in political life. They came from the Rhineland as a rule because school officials thought that men familiar with the region would gain the confidence of the people more quickly and avoid tactless errors more easily than an outsider.[151]

The professional educators in school inspection offices proved to be more competent and thorough during school visitations, more interested in the health and educational achievement of the children, and more active in the improvement of the schools than the clerical inspectors had been. The school inspection reports written by the clergy seldom described school conditions or evaluated the pedagogic skills of the teachers. During the 1860s, the clerical school inspectors in the Aachen district toured schools with more than 100 children crammed in a classroom without a comment on the necessity of expanding the school or appointing an additional teacher.[152]

The new school inspectors were the catalysts of the improvement of the school system in the Rhine Province during the 1870s. On inspection tours they observed carefully the deficiencies of the schools, from insufficient space and desks in overcrowded classrooms to the ill effects of poor lighting and ventilation on the health of the pupils. They recommended specific remedies in their discussion with the mayors after each visitation and in their reports to the district governments. School officials reacted decisively by issuing orders to the communes to renovate old schools, to construct new schools, or to create new teaching positions. The county councillors were instructed to see that the local officials complied and to apply stern pressure on those who stalled or resisted.[153]

The new school inspectors observed the pedagogic skills of the teachers with critical professionalism. They disapproved of the mechanical methods of teaching and the emphasis on rote learning, and commented on the poor performance of teachers who had not graduated from a *Lehrerseminar*. They strove to replace the untrained teachers by licensed teachers as much as possible. Constantly impressing on the teachers the need to continue their education, they opened teachers' libraries and obtained state funds to purchase the books. They organized teachers' conferences, meeting four to six times a year, to enable the teachers to learn and practice better pedagogic methods.

Following the reform of school supervision in the Rhine Province, the school system was rapidly improved and was in many respects the most progressive in the Prussian state. To alleviate the acute problem of overcrowded classrooms, 1,782 new offices for licensed teachers were created from 1873 to 1881. During the same period 953 new schools were constructed and 504 schools were expanded. Overcrowded classrooms remained a problem because of the tremendous growth of the population in the province. The population increased by more than 40 percent in ten counties between the censuses of 1871 and 1885. Despite the expanding enrollments, school conditions in the Rhine Province in 1882 with an average class size of 84 children were less critical than in other provinces, where the average number of pupils per class was 102 in Posen, 100 in West Prussia, 96 in Silesia, and 93 in East Prussia.[154]

The communes in the Rhine Province spent more on school maintenance than in any other province. In 1878 they spent 29.3 marks per pupil in comparison with 22.6 marks in Brandenburg and 19.2 marks in East Prussia. They relied on school fees paid by the parents to a far lesser degree than the school districts in the other provinces. In 1878, 71.6 percent of the costs for school maintenance were covered by communal taxes, 16 percent by school fees, 9.2 percent by state funds, and 3 percent by the income of school endowments. Of the total costs of school maintenance in the provinces of Brandenburg and Saxony, school fees accounted for 33.6 percent and 35 percent, respectively.[155]

In his report to the minister in January 1881, *Schulrat* Hermann Stoeveken of the Aachen district assessed the results of the appointment of professional educators as school inspectors by comparing them with the clergymen who had filled the office in the past. Stoeveken, who was himself a Catholic priest and had been a school administrator for more than a decade, concluded that the change "serves the interests of the school to a great extent." Noting that the Aachen district had earlier twenty-nine churchmen functioning as county school inspectors, he wrote that "the need for so many people did not permit the strict application of principles of selection that would produce the most suitable men for this important office." He observed that "the clergy in densely populated parishes could devote little time and energy to school inspection." He praised the new school inspectors for raising the morale of the teaching profession, correcting school deficiencies, and tightening up the enforcement of compulsory schooling.[156] From the contribution that the full-time school inspectors made to the improvement of elementary education in the Rhine Province can be gauged the loss suffered by the schools in the other provinces where the reform was not introduced.

As the evidence in this chapter shows, the liberal parties that voted for the School Supervision Law of 1872 and supported other *Kulturkampf* measures pursued more ambitious goals of school reform than Bismarck's limited political objectives. The prospects for school reform seemed to brighten when Bismarck chose Adalbert Falk, a judicial official who had once sat in the National Liberal *Fraktion* in the House of Deputies, to head the Ministry of Education in January 1872. In his early years in office, however, Falk confined the appointment of secular school inspectors to the Polish-speaking areas and did not devise any plan for professionalizing the school inspectorate or organizing an interconfessional school system throughout the state. When the school reforms were introduced in the Rhine Province in the 1870s, the initiative came from liberals in the city councils and progressive elements in the school bureaucracy.

Although the struggle against political Catholicism absorbed so much of the energy of Rhineland liberalism in the 1870s, it would be an oversimplification to identify the school reform movement exclusively with *Kulturkampf* politics. For the reformers in the school bureaucracy, the attack on the Catholic church was less important than the positive goal of improving elementary education. They saw the appointment of professional educators as full-time county school inspectors as a prerequisite for making improvements in the school curriculum and pedagogy. In the confessionally mixed counties, they strove to apply the new policy consistently and took issue with Falk's decision to postpone the extension of the reform to the Protestant schools. They spoke out for an equitable treatment of both religious communities and warned that Catholic grievances would arise from the discrepancy in the treatment of Catholic and Protestant churchmen by the Ministry of Education.

The interest of Krefeld's mayor and other liberal politicians in the cause of school reform was aroused to a large extent by partisan politics. The schools became the battleground for their fight against the Center party, which now challenged liberalism's political hegemony in the electoral districts of the Rhineland. Although partisan passion drowned out moral and pedagogic concerns in the school conflicts, liberalism's fight for interconfessional schooling had a deeper purpose than mere opposition to political Catholicism.

In the years immediately after the founding of the German Empire, the interconfessional school seemed to hold great promise for promoting cultural integration and a national civic culture in the new state. The liberals attributed the persistence of confessional particularism in Germany to school instruction that heightened the consciousness of the religious differences and historical antagonisms that separated the Catholics and the Protestants. Interconfessional schools providing a moral education free of religious dogmatism and prejudice, they argued, would promote tolerance and social harmony. The benefits that they expected from interconfessional schooling reflected their moral optimism and faith in progress through the spread of knowledge.

The weakness that the National Liberal and Progressive parties could never overcome was the lack of popular consent to their program of school reform. Only a segment of the Protestant laity supported the interconfessional school. In the city councils elected on the basis of an undemocratic three-class franchise, the liberal bourgeois elite that voted for the reorganization of the municipal schools did not represent well the majority of citizens who belonged to the Catholic faith. Convinced of the moral righteousness of their cause, the liberals were willing to rely on the coercive arm of the state government.

Falk did not carry out school reforms as expeditiously and resolutely as the liberals had expected. By 1876 they were chafing at his cautiousness and concern over the opposition of the Conservatives. To the disappointment of the liberals, he did not execute the School Supervision Law forcefully and exorcise clerical influence from the schools throughout Prussia. In spite of their importunities, he continued to delay the introduction of a school bill. While he concurred with them on the virtues of interconfessional schooling, he preferred to introduce the reform gradually and to rely on local initiative. They were critical of his reluctance to issue a regulation enunciating general principles and binding rules for the establishment of interconfessional schools.

The Ministry of Education ordered school officials in the provincial districts to make decisions in each case after examining the circumstances and to authorize city officials to merge the confessional schools only if such a reorganization would bring about a substantial improvement in school instruction. Judging each case from the viewpoint of pedagogic expediency rather than political ideology, the school bureaucrats in the Rhine Province vetoed the proposals adopted by the city councils to integrate Catholic and Protestant schoolchildren. They advised Falk that the *Kulturkampf* was an inopportune time to introduce interconfessional schooling and that such an innovation would exacerbate political tensions and fuel the Center party's agitation.

The opposition to Falk's school policy was a major cause of his political decline from 1876 on because it extended far beyond the Catholic population. The opposition within the Protestant church was stronger than many liberals acknowledged, and the bold spirit of its leadership astonished state officials. Protestant clergymen had deep-seated apprehensions about the baneful effects of interconfessional schooling on the small Protestant parishes in the Rhineland diaspora and on the Protestant upbringing of children who would be taught by Catholic teachers. Their trust in Falk and their approval of the *Kulturkampf* crumbled quickly when they saw the interests of their own church being jeopardized in the fight against ultramontanism. Their highly organized and vocal opposition convinced King William and Conservatives elsewhere in

Prussia that interconfessional schooling would do grave harm to the religious education of the children.

Tracing the defeat of Falk's school policy to a politically influential Protestant opposition leads to the related question of why his attempt to modernize the school system encountered such strong public resistance and ended up in a state of incompletion. Introducing the change during the *Kulturkampf* politicized the reform process and tarnished the goals of the reformers in the school bureaucracy and the teaching profession. The ideal of the interconfessional school with instruction for each grade in separate classrooms was discredited in the eyes of the Catholic population by being associated with the politics of the *Kulturkämpfer* in the liberal parties. Although Falk was more moderate than the membership of the National Liberal and the Progressive parties, he did not give the school officials in the province the support that they needed to keep school affairs out of partisan politics. The policy that he set in the Cologne school conflict, in the interest of the city's Protestant minority, was not applied consistently. Preferring to handle the interconfessional school question in a case-by-case manner and declining to issue specific regulations to be applied uniformly, he made many decisions out of political considerations. In the school conflict in Krefeld, he ignored the advice of the school officials in the provincial district and conceded to the wishes of the National Liberal politicians in the city.[157]

The failure of Falk, the son of a Protestant pastor in Breslau, to foresee and understand the depth of Protestant opposition to the interconfessional schools in the Rhineland is astonishing. The timing of the school reform was as wrong for the Protestants as it was for the Catholics. The consciousness of confessional differences was still too strong within the Protestant community to accept it. In areas where the Protestants were a minority, their attitude toward the Catholic church was a mixture of bigotry and distrust. The preconditions for the organization of a nonconfessional school system were missing in Prussia in the 1870s, namely tolerance, mutual respect between the religious communities, and a milder articulation of confessional differences.

The manner in which the professionalization of school supervision was carried out gave the reform a pronounced political and anti-Catholic character. The appointment of secular educators as full-time county school inspectors was confined to areas where the Catholics constituted the majority, 48 in the Rhine Province, 34 in Silesia, 25 in Westphalia, 23 in Posen, and 19 in West Prussia. In areas with large Polish populations many Protestant laymen replaced the priests who were dismissed. In Posen 17 of the 23 secular inspectors for the Catholic schools were

Protestants; the Protestant schools, on the other hand, remained exclusively under the supervision of churchmen. In the other predominantly Protestant provinces, the clergy maintained a virtual monopoly of county school inspection offices.[158]

Unfortunately for the cause of school reform, the Catholic clergy experienced these changes in the school system as governmental acts of persecution against the church. The circumstances in which they were ejected from school inspection offices and prohibited from giving and directing religious instruction in the schools left them bitter and aggrieved. The discrepancy in the treatment of the Catholic and Protestant clergy led the Catholics to focus on the inconsistent and discriminatory behavior of the school administration and to respond to the reforms with distrust and indignation.[159]

3

Confessional Schooling and School Politics in the Imperial Era

Reaction against Falk's School Policy

A reaction against Falk's school policy was inevitable when a Conservative belonging to the Pomeranian landowning nobility took over the Ministry of Education in July 1879. During his first months in office, Robert von Puttkamer made several highly publicized gestures to communicate to the nation his disapproval of the school reforms and his intention to end the *Kulturkampf* in the school system. In September 1879 he used the occasion of a reply to a petition signed by more than 400 priests in the dioceses of Münster and Paderborn to announce a policy of reconciliation. He declared, "I wish nothing more fervently than to be able to grant to the clergy of the Christian churches an effective role in the supervision of the elementary school." He pleaded with the Catholic clergy "not to succumb to the mistaken notion that the policy of the state is to be hostile or indifferent to the beneficial influence of the church on the instruction and moral and religious education of the youth." Once their resistance to the May Laws ceased, he promised to reinstate them in their former local school inspection offices.[1]

Another signal of the oncoming reaction was Puttkamer's dramatic intervention in the school conflict in Elbing, a city in the province of East Prussia, where the municipal council decided to organize an interconfessional school system in 1875. Ignoring the objections of the Catholic minority, city officials carried out the first phase of the reform in 1876 with the opening of four interconfessional schools for girls. The Catholic parents protested this change and the forthcoming merger of the confessional schools for boys in a petition addressed to Falk in April 1877. Their petition remained unanswered, and only after they renewed their appeal in February 1879 did the minister request a report from the district governor in Danzig. The report arrived in Berlin on July 28, apparently held back until after Falk left office.

The district government informed the new minister that "the Catholics in Elbing harbor a great distrust toward the interconfessional school, which the city government itself has provoked because it has constantly shown a conspicuous contempt toward all demands made on the school system from a church and confessional standpoint."[2] The harassment of the Catholics began when the Protestant magistrates took an official position against the dogma of papal infallibility and adopted a policy of appointing to teaching offices only Catholics who made a pledge not to teach the doctrine in the schools. By 1872 seven Old Catholics were teaching in the schools. The decision of the municipal school board in 1876 to assign Catholic religious instruction to two of the teachers belonging to this sect added more fuel to the burning conflict.

Deeply moved by this report, Puttkamer immediately opened an investigation and notified the city officials not to proceed further until he had made a decision. They assumed that the minister would not halt the completion of the reform at so late a date. They were stunned when he refused to authorize the opening of the interconfessional schools for boys on October 9. It did not escape his notice in reading earlier correspondence from Elbing that the underlying motives of the city officials were *kulturkämpferisch*.[3] He admitted in the House of Deputies that his decision was determined "to a considerable degree" by his conviction that "it is the duty of the highest administrative authorities to protect confessional minorities in places where their rights and interests are actually threatened."[4]

As much as Puttkamer valued the collaboration of the church and the state in the area of education, he was unbending in his conviction that the church's participation in the supervision of the schools had to be "regulated exclusively from the state's point of view."[5] He intended to rectify the injustices suffered by the Catholic clergy without yielding an inch of the state's sovereignty over the school system. He did not propose the repeal of the School Supervision Law. Nor did he revoke the decree of February 18, 1876, even though its constitutionality seemed doubtful to him.[6] The political course chosen by him was to avoid polemical discussions on constitutional principles and rights, and to terminate the *Kultur-*

kampf in the schools through the discretionary power and initiatives of the state administration.

On November 5, 1879, Puttkamer ordered the district governments to investigate every case in which Catholic clergymen had been excluded from the direction of religious instruction in the schools. State officials in the provinces had to examine whether the reasons for their dismissal were sufficiently grave to warrant such a measure and, if so, to consider whether their recent behavior offered justification for the belief that they would observe the regulations of the school authorities and not subvert the purposes pursued by the state in the education of the youth, should they be readmitted to the schools. Puttkamer's final words of instruction underscored the tolerant and generous manner in which he intended the directive to be carried out. The district governments should "be guided by objectivity and the view that only serious and substantial reasons supported by facts may justify the exclusion."[7]

When Robert von Puttkamer was appointed minister of the interior in June 1881, he ensured the continuation of his policies by the choice of Gustav von Gossler as his successor. During a decade in office, Gossler strove to restore the cooperation of the school administration and the authorities of the Catholic church. He established a cordial relationship with Bishop Georg Kopp of Fulda, whom he proposed for the bishopric of Breslau in 1887. He conceded to the wish of the archbishop of Cologne for the addition of one more hour to the weekly schedule of religious study in the schools.[8] Nonetheless, he declined to annul the decree of February 18, 1876, or to enter "theoretical discussions" on the claims of the church to constitutional rights in the supervision of the schools.[9]

Significant but uneven progress was made in conciliating the Catholic clergy. An increasing number of priests recovered their local school inspection offices and were allowed to direct the instruction of religion once again. It is difficult to graph the progress of this movement because the Ministry of Education, fearful of arming the Center party with political ammunition, disclosed little statistical information about the participation of Catholic and Protestant clergymen in school supervision on the local and county levels. Gossler reported to the House of Deputies that of all the priests who had been removed from the direction of religious instruction during the *Kulturkampf*, 542 were not yet readmitted to the schools as of January 1882. Most of them lived in the Polish-speaking districts of Bromberg and Posen.[10] When the ministry finally published a full report on provisions for religious instruction in 1901, Catholic clergymen were permitted to teach religion in 3,372 schools in the Rhine Province, 819 schools in Silesia, 661 schools in

Westphalia, but only 28 schools in West Prussia and 16 schools in Posen.[11]

By the end of 1883, 2,359 priests were local school inspectors for 4,723 Catholic schools throughout the state. The Catholic clergy in Westphalia were the most successful in recovering their earlier positions; 401 priests were local school inspectors, and only one fifth of the Catholic schools were under the supervision of local magistrates or other laymen. In the Rhine Province 909 priests served as local school inspectors for slightly more than half of the Catholic schools. The government commissioned fewer Catholic clergymen to be local school inspectors in the Polish areas of the eastern territories, for example, with 55 priests in the entire province of Posen and 34 priests in the Marienwerder district. More than 1,000 Catholic schools in Posen were not under the supervision of the local priests.[12] In 1890 a little more than 50 percent of the Catholic schools in the state were under the supervision of the parish clergy. In comparison, about 90 percent of the Protestant schools were inspected by the local pastors.[13]

Apart from the Polish-inhabited areas, Gossler did not expand the appointment of secular educators to county school inspection offices. Pedagogic arguments for the professionalization of school supervision made little impression on him. He took pride in being a pragmatic conservative and told the House of Deputies that in the administration of the schools he was disposed to "avoid a purely doctrinaire standpoint" and to ask how institutions had developed and whether the practices that had evolved over time were worth preserving. It was beyond question "that in the historical evolution of our fatherland *Konfessionalität* has been the leading principle for the organization of the elementary school system and that on this principle everything has been built."[14]

Gossler tried to retain clergymen in county school inspection offices as much as possible. When the bishop of Fulda ordered the clergy in his diocese to refrain from antigovernment activity and to observe the state laws, Gossler was ready to entrust Catholic archdeacons here with school supervision once again. In 1882, after the death of a secular school inspector, he instructed the Cassel district government not to recruit another layman for the vacancy immediately but to consider whether two suitable priests were available for the office. State officials in Cassel had to handle this matter "with a careful consideration of school interests and the desirable collaboration of the state and the church in the educational sphere."[15]

Because the provincial synod in the Rhineland persisted in protesting the secularization of the school inspectorate, Gossler initiated a confidential inquiry in 1889 to find out whether the appointment of Protestant clergymen as county school inspectors would be advantageous. The reply deterred him from contemplating a full-scale reaction. The provincial governor consulted the Düsseldorf district government, which had thirty-one full-time inspectors who had jurisdiction over schools of both confessions. District Governor Hans von Berlepsch emphasized that Protestant churchmen could not be installed in the office once again without extending the same privilege to the Catholics. He argued that "such a change would not be a benefit for the school system, but instead the good progress that it has made since 1872 would probably be impaired." Clergymen frequently did not possess a sufficient knowledge of pedagogy to win the respect of the teachers. Resentment of the clerical school inspectors on the local level was already rampant in the teaching profession, and the teachers would see the appointment of churchmen as county school inspectors as "a reactionary step harmful to the development of the school system."[16]

Until 1890, the professionalization of school supervision still left untouched the predominantly Protestant areas of Prussia, where the traditional link between the offices of church superintendent and county school inspector was preserved. A significant change in policy occurred when Robert von Bosse became the minister of education in 1892. A moderate reformer, Bosse announced in the House of Deputies in 1893 that the school administration was moving in the direction of appointing professional educators as full-time inspectors throughout the state. The occasion was his defense of a budget appropriation for twenty-six additional full-time offices. He observed that developments within the school system were leading toward the formation of a professional school inspectorate. The increasing number of school classes in areas where the population had multiplied and the ever-growing burden of paperwork required of the inspectors made it difficult for many church superintendents to fulfill the responsibilities of this office thoroughly and conscientiously.[17]

Financial and political considerations prevented Bosse from quickly removing the clergymen still serving as county school inspectors. An immense increase in the budget would have been required to implement this change because the average cost of a full-time secular inspector for the state treasury was estimated in 1900 to be 6,400 marks in comparison with the average cost of 400 marks for a part-time clerical inspector. During his seven years in the ministry, Bosse established seventy new full-time offices for densely populated industrial areas, and by 1899 the number of secular inspectors had risen to 310.[18] This trend slowed down thereafter because Catholics and Protestant Conservatives in the House of Deputies formed a powerful coalition against a policy that was driving the clergy out of the schools. For political reasons Bosse's successor, Konrad Studt, conciliated them with assurances that laymen would replace the churchmen only in exceptional cases.[19] Until 1908, only 346 offices for full-time county school inspectors were funded in the state budget, and as many as 839 county school inspectors were still clergymen.[20]

The Persistence of Confessional Schooling

The expansion of the professional corps of school inspectors, restricted to Catholic and heavily populated industrial regions, diminished by no means the confessional character of the Prussian school system. The reaction against Falk's school policy begun by Puttkamer set the school administration on a course that it followed throughout the imperial era. Declaring that the supporters of the interconfessional schools were "defending a lost cause," he announced his adherence to a policy of confessional schooling in the House of Deputies in December 1879. He criticized the coercive manner in which the liberals had established interconfessional schools, and thought that Falk had not protected sufficiently the rights and interests of religious minorities. Observing that the reform had been a partisan issue in city council elections, he stated that matters of school organization must be left up to the ministry, which would make the decision "according to long-established traditions rather than caprice and subjective opinion."[21]

During his years in office, Gossler declined to engage in any pedagogic or ideological discussion of the relative merits of the two types of schools.[22] His school policy was influenced by the significance that he placed on the historical development of the *Volksschule* in Prussia and by his observation that, in areas where Catholics and Protestants lived in close proximity, the parents showed an enduring predilection to educate their children in schools in which the pupils and the teachers were of the same religious faith. As an undersecretary of state in the Ministry of Education in 1879, Gossler conducted an intensive study of the confessional character of the school system. What impressed him in his examination of the statistics gathered by the ministry was that the religious diversity of Prussian society had not produced a large number of schools with confessionally mixed enrollments.[23]

Puttkamer and Gossler worked actively to dissolve the interconfessional schools that had been organized during Falk's years in office, and took a personal interest in hastening a settlement of the school conflict in Krefeld. When approximately 3,000 Catholics in Krefeld petitioned Puttkamer to restore the confessional organization of the school system, he asked District Governor Robert von Hagemeister in January 1880 whether their request could be fulfilled. The district governor urged Mayor Christian Roos to concede to the wishes of the Catholic parents. Besides being weary of the partisan fight over the schools in Krefeld, he thought that the reform had not turned out well. In April the mayor informed Hagemeister that he was prepared to sponsor a compromise, which would reinstate the confessional status of eight schools in the inner city and leave intact five schools in the outlying districts.[24]

Before the city council voted on the mayor's proposal, local Catholic politicians mobilized a popular movement to return the entire school system to its old confessional foundation. Catholics in the city council submitted a counterproposal to abolish all of the thirteen interconfessional schools.[25] At this time the citizens of Krefeld were excited over the annulment of Friedrich Seyffardt's victory in the election of the House of Deputies after the Center party filed a complaint about irregularities in the balloting. A new election was scheduled in May. The interconfessional school became the burning issue in a bitterly fought contest between the two parties. The capture of the seat by the Center party left the National Liberals in an angry mood. In October, the city council's majority rejected the proposal submitted by the Catholic councilmen and took an uncompromising stand in defense of the interconfessional schools.[26]

When the district governor related to Puttkamer what had happened in Krefeld, he criticized the Center party politicians who had exploited the school question for partisan purposes, and advised the minister not to inflict a humiliating defeat on the National Liberal party and order the abolition of the interconfessional schools by administrative fiat. Under these political circumstances Puttkamer did not concede to the wish of the Catholics, but neither did he close the case. He ordered the restoration of the Catholic status of one school, which had no pupils of the Protestant faith, and instructed the district governor to continue his efforts to make the remaining twelve schools confessional once again.[27]

A yearlong stalemate in the conflict was broken by Gustav von Gossler after meeting with a Catholic delegation from Krefeld. On January 2, 1882, he instructed the district government to take into consideration the wish of the Catholic parents to educate their children in confessional schools. Besides appeasing the Catholics, the district governor was now anxious to restore the confessional division of the school system for the sake of the Protestant minority. Because forty-two of the school classes had ten or fewer Protestant children, he assumed that the Protestant consciousness of these pupils was being "repressed" in the overwhelmingly Catholic environment of the schools. In March he ordered the reconfessionalization of three schools for Catholic children and the transfer of the Protestant pupils to the remaining interconfessional schools so that the imbalance between the two confessions would no longer be so great.[28]

Gossler was not satisfied with this piecemeal reorganization of the school system in Krefeld and instructed the district government in April to encourage the city magistrates to reinstate the confessional status of the other nine schools. Impatiently he demanded in September a report on what steps had been taken. During this interval the district governor had waited for Mayor Ernst Küper, who had replaced Roos in May, to take the initiative. Now Hagemeister concluded that the new mayor was "afraid to broach this matter" and that "it had to be settled more by administrative measures." He notified Küper that the confessional organization of the school system was "demanded by the minister as a matter of principle," and ordered the city government to complete this change by the spring of 1883.[29]

Gossler and the ministers who followed him did not apply the confessional school policy consistently. As Chapter 4 relates, the government used an exceptional law in Posen and West Prussia, which placed the authority of appointing schoolteachers in the hands of the state entirely, in order to create interconfessional schools, initially as a means of protecting the German minority from being acculturated by the Polish majority in Catholic confessional schools and then as an instrument for the germanization of the Polish population. The increase in the number of interconfessional schools from 503 in 1886 to 803 in 1901 was concentrated in these two provinces; 403 were located in West Prussia and 169 in Posen.[30]

The idea of organizing elementary education along interconfessional lines never took hold in the other provinces. That interconfessional schools were not established in provinces where Catholic and Protestant inhabitants were intermixed reflected not only the ministry's policy but also the opinions and preferences of the people. Only three interconfessional schools were created in Westphalia. After 1879 most of the interconfessional schools in the Rhine Province became confessional, leaving twenty-three in existence by 1891. The small number of interconfessional schools in Silesia were confined to the heavily Catholic Oppeln district and were intended to protect the Protestant minority.[31]

Berlin was a political stronghold of the left-wing liberals, but its educational system did not actually break with the practice of confessional schooling. In 1901 only 36 of the 249 elementary schools were interconfessional. Each one of the interconfessional schools had a large Protestant teaching staff with the addition of one Catholic or Jewish teacher to ensure that religious instruction would be provided for the religious minority. The education of the Catholic minority took place mainly in Catholic confessional schools, which enrolled 86.8 percent of the Catholic schoolchildren in the city.[32]

The pattern of confessional schooling was sustained throughout the imperial era even though the growth and mobility of the population produced larger minorities in regions where one or the other confession was predominant. The Catholics had a higher rate of growth, increasing from 33.4 to 36.3 percent of the total population between 1871 and 1910. Catholic enclaves formed in the heart of Protestant Prussia, in the city of Berlin, and in the provinces of Brandenburg, Hanover, and Saxony. On the other hand, the Protestant population grew faster in the Rhine Province and Westphalia, where internal migration enlarged the Protestant minority in the Cologne, Düsseldorf, Koblenz, and Münster districts.[33]

Except for the Jewish community, the percentage of children receiving instruction in public schools of their own confession remained high during these years (see Table 1). The statewide average for the Catholic schoolchildren was lower than for the Protestants because the Catholic population was scattered over a wide diaspora area and because a large number of Catholic pupils in Posen and West Prussia attended interconfessional and Protestant schools. In the other provinces the percentages were higher than the statewide average for each confession: for the Catholics as high as 99 percent in the Rhine Province and nearly 100 percent in Westphalia, and for the Protestants as high as 100 percent in

TABLE 1.   Percentage of Children Receiving Instruction in Public Schools of Their Own Confession between 1886 and 1906.

Year	Catholic	Protestant	Jewish
1886	91.4	95.3	37.4
1891	91.2	95.6	31.2
1901	90.4	95.6	28.8
1906	90.6	95.2	27.3

Hanover, most of Pomerania, Saxony, and Schleswig. Catholic and Protestant populations were far less intermixed on the local level than the confessional distribution of the population seen on the provincial or state level would suggest. In only half of the thirty-six provincial districts did the number of Catholic, Jewish, and Protestant children attending schools of another confession altogether exceed 2,000 in 1886 and 1901.[34]

Catholics in School Politics

Despite the ministry's efforts to conciliate the Catholic clergy and return to a confessional school policy, the Center party remained an aggrieved opposition in school politics until the end of the nineteenth century. While economic interests absorbed the attention of other groups in Germany, the Catholics were intensely preoccupied with confessional issues. The experience of the *Kulturkampf* fostered a siege mentality among them and left them with a sense of isolation and marginality in a society that equated German patriotism and national loyalty with Protestantism.[35] The clergy remained embittered and could not forget their injuries. The clerical contingent in the Center party's *Fraktion*, especially Dasbach, Dauzenberg, Mosler, Neubauer, Perger, and Steinbusch, devoted most of their attention to school politics and aired Catholic grievances that arose out of the *Kulturkampf*. During the annual debate on the education budget, they assailed the legacy of the Falk era and called for the repeal of the decree of February 18, 1876, and the restoration of the school arrangements that predated 1872. Denouncing trends in the administration and curriculum of the schools since 1872, they frequently succumbed to inflated oratory about the secularization of the *Volksschule*.[36]

The opposition stance of the Center party developed from distrust and a defensive mentality. The Catholics were deeply suspicious of a school administration that had Protestant personnel from the minister of education down to school officials in the provincial bureaucracy.[37] Although Ludwig Windthorst welcomed Puttkamer's directive of November 5, 1879, he was convinced that officials subordinate to the minister would sabotage his conciliatory policy. Center party deputies repeatedly charged that the *Kulturkämpfer* in the district governments were not executing the directive conscientiously. They complained about the large number of Catholic schools that were still not under the supervision of the parish priests, and called on Gossler to investigate how the provincial bureaucracy was complying with his orders.[38]

Activist priests also kept the school issue burning by ventilating their grievances at the annual *Katholikentag*. Each year they proposed a vote on resolutions protesting the state's encroachment on the rights of the church in the school. In provocative speeches, they denounced Falk's administration for misusing the schools for political purposes and condemned "the school monopoly of the state."[39] Clergymen who were politicized during the *Kulturkampf* took an uncompromising stand against the government's policy of terminating the conflict by administrative measures. The intransigents, who spurned goodwill gestures and demanded the total repeal of the *Kulturkampf* laws, found in Windthorst their chief spokesman in the Center party.[40]

At the *Katholikentag* in 1885, the intransigents launched an attack on the Catholic nobles in the leadership of the Center party, who were eager to move out of opposition and to negotiate a compromise settlement of the *Kulturkampf* with Bismarck. Father Kappan, a political activist in the diocese of Münster, summoned the Catholics to reopen the fight for the church's rights in the school before complete inertia befell the school question. He was part of that group in the church who had said in 1880 that clergymen should not resume activity in the schools until the School Supervision Law was revised and the decree of February 18, 1876 was annulled. Now he contended that as increasingly more priests were permitted to direct religious instruction in the schools, "the fight for the schools on the ground of principles has quieted." He criticized the Center party for abandoning principles in school politics and relying on an amelioration by administrative acts.[41]

A pragmatic wing within the church hierarchy led by Bishop Georg Kopp differed with Windthorst and his coterie of radical priests. Kopp agreed with Gossler that disputes between the church and the state over principles should be avoided. He believed that concessions on both sides had to be made and could be made without damage to the church's independence.[42] At the Bishops' Conferences in Fulda in the 1880s, he opposed any collective manifestation of opposition to the government. In 1887 he succeeded in blocking a movement to address a petition to the government that would have demanded the revocation of Falk's decree. As he wrote to Gossler a day after the meeting, he did "not want the bishops to give the impression of following Windthorst's political watchword," and he considered "any principled treatment of this matter to be the beginning of a new *Kulturkampf*."[43]

In the 1890s the Center's fight to abolish the legacy of the *Kulturkampf* in the school system evolved into a campaign for *Parität*, the equal treatment of the Catholic and Protestant confessions in public life.

During the annual debate on the education budget, the Center party deputies protested the discrimination against the Catholics in the school administration. They drew public attention to the discrepancy between the appointment of laymen as county school inspectors in areas heavily populated by the Catholics and the presence of Protestant clergymen in the office elsewhere. Father Johann Alois Dauzenberg ironically inquired why the state authorities did not appoint professional educators as inspectors for the Protestant schools if the change was so beneficial. He demanded that the government grant to the Catholics the same privilege that the Protestant churchmen possessed.[44]

The Protestant monopoly of offices in the school administration was another Catholic complaint. The Center party pointed out that all but three of the councillors in the Ministry of Education and Religious Affairs and all of the directors of the *Abteilung für Schulwesen* (Department for Public Education) in the district governments were Protestant. Bachem and Dauzenberg contended that the preponderance of Protestants in the school administration gave the Catholics no assurance that matters affecting them were handled with a sympathetic understanding and a generous heart. They demanded that the government appoint a Catholic to head the school administration in the provincial districts where the Catholics constituted the majority of the population and at least one Catholic school official in districts where they were a minority.[45]

The Center's charges of *Imparität* or discrimination, repeated year after year, caused Robert von Bosse much embarrassment. On these occasions he became irritated and lost his composure. He called the complaints unfounded and chided the Center deputies for "pouring only new oil on the fire of confessional sensitivity." Although he insisted that government appointments should be made solely on the basis of professional qualifications and not according to "a mechanical parity," privately he admitted that the ministry had to mollify the Catholics and to defuse the issue of *Imparität*. Between 1893 and 1899, the number of Catholic priests invested with the office of local school inspector increased from 3,830 to 7,305.[46]

The Second Reaction against Falk's Administration

While the Catholics were demanding a return to the status quo ante 1872, the Conservative party spearheaded a fiscal reaction against Falk's administration by calling for a retrenchment in school expenditures. When the district governments started to enforce the General Regulations of

October 15, 1872, rural communities that had long neglected school needs were required to make costly improvements. The General Regulations set eighty as the maximum number of pupils for one-classroom schools and seventy as the maximum size of a class in larger schools. The code prescribed the essential equipment that each school had to have and set standards for the physical structure of the school to ensure that the classrooms had sufficient space, ventilation, and light. Rural school districts in Brandenburg and Pomerania, where school expenses averaged 8–12 marks per pupil in 1871, were spending an average of 17–21 marks for each child in 1878.[47]

Rural householders resented the heavier burden of school maintenance and were hostile toward the school bureaucracy. Bismarck heard many estate owners grumble about the "one-sidedness" of school officials who issued orders for the construction of a new schoolhouse or the appointment of an additional teacher without taking into account the financial resources of the locality.[48] Conservative party deputies aired these complaints during the annual debate on the education budget. In 1885 Wilhelm von der Reck implored the school administration to refrain from ordering the local communities to expand school facilities as long as agriculture was suffering from an economic depression. In a reference to the General Regulations, which required the instruction of history, geography, and natural science, Reck scolded the school bureaucracy for striving to educate children in the countryside beyond the needs of their future occupations.[49]

Puttkamer was all the more sympathetic to these complaints at a time when farm prices during a prolonged agricultural slump were low. In a directive on May 28, 1881, he told school officials in the provincial districts that because the nation was recovering from the disastrous effects of a free-trade policy, they should consider whether their demands for new school facilities had stretched to the limit the financial resources of the local communities. He cautioned them not to expect a considerable increase in state funds for school purposes and instructed them to give careful attention to the economic circumstances of a locality before issuing orders for school improvements and "to postpone them even if they may be desirable and useful insofar as they cannot be carried out without unreasonable pressure on those responsible for school maintenance."[50]

Robert von Puttkamer's policy slowed down the fast tempo at which the school system had expanded during Falk's administration. Adalbert Falk's years in office were an era of unprecedented progress in the school system. To overcome the critical shortage of teachers, he established twenty-one new *Lehrerseminare*, and within a decade students in teachers' training schools almost doubled. The economic depression in the middle of the 1870s made occupations in industry and the trades less attractive to the sons of artisans and peasants, and the rising incomes and pension benefits of the teachers made school employment seem financially more secure. The ministry granted subsidies to assist the local communities in remunerating the teachers, and school officials in the provincial districts applied strong pressure on them to increase the salaries. From 1871 to 1878 the total income of male teachers increased by 24.5 percent in the city and 26.2 percent in the countryside.[51]

Appropriations for elementary education in the state budget increased at an extraordinarily fast pace during Falk's administration. In 1872, the year he entered office, the budget contained an appropriation of 1.5 million marks for the improvement of teachers' salaries. In the following years, a fund earmarked for the salaries of teachers and school subsidies became a regular part of the state budget, increasing from 7.5 million marks in 1873 to 12 million marks in 1877–1878. Whereas 4 percent of the total school expenditures in Prussia came from state funds in 1867, Falk enlarged the state's share of this burden to 12.2 percent by 1878. The state tripled its expenditures for school construction and renovation in the countryside.[52]

The communes and *Schulsozietäten* spent large sums to improve school conditions, occasionally out of civic pride but in most instances after the district governments had ordered and coerced them to build a new schoolhouse or to create a new teaching office. From 1873 to 1881, 9,088 new offices for licensed teachers were established, and 5,975 new schools were constructed. The public investment in elementary education grew at an unprecedented rate. Total school maintenance expenditures rose from 55.6 million marks to 101 million marks from 1871 to 1878.[53]

The government's policy of curbing school expenditures in the 1880s came at a time when the growth of the population in Prussia increased school enrollments. The population grew by 21.3 percent between 1871 and 1890, and the increase was higher than 35 percent in fifty urban and rural counties. The biggest increase in the number of schoolchildren occurred between 1882 and 1886, when the total enrollment rose from 4.3 million to 4.8 million. School maintenance expenditures did not keep pace with the demographic growth and, measured per head of the population, actually declined. The creation of 3,616 new teaching offices from 1881 to 1886 and the addition of 976 new schools fell far below the educational needs of the nation.[54]

The ministry's claim in a statistical survey in 1886 that 53.8 percent of the children were instructed in classes of "normal" size, which it defined as a maximum of eighty pupils in a school with one classroom and seventy pupils per class in larger schools, was a misleading attempt to minimize the deficiencies in the education of a large proportion of rural children. Included in the number of pupils taught in classes of "normal" size were children attending the *Halbtagsschulen*, which were one-classroom schools in which the prescribed thirty-two hours of weekly instruction were divided between two half-day sessions. From 1882 to 1886 half-day instruction was extended from 2,989 to 5,481 schools, with enrollments totaling more than 571,000 children. More than 486,000 children were enrolled in 2,610 schools in which two teachers provided instruction for three classes. In these schools the children in the earliest grade suffered a loss of ten hours of instruction weekly. The worse conditions of overcrowded classrooms were in the countryside, where two thirds of the schoolchildren in Prussia were educated. The average number of pupils per teacher in village schools in 1886 exceeded 80 in fifteen provincial districts and went as high as 110 in Posen, 97 in Minden, and 95 in Breslau. Not admitted to school because of insufficient space were 8,826 children.[55]

Gossler appraised school needs with a greater sense of social responsibility than Puttkamer did. Painfully he struggled with the dilemma of striving to remedy deficiencies and having to respond to complaints about burdening school expenditures. He preferred to eliminate Prussia's old and inefficient system of school maintenance rather than to follow a policy of retrenchment. More than once he instructed the district governments to urge local officials to take over this obligation and put school costs on the communal budget.[56] His ultimate solution was to modernize the system of school maintenance through the enactment of a school law.

In February 1884 Gossler presented the draft of a school law to the cabinet. Objecting to the introduction of a school bill, Bismarck wrote to him: "In my opinion, we run into the danger of taking a leap into the dark and committing ourselves to details which could have a disadvantageous effect on the elections this year and on the contentment of wide circles of the population." Apart from the timing of the school bill just before the Reichstag election, Bismarck disapproved of a law that would require the *Gutsbezirke* as well as the communes to maintain the schools, and was apprehensive about the financial impact of such a law on the estate owners. What the local communities needed more urgently, he thought, was legislation to relieve them of overburdening school costs.[57]

In discussions with Gossler in 1885, Bismarck demanded a legal regulation to restrain the authority of the school bureaucracy to exact higher school expenditures. Under pressure from Bismarck, the ministry drafted a bill that turned over the settlement of disagreements between the local community and the district government to the *Kreisausschuss* in the case of a rural school and the *Bezirksausschuss* in the case of an urban school. The county and district commissions, chaired by the district governor and composed of members elected by the standing committee of the provincial diet, were to reach their decisions "with consideration given to the needs of the school and the financial resources of those obliged to maintain the schools."[58] Within two weeks after the commission's arbitration an appeal could be made to the provincial council headed by the governor.

It was not easy for Gossler to support the passage of this bill in the *Landtag* in 1887. A royal edict in 1817 had invested the district governments with the power of determining the requisite needs of the elementary schools for the local communities. Now the school authorities were binding their hands and relinquishing their responsibilities to the provincial organs of self-administration. Gossler knew of the public's displeasure with the school bureaucracy and bowed to political necessity.[59]

Opposition to the bill ran strong within the teaching profession. The petitions that teachers' associations addressed to the House of Deputies were ignored by all the parties with the exception of the Progressives. The left-wing liberals argued that the bill took decision-making power out of the hands of school officials to whom the *Volksschule* owed its progress and entrusted it to provincial organs that could not be relied on to act with goodwill toward the schools. Under the law, landowners and farmers who were unsympathetic or indifferent to the interests of popular education and the teaching profession would be able to veto school improvements for financial reasons. Because the bill did not prescribe any norms or require the commissions to observe the General Regulations of 1872, the decisions were likely to be arbitrary and inconsistent.[60]

As the Conservatives admitted, the law created "a barrier" against school officials who ordered the local communities to make costly school improvements. The extensive support that this unenlightened measure found among the parties cast much light on the nature of their concerns in school politics. The National Liberals, whose position on the school question was determined more by political objectives than educational interests, swallowed their misgivings about the effect of the law and gave it lukewarm support. The Center party, preoccupied with confessional issues and generally indifferent to the welfare of the *Volksschule* as an institution of learning, defended the bill. The spokesman for the party, Julius Bachem, had long been critical of the scale and pace of school construction during Falk's administration and the coercion that the district governments had employed on the communes in the Rhine Province. He stated that the principal merit of the law was that it put the provincial organs of self-administration in a position to restrain the school bureaucracy. "It would not have been harmful if efforts to improve the schools in the last twenty years had been more cautious and slow," he declared.[61]

Public Investment in the Schools

In 1888 the government devised a more constructive method of relieving the local communities of heavy school expenditures than the Law of May 26, 1887, on the Assessment of Elementary School Requirements. In view of the state's favorable financial situation and the treasury's surplus, Finance Minister Adolf Scholz decided in December 1887 to increase the state's contribution toward school maintenance.[62] He collaborated with Gossler in drafting a law that granted school districts subsidies for the salaries of up to three teachers. When the committee in the House of Deputies revised the government's bill, the state subsidies became more generous: 400 marks for the sole or senior male teacher and thereafter 200 marks for each male teacher and 150 marks for each female teacher in a school district.[63]

With the enactment of this law in 1888, the Prussian government embarked on a new course in its administration of the schools. For years the Ministry of Finance adhered to the policy that state funds were to be used for school purposes "only in adverse circumstances," when a poor school district did not have sufficient resources. Scholz explained that this "narrow point of view" had changed in recent years because of economic conditions and the capacity of the state to acquire larger revenues than the communes were able to do. He acknowledged an obligation falling on the state to contribute to the commune's burden of school maintenance.[64]

The state's increasing appropriations for school maintenance after 1888 helped to offset the unfavorable effects of the law of May 26, 1887 in the rural areas east of the Elbe River. From 1891 to 1901 total school expenditures in Prussia increased by 93.7 percent in the cities and 67.4 percent in the countryside. The average expenditure per pupil rose from 40 to 62 marks in the cities and from 25 to 37 marks in the countryside. The state's role in the immense increase in the public investment for elementary education in the cities was relatively modest. Whereas school funds provided by the local communities rose by nearly 114 percent during this ten-year period, the appropriations in the state budget grew at a slower rate, and the percentage of total school maintenance costs coming from the state actually fell (see Table 2). State funds were unevenly distributed, and the provincial districts in the agricultural east benefited proportionally more than those in the industrial west. In 1901 state grants and subsidies covered 74.1 percent of the total school expenditures in Bromberg, 57.7 percent in Köslin, and 52.7 percent in Gumbinnen in comparison with 16.5 percent in Arnsberg and 13.8 percent in Düsseldorf.[65]

Johannes Miquel, a National Liberal who served as the finance minister from 1890 to 1901, had little sympathy for the interests of elementary education. His outspoken criticism of the schools was superficial and ill-informed. On one occasion, after listening to his assertions that teachers were intoxicated with arrogance and indoctrinated to be Social Democrats in the *Lehrerseminare* and that the reintroduction of Ferdinand Stiehl's curriculum of 1854 would put the schools back on the right path, Bosse wondered how an otherwise intelligent man could "make such amateurish, unstatesmanlike, wrong, and reactionary judgments."[66] Miquel disapproved of the law of June 14, 1888, and thought that Finance Minister Adolf Scholz had erred when he had agreed to a scheme of granting state funds for teachers' salaries to all school districts without setting a maximum for the big cities or making any distinction on the basis of financial need. By 1896 he was striving to return to the policy of confining the state's responsibility for school maintenance to assistance for small towns and villages where financial resources were inadequate. He succeeded in reducing the state's expenditures in 1897 when he withstood the opposition of the *Oberbürgermeister* in the House of Lords and insisted on the passage of a bill regulating teachers' salaries with a provision that limited the state's contribution toward the salaries to a maximum of twenty-five teachers in a school district. The Ministry of Finance estimated that this law, reducing state subsidies to big cities, would save the state treasury more than 4 million marks.[67]

TABLE 2. Percentage of Total School Maintenance Costs Provided by the State.

Location	Year			
	1886	*1891*	*1896*	*1901*
City	4.8	18.6	16	11.3
Countryside	17.5	42.2	38.5	37

From 1891 to 1901 the number of schoolchildren in Prussia rose by more than 754,000 and reached more than 5.5 million. The expansion of the school system during this decade, with the addition of more than 18,000 teachers and about 2,000 schools, reduced the size of overcrowded classes and produced a more favorable ratio of pupils to teachers even in the provinces where the school enrollments increased the most, the Rhine Province, Silesia, and Westphalia. However, the progress of the school system was geographically uneven, a fact that escaped the notice of admiring visitors from America and England.[68] The cities in the western provinces in general spent more for elementary education than the cities in the provinces of East Elbia. The disparity between the cities and the countryside in respect to school provisions grew wider in the 1890s. Within the same provincial district the difference between the average sums spent for the schooling of a child in the city and in the countryside was greater in 1901 than it had been ten years earlier.[69]

Grave deficiencies prevailed in the rural schools despite the ministry's attempts to mask them in its statistical survey in 1901, which claimed that 77.9 percent of the children were instructed in classes of "normal" size. The school administration increased the number of *Halbtagsschulen*, and in 1901 almost 20 percent of all children in the countryside were taught in them. Most of these schools were located in the provincial districts of the east: 928 in Breslau, 868 in Liegnitz, 727 in Posen, and 619 in Frankfurt an der Oder. In the countryside there was also an increase in the number of schools in which two teachers instructed three classes. In comparison, fewer than 1 percent of the children in the cities attended both types of schools. Even with these expedients, extreme conditions of overcrowding were not eliminated. In the *Halbtagsschulen* there were 1,993 classes with 61–90 pupils and 76 classes with 91–120 pupils. Among the other one-classroom schools, 952 had enrollments of 81–100 pupils, and 98 had an attendance ranging from 101 to 150 pupils. In the bigger schools there were 12,251 classes with 71–90 pupils and 740 classes with 91–120 pupils.[70]

An explanation for the uneven and sectional progress of the Prussian school system in the last two decades of the nineteenth century must be sought not only in the unwillingness of the Ministry of Finance to allocate a bigger portion of the state's revenues for elementary education but also in the failure to enact a law that would reform the system of school maintenance. During these years, the local governments in many school districts followed the example set by the Rhine Province and voluntarily took over the responsibility of school maintenance. This trend was strong in urban school districts, and by 1901 school expenses in

17,592 school districts were covered by municipal tax revenues. These districts accounted for 62 percent of the schools. However, 13,567 school districts with *Schulsozietäten* retained the system of school maintenance that had been set by the General Civil Code of 1794. This system with all its flaws prevailed in the rural areas of East Elbia, where the public investment in the schools remained the lowest in the state.[71]

The swift reaction against Falk's school policy ensured that the school system would retain its confessional organization and that Catholic and Protestant churchmen would continue to supervise elementary education throughout the imperial era. The Center party's annual ritual of airing Catholic grievances during the parliamentary debates on the state's budget for education should not obscure the restoration after 1879—except in the Polish-speaking areas—of much of the Catholic church's influence in the schools. Immediately after Puttkamer entered the Ministry of Education, he took steps to conciliate the Catholic clergy who had been driven out of the schools during the *Kulturkampf*. He placed a high value on the collaboration of the school and church authorities while guarding the state's jurisdiction over the schools.

During the 1880s the professionalization of the county school inspectorate was not extended to the provinces heavily populated by Protestants. Arguments about the merits of the reform made little impression on Gossler. His conservative temperament disposed him to respect the tradition of investing churchmen with this school office. In the following decade, Bosse recognized that the increasing burden of work required of the county school inspectors in densely populated industrial regions was making the appointment of full-time professionals inevitable. His efforts to expand the professional school inspectorate produced modest results. The trend slowed down when the Center and the Conservative parties consolidated their efforts to oppose a policy that was eliminating clergymen from the school administration. Until the end of the monarchy in 1918, Protestant churchmen held a firm grip on school supervision. In the Rhine Province and Westphalia, where secular educators were still chosen to be county school inspectors after the *Kulturkampf*, Catholic priests were reinstated in local school inspection offices and were allowed once again to direct the instruction of religion.

Unlike Adalbert Falk, Gustav von Gossler declined to engage in discussions on the pedagogic advantages of the interconfessional school. He was more impressed by the historical development of the *Volksschule* in Prussia and the preference of the parents for confessional schooling in communes inhabited by Catholics and Protestants. The policy enforced by the Ministry of Education under Altenstein as well as the settlement of the Catholics and the Protestants in regionally concentrated masses fostered a confessionally divided school system early in the nineteenth century. Contrary to the expectations of the liberals, interconfessional schooling did not spread after 1870, when the mobility of the population and urbanization produced sizeable religious minorities in many localities. The percentage of Catholic and Protestant children taught in schools of their own confession was astonishingly high. Popular sentiment and will preserved confessional schooling even in regions where geographic segregation alone could no longer perpetuate it.

In another reaction against Falk's administration, Puttkamer introduced a policy of retrenchment in 1881 to curb the rise in school expenditures. During Falk's years in office the school system expanded at an unprecedented rate. The ministry increased the appropriations for elementary education in the state budget, and the school bureaucracy put heavy pressure on the local school boards to increase teachers' salaries and to improve school facilities. Puttkamer gave a sympathetic hearing to rural householders who complained about the growing burden of school maintenance. Unfortunately, his austerity policy came at a time when the growth of the population swelled school enrollments. In the countryside a larger number of pupils were now taught in overcrowded classrooms and in *Halbtagsschulen*.

For Gossler, on the other hand, the solution lay in the reform of the inefficient and anachronistic system of school maintenance. Under the General Civil Code of 1794 the householders in each school district were responsible for school costs. The manorial lords were exempt from the payment of school taxes, a privilege that reduced the financial resources available to rural school districts. Gossler ran into a stone wall when he proposed the enactment of a school law that would require the communes to cover school expenses through their tax revenues. Apprehensive over the financial impact of the reform in East Elbia, Bismarck refused to consent to the introduction of a school bill that would make the big estate owners responsible for school maintenance. The failure to modernize the system of school funding had a detrimental effect on the education of the children in the countryside. Whereas city governments increasingly put school expenses on the municipal budget, the civil code's obsolete system was still widely followed in the provinces east of the Elbe River, where the expenditures for the schools measured per pupil were comparatively low. The critical deficiencies of the schools in this region belied the high reputation enjoyed by the Prussian *Volksschule* abroad.

4

School Politics and
the Polish Nationality in Prussia

In their efforts to suppress the language and nationality of the Polish people in the eastern binational provinces after 1870, Prussian state officials looked to the *Volksschule* to serve as an instrument of germanization. The school's function was not only to teach Polish children to speak German but also to acculturate them into the German nation. Far from spreading the use of the German language and assimilating the youth into German society, this policy bred germanophobia and a repugnance for the school in Polish families. In spite of all the means of coercion at their disposal, the school authorities did not succeed in achieving these objectives. The total bankruptcy of the germanization policy was exposed when the Polish people resorted to political defiance in the school strikes of 1906. While it is true that the increasingly forceful germanization campaign aroused fervent affirmations of Polish national identity and provoked a countermobilization of Polish nationalists, the failure of the government's school policy began before the development of a Polish nationalist movement in the 1890s and the outbreak of Polish resistance after the turn of the century. It was the outcome of a long succession of injustices and mistakes made by state officials. Their first error was to underestimate the difficulties, if not the impossibility, of teaching Polish children to speak and read German in the most impoverished and destitute school system in the Prussian state.

Polish Society and the Schools

Although Upper Silesia was the home of 1 million Polish-speaking inhabitants, the heartland of Polish culture and the center of the nationality
struggle was Posen. Polish society in Posen was predominantly composed
of agricultural laborers and peasants, but there existed also an indige-
nous nobility and middle-class groups that could provide a cadre of
political leaders. The Catholic clergy were Polish and active in public life,
unlike the priests in the diocese of Breslau who were mostly German and
were under orders from Archbishop Kopp to refrain from antigovernment political activity.[1] Clergymen of high rank represented the electoral
districts of Posen in the Reichstag and the House of Deputies. Mobilized
behind the national cause during the *Kulturkampf*, clerical populists
provided the leadership for a network of associations that promoted the
economic self-sufficiency and national consciousness of the Polish community. By using the Polish language in the church and for the religious
instruction given to the children and by indoctrinating the people with a
popular nationalist Catholicism, the local priesthood did more to
heighten Polish national solidarity than any secular political movement
could do up to 1914.

Local cultural life and a large enrollment of Polish-speaking children
gave a Polish character to hundreds of schools in Posen and West
Prussia. When the Ministry of Education conducted the first systematic
statistical study of the family language of the schoolchildren throughout
the state in 1886, 86.5 percent came from exclusively German-speaking
homes, 10.3 percent from families speaking only Polish, and 1.4 percent
from bilingual homes. Polish schoolchildren constituted a large number
in seven provincial districts (see Table 3).[2]

Before 1870 the government's school policy fulfilled the promise made
by King Frederick William III in 1822 to respect the language and
nationality of his Polish subjects. In his edict of December 23, 1822,
Altenstein stated that it would satisfy the interests of the state if the
German language was taught as a subject in every Polish school and if the
teachers and school inspectors took care to see that the pupils achieved
fluency in German before leaving school. Convinced that the most effica-
cious education for Polish schoolchildren would be achieved through
their own language, the minister ordered that the rest of the curriculum
should be taught in the mother tongue.[3]

During the following decades, the Ministry of Education continued to
practice this benevolent and tolerant policy for the education of the

TABLE 3. Distribution of Polish-speaking and German–Polish-speaking
Prussian Schoolchildren in 1886.

Provincial districts	Speaking Only Polish		Speaking German and Polish	
	Absolute	*Percentage*	*Absolute*	*Percentage*
Posen	134,373	65.9	7,628	3.7
Bromberg	53,013	48.4	4,879	4.4
Marienwerder	55,717	37.6	9,195	6.2
Danzig	27,080	29.5	4,576	4.9
Oppeln	159,277	57.5	22,197	8
Königsberg	36,629	18.9	6,017	3.1
Gumbinnen	24,752	19	9,870	7.5

Polish population in Prussia. Eichhorn sought to do justice to the Polish
nationality when he issued his regulation of May 24, 1842 on the language of school instruction in Posen. Schoolteachers were required to
possess a knowledge of German and Polish, and the primary language of
instruction in each school was to be determined according to the nationality of the majority of pupils. In the rural schools attended by Polish
children, the German language had to be one of the subjects in the
curriculum. In urban Polish schools, the language of instruction had to
shift to German in the upper level so that the pupils would be capable of
speaking and reading German with ease when they left school.[4] In later
years German school officials and pedagogues in Posen criticized the
regulation of 1842 for emphasizing the intensive use of German during
the last rather than the earliest years of schooling.

Kulturkampf and the Enduring Alienation of the Polish Clergy

After 1870 state officials increasingly perceived the historical resistance
of the Polish people to assimilation as evidence of weak loyalty to the
Prussian monarchy. Bismarck suspected the Polish clergy and gentry of
being the prime instigators of a movement to restore Polish national
independence, and the presence of priests in the Polish *Fraktion* in the
House of Deputies intensified his aversion to churchmen who mixed
religion and politics. His repeated attempts to conjure up the spectre of a

Polish threat to the German Empire in his defense of the School Supervision Bill presaged the severity with which the law was applied in Posen and West Prussia.[5]

The secularization of school supervision was accomplished with great speed in the Polish-speaking areas. As early as 1872 Polish priests were discharged from county school inspection offices. The new secular school inspectors were invested with great authority. After Polish priests were dismissed from local school inspection offices, the job was not assigned to local dignitaries but to the county school inspectors in order to intensify the state's surveillance of Polish teachers and the parish priests. The government kept inspection districts small because it expected the county school inspectors to function also as "confidential agents who should be constantly informed of the political events and activities within their county and, if necessary, should also assert their influence in this direction."[6]

The secularization of the school inspectorate became a more bitter grievance for the Catholics in Posen and West Prussia than in the Rhine Province. The Polish clergy were replaced by Germans who were not native to the region. During Falk's administration, Protestants were appointed to 17 of the 23 offices in Posen and 9 of the 19 offices in West Prussia.[7] In the House of Deputies, Father Florian Stablewski protested the appointment of German Protestants as school inspectors and reproached them for lacking a sympathetic appreciation for Catholic religious life as well as the linguistic ability to supervise school instruction in Polish. He related that one inspector had introduced in the schools a textbook with a picture of Martin Luther standing alongside the caricature of a monk and that another inspector ordered a teacher to remove the picture of a Catholic saint from the classroom wall.[8]

The interconfessional school policy further alienated the Polish people from the school administration. In 1873 Falk issued a directive encouraging the establishment of interconfessional schools wherever local conditions in Posen permitted such institutions to exist. In the following years, interconfessional schools were opened in cities in Posen and West Prussia at the initiative of mayors and city councilmen who were German Protestants and liberal supporters of the *Kulturkampf*. They brushed aside the objections of the Catholic citizens who had little or no voice in the decision by virtue of the unequal suffrage in the municipal elections. By 1882 there were 200 interconfessional schools in West Prussia and 76 in Posen, and appointed to these schools was a disproportionately large number of German Protestant teachers.[9] From the start the Polish population viewed the innovation with distrust. Ludwik von Jażdżewski, a priest elected to the House of Deputies, called the establishment of interconfessional schools "the first stage in denationalizing the children of Polish inhabitants in the cities."[10]

In the 1880s Gossler took refuge in evasion when he was challenged by the Polish *Fraktion* in the House of Deputies to justify the exception made to the policy of confessional schooling in the binational provinces. The Polish people had good reason for suspecting that interconfessional schools were being opened for the purpose of germanizing the Polish youth. The provincial branch of the Prussian Teachers' Association in Posen criticized the Catholic public schools for working to the benefit of Polish particularism and called for a national school policy that would make "the *Volksschule* become what it should be: a *Pflanzstätte deutscher Kultur und Bildung*" (hotbed of German culture and education). Gustav Lange, a publicist for the teachers' association, contended that "the Polish question would have been settled long ago if the state government had put the school in the service of germanization from the beginning and had proceeded forward with unyielding consistency and firmness." He was convinced that interconfessional schools, by cultivating in the children "the feeling that we are all members of one state and one nation," offered the most promising hope of diminishing the differences that made the two nationalities confront each other like foreign enemies.[11] School officials in the province also considered the interconfessional schools to be "the most effective means at the disposal of the school administration to foster systematically a knowledge of German and a German mentality among the Polish children" and to wear away those cultural differences that obstructed the assimilation of the Polish population.[12]

The school language regulations were another radical expression of the government's determination to give a German character to elementary education in the Polish-speaking areas. In April 1872 Falk ordered officials in the ministry to make an inspection tour of the schools in the eastern provinces. Accompanied by county councillors and school officials, the Berlin visitors observed that Polish pupils in the higher grades were able to speak only a few words of German and that Catholic children of German descent were losing their German identity and becoming Polish. They concluded that the school language regulation of 1842 had doubly failed and recommended a change in policy.[13]

In 1873 the provincial governors of Posen and East and West Prussia (the province was divided in 1876) ordered the introduction of German as the language of school instruction for all Polish children, beginning with the first two years of schooling in the lower level. Whereas Provincial

Governor William von Günther envisioned a gradual germanization of school instruction in Posen, Karl von Horn took a more decisive course in East and West Prussia. His regulation of July 24, 1873 severely restricted the use of the Polish language in the schools. Teachers were allowed to give religious instruction in Polish only in the lower level and were prohibited from using it in the instruction of religion during the six years of schooling in the intermediate and upper levels. Polish reading and writing instruction was permitted only in the final years of schooling insofar as it was necessary to provide the pupils with an understanding of the Bible and church hymns in the mother tongue. This concession was hedged by the discretionary authority of the district governments to order the elimination of Polish lessons in schools attended by German children.[14]

The more moderate regulation of October 27, 1873 in Posen allowed reading and writing in Polish to remain a subject in the curriculum for Polish children, five hours in the lower level and three hours in the intermediate and upper levels each week. Religion and hymns were to be taught in the mother tongue in all three levels. A proviso in the regulation, however, gave school officials the discretionary power to take incremental steps toward an exclusively German education. German could replace Polish in the instruction of religion given in the intermediate and upper levels if the pupils had progressed sufficiently in their comprehension of the language.[15] Thus, the use of the Polish language in teaching religion was not protected against administrative encroachments in the future.

Although the school language regulations of 1873 were an assault on the rights of the Polish nationality, the people did not react with defiance and school boycotts. Their capacity to resist was undoubtedly affected by the state's simultaneous attack on the Catholic church. This struggle waged by the government with vehemence in Posen overshadowed the language issue in the elementary schools. Hundreds of priests were prosecuted for opposing the May Laws of 1873 and the decree of 1872, which required German to be the language of instruction for religion in all secondary schools. The arrest of clergymen and the closing of the seminaries in the archdiocese of Gnesen and Posen left many parishes without a priest. Archbishop Mieczyslaw Ledóchowski, who refused to comply with the May Laws, was deposed by the order of a state court and, after serving a two-year prison sentence, went into exile.[16]

Because government officials tended to blame the willful negligence of the clerical school inspectors for the failure of Polish children to learn German, they underestimated the obstacles to the successful implementation of the language regulations of 1873. The task of instructing in the German language a large classroom of children who came from Polish-speaking homes would have challenged any teacher well trained in modern pedagogy. It was virtually impossible under the school conditions prevailing in Posen and West Prussia. The *Lehrerseminare* in the two provinces provided little training in the methods of language instruction. When officials in the ministry conducted a tour of the schools in Posen in 1887, they encountered Polish teachers who spoke German ungrammatically, with a heavy accent, and who had no skills in teaching the German language.[17]

The schools never attained the educational goals set by the General Regulations of 1872. Polish parents complained that they were maintaining schools that taught their children very little. The mechanical method of instructing German and the teachers' recourse to corporal punishment out of frustration did not make the pupils any more receptive to learning the language. Polish dissatisfaction with the schools voiced by Ignacy von Lyskowski in the House of Deputies in 1877 was corroborated a few years later.[18] School officials in the Posen district excluded history and science from the new curriculum they prepared for Polish schoolchildren in 1887, because school inspectors had reported that the instruction of both subjects had been "given with the least success."[19]

The results of the new school language policy were bound to be disappointing because the ministry made the mistake of underestimating the difficulties of teaching children to read and write German under the school conditions that prevailed in the two provinces. In 1877 the school classes exceeding the "normal" size numbered 869 in Posen and 448 in West Prussia; in 240 of these schools in Posen, there was a ratio of only one teacher per more than 150 pupils.[20] School provisions for German Protestant children were better than those for the Polish Catholics. In 1879 the Posen district government reported that the average size of classes in Catholic schools in five counties ranged from 97 to 136 children per teacher, but for the Protestant schools the corresponding figures ranged from 36 to 79 children per teacher. The same discrepancy existed in the Marienwerder district, where the number of pupils per teacher averaged to 93 in the Catholic schools and 65 in the Protestant schools.[21]

The modest expansion of the school system in Posen and West Prussia was hardly sufficient to relieve overcrowded classrooms in Catholic schools at a time when the rate of growth of the Polish population more than doubled that of the German nationality in the two provinces. The school administration introduced half-day instruction as a temporary solution. In 1882 Posen had already 341 *Halbtagsschulen*, and a third class was added to 105 schools staffed by only two teachers. What began as an expedient measure became a regular feature of the school life of Polish children. By 1891 half-day instruction had been introduced in 817 schools with a total enrollment of nearly 99,000 pupils, and a third class had been opened in 229 schools with a total attendance of close to 38,000 children.[22] The disadvantages of a shortened school day fell hard on the children from Polish-speaking families, who began to learn German when they entered school and practiced it only during school hours.

The winding down of the *Kulturkampf* after 1879 did not affect Posen as much as it did the Catholic Rhineland, where the traditional cooperation between the state and the church in school life was restored. Puttkamer did not append to his decree of November 5, 1879 more stringent guidelines for its implementation in Posen. But officials in Berlin and in the province were in agreement that Polish priests who opposed the school language regulation in the press and in public meetings should not be entrusted with local school inspection or the direction of Catholic religious instruction in the schools. Provincial officials, whose distrust of the Polish clergy had not abated, routinely disposed of each case without examining the concrete facts carefully. As Gossler privately remarked, they "made their decisions on the basis of general political considerations."[23]

Soon after Archbishop Julius Dinder, the first German to occupy the see of Gnesen and Posen, entered office, he took steps to recover the church's influence in the schools. In October 1887 he ordered the parish priests to submit requests to the district governments for permission to direct the instruction of religion in the schools. The provincial bureaucracy did not welcome his initiative. Provincial Governor Robert von Zedlitz-Trützschler feared that the archbishop's order could "serve as a pretext for a large part of the clergy and the population to contrive the idea that the episcopal administration intends to support Polish nationalist agitation from a church standpoint."[24]

For political reasons Gossler wanted to accommodate the archbishop. He and Bismarck had pressed the Vatican to elevate Dinder to the archbishopric in the expectation that he would cooperate with the government in keeping the Polish clergy out of politics. Dinder was obliging even if he did not fulfill all of their hopes. In January 1888 he admonished the clergy in his archdiocese to act with circumspection and reserve in public life and to abstain from any political agitation. Gossler ordered the district governments to grant the requests under the condition that the clergymen observe the school language regulations and use German in their official communications with the teachers. He advised them to keep a close watch on the priests thereafter so that "any misuse of their relationship to the school for nationalist purposes can be nipped in the bud."[25]

The problem of the direction of Catholic religious instruction in the schools was settled to the satisfaction of neither the church nor the state. In the spring of 1888 provincial officials rejected the applications of 241 priests.[26] Active campaigning in elections and delivering inflammatory speeches at public meetings were not the only reasons for denying them admission to the schools. Acting on the basis of county councillors' reports, the district governments excluded clergymen who preached sermons in the Polish language in disregard of the German parishioners and gave catechism lessons in Polish even though the parish had some children of German descent. Also rejected were priests who founded libraries and distributed Polish grammar and spelling books to the children.[27]

After the clergymen received permission to direct religious instruction in the schools, friction between the church and the school administration continued. The priests objected to the requirement to speak German in discussions with the schoolteachers. This requirement seemed to them to be an attempt by the government to put the clergy in the service of suppressing the Polish nationality. Instances of defiance occurred and disturbed the provincial bureaucracy.[28]

The surveillance of the clergymen by the county councillors and the withdrawal of the direction of religious instruction from eleven priests in 1895 strained relations between the church and the school authorities. In a protest to the minister, Archbishop Florian Stablewski, who succeeded Julius Dinder, stated that the government's harassment had "caused such deep disquiet and unhappiness among the clergy" that he might not be able to prevent a collective resignation. He urged Bosse to allow the parish priests to exercise the church's right without petitioning for the government's consent. Following instructions from Berlin, Provincial Governor Hugo von Wilamowitz replied that the government could not discard this safeguard "because the conduct of a segment of the clergy since [1888] has not become more well-disposed toward the state, and because religious instruction is still used in individual instances, sometimes openly and sometimes in a disguised manner, for the purpose of polonizing the children." He implored the archbishop to order the clergy "to confine their attention to religion and church tasks and to refrain from any activity that stands in opposition to the institutions and regulations of the state."[29]

From Anti-Polish Measures to Restraint and Concessions

The different manner in which Puttkamer's decree of November 5, 1879 was executed in the Rhineland and in Posen reveals the anti-Polish tendency that prevailed within the school administration. The Ministry of Education took a sharp anti-Polish turn during Gossler's years in office from 1881 to 1891. Max Kuegler, a young official in the provincial school board of Posen, was summoned to Berlin to be Gossler's adviser on school affairs in the Polish-speaking area. Throughout the 1870s Kuegler had been in the thick of the political conflicts over the schools. He was an active member of the National Liberal party club in the city of Posen and a fervent advocate of the organization of interconfessional schools.[30] In Berlin his career advanced rapidly because Gossler placed more confidence in him than in any other counsellor on his staff.[31] Kuegler advocated a hard line against the Polish population and was the author of the ministry's anti-Polish measures in 1886 and 1887. He represented the ministry on the Royal Colonization Commission, which was created in 1886 to administer the funds allocated to buy out indebted Polish landowners and to settle German farmers in Posen.

Gossler and Kuegler were obsessed with gloomy fears about the future of the German nationality in the east. They thought that the decline of the German population relative to the high rate of growth of the Polish nationality in Posen and West Prussia was a forewarning that the state authorities could no longer ignore. The demographic advance of the Polish population was all the more disturbing to them because little progress was made in breaking down Polish particularism and assimilating the young generation.[32] Neither Gustav von Gossler nor Max Kuegler comprehended the essential reasons for the failure of the schools to teach Polish children to speak German fluently. They saw social and cultural trends in Posen in terms of a conspiracy, namely the subversion of the German identity of the German Catholics by the clergy and the susceptibility of schoolteachers to the influence of ardent Polish nationalists within the nobility.[33] When Bismarck proposed to the cabinet on January 10, 1886 a plan to germanize the countryside in Posen by settling German families on farms carved out of the estates purchased from Polish landowners, Gossler was ready to launch his own offensive. At a cabinet meeting on January 24, he recommended the appropriation of funds to build schools for German children, the enactment of a law to strengthen the state's control over the schools, and a tighter restriction on the use of the Polish language in the schools.[34]

By February Gossler had introduced a bill that placed the appointment of teachers in the Polish-speaking area entirely in the hands of the state authorities. The bill also empowered the school administration to transfer teachers as a disciplinary penalty and thus opened the way for the appointment of Germans to replace Polish teachers. Although this legislation increased the likelihood that the *Volksschule* in the Polish community would fall into conflict with the family and that the confidence of the parents in the schoolteachers would be replaced by distrust, neither the minister nor the progovernment parties in the House of Deputies recognized the folly of this measure. Felix Porsch, a German Catholic representing an electoral district in Upper Silesia, warned that coercive and unjust measures would not bring about the germanization of the Polish people. These words went unheeded. However, the deputies were persuaded to omit the Oppeln district from the jurisdiction of the law. Porsch argued that, because no Polish nationalist movement was hindering the steady assimilation of Polish workers in the industrial area of Upper Silesia, it would be a mistake to confuse the region with Posen.[35] The jurisdiction of the Law of July 15, 1886 on the Appointment of Elementary Schoolteachers was confined to the entire province of Posen and to West Prussia with the exception of those cities and counties that had a German population.

Gossler envisioned a big influx of German teachers in Posen. His plans for the execution of the new law were scaled down after he met with the provincial administrators in Posen on June 23. He solicited their advice on what measures should be taken to dismiss those Polish teachers on whom they could not rely to give the youth a German and patriotic education. Officials in the province informed him that Polish-speaking teachers were still indispensable, so that the transfers had to "be limited to those cases in which the removal of the teacher is especially urgent as a result of specific facts bearing on his political conduct."[36]

Gossler's instructions on the execution of the law ordered the district governments to prepare lists of Polish teachers who should be transferred. He acknowledged that the supply of German teachers with a command of the Polish language was not yet sufficient and that the school administration would have to use Polish teachers of doubtful reliability for the time being. Accordingly, he told the district governments to assign German teachers to urban schools and to relocate Polish teachers to schools in the countryside, where the ability to speak Polish fluently was still essential for teaching. However, in village schools with a small number of German pupils amid a Polish majority, the district governments were to appoint German teachers capable of speaking Polish.[37]

In his instruction on the use of the new budget appropriation for schools in the binational districts, Gossler emphasized the points that "with these funds an improvement of the elementary school system on a general and wide basis cannot be planned" and that "the aim pursued in the appropriation of the funds is solely the protection and strengthening of the German nationality."[38] He recommended that the money be used to offer bonuses in the recruitment of German teachers, to construct separate schools for German Protestant children in localities with an overwhelmingly Polish population, and to eliminate overcrowded classrooms in German schools by the appointment of more teachers. Wherever the German Protestant community was too small to warrant the opening of a separate school, a German Protestant teacher was to be appointed to the Catholic school. In effect, Gossler authorized the introduction of the interconfessional educational structure to Catholic schools in the interests of protecting the German minority.

In 1888 the school administration recruited ninety-four German teachers for the province. The newcomers were assigned to schools where the presence of a Polish teacher on the staff ensured that religion could at least be taught in Polish.[39] Polish parents protested the harm that was done to the education of their children by the importation of German teachers who could not speak Polish and hence could not help the pupils to comprehend the lessons in the early years of schooling. The *Dziennik Poznański*, a daily newspaper in Posen, compared the work of the German teachers to the labors of the mythical Sisyphus and predicted that they would soon become demoralized when they realized that they were mechanically drilling the pupils and relinquishing the noblest ideals of modern pedagogy.[40] A member of the Polish *Fraktion* in the House of Deputies likened the pedagogic methods of the German teachers to the techniques of training a parrot and lamented that the *Volksschule* under the new law was ceasing to be an institution for education. With mounting bitterness he declared that the state government would "not achieve its objective—germanization—because its methods must fill the child with hatred and abhorrence of the German language and with repugnance for the school and its teacher." The moral influence of the teachers would diminish as the parents and children increasingly perceived them "as an instrument of germanization, a part of a coercive germanization apparatus."[41]

After the enactment of the law of July 15, 1886, school officials in the provincial districts, especially in West Prussia, used their new power of appointing teachers aggressively to make the Catholic schools interconfessional. Despite the opposition of the local school boards, they disregarded the relative proportions of the two confessions in the school enrollments and installed Protestant teachers in Catholic schools. In several of the new interconfessional schools the Protestant pupils were fewer than fifteen, and the Catholics formed a big majority of more than 100. As the Danzig district government reported, "the German children are sufficiently protected against Polonization through the appointment of a Protestant teacher and the interconfessional organization of the school."[42]

The provincial bureaucracy exercised its authority under the new law with a bald partiality toward the Protestant confession. Most of the cases of *Imparität* in the school system, which were exposed by the Center party, were located in West Prussia. The increase of the Polish population at a faster rate than the German nationality after 1870 changed the relative proportions of the two confessions in many school districts. School officials ignored the rising enrollment of Catholic children in Protestant schools. They persisted in appointing Protestant teachers to one-classroom schools in which the Catholic pupils were now the majority and to all positions in larger schools in which the Catholics constituted more than 50 percent of the enrollment. They justified their decisions on the grounds that the schools were originally founded with endowments from Protestant estate owners and that the affluent Protestant inhabitants bore a larger share of local taxes than the Catholics. Their essential motive was to protect the German nationality against the advancing Polish masses.[43]

The Center party's attacks on the unequal treatment of the Catholic confession in the school system in West Prussia became a ritualistic part of the annual debates on the education budget. Center party deputies complained that school officials readily made Catholic schools interconfessional for the benefit of a handful of Protestant pupils but took no account of bigger concentrations of Catholic children in Protestant schools. Their charges of discrimination were documented by the party's press.[44] In 1891 the province had 1,084 Protestant schools and 706 Catholic schools.[45] This gross disparity in school provisions led to overcrowded classrooms in Catholic schools and compelled many Catholic children to attend Protestant schools. While the party censured the Protestant oligarchies in the cities for refusing to open Catholic schools, it insisted that the state authorities could rectify the injustices and must be "pressed to apply the principles of tolerance and *Parität*."[46]

The embarrassing publicity arising out of the speech of Anton Neubauer, a priest from West Prussia, in the House of Deputies in 1890 led

Gossler to address an inquiry to Danzig. The district government confirmed the accuracy of Neubauer's criticism.[47] Hoping to defuse the emotional issue of *Imparität*, Gossler instructed state officials in West Prussia on October 30, 1890 to help Catholic parents who demanded the establishment of a separate school for their children, and offered subsidies to encourage the communes to open Catholic schools. He acknowledged that the communes would have to make the decision voluntarily because the school authorities, whose hands were tied by the law of May 26, 1887, could not coerce them.[48]

Besides the appointment of German teachers, the other major item on the agenda of the conference in Posen on June 23, 1886 was the school language question. Provincial officials expressed their wish to ban the use of Polish in the schools. Gossler reacted cautiously and advised them to apply more extensively the proviso in the regulation of October 27, 1873, which granted them the discretionary authority to introduce German for the instruction of religion wherever the Polish schoolchildren had advanced sufficiently in their comprehension of the language.[49]

The Posen district government had already exploited the flexibility of the language regulation and had ordered in 1883 the formation of German language sections for the instruction of religion in schools where German and Polish Catholic children were taught together. Assigned to the German language sections for religious instruction were the children of German descent and Polish pupils whose knowledge of German was judged to be adequate by the school inspectors. With the minister's approval in 1886, the district government ordered the school inspectors to limit the instruction of the Polish language in localities where the population was nationally mixed. Within one year Polish ceased to be taught in the lower level in 541 schools and in the other levels in 19 schools. German replaced Polish as the language for teaching religion in all or some levels in 34 schools.[50]

After a year of such encroachments on the Polish language in the schools, Gossler was ready to act more systematically. On September 27, 1887, he ordered the provincial governors of Posen and West Prussia to eliminate the instruction of the Polish language from all grades in the elementary schools.[51] Political prudence restrained Gossler from banning Polish as the language of religious instruction; he knew of the extreme sensitivity of the Catholic church to this issue. The instruction of religion in the schools laid the foundation for the communion and confirmation lessons that the parish priest gave. The schoolchildren learned the prayers that were recited and the hymns that were sung in the church. Both German and Polish Catholics thought that religion had to be taught in the mother language to reach a child's heart and soul, and that the moral and religious education of the youth was impaired when the truths of their faith were taught to them in a language other than that of their family and church.[52]

For tactical reasons Gossler decided to treat the instruction of the Polish language and religious instruction in Polish as separate matters. He followed a policy of avoiding conflicts with the church without renouncing the possibility that in time German would replace Polish also in the instruction of religion. In the House of Deputies in 1888 he assured the Catholics that the new language regulation did not affect the teaching of religion.[53] A year later he was embarrassed when two Polish priests in the House of Deputies complained that despite his earlier assurances, school inspectors were substituting German for Polish as the language of religious instruction. Testifying from his own experience, Leon Czarliński stated that children in his parish memorized parts of the religion lesson in German without a full comprehension of the meaning. He challenged the deputies to open a parliamentary inquiry of the schools in Posen if they doubted his word or suspected him of exaggeration. Gossler informed the House of Deputies that he would annul the decisions of the provincial officials who had violated his orders.[54]

Responding to inquiries from Berlin, the district governments reported that the innovations made by the school inspectors at their own initiative occurred prior to the minister's injunction. In January 1888 the provincial governor ordered them to refrain from further changes in the language of religious instruction, and thereafter they put a stop to the school inspectors' ad hoc measures.[55] The petitions of protesting Polish parents prompted school officials in Posen to review a few cases. They declined to cancel the changes even when they admitted that nine tenths of the pupils entered the school from Polish-speaking homes and without a knowledge of German. Attributing the petitions to the nationalist agitation of Polish priests, they saw all the more no reason to grant the wish of the parents.[56]

Gossler's successors in the 1890s continued to restrain the school bureaucracy in Posen. At Bosse's request, the provincial governor ordered the district governments again in 1893 not to change the language of religious instruction in the schools "until further notice."[57] The Ministry of Education was able to reassure the House of Deputies in 1893 that, in the schools in Posen attended partly or entirely by Polish children, religion was taught exclusively in Polish in 1,079 schools, exclusively in German in 65 schools, and in both languages in 143 schools.[58]

The provincial bureaucracy was unhappy with the restraints placed on it. Officials in the Posen district had greeted the school language regulation of 1887 as the start of a political course that would lead to the suppression of the Polish nationality if the state authorities followed it with consistency and firmness. Their disappointment was expressed in a report to the minister in September 1889. They argued that, if the province was not to be surrendered to Polish nationalism, the government would have to ban Polish as the language of religious instruction in the schools sooner or later. Once the children were taught religion in German, the schooling of the young generation would "compel the clergy to take account of the German language to a greater extent in the church." They impressed on the minister the urgency of settling this issue soon because the school administration would no longer have a sufficient supply of German teachers who spoke Polish. Observing that the changes made in individual schools had the effect of constantly kindling controversy and keeping the issue aflame, they suggested that it would be better to prohibit the use of the Polish language by a general regulation than through a series of local measures.[59]

The Posen district government urged Gossler to remain uncompromising in his opposition to the efforts of Polish cultural associations to institute private lessons in the Polish language. As early as January 1888, school officials in Posen issued confidential orders to the school inspectors to forbid the teachers to give private instruction. They feared that private schools would indoctrinate the youth with Polish nationalist views by teaching them Polish history and folklore, and would weaken the loyalty of the teachers to the state by putting them on the payroll of Polish associations.[60]

The provincial bureaucracy and the German nationalists in Posen were bitterly disappointed when Leo von Caprivi, who succeeded Bismarck as the Prussian minister president and imperial chancellor in 1890, adopted a conciliatory policy toward the Polish population. His choice of Provincial Governor Robert von Zedlitz-Trützschler as the minister of education and his endorsement of Stablewski for the archbishopric of Gnesen and Posen in 1891 were made with the hope of winning the cooperation of the Polish people who were loyal to the Prussian monarchy. Zedlitz had close personal ties with the Polish nobility, and he optimistically believed that the collaboration of the loyalists with the government would lead to a relaxation of tensions between the two nationalities.[61] Zedlitz listened earnestly when Polish churchmen argued that because of the discontinuation of Polish language instruction in the schools, the youth were no longer able to read the Bible and the catechism and were poorly prepared for the communion and confirmation lessons. To appease the Polish people and to improve the religious education of the children, Zedlitz ordered the district governments on April 11, 1891 to grant public schoolteachers the permission to give private lessons in the Polish language and to allow school buildings to be used for this purpose.[62]

The Polish loyalists wrung a second concession from Caprivi when they gave him the votes that he needed for the passage of the army bill and his trade treaties in the Reichstag. In 1893 Archbishop Florian Stablewski pressed the chancellor to deliver on his promise to reinstate the Polish language as a subject of school instruction. If the expectations of the Polish *Fraktion* were disappointed, he threatened to instruct the clergy to give private lessons in reading and writing.[63] Robert von Bosse, who replaced Zedlitz as the minister of education in 1892, frowned on the chancellor's policy of courting the Polish loyalists and withstood his pressure to appease them. His conflict with Caprivi over the Polish question almost led to his decision to resign in May.[64] Only with great reluctance did he revise the school language regulation.

On March 16, 1894, Bosse authorized those schools in which the children received religious instruction entirely in Polish to offer Polish language instruction at the request of the parents. For fear that the Polish nationalists would use the instruction of religion as a pretext for returning to a bilingual education, Bosse took care to limit the scope of this concession. His directive restricted the instruction of the Polish language to two hours a week (one hour in the half-day schools) for a maximum of two years in the intermediate level and confined it to the schools in the province of Posen in which Polish was the exclusive language of instruction for religion. With this begrudging gesture of conciliation, Bosse found the justification to revoke Zedlitz's decree and to prohibit the private instruction of the Polish language.[65]

Bosse's distrust of the Polish people precluded any conciliatory course in Posen. Whereas Zedlitz dismissed German perceptions of a Polish threat as the exaggerated fears of a ghost, Bosse was convinced that Polish nationalists were cultivating "the bacillus of sedition" in Posen.[66] After 1894 Bosse regretted that the concession had been made. The optional Polish language instruction had to be offered in more schools than he had expected because the clergy roused the parents to request it. The criticism of the German nationalists, who deplored the government's failure to pursue its school policy in Posen with resolution and consistency, deeply wounded him. In public statements he took care to emphasize that the concession of 1894 did not signal a retreat or surrender.[67]

In his efforts to placate the German critics of the concession and to impress on the Polish people the limited purpose of his decree, Bosse repeatedly connected what Gossler had sought to keep apart as separate questions, namely, the instruction of the Polish language and the religious instruction of Polish schoolchildren. In the House of Deputies in 1895, he stated that the German *Volksschule* could not teach the Polish language but was offering the instruction of Polish "only so far as it was necessary in order to enable the children to receive religious instruction fruitfully." He repeated in 1896 that the government made "an exception" in its school language policy "in the interests of the freedom of conscience of the Poles." He elaborated that "we had to introduce Polish instruction to a limited extent if we did not want to exercise any coercion on the consciences of Polish Catholics, because we must prepare the children to participate in Polish religious instruction successfully."[68]

Far from depriving the Polish nationalists of their most potent weapon—the religious issue—the concessions made by Bosse and Zedlitz confirmed the Catholic opinion that Polish schoolchildren should be taught religion in the language of their home and church. The concessions offered too little to redress the grievances of the Poles, who believed that teaching the children the language of their family was a fundamental principle of sound pedagogy and a command of justice. The Polish *Fraktion* in the House of Deputies attacked Bosse's decree as a half-step and declared that the agitation for the cultivation of the Polish language and national identity in the schools would not cease until their legitimate demands were satisfied.[69]

School Facilities for Germans and Poles

Throughout the 1890s, state officials in Berlin continued to underestimate the difficulties of achieving the government's objectives in Posen under the prevailing school conditions. The province's school system remained the most backward in the Prussian state. School officials in Posen had to institute three sessions in some overcrowded one-classroom schools in which the pupils received two hours of instruction. The Posen district had 18 *Dritteltagsschulen* (three-session day schools) in 1893, and the number would have been larger if the admission of children reaching school age had not been postponed for one or two years in some communes. By 1902 there were 33 schools with three sessions, and still about 1,700 children were not allowed to enter school. The *Halbtagsschulen* continued to educate most of the children in the countryside. The Posen district government reported in 1896 that half-day instruction was given for part of the year in 786 so-called *Hüteschulen* (schools for shepherds) because the pupils did farm work and for the entire year in 597 schools because of overcrowded classrooms.[70]

Although the ministry's statistics showed that the state's contribution toward the total school costs in Posen rose to 52 percent by 1901, these funds were actually inadequate to compensate for the extreme poverty of the Polish school districts. Expenditures for the elementary schools in the province were the lowest in the state. Whereas school expenditures in 1901 averaged to 34.9 marks per pupil in Posen, the corresponding figures were 42.6 marks in Pomerania and 49.9 marks in Brandenburg (excluding Berlin).[71]

Nor were the state funds maximally effective with those school districts where the needs were the greatest and where the financial resources were most limited. The new appropriation added to the state budget by the Ministry of Education in 1886 was designated for the promotion of the German nationality in the eastern provinces. In the cabinet meeting Finance Minister Adolf Scholz insisted that the state subsidies should benefit only schools for German children because "the education of Polish children only aids and abets Polish propaganda."[72] In the 1890s Finance Minister Johannes Miquel thought that it was inadvisable to use state money to educate a large Polish middle class.[73] Gossler did not dispute the interpretation of the Ministry of Finance on the purpose of the new appropriation. He had long held the view that provincial officials in Posen should give foremost consideration to "the political side of the matter" when they distributed state subsidies.[74]

The distribution of state funds produced gross disparities in the school provisions for the two nationalities. Subsidies were given to German Protestant school districts to keep the school tax low and to reduce the size of school classes with the appointment of additional teachers. Money was granted also to build Protestant schools for new settlements of German families, which were so small that some of the new schools had fewer than twenty pupils.[75] Between 1886 and 1901, 275 new Protestant schools and 111 new Catholic schools were opened in the province.[76]

When the school fund for the promotion of the German nationality first appeared in the state budget, it was condemned by the Polish population as a measure embodying injustice and hatred. Before long Germans in the province were criticizing the narrow guidelines set by the state government for the distribution of the subsidies. In 1892 Ferdinand von Hansemann, one of the founders of the ultranationalist *Ostmarken-verein*, wrote to Bosse a long letter expressing the views held by German estate owners of his acquaintance:

But on all sides the legitimate complaint is made that the language decree [of 1887] was not followed immediately by measures which would have guaranteed a successful execution of this order. While the state government has given considerable sums for the establishment and equipment of Protestant schools, nothing has happened to improve and expand the Catholic schools, and they remain with conditions which make it impossible even for the most diligent teacher to instruct in the German language successfully.

After comparing the size of classes in Catholic and Protestant schools with figures supplied to him by the county councillor, he urged the minister to appoint more teachers and to reduce the number of Polish children per classroom.[77]

Provincial Governor Hugo von Wilamowitz was another critic of the administration of school funds in Posen. He deplored the use of government grants to construct schools for small German settlements; that thirteen of these schools in the Posen district had fewer than twenty pupils and yet others were being built prompted him to write to the minister in 1894 that "these funds are not administered according to the right principles."[78] A year later he vented his frustration in a long memorandum that pointed out to officials in Berlin that, while the state was spending large sums for the construction of Protestant schools, it was the schools attended by Polish children where the greatest need existed. He lamented that progress in teaching Polish pupils to read and speak German "suffers very noticeably" in overcrowded classrooms.[79]

An epidemic of infectious conjunctivitis that broke out among the Polish schoolchildren in the Bromberg district in 1888 reveals how tragic the consequences of the state's school subsidy policy could be. The physicians whom the district government commissioned to inspect the schools were shocked by the deterioration of the old rural schoolhouses that were constructed out of clay. In a detailed report, they attributed the contagious eye condition to poor lighting and ventilation in classrooms that were too small for the mass of children crammed within the walls, and to the dampness and moisture in school buildings with cracked walls and ceilings and broken floorboards.[80]

In the wake of this misfortune, school officials in Bromberg inaugurated a program to improve school facilities. The county councillors were ordered to initiate discussions with the local school boards and to advise them in planning the construction of new schools and financing the costs. The county councillors had little success and reported that most Polish communities did not have the financial resources to build schools or to provide salaries for additional teachers. What was intended to be a massive renovation resulted in plans to construct nine schools with a special subsidy and eleven schools without state aid. Explaining the disappointing outcome to the Ministry of Education, school officials in Bromberg wrote that more schools would have been built if the district government could have offered poor communities the certain prospect of annual state subsidies for school maintenance costs.[81]

With this experience in mind, the Bromberg district government mentioned repeatedly the inequitable distribution of state funds in its triennial school administration report in 1893. After discussing the favorable ratio of pupils to teachers in the Protestant schools, *Schulrat* Kleve wrote that "significant sums from state funds could be made available for their development in recent years, whereas the Polish school districts are on the average not only much poorer than the German Protestant districts but could be given merely small sums from state funds." Efforts to expand existing schools and to build new ones "frequently fail owing to the fact that up to now the possibility does not exist to grant to Catholic school districts ongoing state subsidies to cover the increased expenses of school maintenance as it is done to Protestant school districts."[82]

School Bureaucracy and the Germanization Program

A mood of pessimism pervaded the reports that the provincial bureaucracy sent to the Ministry of Education in the 1890s. School officials in the Bromberg district began to feel a sense of frustration over the elusiveness of their goals and dwelled on the obstacles to progress in the education of Polish children. *Schulrat* Julius Waschow wrote in 1896 that there were still schools in which one teacher instructed 150–190 pupils and that with such poor school conditions the assimilation of the Polish youth into German society "can proceed only very slowly." In 1899 he lamented again over the "slow and sometimes hardly evident progress" in the schooling of Polish children. He described the mental stress and physical weariness of teachers who instructed two sessions in the *Halbtagsschulen*. He compared the size of classes in Catholic and Protestant schools in which the average ratio of pupils per teacher was 93 : 1 and 60 : 1 respectively, and recommended that teachers instructing Polish children be assigned no more than 60–70 pupils.[83]

Waschow's triennial school administration reports provided officials in Berlin with an unvarnished analysis of the reasons for the poor progress made by Polish children in learning German. He cited the already well-known conditions in overcrowded schools and the irregular school attendance of children who were hired out to tend cattle or to do farm work during the harvest season. He proceeded further and criticized the decision made in 1886 to release the manorial lords from their obligation to provide supplementary assistance when the inhabitants of the *Gutsbezirke* could not raise sufficient funds to support the schools. While the most affluent figures in rural society made no contribution toward school maintenance, those bearing the burden were mostly poor laborers. He advocated the enactment of a school law that would rectify the defects of this system.

The obstacle that seemed to Waschow to defy any solution was the unrelenting opposition of the Polish clergy to the school language regulation. He reported that in recent years their agitation had increased in cities where religious instruction in the schools was given in German. Some priests attempted to give private lessons in reading and writing in Polish. When the district government penalized them, they started to instruct the children for Holy Communion at an earlier age and to teach the Polish language as part of the preparation. Equally disturbing to Waschow was "the harmful influence" of the clergy on the Polish teachers. He reported that in one county a Polish teachers' association was organized by a priest. After citing the example of another priest who scolded a Polish teacher for encouraging the use of the German language, he wrote: "Since they agitate against conscientious teachers in such cases in the most ruthless manner, so it should not be surprising if weak and not very reliable teachers yield to the influence of the clergy for the sake of rest and peace and perform their duty only so far as they protect themselves against disciplinary penalties." He urged the ministry to recruit more German teachers for the Bromberg district.[84]

By the end of the 1890s, the provincial bureaucracy was anxiously looking for ways to make the *Volksschule* a more effective instrument of germanization. In 1896 school officials in the Posen district pressed the minister of education to introduce German as the language of religious instruction in the intermediate and upper grades in the schools of the city of Posen. A year later they proposed again that religion be taught in German in the urban schools and contended that "children from Polish families achieve a complete command of the German language far quicker if they are taught religion in German from the lower level on."[85]

Bosse responded cautiously and ordered the district governments to use their discretionary authority and set up a separate class for religious instruction in German. The school administration itself decided which Polish pupils were to be assigned to the German or Polish language sections for religious instruction on the basis of their knowledge of German. The Posen district government informed the minister that "if nationality is regarded as decisive, then the decision will lie in the hands of the parents and fall in favor of *Polentum*" [the Polish nationality].[86]

The parents protested this innovation in petitions addressed to the minister of education. They disputed the authority of the school inspectors to decide on the nationality of the schoolchildren and defended their right to designate their mother tongue as the language of religious instruction for their children. School officials in the Posen district attributed the opposition of the parents to clerical instigation and suspected that priests had written and circulated the petitions.[87] When Father Ludwik von Jażdżewski's complaints in the House of Deputies prompted Bosse to make an inquiry in 1899, they replied defensively that their recent action amounted to a small change and that the school inspectors took care to select for the German language section only Polish pupils with a good school record. They concluded, "If under such conditions the formation and expansion of German language classes for religion should not be permitted out of consideration for the national origin of the pupils, then it [religious instruction in German] is totally ruled out for them, and a standstill, a retreat in the germanization movement would be inaugurated."[88]

The possibility of taking more aggressive steps to eliminate Polish from the schools altogether began when Konrad Studt replaced Robert von Bosse in September 1899. The new minister of education was personally acquainted with Posen. From 1868 to 1876 he had been a county councillor in the province and had married the daughter of a German estate owner. The experiences of these years left a deep impression on him. More than twenty-five years later he recalled the hostility to the German language cultivated by Polish parents in their homes. He viewed the concessions made during the Caprivi era as a retreat, and thought that the decree of 1894 allowed "politically unreliable" teachers to give Polish lessons in the schools in a manner that was "promoting Polish chauvinistic purposes."[89]

In November 1899 Studt received a letter from Minister of Commerce Ludwig Brefeld, who had recently commissioned an official in his department to conduct an inspection of the continuation schools in Posen. Since 1886 the state government had promoted the establishment of these *Fortbildungsschulen* in the Polish-speaking areas to provide youths over the age of fourteen with vocational skills as well as to further the process of germanization in the interval prior to their induction in the army. The minister's commissar found the performance of the students to be unsatisfactory. The teachers explained to him that they could not work through the entire curriculum because the elementary schools were dismissing the pupils with little knowledge and with poor reading and writing skills in German. The information on the elementary schools that he brought back to Berlin so stunned Brefeld that he immediately related the grim details to Studt.[90]

Brefeld's letter was implicitly a stinging rebuke to the school administration for negligence, and Studt reacted by commissioning an official in the Ministry of Education to conduct a fact-finding tour. From a previous journey to Posen in 1898, Ernst Preische was already familiar with the deficiencies of the schools, which he had inspected in the company of Waschow and other school officials. On his second tour in 1899, Preische visited schools in the Polish-speaking areas of Posen, Upper Silesia, and West Prussia. In a memorandum submitted to the minister of education in January 1900, he reported that the pupils in the schools in Upper Silesia were more advanced in their knowledge of German than in Posen, and attributed the success of the schools in Upper Silesia to their exclusive use of German from the lower grades on. His explanation for the low achievement of the schoolchildren in Posen oddly ignored the poor conditions of the schools and the lax observance of compulsory schooling. Instead he focused on the instruction of religion in Polish as the "cause" and contended, "If during the entire school time instruction in the most important subject is given in Polish, so the training in German and indirectly the education in the other subjects must suffer." He recommended for the future the exclusion of the Polish language from school instruction altogether and for the immediate present the use of the district government's discretionary authority to introduce German as the language of religious instruction in the intermediate and upper levels in those schools where the pupils had attained a sufficient mastery of German. Whether political reasons made such a radical change inadvisable was a question that he pointedly refrained from discussing.[91]

While Preische conducted his inspection tour, Provincial Governor Rudolf von Bitter, who had just replaced Hugo von Wilamowitz, received from Konrad Studt a copy of Brefeld's letter with a request for a report on the schools in the counties cited by him.[92] Upon entering office, the new provincial governor read the school reports filed by the district governments in recent years and was appalled by what he had learned. Because he placed great importance on the role of the schools in the assimilation of the Polish population, Bitter immediately assigned a high priority to the improvement of elementary education. On January 12 he ordered a more comprehensive and probing study of school conditions than Studt subsequently did. When Studt informed the district governments of Preische's findings and recommendations on January 30, he told them to report on the extent to which German had replaced Polish in the instruction of religion and to express their views on whether a limitation on the use of Polish in school instruction was feasible and necessary.[93]

Rudolf von Bitter's letter of January 12, stern and reproachful in tone, ordered the district governments to submit a report on the entire school system "with special attention to all conditions that require an immediate remedy." Stating that the school administration "must strive to eliminate at least the gravest defects as soon as possible," he set forth an immediate reform agenda:

1. The practice of postponing the admission of six-year-old children to school because of overcrowded classrooms should stop.
2. No longer may the number of pupils instructed by a teacher exceed 100.
3. Small classrooms with poor lighting and ventilation should be condemned.
4. School distances requiring the children to travel over 2.5 kilometers should be reduced.

In order to substantiate his demands for state funds, Bitter instructed the district governments to gather material on the financial resources of the school districts and to estimate the sums that would be required for improving the schools in ongoing state subsidies and special grants. He emphasized the confidentiality of this project and told them to refrain from making public inquiries in the communes.[94]

Out of this survey came the boldest and most ambitious proposal for the improvement of Posen's school system in the imperial era. On July 2, 1900, the provincial governor submitted to Studt a long memorandum drafted by *Schulrat* Berthold Thon of the provincial school board. Thon contended that "the continually poor results of the work done in the elementary school correlates with the unfavorable external conditions" and that "with great regularity the visible deficiencies increase in the same degree as the proportion of the Poles in the population." After presenting voluminous statistical evidence to substantiate both assertions, he concluded, "If one would proceed from the idea that assistance is given first where the greatest needs lie, so undoubtedly we must set to work first in the predominantly Polish areas."[95]

With political finesse, Thon answered the objections made by the Ministry of Finance to the use of state funds to improve school life for Polish children. He did not dispute the claims that the improvement of elementary education would redound to the intellectual and economic benefit of the Polish population and produce fresh recruits for the Polish national movement. But from this observation he declined to draw, as the Ministry of Finance had done, "the most extreme conclusion" that a good education for the Polish people did not correspond with the interests of the state and that the government should confine its financial resources to school districts in Posen where the German nationality could be strengthened. He contended that, if the government drew such a conclusion, it would have to dispense with the *Volksschule* as an instrument of germanization. The precondition for a successful assimilation of the Polish population was the spread of the German language, and "this goal can be achieved only with the help of a school system working under favorable physical conditions and capable of rising to the heights of its tasks in its internal organization." To give up the improvement of the schools would "result in a standstill in the germanization work" and in the loss of ground for the German language.

Thon proposed a systematic course of school improvement, beginning with the cities and towns where the prospects for success were the best. Given the magnitude of the deficiencies, he doubted that "normal" school conditions could be achieved in the near future, and listed the immediate reform goals proposed earlier by the provincial governor. He gave estimates of the number of new teaching positions that would be required for reducing the size of school classes and the costs of adding more classrooms to the schools. Stating that the school officials could not demand larger expenditures from poor rural communities, he proposed that the state government appropriate for Posen extraordinary school subsidies for a period of ten years.

The second part of the memorandum covered the teaching profession. Thon wrote that the government could not expect Polish teachers to be politically reliable or to have the capacity to resist the strong influences of their Polish social environment. Polish teachers were cautious in public life and took care to remain aloof from political agitation, but they remained Polish in their hearts. If they did not openly cast their votes for Polish candidates, they abstained and found excuses for not going to the polls.[96] Thon noted that in the Posen district 60 percent of all teachers were Polish and that the language spoken in their homes was for the most part Polish. County school inspectors considered only one third of the Polish teachers to be politically reliable insofar as they encouraged the schoolchildren to learn German. "If the reliability of a segment of the Polish teachers is so limited," Thon exclaimed, "so naturally it cannot be expected that they will educate the children entrusted to their care with a consciously German national tendency and plant German sentiments and patriotism in their hearts."

Thon believed that the school administration could not dispense with Polish teachers in the countryside so long as religion was taught in Polish in most Catholic schools. But he thought that it could "push back Polish teachers gradually" to rural communities by introducing German as the language of religious instruction in city schools. In schools of two or more classrooms in which Polish continued to be used for religious instruction, he recommended the appointment of at least one German teacher and argued that the presence of a German colleague would impose "a certain constraint on the Polish teacher" to refrain from overt Polish propagandizing.

The Failure to Improve School Conditions

Because the school administration could not obtain the necessary funds from the minister of finance, the improvements envisioned by the provincial governor and Thon were not realized. Anti-Polish sentiments were rampant in the Ministry of Finance.[97] Financial preference was given to the support of programs to expand German settlements and to strengthen the German nationality rather than to improve the quality of education for Polish children. When the ministry made funds available for the school system in Polish-speaking communities, political objectives took precedence over educational needs.

In 1903 the state government added to the budget an appropriation to provide bonuses, the so-called *Ostmarkenzulagen*, for teachers who were successfully educating Polish children in the German language in Posen and West Prussia. The distribution of the annual bonuses was a systematic attempt to lure Polish and German teachers into the loyal service of the government's germanization policy.[98] With the *Ostmarkenzulagen*, the school administration rewarded German teachers who had to endure the hostility of the Polish community as well as the emotional and physical stresses of instructing big classes of Polish children. The bonuses were used also to provide an incentive to Polish teachers to sever their cultural and political ties to Polish society. Polish teachers were expected to adopt German as their family language, to have their children receive communion and confirmation lessons in German, and to vote for German candidates in parliamentary and municipal elections.[99]

Parliamentary pressure on the state government to increase its expenditures for elementary education came mainly from the small and politically isolated delegation of Progressives. The most active defenders of school interests in the Progressive *Fraktion* were two school principals,

Albert Ernst from the city of Schneidemühl in Posen and Julius Kopsch from Berlin. In 1899 Kopsch used the ministry's own statistical data and the information that he had collected from teachers and physicians who had inspected the schools to present a disquieting exposé of school conditions in Posen and East and West Prussia. In the following years Ernst and Kopsch continued to publicize the conditions of overcrowded schools in Posen. They argued that the school language regulations and teachers' bonuses would be of no avail as long as school conditions remained so bad. Ernst declared that Polish children would learn to speak and read German more quickly if the teachers instructed classes no larger than thirty to forty pupils.[100]

In many budget debates Ernst embarrassed the minister of education by comparing elementary school expenditures in America and England with the amounts spent in Prussia. He pointed out that England, which had a smaller population than Prussia, had increased school expenditures by over 100 million marks from 1886 to 1896. Although he did not have all the figures at his disposal, he was correct in suggesting that England spent more per capita and more per pupil than Prussia. He criticized the wide disparity in the government's appropriations for the *Gymnasium* and the *Volksschule*. State expenditures, he noted in 1901, averaged to 71 marks per high school student and 17 marks per pupil in the elementary schools.[101]

The Progressives found no allies among the other parties, and officials in the Ministry of Education had no difficulty in fending off their attacks. The deputies listened impatiently to the long speeches of Ernst and Kopsch and were annoyed with them for damaging the reputation of the Prussian *Volksschule* abroad. The National Liberal party dismissed their criticism as exaggerated generalizations drawn from a few individual cases.[102] They were satisfied with the empty assurances of Ministerial Director Philipp Schwartzkopff, who said in reference to the overcrowded schools in Posen that "the situation there is not as critical as it could appear from the statistics."[103]

Wilhelm von Waldow, who replaced Rudolf von Bitter as the provincial governor in 1903, had none of his predecessor's appreciation of the national task falling on the *Volksschule* in Posen. With profound pessimism, he saw Polish hostility to the Prussian state as a pervasive and inveterate frame of mind and thought that the germanization of the province would be achieved not so much by the assimilation of the Polish people as by a policy of displacing them physically and settling German families on the land.[104] Waldow and the district governors were of one mind in believing that the budget appropriation of funds to provide state subsidies for poor school districts should be "put in the service of the German national cause to a great extent."[105] The district governments did not place German Protestant and Polish Catholic school districts on an equal footing in the distribution of their discretionary funds for elementary schools. Subsidies were granted to German Protestant school districts to relieve them of high school taxes. The assessment of school rates in Protestant school districts was half or less than that in the Catholic school districts.[106]

The district governments administered the appropriation earmarked for school construction also to the advantage of the German Protestants. In the Posen district 28 of the 48 new schools built between 1903 and 1905 were in German settlement villages. During the next three years the construction of 39 more Protestant schools, due to the activity of the Royal Colonization Commission, brought the settlement schools to a total of 97 by the end of 1908.[107] The enrollment at many settlement schools was very small. Of the Protestant schools in the province, fifty-six had twenty children or less in 1906.[108]

In view of the political use and inequitable distribution of state funds for elementary education in Posen, none of the goals of the immediate reform agenda could be achieved after 1900. In 1906 about 300 school-aged children were denied admission to school because of overcrowded classrooms. More than 35,000 children attending 1,419 schools were still required to travel distances of more than 2.5 kilometers. Little or no progress was made in eliminating *Halbtagsschulen*. In the Bromberg district alone, 155 Catholic schools were in a critical condition of over-crowdedness and had classes of more than 100 pupils per teacher in 1905.[109] As the school inspectors observed despondently, old school-houses with small, damp, and poorly ventilated classrooms were still in use.[110]

The School Administration's Biggest Error

While the school conditions essential for the successful teaching of the German language to Polish children were not attained, school officials in the province brooded over the slow advance of German culture in Posen. The findings of the statistical survey of the family language of the schoolchildren confirmed what they had noticed since the late 1890s. The germanization of the Polish youth had come to a "standstill." From 1886 to 1901 the proportion of schoolchildren coming from exclusively Polish-speaking families had increased, from 65.9 to 70.2 percent in the Posen district and from 48.4 to 51.4 percent in the Bromberg district. The penetration of the Polish language in the cities—considered to be islands of German culture—was very strong. The progress made by the German language was confined to a few counties and was too little to offer any grounds for optimism. School officials knew that these trends in Posen could not be explained solely by the natural growth of the Polish population because the statistics on the family language of the schoolchildren in Upper Silesia showed a marked tendency of the Polish people in this area to become bilingual and to integrate into German society. An indication that the Polish population in Posen was resisting the assimilation of German culture was the decline in the proportion of schoolchildren from families speaking both languages.[111] An obsession to overcome the impasse in the germanization of the province as well as the desire to substitute more Germans for Polish teachers led the school administration to make its biggest error in Posen—the encroachment on the Polish language in the most sensitive part of the curriculum.

Already in the late 1890s the school bureaucracy had come to the pessimistic conclusion that the efforts of the *Volksschule* to assimilate the young generation would constantly encounter frustration as long as Polish was the language of religious instruction.[112] The religion and optional Polish lessons in the school combined with the church's instruction for Holy Communion and confirmation, which was being extended to four and five years, enabled young Poles to read Polish newspapers and books. School officials in the Bromberg district wrote to the provincial governor in 1898 that the church's instruction was working against the educational goals of the *Volksschule* and abetting the Polish cause. They informed him that in some parishes the lessons included Polish reading and writing instruction and that priests were admitting children under the age of ten. Wilamowitz believed that the government could not interfere in the church's preparation of the youth for the sacraments, but he agreed with them that "in the particular circumstances of Posen the state's interests are hurt by this church instruction." He wrote to the minister that "this instruction serves not only church purposes but pursues at least additionally the aim of hindering the germanization of the children."[113] School officials assumed that the introduction of German as the language of religious instruction for Polish children in the schools would put pressure on the clergy to use German in the church. For reasons that were essentially political in nature, they urged the minister of education to authorize a gradual adoption of German.[114] On this point Thon's memorandum in 1900 repeated what they had already said.

Beginning in the autumn of 1899, school inspectors in the Posen district ordered some teachers to use German in the instruction of religion. When the minister made an inquiry after Polish people protested in the House of Deputies, the district government claimed that the school inspectors had issued the orders without authorization. It is doubtful that they would have taken such independent steps without the consent of their superiors. The district government was embarking on a course of gradually substituting German for Polish as the language for teaching religion and was striving to do so quietly without arousing public excitement. In its reply to Berlin, the district government justified the recent measures on the grounds that the Polish pupils in these schools had a sufficient knowledge of German, and urged Studt to grant ex post facto approval to the change.[115]

The minister's reference to the school language regulation of 1873 in his reply on July 16, 1900 was understood by the Posen district government as an authorization to make a greater use of its discretionary power to eliminate Polish from school instruction in individual cases.[116] On August 18 it informed the school inspectors of its intention to introduce German in the instruction of religion in city schools where the children had acquired a sufficient comprehension of German. The school inspectors were ordered to assess the ability of the pupils and to name those schools in which the change should be made.[117] The protests of the parents and the first signs of resistance in the fall of 1900, when Polish children refused to read Bible stories in German, did not deter the school administration from going forward.

On March 31, 1901, Provincial Governor Rudolf von Bitter informed the minister that the district governments intended to change the language of religious instruction in a selected number of schools. Because the provincial governor raised no objections, Studt gave his approval on April 11.[118] With the beginning of the school semester after Easter, the Posen district government carried out its plans swiftly without giving any notice to the local school boards. By the end of 1902, religion was taught to Polish children in German on all or some levels in 252 schools.[119] Although Polish continued to be the exclusive language of Catholic religious instruction in 853 schools in the countryside, the change affected more children than the statistics suggest because the city schools had large enrollments.

School administrators in the Bromberg district proceeded less aggressively. They took the precaution of sending out inquiries marked "secret" to ask whether the county councillors had any misgivings of a political nature to express.[120] Their plan to introduce German first in the upper level of schools in the binational counties and then gradually in the predominantly Polish counties was approved by the minister on September 27, 1901.[121] By the end of 1902, school officials reported that since Easter 1901 German had replaced Polish as the language of Catholic religious instruction in the intermediate and upper levels of 39 schools. Now Catholic children were taught religion in German in all or some levels in 394 schools and exclusively in Polish in 344 schools.[122]

The parents protested that the change was implemented in a secretive and furtive manner. Some parents defiantly asserted their right to decide the language of their children's religious education and forbade them to read biblical storybooks in German or to speak in German during the religion lessons. Through the moral support of the clergy and the unifying effect of mass popular assemblies, the sporadic resistance of a few families mushroomed into an organized protest movement. Clergymen participated conspicuously in the public meetings. Religious and national interests intertwined when they defended religious instruction in the mother tongue and assailed the school administration for striving to suppress the Polish language and nationality.

The school strike, as the resistance of the Polish schoolchildren was called, received nationwide publicity because of the events in the border town of Wreschen.[123] In the spring of 1901, the Posen district government introduced German as the language of religious instruction in the upper level of the Catholic school in Wreschen. Throughout April and May an increasing number of children refused to use the religion books in German. After repeated admonitions from the school inspector, most of the defiant pupils deferred. The others who persisted in their disobedience were detained after school hours and struck with a rod.

At a public meeting in the town on May 16, two Polish radicals in the House of Deputies exhorted the crowd to resist the suppression of the Polish language in the schools. The indignation of the parents, stimulated by the mass meeting, exploded when the teacher caned fifteen pupils on May 20 for refusing to recite a Psalm in German. The punishment of the children drew to the school later in the day a crowd of parents who hurled threats and insults at the teacher. One mother leading a gang of teenagers entered the school and quarreled with the teacher. The school inspector then summoned the police to disperse the mob. The police patrolled the street, and the only act of violence that occurred that evening was committed by someone who threw a stone at the window of the teacher's house.

The state prosecutor indicted individuals in the crowd who had entered the school or had not obeyed the police order to disband on the charge of disturbing public order and rioting. The trial ended in November 1901 with the court handing down the verdict of guilty and sentencing the accused to imprisonment for various terms extending as long as thirty months. The injustice of such severe penalties for parents who had acted to protect their children and had not rioted made the Wreschen affair a cause célèbre. The domestic and foreign press criticized the court's judgment. The minister of justice himself acknowledged the harshness of the punishment and attempted to persuade the cabinet to pardon the offenders. Even those ministers who had doubts about the humaneness of the court's decision thought that a pardon would have a damaging effect on the state's prestige, and agreed with the minister of finance that the government should not give the public the impression that the state had committed an injustice.[124]

In the aftermath of the Wreschen affair, Studt did not examine afresh the feasibility and political wisdom of introducing German as the language of religious instruction for Polish schoolchildren in Posen. A memorandum written by Max Kuegler in December 1901 presented the minister with a superficial analysis of the recent school disturbances. Kuegler made no attempt to understand the religious sensibilities of the parents. His perceptions of Polish agitators spreading the seeds of sedition prevented him from drawing any lessons from the school strike. Nor did he make any constructive proposals for improving school conditions.[125]

The press coverage of the Wreschen affair made Studt very defensive and inflexible. It was difficult for him to see any compromise with, or conciliation of, the Polish population as anything other than a defeat for the Prussian school administration. The newspaper accounts of the use of corporal punishment in the schools had hurt the reputation of the school authorities and teachers in Posen. Studt was piqued at "the slander and lies" in the press.[126] At the same time he felt the pressure of German nationalist opinion. The *Ostmarkenverein* responded to the school strike in Wreschen by calling for a more resolute language policy for the schools in Posen and by impressing on the school administration that a reoccurrence of such public resistance to the state authority could not be tolerated again.[127]

An interpellation sponsored by the National Liberal party opened a debate on the Wreschen affair in the House of Deputies on January 13, 1902. With the gallery packed and the government bench fully occupied, the National Liberals asked what measures the government intended to take to promote German culture in Posen. Their purpose was to apply pressure on the government to pursue its *Polenpolitik* decisively and to warn the minister of education against any concessions. Arthur Hobrecht, who represented an electoral district in West Prussia, stated that "no possible advantage of a change [in policy] can compensate for the grave damage which would arise if the confidence of our German countrymen in the East in the firmness and constancy of the government and its conduct is shattered."[128]

The only German deputies who called for a radical revision of the government's school policy in Posen were the Progressives. Hugo Kindler, who came from the city of Posen, criticized the tendency of the school administration since 1886 to suppress the Polish language in the schools. He argued that this repressive policy was having the opposite effect of what the government intended. It was reviving Polish particularism just as the *Kulturkampf* laws and the antisocialist legislation of 1878 had strengthened the Center and Social Democratic parties. The school language conflict had aroused an antipathy to the German language that penetrated deeply into Polish family life and made all generations resist the use of German. Besides deploring the school administration's failure to accommodate "the legitimate wishes" of Polish parents, Kindler advocated the introduction of Polish as a subject in the school curriculum in Posen so that both German and Polish children would learn the language. He asserted that such a tolerant policy would remove the cause for Polish agitation against the state authorities and was more likely to strengthen the government's position in Posen and to assimilate the Poles into German society rather than to polonize the province.[129]

The leaders of the Center party chose Alois Fritzen, a native of the Rhineland to be the spokesman for the *Fraktion*. They deliberately passed over Hermann Roeren, who had delivered earlier in the Reichstag a passionate condemnation of the government's school policy in Posen and the use of corporal punishment against the children during the school strike. Fritzen declined to discuss the Wreschen affair and thereby avoided a posture of opposition. He appealed to Studt to be conciliatory and pointed out that "the Achilles' heel of the government's school policy" in Posen was that the new language measures affected the instruction of religion. Because the clergy in Polish communities preached in Polish and prepared the youth for Holy Communion and confirmation with Polish catechisms, he saw no purpose in forcing religious instruction in German onto the schoolchildren.

Much of Fritzen's speech otherwise created a distance between the Center party and the Polish opposition. He censured the Polish press for attacking the German nationality and cultivating the treasonous idea of restoring a Polish national state, and he pointedly added that the government was justified in legally prosecuting the excesses of Polish journalists. He announced to the House of Deputies that the Center party was "not absolutely disinclined to approve of measures to strengthen and elevate the German nationality, customs, and culture in the Eastern Marches." As long as consideration was given to Catholic religious life in Posen, he saw no injustice in the assimilation of the Polish people into German society. He assured the government that the Center party would support efforts to promote German culture in the province "under the condition that *Parität* prevails and that the rights of our Polish fellow citizens are not violated."[130]

In his response to the interpellation, Studt assured the German nationalists that the school administration would not retreat and alter its policy in Posen. Blaming the school strike on the agitation of the Polish press and the clergy, he contended that the change in the language of Catholic religious instruction would have been carried out without disturbances if political provocateurs had not incited the parents. Because he saw the Polish opposition as "a test of strength" and thought that any concession would be a triumph for the agitators, he rejected the appeals of the Center and the Progressive parties to accommodate the wishes of the parents.[131]

The School Strike of 1906

In the following years neither the minister nor the provincial bureaucracy took seriously the Center's warning that measures affecting the language of prayer and religious instruction in the schools would be "the Achilles' heel of the government's school policy" in Posen. In a gradual and cautious manner the district governments extended the use of the German language in religious instruction. The pace was accelerated beginning with the spring of 1906, when German replaced Polish in the instruction of religion in all or some levels in 183 schools in the Bromberg district and 20 schools in the Posen district. By the end of 1906, among nearly 241,000 Polish-speaking pupils in the province, 88,500 were taught religion in the German language.[132]

Because the petitions of the parents had proven to be of no avail, the Poles were confronted with the choice of accepting passively the suppression of their language in the religious education of their children or insisting on their parental rights and resisting. By the time the schools reopened after the summer recess, Polish newspapers and a wave of protest demonstrations had produced a consensus in the Polish community that a school strike was a morally justified defense of the rights of the parents and an effective means of forcing the government to rescind the new measures.[133] In the wake of the mass meetings came a proliferation of school strikes. During the month of October, a total of 31,739 children in 473 schools refused to speak in German during the religion lesson. The number rose daily and reached a peak of 46,886 children in 755 schools by November 14. Although the resistance thereafter steadily declined, as late as March 1907 more than 31,000 children were still defiant. During this time the school strikes spread to West Prussia, where more than 14,000 pupils were estimated to be participating in the movement at its greatest strength.[134]

The strike movement owed its rapid growth in October and November 1906 in large part to the activism of the lower clergy. The archbishop's pastoral letter of October 14, which stated that it was a principle of the Christian church that religion had to be taught in a child's mother tongue to ensure a full understanding of its spiritual and moral truths, had the effect of lending a certain legitimacy to their public opposition. Polish priests organized and led two thirds of the protest meetings. The exclusion of Polish clergymen from local school inspection offices and the direction of Catholic religious instruction in the schools and the government's surveillance of their parish activity had alienated and embittered them.[135] Not without cause did they fear that the government was attempting to coerce the Catholic clergy in Posen to adopt the German language in parish life.[136]

The outbreak of the second school strike on a scale that exceeded the local incidents of 1901 shocked high state officials. When the cabinet met on November 27 to discuss the use of more forceful countermeasures, the ministers knew that the school strike was not a straw fire that could be extinguished quickly. The cabinet was impressed by the scale of the movement, the solidarity of the Polish people, their bitter feeling toward the school administration, and their inward conviction that justice was on their side. The two ministers of the interior, Theobald von Bethmann Hollweg for Prussia and Arthur von Posadowsky for the Empire, doubted that the state government could successfully wage a political fight on the question of teaching religion in German to schoolchildren whose family and church language was Polish. Chancellor Bernhard von Bülow was likewise pessimistic in his appraisal, remarking that "the language question in the instruction of religion is an extremely ill-chosen ground for conducting the national conflict." Posadowsky's criticism of the government's school policy in Posen, as the protocol of the cabinet meeting recorded, was blunt and sharp:

The ground on which the govenment's measures in the school strike stand is a morally weak one. The policy that has been pursued in the language question is by no means irreproachable. It is an illusion to assume that Polish children can be germanized by forcing on them German instruction. If the school can teach them the German language to the extent that they are able to use it as the legal official language in their dealings with the authorities, then it has fulfilled its task. He considered the substitution of [German] in place of the mother tongue in the instruction to be politically very questionable and the source of continual disturbance and not unjustified complaints.

He advised Studt to eliminate the cause of Polish discontent and "to make it possible for the two nationalities to coexist peacefully."[137]

Konrad Studt could not appreciate Posadowsky's political insight. Instead of seeing the school strike as the reaction of Poles with religious grievances, he contended that the movement was instigated by politically subversive Polish nationalists. He declined to restore Polish as the language of religious instruction in schools where the change had been made. Such a concession, he told the cabinet on October 23, "would mean a defeat for the school administration vis-à-vis the Polish school-children and would endanger the authority of the state." His strategy for ending the strike was to employ firm but prudent measures and to prevail on Archbishop Florian Stablewski to order the clergy to cease their agitation. Bearing in mind the unfavorable publicity during the Wreschen affair, he was determined "not to create any martyrs" this time and instructed school officials in the province to avoid the use of corporal punishment.[138]

Studt rejected the provincial governor's proposal to discontinue Catholic religious instruction for Polish children in the schools of Posen and to turn it over to the church completely. When Provincial Governor Wilhelm von Waldow and the two district governors discussed the proposal in a mood of despondency at a meeting on October 10, it seemed to them to be the only nonviolent way out of the crisis.[139] Studt thought that if the religious education of Polish children was left entirely to the Catholic church, it would be removed from the supervision of the state; he feared that Catholic religious instruction would assume all the more a Polish nationalist orientation. The decision made in Posen would set "a highly dangerous precedent." Polish parents in Upper Silesia and West Prussia would then demand the exemption of their children from the instruction of religion in the schools, and socialist parents would be tempted to adopt the tactics of passive resistance to exclude the subject from the school curriculum altogether.[140]

Astounded by the scale of the school strike, Wilhelm von Waldow was very pessimistic about the government's capacity to break the resistance quickly.[141] He did not authorize the use of forceful countermeasures for fear of making the situation more inflammable and provoking a revolt. Although newspaper editors and priests were prosecuted on charges of inciting the parents to resist, he ruled out the prosecution of the parents and the imposition of executive fines, which under the law the state authorities could levy up to 300 marks. The countermeasures at first were mild. State subsidies were withheld from school districts where school strikes broke out. Children who refused to speak in German during the religion lesson were detained after school hours. Wherever the strikers disrupted orderly school life, they were put into a separate classroom and taught by people hired especially for this purpose. School officials were under orders to "avoid any harshness which could give cause for justified reproaches against the school administration and could endanger the health of the children."[142]

German and Polish teachers generally stood on the government's side during the school strike. School officials attributed the dutiful conduct of the Polish teachers to "the fear of losing the *Ostmarkenzulagen.*" The school inspectors reported that "under the beneficial influence of the *Ostmarkenzulagen* German is spoken in the families of Polish teachers more now than before 1903" and that "the number of nationally unreliable teachers is becoming fewer." The strains of teaching during the school strike seem to have affected the morale, if not the outward conformity, of the Polish teachers. The Posen district government deprived 110 teachers of bonuses between 1906 and 1908, in most cases for poor school performance.[143]

More than financial rewards motivated the German teachers to support the state government. They fully endorsed its school policy. As early as 1898 the teachers' association in Posen was speaking out for the use of the German language in the instruction of religion in all schools in the province. Its leadership urged the school administration to initiate the change and argued that the elimination of Polish from school instruction would make it easier to appoint German teachers.[144] In the conflict between the nationalities the German teachers supported the side of the extreme German nationalists. More than 1,000 elementary schoolteachers in the province were members of the *Ostmarkenverein* in 1906–1907.[145]

Polish hostility to the teachers during the school strike intensified. The parents thought that Catholic teachers had a duty to inform the school inspectors honestly that religious instruction in German did not touch the hearts of Polish children. The Polish press rebuked the teachers for currying favor with the school inspectors and promoting the use of German in order to obtain bonuses.[146] In public places the teachers were insulted, threatened, and assaulted. Frequently the anger of the local community was vented by throwing stones at the windows of the teacher's home. In many localities the police stationed a guard outside the school and the teacher's house to prevent vandalism and to protect the teacher from physical injury.[147] Libelous offenses to teachers in the press, threats, and physical assault accounted for a large number of the convictions in cases connected with the school strike that were prosecuted by the state.[148]

By the end of March 1907, the provincial bureaucracy had grown impatient with and weary of the stubborn resistance of the Poles and was now prepared to apply the strong countermeasures that had been used effectively to suppress the school strikes in Upper Silesia and West Prussia. District Governor Emil Krahmer of Posen requested authorization from the minister of education to impose executive fines on the parents.[149] With the cabinet's consent, he ordered the county councillors to warn the fathers who were ringleaders of the school strike that they would be fined. He also weighed the possibility of removing children from the custody of their parents and instructed the school inspectors to report on cases in which there was concrete evidence that the father's political conduct was harming the moral welfare of his children.[150]

Threatened with financial penalties, Polish parents gave up their resistance in May and June 1907. By this time the continuation of the school strike seemed futile. The Polish people knew that their struggle found little support in influential German Catholic circles. Exposed in the newspaper, *Kurjer Poznański* (Posen Courier), were the "intrigues" and "perfidy" of the Center politicians who tried to prevent the Polish *Fraktion* from opening a debate on the grievances of Polish parents.[151] The announcements of the end of the school strike were bitter and defiant. The parents declared that they had not and would never reconcile themselves to the religious education of their children in the German language. In the words of the newspaper, *Gazeta Polska* (Polish Gazette), the end of the school strike was just "a cease-fire in the conflict with the Prussian government."[152]

The school strike was not completely without effect. Quietly and without publicity in October 1906, the provincial governor ordered the Bromberg and Posen district governments not to change the language of religious instruction in any other schools until further notice.[153] In June 1907 Konrad Studt's request to resign was accepted. Bülow and the rest of the cabinet had long awaited his departure. Studt had come to regard the administration of the schools in Posen as the thorniest responsibility shouldered by the minister of education. He left office with bitterness and was aggrieved that he had borne "the most slanderous attacks of the opposition press on [his] character and 'system' alone without any official support" from his cabinet colleagues.[154]

The two strikes had shown the irreconcilable opposition of the Polish people to the government's policy of germanizing the schoolchildren, and yet in the aftermath of nearly one year of passive resistance Ludwig Holle, the new minister of education, was no more willing to alter this policy than Studt had been in 1901 and 1902. Raising fearful prospects of the consequences of any change in policy or conciliatory gesture, officials in the ministry imposed on themselves an immobility that prevented them from making any concession that would overcome Polish alienation from the *Volksschule*.

Chancellor Bernhard von Bülow ran up against the ministry's inflexible position when he raised the question of conciliating the Polish people in 1908. His personal friend, Theodor Schiemann, approached him with a proposal to grant a pardon to persons convicted of breaking the law during the school strike and to concede to the Polish people in Posen the freedom to open private schools in which the Polish language would be taught. A professor of Russian history and a political columnist for the Conservative party organ, the *Neue Preussische Zeitung*, Schiemann was convinced that the coercive policy of germanizing the Polish population had failed and that success would not crown the government's forceful measures in the future. He advised Bülow to abandon this elusive goal and to set for the schools simply the task of instilling in the Polish youth a consciousness of being Prussian state citizens, from which would come a voluntary assimilation. "The self-germanization of the Polish nobility and middle class," he said, "will be carried out more easily if it happens out of their own choice than if it is coerced." He contended that the concession to open private schools would weaken the opposition to the German *Volksschule* and take the wind out of the sails of the Polish agitators.[155]

Minister of Education Ludwig Holle and Minister of the Interior Theobald von Bethmann Hollweg, together with the provincial governors of Posen and West Prussia, urged the chancellor not to grant a pardon to individuals convicted of breaking the law during the school strike. They thought that such a conciliatory gesture would be misrepresented by Polish propagandists as a sign of the government's weakness and a belated confession that injustices had been committed by the state authorities in fighting the school strike. More disturbing to them was the likelihood that the government's action would leave its German supporters uncertain and bewildered. The concessions would upset the Germans in the *Ostmark* and shatter their confidence in the government's will to pursue a firm *Polenpolitik*.[156]

Holle expressed his disapproval of private schools for Polish-speaking children in a letter to the chancellor on January 17, 1908, and a discussion with the Berlin professor two weeks later did not alter his views. The minister of education, guarding the school monopoly of the state, was bolstered by Bethmann Hollweg, who wrote to him on January 30: "One may be of the opinion that the Prussian school policy toward the Poles has not always been correct and in its results has not fulfilled the expectations placed in it, but in my opinion there can be no doubt that at the present time it may not be changed." Knowing that influential people were advising Bülow to adopt a conciliatory policy, he urged Holle on April 16 to send the chancellor another letter with a stronger rebuttal to Schiemann's argument. He contended that "today the school and language policy is no longer separable from the general *Polenpolitik*" and that a change in school policy "would be perceived as a weakness and would make the continuation of an energetic *Polenpolitik* impossible."[157]

The minister of education stated his objections to Schiemann's proposal with such vigor that the chancellor was persuaded to discard it.[158] Holle pointed out that to concede to the Polish population an unlimited right to establish private schools would be a radical break from the state's long-standing policy and would set a dangerous precedent. The same liberty could not be withheld from German citizens, and the inevitable consequence would be socialist and ultramontane private schools. He contended that national conderations in Posen and West Prussia made Schiemann's proposal "a dangerous experiment." The Polish people had already shown a great capacity to make sacrifices and would certainly raise immense sums to open numerous private schools "in order to devastate the Prussian *Volksschule* in their homeland." Operating apart from the tight supervision of the state authorities, the private schools would be misused to abet the Polish nationalist movement, to fill the youth with bitter hostility toward the German nation, and to kindle the hope of resurrecting the Polish fatherland. The school administration would in effect renounce all prospects of germanizing the young generation.

Ludwig Holle disputed Theodor Schiemann's contention that a change in school policy would reconcile the Polish population to the Prussian state. Although he repeatedly referred to the futility of unspecified concessions made to the Polish people in the past, what concerned him was how an accommodation to the wishes of Polish parents would affect the government's policy of germanizing the eastern districts. He argued that "a change in policy in the school sphere would be interpreted only as indecision and weakness," an impression that would make German support for a vigorous *Polenpolitik* waver. He also thought, like Bethmann Hollweg, that the question of whether the school and language policy that had been followed since 1886 was pedagogically and politically sound was a mute issue now. The *Volksschule* had been drawn so deeply into the conflict between the nationalities that educational policy could no longer be separated from the Prussian government's fight to suppress the Polish nationality.[159]

Historical explanations of the antagonistic relationship between the Prussian Poles and the state authorities that focus on Bismarck's virulent hostility toward the Polish nationality and the policies devised by leading officials in Berlin overlook the central role played by resolute advocates of the germanization policy in the provincial bureaucracy. The radicalization of the government's school language policy from the 1880s to the outbreak of the school strikes in 1906 was to a large extent the result of aggressive measures taken by school officials in the provincial districts, frequently acting on their own initiative and employing broad discretionary power. Far from being mere cogs in a governmental machine, they pressed their views on officials in the Ministry of Education and sought to steer them on to an unwavering course of suppressing the language and nationality of the Poles. Although they politicized school policy in the Polish-speaking east, they did not succeed in making the school an effective instrument of germanization. The stubborn resistance of the Polish population explains much, but not all, of the failure of this school policy. The school administration in the province could not implement the school language regulations of 1873 and 1887 well; it was hamstrung by the refusal of the state government to make the necessary financial investment in the education of Polish schoolchildren that would have made the schools a noncoercive agency for the assimilation of the youth into German society.

Because state officials blamed clerical school inspectors before 1872 for the poor progress made by Polish schoolchildren in learning the German language, they underestimated the internal obstacles to a successful implementation of the school language regulations. Under the school conditions prevailing in the province, it was virtually impossible for the schoolteachers to equip the Polish pupils with a command of the German language. School expenditures per pupil in the Polish school districts were the lowest in the state; therefore, the most unfavorable ratio of children to teachers existed in these overcrowded classrooms. The size of classes in Polish school districts was larger than the statistical averages for the provinces published in the ministry's massive two- and three-volume reports in the *Preussische Statistik*. These reports are unreliable for the school system in Posen because the official statisticians did not make any distinctions between schools for the German and Polish nationalities. As the unpublished reports of the school bureaucrats in the province indicate, educational provisions for German Protestant children were far better than those for Polish Catholics.

The disparities in school facilities for the two nationalities grew even greater after 1886, when the Ministry of State decided to appropriate school funds for the protection and strengthening of the German nationality in Posen. Although the Polish school districts had poorer financial resources and greater needs, it was the German inhabitants who benefited the most from the state's assistance. Provincial administrators deplored the narrow guidelines set by the Ministry of State for the distribution of the state's school subsidies and repeatedly urged Berlin to allocate more money for schools instructing Polish children. Officials in the Ministry of Finance could not be budged from their fixed opinion that any improvement in the education of the Polish youth would only serve the cause of Polish nationalism.

The school administration in Posen made its task all the more difficult by alienating the Polish clergy. During the *Kulturkampf*, the state authorities employed more coercion against the Catholic church in Posen than in other Catholic regions in the west. A reconciliation did not occur during the years after 1879 because of the provincial bureaucracy's ingrained suspicion of Polish churchmen. The Bromberg and Posen district governments did not execute Puttkamer's order of November 5, 1879 in a generous and conciliatory manner. Polish priests did not recover their local school inspection offices. The requests of many clergymen to direct the instruction of religion in the schools were rejected. The permission granted to some of the other priests in the late 1880s was soon revoked. In the course of the 1890s, a declining number of priests were allowed to exercise the church's right to supervise religious education in the schools. Deprived of an official relationship to the schools and indignant at the district government's surveillance and harassment, Polish clergymen were bitterly aggrieved by the end of the decade. In the pulpit and at public meetings they became outspoken critics of the school authorities, the school language regulations, and interconfessional schooling.

The provincial bureaucracy once again played a fateful role in the escalation of hostility that led to the school strikes of 1906–1907. In a conference with Minister of Education Gustav von Gossler in June 1886, school officials in the province urged that the Polish language be banned in the schools altogether. Gossler knew of the sensitivity of the Catholic episcopacy on the issue of religious instruction, and political prudence guided him when he issued the school language regulation of 1887, which left untouched the use of Polish in teaching religion. His successors, Robert von Zedlitz-Trützschler and Robert von Bosse, were also cautious and prohibited the district governments from changing the language of religious instruction throughout the 1890s. The school bureaucrats chafed at this restraint. They were, furthermore, disappointed when Imperial Chancellor Leo von Caprivi adoped a conciliatory policy toward the Poles. The Prussian government's concession in 1894, a halfmeasure in the eyes of the Poles, permitted optional Polish lessons on a limited scale in the schools.

In the 1890s school officials in the province became frustrated and despondent over the slow progress of germanization. In their discussions of the obstacles to the achievement of this goal, they dwelled on the opposition of the Polish clergy to the school language policy and on the use of Polish for religious instruction in the schools and for the lessons given to the children in preparation for Holy Communion and confirmation. These lessons, now beginning at an earlier age and including Polish grammar, were promoting Polish literacy and working against the goals of the school. In their search for a more effective way to assimilate the Polish youth into German society, the school officials began to prod the ministry to introduce German as the language of religious instruction in the schools. Through this change they intended to open the way for the appointment of more German teachers and to put pressure on the clergy to use German in their parish instruction of religion. In the autumn of 1899 and in 1900, the Posen district government took the initiative in ordering the teachers to use German in the instruction of religion at selected schools.

These bureaucratic measures did not cease when the protests of the parents in Wreschen led to a highly publicized trial of the Polish residents who were arrested on the charges of rioting. In the aftermath of the Wreschen affair, Minister of Education Konrad Studt did not reevaluate the school policy in Posen. Unable to appreciate Polish feelings on this issue, he could not gauge well the determination of the parents to defend their right to decide on the language of religious instruction for their children. Neither could he see how the school policy was provoking a more political affirmation of Polish national identity and an antipathy to the German language in Polish society. On the other hand, he was far more sensitive to the views of anti-Polish hard-liners in the *Ostmarken-verein* and the National Liberal party who warned the government that any concessions to the Poles would shatter public confidence in its capacity to carry out the *Polenpolitik* with firmness and consistency.

The scale of resistance in the school strikes that broke out in October 1906 dismayed government officials in Berlin and in the province. The continuation of the children's defiance into 1907 testified to the government's difficulties in repressing the movement. State officials could have ended the school strikes sooner by conceding to the demands of the parents or by removing religion from the schools in Polish localities and leaving the instruction completely in the hands of the church, as Provincial Governor Wilhelm von Waldow and Archbishop Florian Stablewski had separately proposed. Konrad Studt would accept neither one of these solutions. He equated any concession restoring Polish as the language of religious instruction as a defeat for the school administration that would undermine the state's authority. The exclusion of religion from the curriculum of Catholic schools in Posen seemed to him to be a dangerous precedent, encouraging the Social Democrats as well as the Polish communities in Upper Silesia and West Prussia to resort to similar tactics. What troubled him even more was that this solution would remove the religious instruction of Polish children from the supervision of the state. Distrustful of the political loyalty of the Polish clergy, he feared that religious instruction outside the jurisdiction of the state's administration of the schools would serve Polish nationalist purposes.

5

Confessional Particularism
in Prussian Society and
the Making of the School Law

More than half a century passed before the promise of a school law contained in the Prussian constitution of 1850 was fulfilled. The dissatisfaction of the Catholic bishops with Adalbert von Ladenberg's draft of a school law in 1850 and the unhappy fate of Heinrich von Mühler's school bills of 1868 and 1869 revealed the deep division of opinion within Prussian society on the school question and the conflicting interpretations that state officials, church leaders, and the liberal parties gave to those articles in the constitution that provided the fundamental principles for a school law. The experience of the *Kulturkampf* engendered in the Catholics an enduring distrust of the school administration, and in the following years a school law was always one of the prime concessions that the Center party sought as a quid pro quo for their support of government bills in the Reichstag. Catholic politicians looked to a school law to provide a secure foundation for a confessional public school system and solid protection for the rights of the church and confessional minorities in school districts. The possibilities of winning such a concession were enhanced after 1890 when the massive electoral vote of the Social Democrats increased the strategic value of the Center party's seats in the Reichstag, which now held the balance between the Left and the Right. Assuming that this pivotal position gave the Center party more political power than it actually had, historians have generally seen the School Law of July 28, 1906 as a reactionary, Clerical measure, which was introduced by the government as a concession to the Center party and passed by a coalition of parties strongly motivated by antisocialism.[1] An examination of the making of the school law from 1890 to 1906 produces a more detailed and complete picture of what happened and a more profound view of the society of imperial Germany.

Public Pressure for a School Law

No progress was made in putting the school system on a modern legal foundation during the 1880s because of Bismarck's political objections to the reform of school maintenance. While his concern for the financial interests of the landowning nobility blocked the introduction of a school bill, public pressure for the reform of school maintenance was steadily growing, especially in Silesia where the defects and inequities of the system prescribed by the General Civil Code of 1794 were more visible than in any other province. A decision of the provincial diet in 1829 extended to the Protestant schools the provisions of the Silesian Catholic School Regulation of 1801, which made the communes and the estate owners in the *Gutsbezirke* responsible for paying for school costs. When the High Administrative Court ruled in 1876 that this decision did not have the force of law, the administration of school finances was thrown into confusion. The effect of the court's judgment was to return the Protestant schools to the jurisdiction of the civil code, which required the householders in each school district—the *Schulsozietät*—to provide for school expenses.[2] Because Silesia had over 3,800 *Gutsbezirke*, the restoration of the old system reduced the financial resources available for the support of the Protestant schools. The civil code did not consider the *Gutsherren* or the *Forensen*—landowners who did not reside in the school district—as householders and exempted them from paying the school tax.

The unfair manner in which the burden of school maintenance was distributed in Silesia caused much discontent. The assessment of school taxes was frequently higher for Protestants than for Catholics living in the same area.[3] School districts located in the industrializing regions of Silesia were affected by the rapid expansion of the working-class population and thus found their expenditures increasing without being able to tap the wealth of the joint-stock companies. The privileges enjoyed by the estate owners in the school districts under the civil code made the school tax paid by the other landowners seem all the more burdensome.

A petition from Protestant householders in Silesia, which demanded that estate owners be made legally liable to contribute to school maintenance, forced the Ministry of Education and the House of Deputies to examine their grievances in 1887. In the House committee on education the spokesman for Gustav von Gossler stated that the problems in Silesia could be remedied only through a law applying to the entire state.[4] The committee's majority recommended that the petition be forwarded to the minister with the request to introduce a school bill as soon as possible. The deputies from the province reacted to this report with angry impatience. One deputy snapped that the people in Silesia should not be told to wait until the enactment of the "legendary" school law.[5]

A year later Baron Octavio von Zedlitz und Neukirch, a Free Conservative party member from Silesia, sponsored a resolution that urged the government to propose legislation that would make school maintenance, in accordance with Article 25 of the constitution, a responsibility of the commune. "To bring about the same obligations and legal equality in respect to school maintenance between the diverse citizens of a locality," he contended, "it is necessary that school expenses be covered by a communal tax." The Conservative party declined to take a position in principle; it still had deep misgivings about the effects of such a law on the big landowners. The Center party chided Zedlitz for ignoring other parts of the constitution that guaranteed the rights of the communes and the churches, and insisted that the school law had to implement Articles 22–25.[6]

Appeals from the teaching profession for a uniform regulation of salaries provided the House of Deputies in 1889 with another occasion to prod the government to introduce a school bill. The prevailing system of setting salaries in each school district resulted in gross disparities in the earnings of teachers in the cities and the countryside and in the flight of experienced teachers from underpaid positions in village schools. In the committee on education the Progressive party members, who were by now pessimistic about the prospects of enacting a comprehensive school law, spoke in favor of improving the income of the teachers by a special measure. A councillor in the Ministry of Education replied that it was not possible to regulate the salaries of the teachers without enacting a law on school maintenance because both matters were interrelated. Annoyed by the government's inaction, the Progressives on the floor of the House of Deputies raised the question of what tactics should be employed to obtain school legislation. Heinrich Rickert, a Progressive party leader, proposed that they use their budgetary power to force the ministers of finance and education to introduce a school bill. Baron Octavio von

Zedlitz und Neukirch urged the House of Deputies to seize the initiative and vowed to submit a legislative proposal in the next session if the government continued to stall.[7]

By the end of the 1880s the cabinet could no longer ignore the impatient demands of the House of Deputies, the complaints of the Silesians, and the disputes over school maintenance that disturbed the social harmony of many communities—disputes that had to be settled in the courts because the antiquated school regulations of the Prussian monarchy seemed irrelevant or unfair. After Bismarck's resignation in March 1890 cleared the way for the introduction of a school bill, Gustav von Gossler sought the cabinet's authorization to prepare a school law. These circumstances account for the government's decision to introduce a school bill in November 1890 more than any intention to use the elementary school as a *Kampfinstrument gegen Sozialdemokratie* (instrument in the struggle against Social Democracy).[8] Although the Cabinet Order of May 1, 1889 expressed the emperor's wish "to make the elementary schools useful in counteracting the spread of Socialist and Communist ideas," no trace of assigning them a role in the class conflicts of imperial Germany appeared in the *Begründung* (argument) appended to the draft of the school law.[9]

The Political Battles over the School Bills

The Free Conservative and National Liberal parties greeted the school bill and praised the skill with which Gossler avoided controversial principles. The school bill omitted any mention of confessional and interconfessional schools and did not explicitly require that schoolchildren be taught by teachers of the same confession. Because Falk's decree of 1876 on the state's supervision of Catholic religious instruction in the schools was in no way annulled, the National Liberal party took satisfaction in seeing that the school bill upheld "the principles that the school is a *Staatsschule* and that neither out of consideration for the rights of the churches nor out of consideration for the self-government of the communes should the state be restricted in respect to its right to appoint teachers and to exercise school supervision."[10]

The Center vowed to wage an unrelenting fight against the school bill, which did not place the *Volksschule* securely on a confessional foundation. It did not require the school administration to order the establishment of a separate confessional school if the Catholic minority attending a Protestant school exceeded sixty pupils or vice versa. Neither did the provisions on religious instruction offer sufficient guarantees for an effective supervision by the churches. The Center demanded that greater influence be granted to the church authorities in the examination of candidates for teaching licenses and in the appointment of teachers. In an appeal for Conservative party support, Ludwig Windthorst justified his party's insistence on ironclad guarantees:

> The Catholics are in a very insecure position because our entire school system up to the top is led by Protestants, and even with the best will these gentlemen are not able to free themselves of their Protestant feelings and convictions . . . and if we now see that not only the minister but almost all of his councillors are Protestants and that even the school officials in the provincial districts are Protestants, so it is clear why Catholics view school legislation with concern and apprehension.[11]

The future of the school bill depended on the alignment of the Conservatives, and both sides listened attentively to the words of their leader in the opening debate on December 5 and 6. Count Leopold von Buch's cool reaction to the school bill led to much speculation in the press that Gossler's days in office were numbered.[12] Although the Conservatives accepted reluctantly the obligation of the *Gutsherren* to provide for school maintenance, they were intent on limiting the tax liability of these landowners. They objected firmly to the provision that school costs in districts uniting communes and *Gutsbezirke* were to be divided according to the standards used in levying communal taxes, the assessment of the state tax on incomes and property. The estate owners preferred a division of school costs that took into account the number of households or schoolchildren in each part of a joint school district. The Conservatives were also dissatisfied with the section of the school bill concerning the confessional communities and church interests. The hopes of the Catholic opposition were lifted by Count Buch's remark that it was doubtful that a school law could be enacted in the present parliamentary session.[13]

For many months Ludwig Windthorst had suspected Baron Octavio von Zedlitz und Neukirch of maneuvering to enact a school law on the basis of a pact among the *Kartell* (cartel) parties, which included the Conservatives, the Free Conservatives, and the National Liberals. In 1889 he warned them that the Center party would not stand aside in weakness but would "seize any opportunity to demonstrate its power." Now he warned the state government that the Catholics would conduct an unrelenting agitation campaign if the *Kartell* parties passed the school bill against the Center's opposition. He told the House of Deputies that "the grounds would be laid for a fight whose end I do not see and whose contamination will go far deeper than that of the earlier *Kulturkampf* legislation."[14] Windthorst repeated this threat in a private conversation with Secretary of State Marshall von Bieberstein on January 14, 1891, and asked him to communicate to Chancellor Leo von Caprivi that if the school bill was accepted the Center would no longer follow a progovernment course and provide the votes that the chancellor needed in the Reichstag.[15]

Gossler's introduction of the school bill without consulting the Catholic bishops in Prussia strained relations between the church and the government. At a special conference summoned by Archbishop Philipp Krementz of Cologne on November 27, 1890, the bishops drafted a petition to the Ministry of State, protesting that the proposed law did not do justice to the church's constitutional right to direct the instruction of religion in the schools. It did not recognize the church's right to select the books for the subject of religion or to confer a special commission on the teachers who gave the instruction. Because it empowered school officials to remove clergymen from the direction of religious instruction at any time, the bishops thought that "the danger of conflicts can hardly be avoided" in view of "the wide scope given to the discretionary judgment of the state's administration of the schools." They urged the government to withdraw the school bill and to introduce a new draft law after reaching an understanding with the church.[16]

When the cabinet discussed the petition on December 7, Gossler was angry about the Center's opposition and advised his colleagues not to reply to the bishops' "exorbitant" demand to be consulted prior to the introduction of a school bill. Caprivi and the other ministers thought that "the pretensions of the episcopacy could not be left unanswered," and instructed Gossler to draft a reply. The letter sent by the chancellor rejected the petition with the sharp rebuke that previous attempts to arrive at an understanding with the bishops on the implementation of Article 24 of the constitution had only led to theoretical disputes and "hindered an agreement on the basis of actual practices."[17]

The bishops were not of one mind on how the church should fight the school bill. From the middle of December through February 1891, they watched closely the work of the committee to which the school bill had been sent for revision. The amendments proposed by the Center party deputies, Victor Rintelen and Ludwig Windthorst, were voted down when the Conservatives decided to align with the Free Conservatives and the National Liberals rather than to desert the government.[18] The bishops in the Rhineland saw in this political alignment in the committee the alarming prospect that the school bill would find a majority in the House of Deputies. At a meeting on February 17, the bishops of Cologne, Münster, and Trier agreed to issue in their dioceses pastoral letters opposing the school bill and impressing upon the faithful that the instruction of religion given by schoolteachers without the *missio canonica* could not be recognized as Catholic teaching. This plan for a public protest was discarded after the other bishops demurred. They thought the pastoral letters with an implied threat to rally the Catholic population to boycott the instruction of religion in the schools would be perceived as "a declaration of war" against the government and provoke a backlash. Bishop Georg Kopp of Breslau told Archbishop Krementz that Gossler "would denounce us to the emperor and the chancellor as disloyal agitators who preach sedition" and would push the school bill through the *Landtag* by arousing the indignation of the Protestants in the Conservative ranks.[19]

Gossler's resignation on March 10 was immediately seen as a victory for the Catholics and produced a flurry of rumors that the school bill would be withdrawn.[20] The speculation in the press was confirmed when his successor, Robert von Zedlitz-Trützschler, announced in the House of Deputies that the government no longer saw any purpose in continuing the deliberations. The resolute opposition of the Center made the school bill a hindrance to Caprivi's efforts to establish friendly relations with the party that commanded a pivotal position in the Reichstag. In the election of February 1890, the strength of the *Kartell* parties had fallen to 135 seats of a total of 397 in the Reichstag. The chancellor knew that the support of the Center's leadership, who controlled 106 votes of their own *Fraktion* plus those of the Polish representation, would be essential for the passage of the army bill that he intended to introduce in November 1892.[21]

The dissatisfaction of the Conservatives contributed to the failure of the school bill as much as the opposition of the Catholics. As early as December 4, 1890, the *Neue Preussische Zeitung* informed its readers that the school bill needed "a fundamental revision" and was not likely to be passed in the current legislative session. The newspaper, which spoke for the orthodox Protestant wing of the Conservative party, doubted that the diverse views among the *Kartell* parties could be bridged and declared emphatically that the Conservatives would not surrender their principles and concede to the views of the National Liberal party.[22] The Conservatives were displeased with the work of the House of Deputies committee. The amendments proposed by the Center party made them all the more conscious of the flaws of the school bill. The representatives of their party on the committee showed little courage when they yielded under the government's pressure and withdrew their amendment to require the establishment of a separate school at the request of the parents if the number of children attending a school of another confession exceeded sixty. They voted against this proposal when Ludwig Windthorst subsequently sponsored it. To the vexation of their party comrades, they accepted a National Liberal party amendment, which was intended to make the opening of schools for confessional minorities more difficult.[23]

Robert von Zedlitz-Trützschler knew that the Conservatives were disappointed that Gossler had not adopted their "Christian-conservative standpoint" in drafting the school law. He had no sympathy for it himself. When the cabinet discussed the future of the school bill on April 12, he recommended that the government end further parliamentary deliberations. He pointed out that the Conservatives on the committee had not represented their party well and that the committee had not revised the school bill as the Conservatives had wished.[24]

Zedlitz had close ties to the orthodox Protestant wing of the Conservative party. His daughter was married to the son of Hans von Kleist, and one of his confidants was Wilhelm von Hammerstein, the editor of the *Neue Preussische Zeitung*. The new draft of the school law presented to the Ministry of State in October 1891 reflected the high value that Zedlitz placed on the church's influence in the schools and his conviction that the *Volksschule* was, next to the church, the best place to cultivate the religious and moral consciousness of the nation upon which the health and very existence of the state depended.[25]

In his draft of the school law, Zedlitz strove to implement conscientiously all of the articles on education in the constitution. Whereas Gossler excluded the sphere of private education from his school bill, the new draft law entitled any citizen who possessed sound moral character and proper professional qualifications to establish a school with the consent of the state authorities. Defending this section of the school bill, Zedlitz wrote to the Ministry of State on October 16 that the present practices of the school administration did not stand in accord with the freedom of teaching guaranteed in the constitution. He thought that "the hostility which the previous bill had encountered from the Center party on this point [was] justified." He assured his colleagues that Articles 81–83 contained sufficient precautions to "ensure a patriotic and Christian organization for private instruction and [to] prevent the development of the private school into a competitor against the public school."[26] Private schools were placed under the supervision of the district governments and could be shut down if the county commission decided that any one of them no longer fulfilled the legal preconditions under which the state license was granted.[27]

Because Zedlitz believed that the instruction of religion should influence the entire life of the school, he applied the confessional principle extensively in his school bill. The schoolchildren were to be taught, as a rule, by teachers of their own faith. Teachers' training schools were also required to have a staff belonging to the same confession. Generous rights were granted to religious minorities in the school districts. Wherever more than thirty Catholic or Protestant children attended a school of another confession, the district governor was empowered to order the establishment of a separate school for them at the request of their parents. Such an order was mandatory if the confessional minority in a school district numbered more than sixty pupils. In drafting the provisions for confessional schooling, Zedlitz was guided by what he had learned as the provincial governor of Posen:

> The assumption that the education of children [of different religions] in the same schools fosters and strengthens confessional peace has not proven to be true. School officials encounter again and again the difficulty of finding the right form for religious devotions, setting the proper tone for teaching history, and selecting reading books for the instruction of the German mother tongue so that no one's conscience is violated. . . . And another factor is to be added to this one. The educational effect of the instruction depends to a great extent on whether the teacher succeeds in affecting the feelings of his pupils in the right manner and on whether the teacher, the school, and the home stand in the right relationship to one another. It is of considerable importance that the teacher, children, and parents be of the same faith so that mutual trust is nourished.[28]

Proceeding from the premise that religion could be taught in the *Volksschule* only in cooperation with the church authorities, Zedlitz defined the rights of the church in his draft of the school law more broadly than Gossler was willing to do. Under Article 18, church officials could commission the parish pastor or priest not only to supervise the instruction of religion but also to teach the subject instead of the schoolteacher. Article 112 entitled a representative of the appropriate church to be a voting member of the commission examining candidates for the teacher's license. If he declined to certify the candidate's qualifications to teach religion in contradiction to the judgment of the majority, then the issue was to be settled by the provincial governor in agreement with the church authorities.

Within the cabinet, Finance Minister Johannes Miquel raised strong objections to the school bill. He disapproved of the provisions for the establishment of separate confessional schools for religious minorities and contended that the increasing mobility of the population and the financial interests of the confessionally mixed cities would require the organization of interconfessional schools. He pointed out that Article 112, in effect, conceded to the church authorities the power to veto the appointment of any teacher. The section on private education seemed to him to be another threat to the state's control of elementary schooling. He argued that many private schools under the direction of Catholic priests would be opened in competition with the public schools. Catholic private schools "would conflict with the interests of the state the most" wherever "strong national and politico-ecclesiastical divisions" existed in Prussia. Dismissing Zedlitz's comment that the implementation of liberty of teaching in the school law was a necessary guarantee for freedom of conscience, he advised the Ministry of State to strike out Articles 81–83.[29]

A man of strong character and firm principles, Robert von Zedlitz-Trützschler defended his school bill and asked the cabinet to settle the issues over which he and Miquel disagreed. At a meeting on December 23, Miquel restated his objections and argued additionally that it would be a mistake to introduce a school bill in opposition to the Free Conservatives and the National Liberals because the two "middle parties" represented the mainstream of Protestant opinion. Johannes Miquel, the erstwhile National Liberal party leader, was unhappy at the prospect of an alignment of the Conservatives with the Center in the Reichstag and the House of Deputies. Caprivi replied that the school bill had to be passed with the support of the Center party.[30] Since 1890 the strategy pursued by this Catholic party was to barter their votes for government bills in exchange for the concession of a school law. Caprivi was hoping to conciliate them and to clinch their position as a progovernment party. The chancellor's need for Center party votes in the Reichstag played into Zedlitz's hand. The other ministers were readily persuaded that the school bill contained sufficient safeguards against the proliferation of private schools. Miquel was now in a difficult position, faced with the choice of resigning or supporting the government's policy. Reluctant to sacrifice the completion of his vast scheme of tax reform by resigning, he decided to abstain in the cabinet's vote on the school bill.[31]

The Center party press and Catholic churchmen greeted the school bill of 1892 with warm praise and identified at once the advantages that it offered in comparison with Gossler's draft law. The *Kölnische Volks-*

zeitung informed its readers that the new school bill expressed more effectively the confessional character of the *Volksschule* and provided greater protection for religious minorities in diaspora areas. It surrounded the instruction of religion with many more guarantees for the exercise of church influence in the school system.[32] Archbishop Krementz wrote to the episcopacy that even if his misgivings were not eliminated by the amendments of the Center party, "the acceptance of the entire law could be permitted as a *minus malum* in comparison with existing conditions." In his reply the bishop of Trier itemized the virtues of the school bill and observed that no other school law in Austria or France contained all these advantages. "We will hardly ever receive in Prussia a better law corresponding to our wishes entirely," he remarked.[33]

When the Free Conservative and the National Liberal parties turned the general budget debate in January 1892 into an attack on the school bill, Caprivi reacted with a sharp counteroffensive. In the public perception he was now as closely linked to the school bill as Zedlitz was. The chancellor's remarks left the impression that he was determined to push the school bill through the *Landtag* and did not care whether the National Liberal party opposed it. He stated openly that the government's intention in drafting the law was "to make peace with Catholic citizens and to create conditions in the *Volksschule* with which the Catholic church can be satisfied." To take the wind out of the sails of the National Liberal party opposition, he called the schools one of the most important means of repelling socialism and argued that they could "not dispense with religion" if they were "to fulfill their task from this special point of view." He reminded the National Liberals that the schools could not teach religion without the cooperation of the churches, and in a cutting rebuke he told them that if they carried their opposition to its logical conclusion, they would find themselves demanding the removal of religion from the school curriculum altogether.[34]

In the first debate on the school bill from January 25 to 29, the Free Conservatives and the National Liberals assailed the "extreme confessionalism" of its provisions. They contended that the concessions to the church amounted to a *Mitherrschaft* (codominion) in the school system that exceeded the limits of what the interests of the state and the unity of school supervision should permit. They objected especially to the power granted to the church in the examination for the teacher's license and to the formation of local school boards under the chairmanship of the parish priests or pastors. With similar vehemence they deplored the school bill's weak precautions against the misuse of the freedom to teach and warned that the Poles and the Social Democrats would seize the opportunity to open private schools in competition with the public schools.[35]

The political passion with which the Free Conservatives and the National Liberals waged an unrestrained battle against the school bill in the *Landtag* and in the press was aroused by their wrath over Caprivi's intention to abandon the *Kartell* strategy of the Bismarck era and to embark on a "new course" that threatened to relegate them to an insignificant position in parliamentary life. Robert Friedberg, a National Liberal, reproached the chancellor for making concessions to the Center party in school legislation in return for their support for the army bill and the trade treaties. Complaining bitterly about Caprivi's disregard of the Free Conservatives and the National Liberals, he said, "Even if the middle parties are at the present time in the minority, so they have always formed a solid foundation on which the government could rely in all national questions."[36] The passage of the school bill against their votes was a humiliating prospect, and the leader of the Free Conservatives, Wilhelm von Kardorff, warned the Center and the Conservatives "not to overrule those parties which have a greater importance in the German fatherland than their current number of parliamentary seats would indicate."[37]

The National Liberals were disappointed when the speakers for the Conservative *Fraktion* praised the school bill and immediately excluded the possibility of any pact with them.[38] Knowing that ideological differences made the enactment of a school law with a *Kartell* majority impossible, the middle parties began to apply pressure on the government to withdraw the school bill. Baron Octavio von Zedlitz und Neukirch emphasized the depth of public opposition in the advice that he gave to Caprivi:

> If one wishes to adhere to the policy that it is the task of our times to unite all groups supporting the state in the fight against Social Democracy, so I believe that it is not advisable to solve the questions that stir our nation very deeply today according to the views of one party or another party; if we achieve no agreement today, then, in the interests of uniting all groups loyal to the state, it is advisable to exclude this matter from legislative action and, as we have continually demanded, to introduce a law on school maintenance, leaving the big questions involving controversial principles pending at this time.[39]

The National Liberals succeeded in creating a crisis when Miquel submitted a letter of resignation on January 21. The request was withdrawn after Emperor William declined to accept it. Besides enhancing his popularity with the liberal public, Miquel's attempt to resign strengthened his influence in the Imperial Palace. William now decided that the school bill had to be passed with the support of the middle parties. On January 23 he told the minister of education that he would visit him that evening for beer and suggested that certain members of the House of Lords and the Reichstag be invited also. At the *Bierabend* the conversation focused on the school bill, and William remarked that he would never sign a school bill that was passed with Center and Conservative votes alone.[40]

The public hue and cry did not subside after the school bill was sent to the committee. Throughout February the House of Deputies was deluged with petitions demanding a fundamental revision of the school bill or its defeat. The school bill offered the National Liberal party leaders a welcomed opportunity to unite their middle-class ranks—divided on many of the important economic and political issues of the day—in the defense of freedom of thought and educational progress. The party's press seized its old battle flags to fight what it depicted as a reactionary, Clerical school bill that would deprive Catholic teachers of moral autonomy and force them into religious hypocrisy and servility to the clergy. Much of the emotional excitement over the school bill was grounded in anti-Catholicism and fear of the Roman church, which the National Liberal press exploited with hollow slogans.[41]

The officials of the big cities who protested the school bill did not confine their attention to urban interests. At the *Städtetag* (a congress of the mayors) in the province of Westphalia, the keynote address of the mayor of Hagen was essentially an attack on the school bill's concessions to the Catholic church. He contended that the school bill broke with the traditional concept of the *Volksschule* as a state institution and was surrendering important state powers to the church "so that a kind of dualism in school supervision will arise." Asserting that the schoolteachers would become dependent on the clergy throughout their professional life, he portrayed the plight of the Catholic teacher under the subordination of "a religious or political fanatic or even a person who puts his confessional point of view before his love for the fatherland." He declared that freedom of teaching, however right it sounded in theory, was harmful in practice because it would result in the establishment of Catholic private schools in competition with the public schools. "The fear that it will be used vigorously to cultivate and foster confessional intolerance and confessional division within the nation has seized hold of wide circles," he observed.[42]

Helping the National Liberal party to propagate the notion that the bill was surrendering the elementary school to the Catholic church was the *Evangelischer Bund zur Wahrung der deutsch-protestantischen Inte-ressen* (Evangelical Union for the Protection of German-Protestant Interests), founded in 1886 for the purpose of continuing the struggle against "ultramontanism." The propaganda of the Evangelical Union stirred up popular prejudice against the Papacy and the Jesuits, and cast a cloud of suspicion on the national loyalty of Catholic churchmen whose supreme authority resided outside the German Empire. The large membership that it recruited (76,000 by 1890) suggests the extent to which anti-Catholicism was still smoldering within the educated bourgeoisie a decade after the *Kulturkampf*. From its founding the leaders of the Evangelical Union identified the German nationality exclusively with the Protestant confession, and after the turn of the century their polemics against Catholicism exhibited a vulgar chauvinism. To wage their fight more effectively, they put "ultramontanism" in the same company with Polish nationalism and collaborated with the *Ostmarkenverein*.[43]

A widely circulated manifesto of the Evangelical Union criticized those provisions of the school bill that were "not required for the sake of Protestant church interests, but instead granted to the Roman church an augmentation of power that would be dangerous to the state as well as to the Protestant church." It impressed on the public the distinction between the Protestant church authorities, who were closely bound to the royal government, and the Catholic hierarchy, which had greater independence and aspirations for power. Asserting that the clergy would gain control over the Catholic teaching profession, it warned that "given the ideological orientation in the Roman church today, the cultivation of patriotic feeling and national culture could not be expected from such teachers."[44]

With exaggerated predictions about the proliferation of Jesuit schools, the Evangelical Union heightened public fears of the consequences of the proposed law. Willibald Beyschlag, one of its founders and a professor of theology at the University of Halle, argued that conceding the right to open private schools to Catholic religious orders would put into the hands of the "ultramontanes" a mighty weapon for fighting the Prussian state. He demanded that the school bill disqualify Catholic priests from teaching in private schools, explaining contemptuously that "persons who alienate themselves from the fatherland by the oaths of their religious order and are obliged to unconditional obedience to a foreign authority cannot fulfill the task of the German *Volksschule*."[45]

The political following that the National Liberal opposition gained by inciting Protestant fears of the Catholic church troubled the Conservative supporters of the school bill. Pastor Friedrich Zillessen, the founder of the *Freunde der evangelischen Volksschule* (Friends of the Evangelical Elementary School), deplored how Protestants were being misled by anti-Catholic attacks on the school bill into helping the partisans of the interconfessional school to defeat it.[46] In March the Conservative party organ could no longer ignore the effectiveness of the National Liberal party propaganda and published an article under the headline "the school bill and the fear of the Catholic church." The *Neue Preussische Zeitung* lamented how much hysterical apprehension of the Catholic church, grounded in bigotry and ignorance, pervaded the school bill controversy, and chided Protestant pastors who joined the liberal opposition because of imaginary fears that the new law would enhance the power of the church hierarchy and enable it to threaten Protestantism.[47]

The bitter and unyielding opposition of the National Liberal party to the school bill and the destabilizing effects that the government's new strategy was having on domestic politics disturbed a small circle of high state officials with easy access to the Imperial Palace. Count Philipp zu Eulenburg, a friend of the emperor and the Prussian ambassador to Bavaria, and Friedrich von Holstein, a privy councillor in the Foreign Office, frowned upon Caprivi's courtship of the Center party in order to win their votes in the Reichstag. Hostile to the Center party, both men favored a government alliance with the Free Conservatives and the National Liberals whom they regarded as the most reliable supporters of the German Empire. They were worried that the passage of the school bill would drive the National Liberals into an alignment with the Progressive party, which was further to the Left. Their determination to kill the school bill acquired a sense of urgency when the press reported Bismarck's comment that the school bill was an "apple of discord unnecessarily thrown among the parties." The possibility that the former chancellor would exploit the agitation against the school bill for his own purposes and lead the fight in the House of Lords alarmed them. By the end of February they were intriguing to remove Zedlitz-Trützschler from office and to use the appointment of a new minister as a pretext for the withdrawal of the school bill.[48]

Otto von Helldorf, Eulenburg's other informant in Berlin and a Conservative party member in the House of Lords, likewise thought that the introduction of the school bill was a blunder. He was critical of the *Kreuzzeitung* group whom he accused of striving to refashion the Conservatives as "a Protestant Center party." As the chairman of the party's executive committee, he was worried that an alignment with the Center would cost the Conservatives the loss of many seats to the National Liberals in the next election. He was one of the guests at the *Bierabend* at Zedlitz's home on January 23 and with great relief heard the emperor say that the school bill had to be passed with the support of the middle parties. At other social occasions on February 3 and 13, he seized the opportunity of conversations with William to strengthen his adherence to this position.[49]

In March Eulenburg, Helldorf, and Holstein worked in tandem to kill the school bill. Writing to the emperor at Holstein's urging, Eulenburg called the introduction of the school bill a "political mistake" and reproached Caprivi for building a Reichstag majority for the army bill with the Center party. He advised William to instruct the Conservatives "to bury the bill in the committee if it cannot be enacted by a compromise" with the middle parties.[50] At the same time Helldorf requested an audience with the emperor. When they met on March 16, William was psychologically depressed. Helldorf told him that the political crisis could be resolved if a substantial part of the Conservative party *Fraktion* amended "the all-too-pro-Catholic sections" of the school bill in an agreement with the middle parties. Otherwise the school bill would have to be bogged down in the committee. He urged William to lose no time in telling Wilhelm von Rauchhaupt, the leader of the Conservative party *Fraktion*, how the school bill should be handled lest the deputies on the committee from the Conservative and Center parties reach an agreement beforehand. He proposed that Miquel should encourage the National Liberals to negotiate with the Conservatives, and he named several deputies who would be suitable for such confidential talks.[51]

On the following day, just when the business on the agenda of a routine meeting of the Crown Council was finished, the emperor unexpectedly brought up the question of the school bill. He commented that the opposition was very strong and that the chancellor's defense of the school bill in the House of Deputies had been too uncompromising. He stated that the school law had to be enacted in agreement with the Free Conservative and the National Liberal parties. Miquel seconded the emperor's wish and called for a return to the government's earlier strategy of relying on the *Kartell* parties, which had supported all the important legislative measures in Prussia and the German Empire since 1866. Caprivi replied that the *Kartell* policy was no longer practical and that the government had to obtain the cooperation of the Center party if it expected to operate effectively in the Reichstag. The school bill would lose its political usefulness if it was amended in a manner unacceptable to the Catholics. William insisted that the school bill had to win the approval of the middle parties, and he did not care whether it was passed in the current session or not.[52]

Zedlitz-Trützschler was offended by the emperor's remarks and understood them to mean a loss of confidence in him. He was in the midst of arranging an agreement in the committee to delete the section on private education and to revise other articles that applied the confessional principle too rigorously. However, an amendment of the school bill suitable to the anticlerical liberals would be unacceptable to the Center and the Conservatives and contrary to his own convictions. The condition laid down by William left Zedlitz-Trützschler with no other alternative than to resign.[53] Silently he left the Crown Council meeting and sent in his resignation. Caprivi, who was vexed by Miquel's intrigues, submitted his resignation also on March 18.[54]

A weeklong ministerial crisis ended unsatisfactorily when Caprivi was persuaded to remain in the office of the imperial chancellor. Because he stubbornly refused to work with Miquel in the Prussian Ministry of State, Count Botho Eulenburg agreed to serve as the minister president under the condition that Robert von Bosse, the state secretary of the Imperial Department of Justice, be appointed as Zedlitz's successor. By his choice of a conservative bureaucrat known to be a devout Christian, Eulenburg hoped to conciliate the Conservatives and to reassure the Catholics that the new minister would not create difficulties for the Catholic church. He intended to withdraw the school bill and wanted to signal to the House of Deputies that the school administration was not changing its course.[55]

When Count Botho Eulenburg announced the withdrawal of the school bill on April 28, his terse statement communicated to the House of Deputies that the government would not introduce another one for a long time to come. The experience of two school bills revealed the sharp division of opinion in the nation, and state officials doubted that a majority vote would bring the controversy to a rest.[56] The ministers had not expected such a passionate ideological clash over the school bill in 1892. Besides making a lasting impression, the conflict taught them that at a time when the government had to unite all sections of society loyal to the monarchy against Social Democracy, the enactment of the school law did not serve the interests of the state.

The withdrawal of the school bill was a bitter disappointment for the Center and the Conservatives who thought that they had been cheated of a major legislative achievement because of intrigue. The Conservative press blamed the emperor's unscrupulous advisers who "deceived" him with false reports that a growing number of Conservative deputies were wavering in their support for the school bill.[57] The Center and the Conservatives were close to reaching a compromise on the revision of the school bill. Knowing that an agreement between themselves was possible and that they constituted a solid majority, they reproached Eulenburg for dispatching the school bill.[58]

The manifestations of anti-Catholicism in the conflict over the school bill left the Center party supporters feeling both aggrieved and vulnerable. Throughout the debate they had observed with indignation the anticlerical propaganda in the liberal press.[59] They resented the government's new dictum that the school bill had to be passed with the support of the middle parties and that the National Liberals, which represented the opinion of the Protestant bourgeoisie, should not be overruled by a majority based on an alliance between the Clerical and Conservative parties. A Catholic deputy commented ironically that the government had not been afraid of Center party votes earlier, when bills in the Reichstag would not have been passed without the backing of his party.[60]

Renewed Parliamentary Demands for a School Law

Robert von Bosse's policy of dealing with the problems of school maintenance through piecemeal legislation was unacceptable to the Center and the Conservatives. Because the outcome of the 1893 election strengthened the two parties in the House of Deputies, they continued to press their demands for a comprehensive school law. The tactics that they adopted to compel the government to introduce a school bill made it difficult for Bosse to navigate in the House of Deputies. In 1893 they defeated his bill for an appropriation of state funds to provide subsidies to poor school districts for the improvement of teachers' salaries. A Center party deputy said that to pass this bill would mean "nothing other than to take from the ministry any incentive to present to us a general school law." For their part, the Conservative party members explained that it was "not possible to settle the big school question piecemeal."[61]

In 1896 Bosse aroused the wrath of the Center and Conservative parties by proposing another bill that only regulated teachers' salaries. Frankly, he told the House of Deputies on January 30 that he did not expect to present the draft of a comprehensive school law in the foreseeable future and that "the present government does not believe that the time has yet come to revive anew the complex, deep, and passionate conflicts which the introduction of the last school bill had provoked."[62] Bosse's speech was interrupted by loud dissent. Ernst von Heydebrand und der Lasa, the Conservative party leader, berated Bosse for being timid and hinted that another minister with more courage and pluck should replace him.[63] The two parties, recognizing the need to redress the grievances of the teaching profession, finally voted for the bill with mixed feelings. Felix Porsch admitted that many Center party deputies wondered whether it was wise "to give up a trump card which should be saved in order to compel the government to introduce a school law."[64]

Wounded by Heydebrand's criticism, Bosse brought up the question at a cabinet meeting on March 7 and found among his colleagues unanimous agreement that the government could not risk another fight over the school law.[65] The government's inaction caused public confidence in Bosse to decline. The image of him as a weak minister was fixed from 1896 on. The criticism of him from the Center party became harsher in each succeeding annual debate on the school budget, and he entered the House of Deputies on these occasions with tenseness and anxiety.[66] In the budget debate on March 9, 1899, Dauzenberg repeated the demand for a courageous minister of education who would be willing to introduce a school bill. The deputy was venting the irritation of the Center party, which had provided the votes in the Reichstag that the government had been using without making the slightest concession to their demands for a Prussian school law. Bluntly he stated that the Center party was justified in expecting a quid pro quo.[67]

Dauzenberg made these remarks several days after two deputies from Silesia had proposed two competing resolutions urging the government to introduce school legislation. Bosse discussed the two motions with the vice-president of the Prussian Ministry of State, Heinrich von Bötticher, prior to the House of Deputies debate on April 19. Bötticher had no objections to the introduction of a bill confined to matters of school maintenance. For tactical reasons, he thought that it would be better if the provisions on confessional matters were added to the bill by the initiative of the House of Deputies. Observing that "the trend in public opinion in the last seven years has become more conservative," he predicted that the amendments of the majority formed from the Center and Conservative parties would "not run up against as much opposition" as the school bill of 1892 had.[68]

With Bötticher's reassuring conjecture in mind, Bosse announced his readiness to draft a school law to the House of Deputies. He acknowledged the urgent need for a school law and confessed that the government could "not evade this task for long." His words left the impression that apart from certain controversial issues that led to the failure of the school bill in 1892, he would otherwise follow Zedlitz's draft closely. He declared that in the last seven years "the general opinion on the confessional character of the school has become almost unanimous so that there is hardly anyone—at least in this House—who disputes the view that constitutionally and in actuality the confessional school is the rule."[69]

The adoption of Heydebrand's resolution for a comprehensive school law by a majority formed from the Center and Conservative parties over the opposition of the National Liberal party was not likely to convince Miquel that the time had come for the enactment of a school law. The substantial funds that the parties expected the government to appropriate with the reform of school maintenance made the finance minister all the more wary. On August 27 he informed Bosse that the emperor was no longer satisfied with his performance in office and that the reasons were not known. Following this conversation Bosse decided to wait a few weeks and then to resign for reasons of health. In a letter on August 30, Miquel advised him to resign at once because Emperor William desired a change in the Ministry of Education. Later on the same day Miquel hastily dispatched a second letter, informing Bosse that Konrad Studt—the provincial governor of Westphalia—had been selected as his successor. Bosse learned later from other members of the Ministry of State that Miquel had been intriguing for weeks to bring about his resignation.[70]

Johannes Miquel and other high state officials were mistaken in assuming that the government could delay the enactment of a school law indefinitely. With growing impatience, the House of Deputies demanded the introduction of a school bill throughout the 1890s and after the turn of the century. The deputies from Silesia formed a politically influential bloc that kept the issue alive. It was no accident that, in the 1899 debate in the House of Deputies on the two resolutions proposed by Ernst von Heydebrand and Julius Reinecke, many of the speakers came from this province. With deep feeling, Heydebrand described the discontent in the rural school districts of Silesia and the hostility of small farmers and other inhabitants toward the estate owners who had an "objectively unjustified special position" in respect to the financial burden of school maintenance. He deplored "the constant strife and dissension" and the continual round of litigation arising from the anachronism and unfairness of the regulations in the General Civil Code of 1794. The unhappy experience of his party in recent election campaigns in Silesia convinced him that harmonious class relations and social stability in the countryside made the elimination of the exemption of the big landowners from the obligation of school maintenance a matter of interest to Conservatives throughout East Elbia.[71]

The Center party *Fraktion*, which had a membership from the middle 1890s to 1906 that included a stable contingent of eleven priests (not counting the Polish clergymen from Posen), formed another pressure group lobbying for the enactment of a school law. A comprehensive school law seemed to the Catholics to be the most effective means of obtaining solid guarantees for confessional schooling and equality in school provisions for the Catholic and Protestant confessions. Although more than 90 percent of the Catholic children attended schools of their own confession, the Catholics were sensitive to the discrepancies in the school facilities for the two confessions because the number of Catholic pupils attending Protestant schools was more than three times greater than the number of Protestant pupils in Catholic schools. Many industrial towns in the predominantly Protestant provinces of Brandenburg and Saxony had sizeable Catholic minorities. In cities that provided for school maintenance through municipal taxes, Catholic parents experienced years of frustration in their efforts to prevail on the local authorities to establish separate schools for the Catholic minority or to take over the costs of existing Catholic private schools and give them the status of public schools.[72]

In the 1890s the petitions sent by Catholic parents to the House of Deputies and the annual debate on the education budget provided the Center party with opportunities to air Catholic complaints. The Center charged that Protestant liberals in city governments did not place a high value on confessional schooling and expected the Catholic citizens to send their children to the Protestant communal schools. They criticized the reluctance of the school administration to apply the law of May 26, 1887, and to appeal to the provincial organs of self-administration to arbitrate these local disputes.[73] Because the district governments knew that the fiscally conservative county and district commissions would decline to impose higher school expenditures on the communes, they did not want to fall into an adversary relationship with them by submitting cases on behalf of the Catholic parents.[74]

Discussions of Catholic grievances in the House of Deputies often ended with a call for a school law that would set uniform standards requiring the communes to maintain schools for each confession. In 1895 a priest in the Catholic *Fraktion* declared, "We must have a school law which is able not only to break the unjustified resistance of the city governments to the justified demands of the confessional minorities but also to prescribe for the district governments fixed norms on how they can fulfill properly the constitutional principle that confessional conditions are to be considered as much as possible in the organization of the schools." With such a law, Catholics would not always need to appeal to the minister to reverse the decisions of the district governments and to vindicate their rights.[75]

When Konrad Studt entered office in September 1899, the school law issue had already led to the resignation of his three predecessors. A solution that all parties could approve or tolerate seemed unattainable. The new minister had no intention of undertaking a task with such a high probability of failure. Very quickly he learned that the use of dilatory tactics and evasive pretexts would cost him the confidence and cooperation of the House of Deputies. Given the frustration and the aggressive temperament of the deputies now, his tenure in office was likely to be much shorter than Bosse's seven years.

When the House of Deputies confronted Studt with an interpellation to find out what measures the government expected to take "to eliminate the defects and injustices in respect to the maintenance of the schools," he gave an evasive answer on March 29, 1900, as the Ministry of State had authorized him to do. His noncommittal statement that the government had to examine the expenditures of the school districts and to gather statistical data before it could take any legislative action was received with skepticism on all sides of the House of Deputies. Felix Porsch derided his transparent protest with sarcasm. Two other Silesians, Ernst von Heydebrand and Hugo Seydel, were disappointed by the coolness and apparent indifference of his reply and reproached him for ignoring the inequities in the system of school maintenance and the urgent need for reform.[76]

It was Baron von Zedlitz und Neukirch who took the intiative to open the way for the passage of a school bill. Departing from their earlier position, the Free Conservatives were now willing to support a comprehensive school bill in an alignment with the Center and the Conservatives. Zedlitz offered to negotiate an agreement with them on the draft of a school law that included the confessional organization of the schools, safeguards for the interests of the Catholic or Protestant minority in any school district, and guarantees for the participation of the churches in the local administration of the schools.[77] His speech caused a stir of excitement. Immediately the Conservatives pointed out that one of the middle parties had edged closer to them. Studt remarked that Zedlitz's clarification of his party's position would "make it easier for the government to make decisions on this issue."[78]

The enactment of a school law was now a matter of high priority for the Conservatives, and on January 15, 1901 Heydebrand and other members of his *Fraktion* proposed a resolution to prod the state government to introduce a school bill. Studt knew that the Ministry of State had decided not to present a school bill in the current session, but he could not forget his unhappy experience a year ago, when the House of Deputies had spurned his evasive announcement. He had enough political astuteness to know that a replay of the same speech would damage his relationship with the parties beyond repair. He decided to speak for himself, if not for the Ministry of State, and to dispel all doubts about his commitment to the reform of school maintenance and his intention "to achieve this goal as soon as possible."[79]

When Studt communicated his plan to the Ministry of State, Miquel disagreed and thought that he should confine his statement to "a clarification of the present stage of preparations." In a memorandum sent to his colleagues, Miquel contended that Studt could not discuss the specific content of the school bill because the cabinet had not made any decisions. He feared that the government's freedom of action in the future would be "prejudiced in an unfavorable way" by Studt's remarks, and hinted that there were points over which the Ministries of Education and Finance disagreed.[80] Miquel's interference irritated officials in the Ministry of Education. Max Kuegler told Konrad Studt that "a repetition of the dilatory statement" that he gave a year earlier would bring down on him the wrath of the House of Deputies. This body would "conclude that the state government completely rejects its wish." Besides coming into a collision with the Conservatives, the government would have "to reckon with the possibility that the Landtag on its own initiative would propose the draft of a school law, for which Zedlitz's school bill [of 1892] would easily provide the model."[81]

Kuegler was not indulging in wild speculation when he warned that the House of Deputies would take greater initiatives in making a school law. There were many signs that the Center and the two Conservative parties were moving closer together in school politics. Changes in the tactics of the Center's leadership did much to reduce the differences that had once separated the parties. Karl Bachem and Felix Porsch had a keen political appreciation of the importance of eliminating the mutual distrust between the state government and the Catholic church and stressing the common interests of Catholics and Protestants in the struggle against socialism.

The younger generation of politicians who took over the party's leadership after Ludwig Windthorst's death in 1891 made a conscious effort to dispel Protestant fears of the Catholic church. When they discussed the church's participation in the administration of the schools, they took care to reassure government officials and the other parties that they neither expected nor demanded that the state relinquish its rights. They adopted a more restrained tone in airing Catholic grievances and were inclined to offset their complaint with an affirmation of the patriotism of Catholic citizens.[82] The desire of the Center party to move out of the political isolation that the *Kulturkampf* had forced on the Catholics and to assimilate into the national community of the German Empire did not go unnoticed. In 1901 Studt commended the "moderate and conciliatory tone" of the Center party deputies during the budget debate and observed that they had maintained an aloofness from the attacks on the school administration made by the Polish *Fraktion*.[83]

While the Center party strove to appear less "ultramontane," the Free Conservative party was shedding the anticlericalism of its earlier years. In 1901 Baron von Zedlitz und Neukirch greeted Karl Bachem's statement that Catholics and Protestants should join hands in combating the forces of revolutionary socialism, and he assured the Center party that he harbored no hostility toward the Catholic church. "I recognize completely the justification of the idea that the church and the school must be kept in a certain bond and that even the servants of the church must be kept in the closest relationship with the school," he said.[84]

The Debate within the Government

Mounting pressure from the House of Deputies together with the observation that the differences between the parties had narrowed since 1892 led Studt to begin the preparation of a school bill. In June 1900 he sent Max Kuegler's outline of fundamental principles for a school law to the Minister of the Interior, Eberhard von der Recke, and requested that officials representing them meet to discuss it. Kuegler proposed a reorganization of the school districts to create larger and financially stronger units of school maintenance than the communes. Under his plan, cities with more than twenty-five teaching offices would continue to be individual school districts, but the smaller communes and *Gutsbezirke* would be united into *Kreisschulverbände* (countywide school districts).[85] Besides obtaining support for this innovation, Studt hoped that representatives of the two ministers would agree on the need for a substantial increase in state funds for school maintenance. He wrote to Recke that the enactment of the school law would place new financial obligations on the estate owners and that the Conservative party would accept the change only if it was assured that the appropriation of state money for school subsidies would lighten the burden of school taxes.[86]

The minister of the interior declined Studt's request. He doubted that the differences between the parties had diminished sufficiently to ensure a smooth passage for the school bill in the *Landtag*. The Center and the Conservative parties would certainly propose controversial amendments concerning the rights of confessional minorities and the church's participation in the schools. "A repetition of the conflict that was ignited in 1892," Recke contended, "could result in an enduring division between the parties on whose harmonious collaboration the government is dependent for the execution of its policies in the Reichstag." He regarded the creation of countywide school districts as an innovation that would only produce more bureaucratic obstruction and red tape, and questioned whether such a reform would be consistent with Article 25 of the constitution.[87]

The expectation that the House of Deputies would renew its demands for a school law in the forthcoming budget debates led Studt to appeal to Miquel and Recke in December 1900 with a second request to open interdepartmental discussions for the preparation of a school bill. Once again he expressed deep concern about the financial burden that would fall on the estate owners after their exemption from school tax levies was abolished. He wrote that the representatives of the three ministers should discuss in detail how "the hardships" arising from the enactment of the new law could be "alleviated by the distribution of state subsidies for school costs." He suggested that the government would have to grant bigger subsidies than what would be required simply to assist poor communes.[88]

Although both ministers consented after a long delay to participate in the interdepartmental discussions, the first meeting held on May 22, 1901 served only to underscore the sharp division of opinion between the Ministry of Education and the Ministry of Finance. Christian Germar, the senior councillor in the Ministry of Finance, fell at odds with Kuegler when he declared that Kuegler's proposal offered no sound basis for a school law. He stated that Finance Minister Georg von Rheinbaben, who had recently replaced Miquel, could not accept any school law that "would be feasible only with a very considerable increase in state expenditures."[89] The relations between the two ministries were further strained when Germar absented himself from the next meeting in June, and each side blamed the other for breaking off the talks.

On October 10, 1901, Max Kuegler forwarded his proposal to the provincial governors and solicited their opinions on the advisability of forming countywide school districts and on the likelihood of public agitation against a school bill that omitted provisions concerning confessional and church matters.[90] The replies to this inquiry were overwhelmingly negative. In the provinces where the confessional *Schulsozietäten* were deeply rooted in community life, the provincial governors reported that the people would resist the transfer of school property to the communes if the law did not include provisions that safeguarded the confessional character of the schools.[91] The formation of countywide school districts appeared to the provincial governors as a radical change that would encounter strong opposition wherever citizens had an affectionate attachment to the schools in their communes. The provincial governor of Hesse–Nassau contended that such a change would violate the language and spirit of the constitution. The statesmen of 1848 and 1849 placed the responsibility for school maintenance on the communes "for profound reasons of an ethical nature." They regarded the *Volksschule* as a communal institution and saw in the commune an association of parents who had as much an interest in the education of the youth as the state.[92] Studt scrapped Kuegler's draft of the school law as a result of the unfavorable reports of the provincial governors.

In 1902 Studt made a personnel change in the ministry that had a decisive effect on the making of the school law. He decided to remove Kuegler from the office of the director of the department for elementary school affairs and arranged to have him transferred to another post. Kuegler did not possess the skill of maneuvering in parliamentary politics, and his relations with the Center party *Fraktion* were very cool. In the Center's press he was described as a foe of the Catholic confession and "a staunch adherent of Falk's *Kulturkampf* ideas in the Ministry of Education."[93] Studt was no longer confident that Kuegler would be able to negotiate successfully with the party leaders and pilot the school bill through the *Landtag*.

The political abilities required for this task led Studt to choose Philipp Schwartzkopff as Kuegler's successor. As the director of the department for church affairs in the Ministry of Education and Religious Affairs, he had already won respect in the House of Deputies for his politically tactful speeches. As an orthodox Protestant and a patron of the Inner Mission and other church philanthropies, he enjoyed cordial relations with the Conservative party.[94] In his new office Schwartzkopff proved to be more knowledgeable in parliamentary politics than Studt himself. He acquired a reputation as a quick-witted thinker and an adept politician who operated in the parliamentary corridors with great self-assurance. Because Studt possessed neither a strong will nor independent convictions, he was able to act on his own initiative. It was Schwartzkopff who gave the school bill that was finally introduced in 1905 its confessional coloring.[95]

When Schwartzkopff drafted a new school law in the spring of 1903, he took earnestly the statements made by Center and Conservative deputies that the confessional organization of the school system and the internal administration of the schools were matters that could not be circumvented. He incorporated into the law provisions concerning confessional interests but confined these regulations to matters on which the Free Conservatives and the National Liberals were likely to compromise. His draft law dissolved the confessional *Schulsozietäten* and transferred school property and the responsibility for school maintenance to the communes. He coupled this reform with solid guarantees for the confessional character of the schools. He excluded all regulations on the instruction of religion because he knew that the middle parties would not yield to the Catholic bishops the power to certify the qualifications of the schoolteachers to instruct the subject.[96]

The new draft law laid down the general rule that Catholic and Protestant schoolchildren should receive instruction from teachers of their own faith and that only teachers of the appropriate religion were to be appointed to the confessional schools. It required the establishment of a separate school for the Catholic or Protestant minority in a school district if there were more than sixty pupils of that faith for five consecutive years. In cities and rural communes with more than 5,000 inhabitants, a confessional minority was entitled to have its own school if the number of pupils exceeded 100. Existing interconfessional schools were left intact, but in the future the opening of interconfessional schools was allowed only in the former Duchy of Nassau and, "insofar as national interests require it," in the provinces of Posen and West Prussia.[97]

Officials in the Ministry of Education did not expect the National Liberal party to put up serious resistance to this section of the school bill. When Studt submitted the new draft law to the finance and interior ministers in May 1903, he wrote, "The fight for the interconfessional school, which raged a generation ago, no longer stands in the foreground of the activities and interests of the middle parties. People have recognized that the interconfessional school carries with it disadvantages insofar as it is apt to impair not only religious and moral education but also the cultivation of patriotism." He pointed out specifically that in the instruction of history the great achievements of the Reformation could not be related "without the constraints which are required out of consideration for the other confession."[98]

The school bill was not introduced in the 1904 legislative session as Studt had hoped; instead the discussions between the three ministries dragged on for two years. Officials in the Ministry of Finance and Ministry of the Interior did not see the urgency of reforming Prussia's antiquated system of school maintenance and paid little heed to the impatient demands of the House of Deputies. For over a half century doubts about the political wisdom of enacting a school law had prevailed within the government. Apprehensions and uncertainties about the consequences of the law made officials in both ministries hesitant. They preferred not to take legislative action and to bind the hands of the state administration so long as they did not know its future effects.[99]

In the discussions on the draft of the school law in 1903 and 1904, officials representing the finance and interior ministers repeatedly argued for the removal of the section on the confessional organization of the schools. Hans von Hammerstein, the current minister of the interior, thought that the school bill should not be drafted to suit the Center party because the agreement of the middle parties was an essential condition for the enactment of the law. Although he agreed with Studt that the enthusiasm of the National Liberal deputies for the interconfessional school had diminished since 1892, he doubted that they could escape the pressure of the liberal press and accept the articles that restricted the opening of new interconfessional schools. Finance Minister Georg von Rheinbaben objected that the provisions for confessional schooling would limit the discretionary power of the state administration and lead to a big increase in school expenditures. Schwartzkopff firmly rejected their demands to cut this section out of the school bill. From his confidential discussions with members of the *Landtag*, he knew that a school bill that did not designate the confessional school as the norm would have no prospects of being passed.[100]

It was the question of money rather than confessional schooling that dominated the discussions between the three ministries. Rheinbaben declared flatly that he could not consent to the introduction of a school bill until he knew precisely what its consequences would be for the state's treasury. Christian Germar, his representative in the interdepartmental discussions, said repeatedly that larger budget appropriations for the execution of the school law could not be made in view of the state's current unfavorable financial situation. He was especially concerned about the impact of the school law on the *Gutsherren* because he knew that the Conservatives were expecting state subsidies to relieve the estate owners of heavy school taxes. In order to distribute school costs justly, Schwartzkopff made the assessment of state taxes on income and property the basis for levying the school tax in rural school districts uniting a

Gutsbezirk and a commune. Germar objected that under this method of assessment the school tax would fall too heavily on the estate owners. He demanded that the district governments conduct trial assessments of the school tax in the countryside in order to ascertain how the school law would affect the big landowners.[101]

Officials of the Ministry of Finance were also disturbed about the unfavorable effects of the school law on the German nationality in Posen. The financial liability of the Germans for school costs would increase when Polish Catholic and German Protestant *Schulsozietäten* were dissolved and the communes took over the obligation of school maintenance. Germar lamented that "in Posen the politically loyal circles of the population would be harmed by the law to the advantage of the less loyal." He questioned whether the government should "proceed with such a law at a time when it was urgently necessary to strengthen the German population in its difficult situation."[102]

Anxious about rising school expenditures, the Ministry of Finance raised strong objections to the clauses that set minimal standards for the schools. Schwartzkopff's draft of the school law required the appointment of a second teacher to a one-classroom school if the number of pupils exceeded eighty over three consecutive years, and the appointment of a full-time teacher for every seventy children in larger schools. It laid down the rule that neighboring villages forming a joint school district had to have individual schools if the children were traveling more than 2.5 kilometers from their homes to the school. Officials in the Ministry of Finance complained that the first regulation alone would force the state government to open eighteen new *Lehrerseminare* and the communes to create over 10,000 new teaching offices. The unconditional wording of the articles would not allow the provincial organs of self-administration under the law of May 26, 1887 to examine whether the commune had the financial capacity to fulfill the requirements.[103]

Schwartzkopff insisted on incorporating in the school bill legally compelling standards for school facilities. Eduard von Bremen, who assisted him in the interdepartmental discussions, told Germar that the landowners in the countryside were generally unsympathetic to popular education and that the school administration had to have "guarantees" that the responsibility of school maintenance would be properly fulfilled. He contended that because the county commissions were able to obstruct the improvement of the schools by using "the excuse" that the communes had inadequate financial resources, it was necessary to set down in the law the conditions in which the teaching staff of a school had to be expanded.[104]

The School Bill Compromise of 1904

After months of formal discussions Schwartzkopff had made no progress in obtaining the consent of the finance and interior ministers to introduce the school bill. It was clear to him that the Ministry of Finance would continue its obstructionist tactics and demand reports on the probable effects and consequences of the school law. He decided to offer the government compelling evidence that a school bill could be pushed through the *Landtag* without provoking the acrimonious partisan conflicts that occurred in 1892. On January 22, 1904, Studt requested royal authorization to open confidential negotiations with the party leaders. In the following weeks Philipp Schwartzkopff met with Heydebrand and Zedlitz as well as with Albert Hackenberg, who represented the National Liberal party, to reach a compromise on how far the school law should go to implement Article 24 of the constitution.[105] The leaders of the Center party *Fraktion* were informed of the negotiations but chose not to join the political bargaining. They wanted to retain their freedom to oppose interconfessional schooling without any exception for Nassau and the provinces of Posen and West Prussia.[106]

By early May, Hackenberg, Heydebrand, and Zedlitz agreed to a compromise proposal just in time to substitute it for Zedlitz's routine motion on the introduction of a school bill, which was scheduled for debate in the House of Deputies on May 13. The new proposal defined the boundaries within which the section on church and confessional matters had to be kept and laid down four principles for the execution of Article 24. Pupils of one school were as a rule to belong to the same confession and to be instructed by teachers of their faith. Interconfessional schools, designated as "exceptions," were to be permitted only for such "special reasons" as national considerations in the Polish-speaking area and historical circumstances in the former Duchy of Nassau. Separate schooling was to be provided for the Catholic or Protestant minority in a school district if the number of pupils of that faith rose to an appropriate level. Representation was to be granted to the church in the local school boards formed in the countryside and the cities.[107]

Schwartzkopff achieved an agreement between the political parties because he found a disposition to compromise on all sides. The National Liberals made concessions to the Conservatives on the issue of confessional schools. The Conservatives, in return, accommodated the middle parties by setting aside their other demands for the church's participation in the administration of the schools. They agreed to a compromise that offered "the minimum of what must be granted to maintain the confessional character of the schools." The Center deputies, apart from their weak objections to the proposition on the interconfessional schools, accepted the proposal as "the minimum of what their party must demand."[108] To enable the Center party to endorse the rest of the agreement, the sponsors made arrangements for a separate voting on each part of the proposal.

The most important political concessions were made by the National Liberals whose endorsement of the compromise proposal of May 13, 1904 meant the abandonment of their traditional defense of interconfessional schooling since the 1860s. Their representative in the negotiations was a Protestant pastor from the Rhineland who stood close to the Conservatives on the issue of confessional schools. Hackenberg believed that the Christian ethos had to permeate the instruction of history and other subjects in the curriculum if the *Volksschule* was to fulfill its task of educating the youth for life. In the House of Deputies on May 13, he disdainfully censured the liberals of the 1870s for comparing an idealized interconfessional school with a caricature of the confessional school and exaggerating the cultural and social benefits of interconfessional schooling. The experience of the Rhine Province had taught him that the introduction of the interconfessional schools had not attenuated confessional differences or promoted social harmony.[109] As a member of the Evangelical Union, he had good reason to believe that the school system would not prosper on an interconfessional basis in a country where the confessional division of society was sharp and intensely felt.[110]

Recognizing pragmatically that the confessional school was the prevailing form of elementary education in Prussia, the leaders of the National Liberal party *Fraktion* declined to take a doctrinaire stance. Robert Friedberg and Karl Sattler treated the school bill compromise as a matter of practical politics and decided for tactical reasons to come to terms with the Conservatives. Their aim was to remove the Center party from its pivotal position in the Prussian House of Deputies by collaborating with the parties of the political Right in passing the school bill and other measures. They thought that the National Liberals would achieve nothing if they fought for an equal legal status for both types of schools. By accepting the compromise, however, their party could prevent the enactment of a Clerical school law by a coalition of the Center and Conservative parties.[111]

The liberal press and the left wing of the National Liberal party reacted with outrage to the opportunistic conduct of the *Fraktion*. The *Kölnische Zeitung* deplored the surrender of the party's liberal principles and declared that "school questions are no area for compromises" but the ground on which "two irreconcilable *Weltanschauungen* must confront each other."[112] Squabbling broke out among the National Liberals after the House of Deputies debate on May 13. Ernst Bassermann and the National Liberals in Baden criticized the *Fraktion* in the Prussian House of Deputies for helping the right-wing parties to put clerical influence in the schools on a more solid foundation.[113] Reports of a split within the *Fraktion* were leaked to the press. Under the pressure of the public outcry several deputies hastened to disclose their disapproval of the school bill compromise. When Hackenberg first informed his comrades of the agreement that he had concluded with Heydebrand and Zedlitz, strong opposition was voiced by Ernst von Eynern and the deputies who represented electoral districts in Hesse–Nassau. They argued that the party could only support a school bill that granted the communes the right to open interconfessional schools. When the *Fraktion* met for a second discussion, some of the dissenters preferred to be absent, and the others acquiesced in the endorsement of the compromise with a heavy heart.[114]

The opposition to the school bill compromise soon threatened to become a rank-and-file revolt. The centers of dissent were the cities in Hesse–Nassau and the Young Liberal clubs in the Rhine Province and Westphalia, which defied the conservatism of the party leaders by agitating for the reform of Prussia's three-class franchise. The efforts of Robert Friedberg and Karl Sattler to defend their actions on the grounds of political strategy did not persuade the members of the *Reichsverband der Nationalliberalen Jugend.* The Young Liberals reproached them for debasing the National Liberals to a governmental party that had neither convictions nor courage. At a stormy meeting in Cologne, they hissed Sattler's speech and censured the *Fraktion* in a resolution that called for a national party congress to discuss the school bill compromise.[115]

Confronted by a storm of indignation, the party leaders retreated and began to minimize the significance of the school bill compromise. Hackenberg told a party congress in the Rhine Province that the *Fraktion* still had "a free hand in all aspects of the school bill." The *Nationalliberale Korrespondenz*, the party's official organ, declared that it was "a mistaken view and interpretation" to see the compromise as a vote against the interconfessional school.[116] To ward off the threat of a rank-and-file revolt at a national congress, the party's executive committee convened on June 12 and after a six-hour-long debate placated the left wing with the reassuring promise that the *Fraktion* would strive "to secure for the interconfessional school a legal status which not only maintains the existing interconfessional schools but also makes possible the continuation of this school system on the basis of its legal equality [with the confessional schools]."[117]

The Progressives (divided since 1893 into two parties) were the solitary defenders of the interconfessional school in the House of Deputies debate on May 13. Afterwards they watched the bickering within the National Liberal caucus with lively interest. They were hoping that the criticism of the liberal press and the Young Liberals would force the *Fraktion* to disavow the school bill compromise and to align with them in opposition to a school bill supported by the Center and Conservative parties. The events of May 13 had shattered their assumption that similar principles united all liberal parties on the school question. The other parties had negotiated the agreement in secrecy and had not informed the Progressive People's party and the Progressive Union of the compromise until May 13. The Progressive deputies were taken by surprise when the substitute proposal was circulated in the House of Deputies. They blamed Hackenberg for the suddenness and haste with which the compromise proposal had been adopted. They thought that if the vote had taken place a week later, after the National Liberal party press and local clubs had had time to express their views, the *Fraktion* would not have supported it.[118]

The agitation of the Young Liberals did not affect the *Fraktion* as much as the Progressives had hoped. The National Liberal party leaders had no intention of disavowing the school bill compromise and aligning with the Progressive parties. The consequences of such a course were made clear to them when the *Neue Preussische Zeitung* reminded the National Liberals that they no longer commanded a decisive position in the *Landtag* and that if they broke the agreement, the Conservatives would make the school law with the Center party.[119] Robert Friedberg took this warning to heart. At a party meeting in Berlin he pointed out that a coalition of the Center and Conservative parties could form a majority for the passage of a school bill. National Liberal opposition to it, he argued, would not have the same impact on the government as it had in 1892 because the influence of the Center party in parliamentary politics had become greater since then. He doubted that one large liberal party uniting the National Liberals and the Progressives would become a parliamentary power in the near future. He had good reason to hope, on the other hand, that the National Liberals could still play an important role in the *Landtag* if they revived the *Kartell*.[120]

By August 1904 the Ministry of Education had drafted a school law based on the compromise proposal and had submitted it to Hammerstein and Rheinbaben for their comments. Both ministers were slow to respond. When the three ministers finally discussed the school bill in

December, the conference ended inconclusively with the decision to elicit the views of the party leaders on the provisions for confessional schooling. Hammerstein was impressed by the National Liberal opposition to the school bill compromise and questioned whether the party would adhere to it.[121]

The Provincial Bureaucracy and the Draft School Law

Hans von Hammerstein and Georg von Rheinbaben withheld their final decision on the introduction of the school bill until they had read the reports from the provincial governors. On June 30, 1905, Studt forwarded copies of the draft law to the provincial administrators for their comments. At the request of the finance minister, whose objections to the extension of the school law to the Polish-speaking districts had grown stronger, Studt sent a second letter to the provincial governors of Posen and West Prussia, asking them specifically whether the immediate execution of the law would "be beneficial or disadvantageous to German national interests" and whether it would be advisable to exclude the two provinces from its jurisdiction.[122]

The impact of the school law was bound to be uneven because of the diversity of school conditions in Prussia. The provinces east of the Elbe River would experience the most extensive change. In 1906 there were 15,672 *Gutsbezirke* with nearly 2 million inhabitants in the Prussian state, but the largest number were concentrated in Brandenburg, Pomerania, Posen, and Silesia. Although the city governments had increasingly assumed the responsibility of providing for school costs through their tax revenues, still existing were 10,811 *Schulsozietäten*, of which 2,110 were located in Brandenburg, 1,811 in Posen, 1,474 in Schleswig–Holstein, 1,258 in Pomerania, and 1,237 in Silesia. Apart from the Rhine Province and East and West Prussia, where provincial regulations had required the communes to maintain the schools since 1845, the practice of putting school expenditures on the municipal budget had been adopted widely in Hesse–Nassau and to a lesser degree in Westphalia.[123]

The Catholics, whose diaspora in the Prussian state extended further than the Protestant majority, could expect to gain more from a law entitling confessional minorities in the school districts to their own school. In 1906, 95.2 percent of the Protestant and 90.6 percent of the Catholic pupils in Prussia attended schools of their own confession. The benefits of this provision for the Catholic population would be especially significant if the law applied to Posen and West Prussia. More than

50 percent of the total of the 70,053 Catholic children instructed in Protestant schools lived in the provinces of West Prussia (16,609), Posen (14,543), and Silesia (10,350). In the enrollments in the interconfessional schools the proportion of Catholic pupils had increased since 1891, from 45 percent to 50.3 percent by 1906, whereas the percentages for the Jews and the Protestants had declined.[124]

Apart from the binational areas of the east, the provincial administrators subscribed to the provisions for confessional schooling. They observed that this section of the law corresponded to historical development and existing practice. The district governor of Koblenz remarked crisply that the controversy over confessional and interconfessional schools had been "decided already not only by the political parties but also through practice." Provincial Governor Eberhard von der Recke reported that in Westphalia "the disinclination of Catholics and Protestants to send children to schools of another confession is great" and that the establishment of confessional schools for minorities of fewer than sixty children very seldom encountered resistance in the communes.[125]

The reaction to the article in the draft law requiring the establishment of a separate school for the Catholic or Protestant minority—if there were at least 120 children of that faith in cities and rural communes with a population of more than 5,000 and at least 60 children in smaller school districts—reveals how much the state bureaucracy in the provinces had come to accept confessional schooling as the norm. Officials in Saxony and Westphalia thought that the figures set in the draft law were too high. The district governor of Merseburg pointed out that the provincial council of Saxony had ruled in many cases that a confessional minority had a justified claim to its own school if there were at least sixty pupils. The district governor of Münster recommended that the figure for big communes be lowered to sixty "in order to satisfy, in our opinion, the legitimate interests of confessional minorities and to ensure the acceptance of the law." He contended that "this provision would not be felt by the communes of our district as a particular oppression but instead would be accepted quietly as the necessary consequence of confessional schism."[126]

Officials in Brandenburg and Pomerania were deeply concerned about the effects of the school law on the finances and social standing of the landed nobility. They were disappointed in the small sum allocated by the Ministry of Finance for the implementation of the law, and stated emphatically that more money would have to be appropriated to assist rural communities. The district governor of Frankfurt an der Oder wrote that "the means and the way must be found to prevent the overburden that threatens the big estate owners." He recommended that the law fix a ceiling on the assessment of the school tax in school districts uniting communes and *Gutsbezirke* and that state subsidies cover the rest of the school expenditures. Officials in both provinces objected also to the election of the school boards in the *Gutsbezirke* and the designation of the local school inspector rather than the *Gutsherr* as the chairman. The district governor of Potsdam pointed out that the *Gutsherren* in their capacity as church patrons appointed the pastors and were "not accustomed by virtue of their social station to make decisions and to act under the direction of the local inspectors." He saw no compelling reasons "to carry out a coercive displacement and to rob the *Gutsherren* of their old rights."[127]

What disturbed the provincial bureaucracy the most was the section of the draft law that granted the communes the right to nominate teachers for school offices. Because the teachers in more than half of the school offices were selected by the state authorities, the district governments regarded the *Vorschlagsrecht* (right of nomination) given to the communes as a curtailment of their powers. In Brandenburg, East Prussia, Pomerania, and Saxony, the local governments possessed a legal right to appoint the teachers only in the cities, and in Silesia the city magistrates exercised this *Wahlrecht* only for the Protestant schools. The cities of the Rhine Province exercised a *Vorschlagsrecht* merely as a concession from the district governments. In the other school districts in the state the school bureaucracy appointed the teachers after consulting or without consulting the local magistrates.[128] In 1903 all teaching appointments were made by the state authorities except for 12,602 offices under the patronage of the *Gutsherren* and 25,744 offices filled by the city magistrates.[129]

The school bureaucracy in the provinces wanted to have a free hand in the selection of the teachers. "For political reasons," admitted the district governor of Breslau, "the school administration must be assured of the greatest possible influence in the appointment of the teachers." Armed with broad appointment powers, school officials would halt the tendency in the big cities to select principals and teachers holding liberal political opinions and would inhibit members of the teaching profession from manifesting their support for the Progressive parties. Only in Saxony did the provincial and district governors defend the *Wahlrecht* exercised by the cities in the appointment of the schoolteachers and warn that Magdeburg and other cities would oppose the loss of their rights.[130]

Schwartzkopff's draft of the school law included Posen and West Prussia within its jurisdiction but empowered the school administration to suspend the application of the articles on the confessional organization of the schools, the rights of confessional minorities, and the formation of local school boards if it decided that national interests warranted such exceptional measures. Even with this precaution the provincial bureaucracy had profound apprehensions about the draft law. In the administration of the schools, the district governments were accustomed to broad discretionary authority, which they exercised for political purposes and to the advantage of the German nationality. They could not easily accept a law with norms that would limit the latitude of their discretionary powers and grant equal rights to the Germans and the Poles. Provincial Governor Wilhelm von Waldow stated, "Up to now the authority of the school administration to regulate the confessional conditions of the schools according to its own judgment and reasons of expediency has formed one of the most important means of executing a national school policy and is presently indispensable."[131]

The district governors of Bromberg and Posen contended that the principles embodied in the draft law would mean in practice a sharp departure from the current policy of promoting a German school system and protecting the German nationality. District Governor Georg von Guenther explained that over the years officials in Bromberg held the point of view that it was "not practical in our region, where the German nationality has to struggle hard, to create more footholds for the Polish nationality than necessary by establishing new Catholic schools." He disapproved of the provision that would permit the appointment of a Catholic teaching staff at a hitherto Protestant school if the Catholic pupils outnumbered the Protestants for five consecutive years. Many Protestant schools had been preserved even though the growth of the Polish population in the locality had caused the enrollment of Catholic children to swell. For years the Poles had agitated for the appointment of Catholic teachers to these schools without success. Guenther predicted that the Poles would fight harder once the law was on their side and that there would be a mass exodus of German Protestants if they lost their schools to the increasing Polish population.

The district governors pointed out that a large number of Catholic schools had been made interconfessional and warned that the Polish community would strive to restore the confessional character of these schools after the enactment of the school law. "In view of the fanatical hatred of the Polish Catholic clergymen against the interconfessional schools, which they see as the most dangerous institution in the germanization efforts of the state," Guenther feared that this agitation would not cease until the Poles had achieved their goal. He argued that Protestant teachers had to be appointed to these Catholic schools because "even the best Catholic teacher of German descent cannot free himself from the Polonizing influence of the Catholic clergy." Continuing to justify the creation of the interconfessional schools on political grounds, he wrote:

> One must constantly keep in mind that every Catholic school is a foothold for the Polish nationality because of the inevitable influence of the Catholic clergymen who are almost always hostile to the state. Solely for this reason and not merely for pedagogic and financial reasons is the interconfessional school of great importance in our district. Through it the possibility is opened in predominantly Catholic areas to appoint a German Protestant teacher, who constitutes not merely a support for the scattered settlements of Germans but compels the opposition by his mere presence to maintain a certain moderation and cautiousness in its activities.[132]

The district governors also raised strong objections to the provisions of the draft law that would restrict their discretionary authority in the distribution of state subsidies. Guenther wrote that up to now in the administration of state funds appropriated to assist poor school districts, "it has been possible to put this money in the service of German national interests and to use it for strengthening the economic position of the German Protestant school districts without having to fear that complaints will be raised by the Poles." Once the distribution of the state subsidies was entrusted to the county commissions in accordance with the school law, the funds would be apportioned according to "a rigid formula" based on the financial circumstances of the communes. District Governor Emil Krahmer of Posen stated that the effects of this schematic system would be to put both confessions on an equal footing and to increase the school taxes of the German Protestants, who were presently relieved of a large part of their school costs by state grants.

The provincial governor informed officials in Berlin that it was not accidental that in Posen only a few cities had taken over the responsibility for school maintenance. Besides the confessional diversity of the population, the other reason for the prevalence of the *Schulsozietäten* was that the German Protestants paid lower school taxes than Polish Catholics because of the distribution of state subsidies. Under the school law, state officials could no longer treat the two confessions differently without provoking complaints, and the more affluent German inhabitants in the communes would be taxed more heavily for school costs than the Polish population. He concluded that "political objections of a national nature" made it inadvisable to extend the school law to Posen.

The district governors in West Prussia took opposing sides in their judgment of the school law. District Governor Jaroslaw von Jarotzky of Danzig thought that it would not be proper to exclude the Polish-speaking areas from the jurisdiction of the school law. Supporting the provisions that corresponded "to the requirements of equity between the confessions," he contended that the execution of the school law would have a healthy political effect and would "demolish the impression held especially by the Poles that the Catholic confession in these provinces is treated unfavorably by the state." Arguing for the exclusion of the two provinces from the jurisdiction of the school law, District Governor Ernst von Jagow of Marienwerder wrote that "if [the school administration] is bound to the regulations of the draft, in many cases it would have to take measures which turn out to be harmful to the German nationality and beneficial to the Polish movement." The provincial governor concurred with Jagow. He estimated that under the proposed law the school taxes of the estate owners would increase by 50–100 percent, a matter that disturbed him all the more because "the political and national point of view" would not be taken into account when the county commissions were put in charge of allocating the state subsidies.[133]

The problem of Upper Silesia was raised by District Governor Ernst Holtz, who contended that the school authorities in the Oppeln district should also be empowered to suspend the application of certain articles of the school law. Provincial Governor von Zedlitz-Trützschler rejected his recommendation that the exceptional clauses for Posen and West Prussia be extended to Upper Silesia. The deputy, substituting for Zedlitz who was ill, wrote in his report that the Catholic clergy, except for a small number of Polish nationalists, posed no obstacles to the execution of the school law and that "the nationality question could be settled in another manner than by fighting in the school domain." He warned officials in Berlin that the Center would mobilize a massive popular movement in opposition to a school bill that contained exceptional clauses for Upper Silesia. The state government would pay "a high price." Not only would the opposition of the Center party put the passage of the school bill in jeopardy, but the discriminatory treatment of the Oppeln district would arouse the indignation of Cardinal Kopp and antagonize the Catholic clergy. "A Catholic *Volksschule* in any village in Upper Silesia poses a danger for the state once the local pastor is excluded from its administration by a government decree," he remarked.[134]

The reports from Posen and West Prussia confirmed the misgivings expressed by the finance minister since 1903. Now Rheinbaben found a stout ally in the newly appointed minister of the interior. After Bethmann Hollweg read the reports, he informed Studt immediately that the political objections raised by the provincial administrators were too weighty and compelling to be set aside. He also hinted that it might be advisable to extend the exceptional clauses in the school law to the counties in East Prussia encompassing the Catholic diocese of Ermland.[135]

Studt discussed the school law with the governors of Posen, Silesia, and West Prussia at a special conference on October 14, 1905. Officials in the Ministry of Education were reluctant to exclude the Polish-speaking area from the jurisdiction of the school law. They surmised that the underlying reason for the provincial bureaucracy's resistance was the heavier burden of school taxes that the German inhabitants would pay to the benefit of the Polish population. Schwartzkopff was confident that a larger budget appropriation for school subsidies would eliminate the dissatisfaction of the Germans. To dispel the apprehension that the provisions for confessional schooling would hurt the interests of the German nationality, he offered to amend the draft law so that the school administration in Posen and West Prussia would have complete freedom to make the schools interconfessional. This concession did not appease the finance and interior ministers, so that finally Studt yielded to their demand for the exclusion of both provinces from the jurisdiction of the law. He stood firm, however, in opposing a qualifying clause for the execution of the law in Upper Silesia. He contended that the exceptional treatment of the Oppeln district would "make the introduction of the school bill impossible" because the Center would see in such a provision a vote of no confidence against Cardinal Kopp and the Catholic clergy and would fight the school bill from the start.[136]

Schwartzkopff rewrote several articles in the draft law in response to some of the political objections voiced by the provincial administrators. The most significant amendment diminished the role of the communes in the appointment of the teachers by the school authorities. Article 40 now granted a *Vorschlagsrecht* to the school boards in the cities with more than twenty-five teaching offices and left the school boards in the smaller communes merely with the right to be consulted. Bearing in mind the Polish-speaking Catholic parishes of Upper Silesia, Schwartzkopff inserted a clause empowering the state government to expel clergymen from the local school boards if they disturbed the peace and order of school life. He weakened the unconditional wording of Article 19, which provided for the appointment of Catholic teachers to a Protestant school if the Catholic pupils constituted at least two thirds of the enrollment for five years and vice versa, by adding the phrase "as a rule" and the requirement of the minister's consent. This amendment allowed school officials to make exceptions to the rule and to preserve the

Protestant schools in Upper Silesia.[137] Once these revisions were made, Studt obtained the approval of the Ministry of State to introduce the school bill.

The School Bill and the Opposition in the Cities

Just before the legislative session of 1905–1906 started, a crisis created by the National Liberal *Fraktion* threatened to break up the coalition that had agreed to the school bill compromise of 1904. Standing in fear of criticism from the liberal press and the left wing of their own party, the National Liberal deputies reopened the interconfessional school question in their talks with Schwartzkopff in October and demanded that the law permit the communes to organize interconfessional schools for "special reasons." Schwartzkopff was upset and thought that the National Liberals were now twisting the meaning of the compromise proposal.[138] He and Studt were put under heavy pressure to conciliate the National Liberals on November 13, when Emperor William authorized the introduction of the school bill under the condition that the minister continue his negotiations with the party's representatives and reach an agreement on the issues still in dispute.[139]

Schwartzkopff's negotiations with the National Liberal leaders were prolonged and wearisome because the Conservatives refused to make any concessions that went beyond the agreement of 1904. Finally, he persuaded Heydebrand to make a gesture of accommodation by devising a compromise that gave the National Liberals far less than what they really wanted—an unrestricted freedom to open both types of schools. His revision of Article 20 allowed the communes to establish new interconfessional schools for "special reasons." This concession lost much of its value because the clause that entitled a Catholic or Protestant minority to confessional schooling applied to these schools.[140]

While Schwartzkopff rewrote the draft law, he took care to secure the support of the Center party. In a private meeting with Cardinal Kopp on October 28, Schwartzkopff asked him whether it was advisable to introduce the school bill. Kopp raised no objections. He related that in a confidential discussion with Felix Porsch earlier, he was told that no member of the Center party *Fraktion* would attempt to insert into the school bill a paragraph defining the rights of the church in the supervision of the schools. Some Catholic deputies were likely to contest the clause in Article 20 permitting the establishment of interconfessional schools under exceptional circumstances, but this opposition would not prevent the entire party from voting for the bill.[141] Shortly thereafter Schwartzkopff discussed the revision of Article 20 with Porsch himself and was informed that the Center party could not vote for it but would "tolerate" it.[142] With this assurance from the chairman of the *Fraktion*, Studt wrote to Emperor William on November 28 that "it can be assumed from confidential inquiries ordered by me that [the Center] will vote for the enactment of the law even in its newly expanded form."[143]

The school bill presented to the *Landtag* in December 1905 made the confessional school the rule in Prussia. It required that schoolchildren should receive instruction from teachers of their own confession and that teachers of one and the same faith should be appointed to a school. The interconfessional school systems in the former Duchy of Nassau were left intact. Elsewhere the establishment of new interconfessional schools was restricted to places where such schools already existed.[144] This clause in Article 20 permitted the expansion of interconfessional school systems in thirty school districts located mainly in the binational areas of East Prussia and Upper Silesia.[145] Otherwise the communes could open interconfessional schools only for "special reasons" and with the consent of the school authorities. The ministry's interpretation of this concession to the National Liberal party was revealed in the reference to those interconfessional schools as "an exception" to the rule in the *Begründung* appended to the school bill. Its intention to limit the opening of interconfessional schools was disclosed again when Schwartzkopff told the House of Deputies committee that "the 'special reasons' could not be of a general nature and could not be based on the preference that people give to the interconfessional over the confessional school system."[146] If the Catholic or Protestant pupils in a school district where public schools had only teachers of the other confession counted more than 120 in cities and rural communes with a population of over 5,000, or more than 60 in smaller communes, then Article 23 required the establishment of a separate school for them when their parents submitted such a request to the school administration. This provision for the schooling of confessional minorities was a strong deterrent to the evolution of an interconfessional school system in the cities.

Fear of socialism affected Schwartzkopff's draft of the school law more than the school bills of Gossler and Zedlitz. A distrust of the self-governing bodies of the big cities pervaded the articles on the local administration of the schools. Two events in Berlin that alarmed the Ministry of Education were the election of city councilman Paul Singer, a Social Democratic party member, to the municipal school board in 1898 and the board's decision to permit gymnastics clubs of the Social Democratic party to use the school auditoriums. Immediately after Singer's election Bosse issued instructions to the district governments not to confirm the election of Social Democrats to the municipal school boards.[147] Because the district governments did not exercise this right in the big cities, other cases involving city councilmen who espoused radical pedagogic views on the elimination of religious instruction from the schools followed the Singer episode.[148] The school bill provided a safeguard against the entrance of Socialists and radical pedagogues into the school board by requiring that the election of those members drawn from the city council and the teaching profession be confirmed by the state government. To prevent Social Democratic party clubs from using school facilities, it stipulated that the communes could not make school property available for other purposes without the permission of the school authorities.

For the protection of religious interests, Article 29 granted the city governments the right to form smaller school committees for the Catholic and Protestant confessions under the jurisdiction of the school board. The establishment of confessional school committees was mandatory in cities where the *Schulsozietäten* made such a request prior to their dissolution. The membership of the committee included an executive officer in the city government presiding as the chairman, the city's school inspector, the eldest pastor of the appropriate confession, and several citizens of the same faith elected by the school board. Lest the confessional school committees become a wellspring of political strife, the state authorities assumed the power of confirming the election of the members and unseating them at any time. Article 29, a concession to the Center party, offered the Catholics the prospects of having a voice in school affairs in cities where Protestant liberals controlled local politics. For the city governments in the eastern provinces this provision represented a disturbing innovation. Most of the cities that had confessional school boards functioning alone or under the jurisdiction of a nonsectarian school commission were located in the Rhineland in the west.[149]

In the countryside the clergy in their capacity as local school inspectors retained their strong position in school affairs. Article 31 on the formation of the local school board for each school in the rural communes designated the local inspector as the chairman. The other members were the village mayor, a teacher named by the school administration, and parishioners of the same confession as the school who were elected by the village council. The wording of Article 31 underscored the commanding position of the local school inspector by requiring the school board to support him in the fulfillment of his duties.

The school bill was a bitter disappointment to the teaching profession. The Prussian Teachers' Association with a membership of over 62,000 was offended because at no point in the preparation of the draft of the school law had officials in the ministry consulted its leaders.[150] Schwartzkopff and Studt saw no purpose in soliciting the views of representatives of the teaching profession because the association's executive committee had issued a public statement in opposition to the school bill compromise in 1904. While the school law was being drafted in 1905, the provincial branches of the association adopted resolutions demanding that confessional and interconfessional schools be put on an equal footing. Studt disapproved of the teachers' agitation for the interconfessional school and dismissed their pedagogic views as naive and uninformed by practical experience.[151] Neither the Ministry of Education nor the party leaders who were involved in the negotiations over the school bill felt any need to take into consideration pedagogic theories that deviated sharply from the opinion of the majority of the nation.[152]

Throughout December the Prussian Teachers' Association organized rallies to protest the school bill in numerous cities. The teachers were disgruntled because the proposed law did not redress their old grievances. Neither the appointment of clergymen as school inspectors nor the connection of teaching offices with church duties was eliminated. The leaders of the association criticized the provisions for confessional schooling and assailed the National Liberals for making a political compromise with the parties of the political Right.[153] In their attack on the school bill, they took care to distinguish their defense of the interconfessional school in which religion was a subject of instruction from the agitation of the Social Democratic party for the secular school. An unwillingness to take the instruction of religion out of the province of the public school and to put it in the hands of the church alone led them to oppose the secularization of elementary education. They did not see the secular school system of France or Holland as a model for the Germans. During the school bill debate Johannes Tews, a publicist for the Teachers' Association, contended that "the abandonment of religious instruction by the state means in reality a capitulation before the external power of the church." He thought that the removal of religion from the curriculum would diminish the moral and cultural influence of the school.[154]

The Prussian Teachers' Association criticized sharply the school bill's encroachment on the self-government of the communes and showed a deeper distrust of the state than earlier generations of teachers had felt. Liberals in the teaching profession were now convinced that in Prussia the *Verstaatlichung* of the school system would be a reactionary development.[155] Especially disturbing to them was the curtailment of the rights of the cities in the appointment of school principals and teachers. Knowing that suspicion and hostility toward the Prussian Teachers' Association prevailed within the state bureaucracy, they feared that under the new law the government would possess an effective instrument to inhibit the public activity of teachers and that, as a result, ambitious place-seeking and hypocrisy would flourish in the profession.[156]

The opposition of the schoolteachers gained much strength from the agitation of the Progressives in the city councils in Berlin, Breslau, Frankfurt am Main, Königsberg, and other cities. The city councilmen put the school bill on their agendas and voted for resolutions protesting its encroachments on local self-government.[157] They flooded the House of Deputies with petitions that proposed amendments to the school bill and called for its defeat if the provisions curtailing the rights of the communes were not revised.[158] The culmination of this agitation was the *Städtetag* that convened in Berlin on January 15, 1906; this congress united the mayors of the big cities throughout Prussia in opposition to the school bill. The mayors detected in the school bill a distrust of the city governments and suspected that a fear of Social Democratic influence in the city councils had affected the drafting of the law.[159]

The protest demonstrations were confined mainly to Progressive party circles in the cities. The countryside was politically quiescent during the debate on the school bill in the House of Deputies.[160] Indifference prevailed likewise among the Social Democratic party rank and file. The Social Democrats did not fight the school bill in tandem with the Progressives. The big demonstration in Frankfurt am Main on February 4 organized by the two parties was a late and isolated manifestation of cooperation. City councilman Max Quarck, a Social Democratic party member who addressed this rally, later criticized his own party. He regretted that the Social Democrats had not recognized early enough the danger of a reactionary school law and had not mobilized working-class families in opposition to the confessional school.[161] Johannes Tews was correct when he observed that the working classes took no interest in the school bill because school policy had been assigned a subordinate place in Social Democratic party politics for many years.[162]

After the Social Democrats were released from the constraints of the antisocialist law of 1878, they did not agitate against clerical influence in the schools or make any special effort to reform the schools. When the Erfurt program of 1891 was adopted, Karl Kautsky did not put any emphasis on abolishing the church's relationship to the school, as Friedrich Engels had recommended.[163] Party leaders noticed that workers were not antireligious and that polemics against Christianity and the churches frightened away many voters. Moreover, they did not look to the public school system to elevate the proletariat. Wilhelm Liebknecht did not share the optimistic faith of the liberals that better social conditions would arise from the spread of formal education. Instead he relied on social and economic forces to bring about the emancipation of the working class and believed that a worker's essential political education would be acquired in the associations of the Social Democratic party. The Social Democrats remained aloof from the controversies over the school bill in 1892 and left the task of defeating it to the liberal parties.[164]

In the following years, circumstances did not encourage the Social Democrats to become involved in the politics of school reform. The three-class franchise blocked their entry into the Prussian *Landtag* until 1908 and prevented them from challenging the political hegemony of the liberals in the big cities. The Social Democrats, who could not influence school policy in the parliamentary arena, were all the more inclined to underestimate its importance.[165] They concentrated their energies instead on the creation of educational alternatives to the *Volksschule*, with youth groups, cultural clubs, lecture programs, party and trade union schools, and extension courses for *Arbeiterbildung* (the education of workers).[166]

The aloofness of the Social Democrats from school politics did not cease until late in 1904. At a party congress in December, Leo Arons delivered a speech on the school bill compromise adopted by the House of Deputies. Although he reproached the National Liberals for allying with the Conservatives, most of his invective was directed at the Progressives for advocating the halfway reform of interconfessional schools instead of a bolder program to secularize the schools and to abolish the *Vorschulen* and class distinctions in elementary education. The congress decided to make the separation of the school from the church, the removal of religion from the school curriculum, and the establishment of comprehensive schools for the education of all social classes from the age of six to fourteen, the focal points of Social Democratic party agitation in school politics.[167]

The Social Democrats did not move quickly to contest the school bill. Reports in the party press on the opening debate in the House of Deputies in December 1905 belittled the opposition of the Progressives as a "lame defensive" and scornfully depicted them as half-hearted reformers who were afraid to speak out for the exclusion of religious instruction from the schools.[168] Leo Arons and Paul Göhre thought that the Social Democrats should manifest their opposition to the school bill by disaffiliating themselves from the church and withdrawing their children from religious instruction. The party's executive committee did not issue, as Arons proposed, a call for a mass exodus from the Protestant church as Social Democracy's answer to the school bill. When the Social Democrats staged mass demonstrations on January 21 and March 18, 1906, the demand for suffrage reform in Prussia pushed the school bill issue to the sidelines.[169]

The School Bill in the Prussian Parliament

The opposition mobilized by the Progressives in the cities put the National Liberal party deputies in an uncomfortable situation. The left wing of their own party applied pressure on them to amend the school bill. The *Kölnische Zeitung* complained that the school bill was the outcome of a compromise made by party politicians rather than the product of a progressive and enlightened school policy and reminded the National Liberal deputies of their duty to revise it.[170] At a party congress in the Rhineland early in January, the delegates adopted a resolution demanding that the *Fraktion* secure for the interconfessional school a legal status of equality with the confessional school.[171] Because Robert Friedberg and Eugen Schiffer—who sat on the House of Deputies committee that was formed to revise the school bill—were bound to the bargain that they had made with Heydebrand in November, they did not support the amendments of the Progressives. Neither in the committee nor later in the deliberations of the full session of the House did the National Liberals break their coalition with the Conservatives and vote for amendments that would have given the communes greater freedom to establish interconfessional schools. The Progressives were astounded that the National Liberals ignored the declaration of their party's executive committee on June 12, 1904, and sharply rebuked them for not fighting for the interconfessional school.[172]

Friedberg's response to their criticism was a confession of his own ambivalence toward the school bill as well as a justification of his tactical decision to align with the Conservatives. He conceded openly that the ideals of the National Liberal party "deviate somewhat far" from the school bill coming out of the House committee. "If we had a big liberal majority here in the House and a state government which follows the same course as we," he said, "then we would have wished that the full legal equality between the interconfessional and confessional schools was expressed in this bill." At the same time, he contended that a law drafted under the influence of the Center party would have brought far more harm to the Prussian school system. The National Liberal party leaders could not help seeing that their party was not needed to create a majority for the passage of a school bill because the Center and the Conservatives could have reached an agreement without them.[173]

Having made a politically embarrassing compromise on one section of the school bill, the National Liberals were all the more determined to obtain concessions from the Conservatives and to amend other parts that were unacceptable to them. The opposition of the academic intelligentsia and the liberal Protestant bourgeoisie in the cities gave the National Liberal party more political leverage than the Conservatives were willing to acknowledge in public. In the middle of March twenty-seven prominent scholars, including Lujo Brentano, Otto Harnack, and Max Weber, submitted a petition to the House of Deputies, criticizing the articles on the confessional organization of the schools in the proposed law. Although some of the signers taught at the universities in Freiburg, Heidelberg, and Munich, they thought that no progressive-minded person in Germany could be indifferent to the enactment of a school law that would perpetuate the influence of clericalism and religious particularism in the largest educational system in the country. Within a short time more than 800 signatures from the academic and literary world were added to the petition.[174] This protest came too late to have a great effect on the making of the school law, but it indicated to the state government that the passage of a school bill by a Center-Conservative majority would violate the sensibilities of the educated elite.

The National Liberals sought to strengthen their bargaining power by threatening the government and the Conservatives with the possibility that they would swing over to the opposition. At a party meeting in Magdeburg just before the second reading of the school bill in the House of Deputies committee, Eugen Schiffer gave a widely publicized speech in which he identified three shoals on which the school bill could be shipwrecked. Optimistic that ultimately concessions would be made to National Liberal party demands, he declared that the Conservatives had to be reminded constantly that in Prussia a school law could not be made with their large block of votes alone. The government knew that the school bill had to be passed with the support of the National Liberals "because far beyond the extent of our mandates the weight of importance of the progressive and nationally-minded bourgeoisie is asserted by us, and because there is a feeling that a new regulation of the school system can proceed in a beneficial manner only with the agreement of this bourgeoisie." He would strive earnestly to reach an accord with the

Conservatives, but he warned that "if we encounter objections to our minimal demands, then the law fails, and if it passes, then it comes about without us and against us."[175]

In March and April, the National Liberals with the help of the Free Conservatives succeeded in prying concessions from the Conservatives in the House committee. The Center party deputies, who stood alone in their defense of the government's bill, were frustrated and angry. They complained that the amendments were eliminating provisions that were essential for preserving the confessional character of the schools.[176] The interest of the Center party in the enactment of the school law was almost shattered when a National Liberal party motion to strike out Article 23 on the opening of schools for confessional minorities was passed in the committee's first reading of the school bill. A compromise arranged by the Free Conservatives restored this paragraph in the second reading. In return, the National Liberals gained the support of the two conservative parties for the revision of Article 31. The designation of the local school inspector as the chairman of the rural school board was deleted. The selection of the presiding officer of the school board was now left up to the school administration. Schwartzkopff consoled the Center party with the remark that the amendment was of "no practical importance" because the state government could "not find in most school districts any other suitable person for this position than the clergy."[177]

The National Liberals achieved their biggest triumph in the revision of Article 40. Very unwillingly did Studt "sacrifice" the power of the state and accept the amendment that granted to the communes the right to select the teachers appointed to the schools. Because Studt thought that "the state's influence in the appointment of the teachers and hence in the schools had been pushed back hard" by this amendment, he resisted the demand of the National Liberal party that the communes be granted the right to choose the school principals as well.[178] The school authorities selected the principals for 3,500 offices without consulting city officials. Studt was dissatisfied with the manner in which the city governments exercised the right to propose candidates for appointment to the other 2,100 offices. He complained that they nominated principals, like Kopsch and Tews, who were affiliated with the Progressive parties.[179]

A crisis arose when the National Liberals threatened to vote against the school bill if their demands were not entirely fulfilled. This threat posed a grave problem for the Ministry of State because Emperor William told Chancellor von Bülow that he would sign the school bill only if it was passed with the support of the National Liberals.[180] When the cabinet discussed the crisis early in May, the consensus of opinion was that the school bill had to be accepted by the National Liberal party. The ministers thought that the enactment of the school law without the National Liberals would give the opposition "a welcomed pretext to reinforce the widespread view in the public that the law was simply a Clerical–Conservative makeshift piece of work."[181] Because they feared that the Center party would seize this opportunity to form a majority with the Conservative party and to pass a school bill that was more to its liking, they authorized Studt to negotiate an accord with the National Liberal party as quickly as possible. In the negotiations that produced the final revision of Article 40, the minister of education made concessions that few school officials would have imagined a year earlier. The law granted to the cities with over twenty-five teaching positions the right to make the appointment. In the smaller communes the school boards selected the teacher from among three candidates proposed by the school administration. The power of appointing the principals left to the state authorities was also truncated when the government made its last concession to the liberals. To placate the mayors of the big cities in the House of Lords who fought to retain the rights that they presently possessed, Heydebrand and Zedlitz sponsored an amendment granting to the communes the right to appoint the principals as well as the teachers if they had exercised it for at least five years prior to the enactment of the law.[182]

Throughout the deliberations of the school bill in 1906, the government and the Conservatives yielded one concession after another to the National Liberals. Fear of the enactment of a school law by a majority dependent on Catholic votes and concern about the sensibilities of the Protestant bourgeoisie led the government to accommodate the National Liberal party *Fraktion* far beyond what its size—74 votes out of 433—warranted. The same anxiety held the *Kartell* parties together. When a Free Conservative party newspaper chided Schiffer for "sitting on a very high horse" and exaggerating the importance of his party with his threats of voting against the school bill, the *Nationalzeitung*, the organ of the National Liberal party, replied: "The Center party stands ready with open arms. Why do the Conservatives and the government hesitate to sink in its bosom if the National Liberals are really a negligible quantity, which must be evaluated simply according to their number of mandates."[183]

The Free Conservatives knew that there were two majorities for the passage of the school bill, and strove to forestall a coalition of the Conservative with the Center. Zedlitz mediated continually between the leaders of the Conservative and National Liberal parties and devised compromise proposals to bridge their differences. He held the *Kartell* together by continually reminding the other parties that if the Center party influenced the language and spirit of the school law, it would make concessions to the Catholic church that would be unacceptable in the Prussian state. In the House of Deputies he warned the government that the middle parties would never reconcile themselves to a school law made by a Clerical–Conservative majority "because we would believe that the spirit in which that law was carried out would not correspond to our views of the Prussian school administration."[184]

Although the Conservatives did not publicly express such apprehensions of the Center party, they yielded to the demands of the National Liberal party in respect to Article 40 in order to keep their coalition together. They defended the authority of the state in the appointment of schoolteachers and voted against amendments proposed by the National Liberal party members in the committee's first reading of the school bill. After the Conservatives had accepted the amendment expanding the rights of the commune in the committee's second reading, Heydebrand insisted that his party had reached the extreme limit of what it could concede to the National Liberals.[185] On May 12 Studt informed Heydebrand of the decision of the Ministry of State and solicited his support for the negotiations that Schwartzkopff would soon begin with Friedberg and Schiffer. In another conversation on May 13, the minister impressed on Heydebrand "the necessity of a hasty settlement in the interest of quieting public opinion and [avoiding] the dangers to which the bill would be exposed from the greater demands of the Center." Heydebrand promised "to take a more accommodating position toward the wishes of the National Liberal party" after a long discussion with Studt on May 26.[186]

It was easy for the Conservative party to be obliging at this time because the section of the bill dealing with school maintenance had been amended in the House of Deputies in accordance with the wishes of the big estate owners and to the advantage of rural villages and small towns. The Conservatives on the school bill committee were successful in revising the regulation for the school tax in the joint school district so that now one half of the school tax payment was to be based on the number of children attending the school from each commune or *Gutsbezirk* and the other half according to the tax assessment on property used for the levy of the county tax. For the school tax, real estate was to be assessed at half of its taxable value.[187]

New provisions for state appropriations in the amended school bill made it a more generous measure than the Ministry of Finance intended.

The beneficiaries of the state's largesse were the countryside and small towns. Densely populated cities were not eligible for several categories of state assistance. State grants to cover one third of the costs of constructing new schools were limited to school districts with no more than seven teachers. State subsidies in three other categories were confined to school districts with no more than twenty-five teachers. Subsidies "for the purpose of eliminating unfair displacements in raising school taxes which arise as a result of the school law" promised relief to estate owners on whom the responsibility for school maintenance in the *Gutsbezirke* was placed. With statistical material available to prove his point, Count Alfred von Strachwitz, an estate owner in Silesia, told the House of Deputies that through the decisions of the school bill committee the burden of many in the countryside, especially the big landowners, had been considerably lightened.[188]

The assertions in the liberal press that the government had made concessions to the Clerical party in the school law were misleading. Studt called these statements "fables" in a letter that he wrote to the chief of the emperor's Civil Cabinet. He added that "the wishes of the Center have been fulfilled only to a very small extent, and continual influence must be exerted to prevent them from rejecting the bill."[189] In the final vote on the school bill the Center deputies abstained. They thought that the revision of the government's bill in the House committee had done much damage to the school law.[190] One amendment to Article 20 made it difficult for a commune to reconfessionalize an interconfessional school. Another new clause permitted a commune that did not obtain the school administration's approval to open interconfessional schools to file a complaint with the provincial council and then to appeal to the High Administrative Court as the final arbiter. The existing practices for the establishment of separate schools for confessional minorities were more advantageous for the Catholics in some provinces than the conditions laid down in the law. In a petition to the House of Deputies, Catholic clergymen in Saxony protested that Article 23 put in jeopardy several Catholic public schools that had been recently founded in this predominantly Protestant province because their enrollments were fewer than 120 pupils.[191]

The school law left unredressed the grievances of the Catholic population not only in the provinces of Posen and West Prussia but also in Nassau. More than 34,000 Catholics in the Wiesbaden district signed a petition to the House of Deputies, urging that the provisions for confessional schooling be applied to their area. Another petition signed by 6,000 Catholic fathers in Frankfurt am Main demanded that more of the city's schools should be organized on a confessional basis to fulfill the wish of those parents who wanted to send their children to confessional schools.[192] The schools in Frankfurt were confessional before 1870, and the establishment of interconfessional schools during the *Kulturkampf* years became an issue of enduring contention between the city government and the Catholic minority.[193]

The enactment of the school law was a bitter experience for the Center party. Although the Center party formed the second largest *Fraktion* in the House of Deputies, the school law was made by an agreement of the *Kartell* parties without them. The *Kölnische Volkszeitung* remarked ironically that "fear of the Center" did not prevail in the Reichstag and suggested that the Center deputies there should take note of the history of the school bill compromise in the Prussian *Landtag* and let the middle parties try more often to pass major pieces of legislation without Catholic votes.[194]

Some General Conclusions about the School Question in Wilhelminian Germany

The history of the school law from 1890 to 1906 reveals the persistence of anti-Catholicism in Prussian society. During these years the Center party gradually moved out of its defensive attitudes and thinking, deeply marked by the experience of the *Kulturkampf*. The Center party became progovernment and avoided any action that could give cause to doubt the national loyalty and patriotism of the German Catholics. And yet the Center party got few political rewards for the indispensable support that it gave to Chancellors von Hohenlohe and von Bülow in the Reichstag. It gained minor concessions in its fight for Catholic interests in the school system. Unacceptable to Emperor William and the Protestant ruling elite was the possibility that the language and spirit of a school law for the Prussian state would be influenced by the Catholic party. When the school law was enacted, the outcome was determined far more by Protestant interests and sensibilities than by Catholic demands and political power.

In comparison with the passionate ideological conflict over the school bill of 1892, the opposition to the school bill in 1905–1906 was smaller in scale and emotionally more subdued. By 1906 the partisans of the interconfessional school were reduced to a small coterie of the liberal leadership of the Prussian Teachers' Association, the advocates of school reform in the two Progressive parties, and interest groups representing the Jewish community in public life.[195] These groups had no influence on the government's school policy or on public opinion. Moreover, the Catholic and Protestant teachers did not think alike; the members of the German Association of Catholic Teachers founded in the Rhineland in 1889 were steadfast supporters of confessional schooling.[196]

The making of the school law in 1906 intensified the sense of isolation and impotence that the liberal school reformers felt. When the National Liberals stood firm in supporting the school bill in an alliance with the Conservatives, Johannes Tews wrote bitterly: "To us remains only the possibility of either capitulating and seeking shelter in the currently very large army of supporters of a confessionally divided, clerically stamped, internally and externally confessionalized public school system or continuing to fight for our ideas and demands without having the necessary propping and patronage of the bigger parties."[197] He lamented that the fear of socialism had dampened the interest of the liberal bourgeoisie in school reform. He observed that the claims of the Center and Conservative parties that the close association of the school with the church was essential to combat Social Democracy had found greater credence among the educated middle class since 1890.[198]

The *Bildungsbürgertum* (educated bourgeoisie) did not stand in the foreground of the political fight for the interconfessional school in 1892 and 1905–1906. The 102 professors at the University of Halle and the 69 professors in Berlin who addressed petitions to the *Landtag* in 1892 were concerned about preserving the school monopoly of the state; they were not motivated by any commitment to liberal school reform. The academicians ignored Article 22 of the Prussian constitution, which proclaimed freedom of teaching as a fundamental right, and protested that Zedlitz's school bill slackened the existing restrictions on the opening of private schools. They thought that the draft law granted to the church a *Mitherrschaft* in the direction of the schools at the expense of the state's authority.[199]

Neither of the two petitions contested the provisions for confessional schooling or spoke out for the right of the communes to establish interconfessional schools. On this issue the professors in Halle had no quarrel with Zedlitz:

> We agree that "the consideration of confessional conditions as much as possible," as the constitution prescribes, is the proven way to fulfill the task set for the *Volksschule*. We consider, whether it be out of principle or for

practical reasons, the confessional school appropriate for our present-day conditions and gladly observe the draft law in all provisions which are really necessary to protect it as the rule valid for Prussia.

They demanded simply that the law permit the opening of interconfessional schools "as a *Nothilfe* [expedient] in proven exceptional cases," wherever the Catholic and Protestant communities were not big enough to have separate schools. The petition from Berlin, which included Rudolf Gneist, Theodor Mommsen, Heinrich von Treitschke, and Rudolf Virchow as signers, concluded with the wish that "the long-preserved principles on which the prosperity of our school system depends and which take into account the importance of religion for popular education as well as the justified influence of the religious communities on it would remain in effect." These views explain why only fifteen professors in Prussian universities joined Max Weber and other scholars who submitted a protest to the House of Deputies in March 1906.

In the years after 1890 support for the interconfessional school had declined among the National Liberal bourgeoisie. The *Pädagogische Zeitung*, a newspaper published by the Berlin Teachers' Association and the main organ of the nationwide German Teachers' Association, was far from giving the public a full or satisfactory explanation when it asserted that "opposition to Social Democracy" led the National Liberals to align with the reactionary parties in school politics to enact the school law, whose most important provisions were influenced by "hidden political motives"—the belief that a dam could be erected against the political strivings and economic demands of the working class by means of education.[200] In the past the ideological passion with which the politicians of the National Liberal party fought for the interconfessional school was kindled by anti-Catholic sentiment and specifically by the suspicion that Catholic public schools were not educating the youth to be patriotic Germans and loyal subjects of a Protestant monarch. The generation after the *Kulturkampf* saw the folly of using the interconfessional school "for the polemical purpose of fighting ultramontanism." Experience taught them that in the political battles over the school the Center party had been strengthened and the Catholic clergy had been turned into political firebrands. They thought that liberal politicians who took up the interconfessional school cause in pursuit of "a negative and ephemeral goal" were unwittingly undermining the school's primary function of giving the youth a moral and patriotic education grounded in religion.[201]

The National Liberals of the Wilhelminian era had a deeper sense of the strength of confessionalism in the religious and cultural life of Germany than the political liberals of the 1860s. No longer did they look to the interconfessional school to foster religious tolerance and social cohesion. Albert Hackenberg and other National Liberals who belonged to the Evangelical Union had an intense consciousness of the religious segmentation of German society and believed that the differences between the Catholics and the Protestants were too great to be bridged by a common school experience. Theodor Kaftan, a general superintendent in the Protestant church and a supporter of the National Liberal party, thought that the Protestants who championed the interconfessional school made the mistake of assuming that "the division between Romanism and Protestantism is only a matter of differences in a few religious doctrines." He contended that "the division is not only a religio-ecclesiastical one but also a moral and cultural one, and because this exists, there is really no Christian interconfessional school."[202] The extent to which this outlook prevailed among the bourgeoisie of the National Liberal party can be gauged by the membership of the Evangelical Union, which formed a part of the party's political constituency and reached over 294,000 by 1905. The rate of growth of its membership was stronger in Prussia than in any other state in the German Empire.[203]

In Prussia there was no popular support for a complete break between the school and the church. Johannes Tews acknowledged the strong position of organized religion in public life when he criticized the Social Democratic party propagandists of secular schools. He saw no prospect of success for a school reform movement that was based on an antichurch and antireligion standpoint.[204] Very slowly and unevenly did secularization advance in imperial Germany and erode confessional identity and solidarity. Attendance at church worship and passage through the church rites of baptism, confirmation, marriage, and burial showed a high level of religious conformity even though the clergy observed a decline in personal piety. Social Democracy's popular following consisted mainly of Protestant workers in the cities. The Social Democrats did not make inroads among the agricultural workers and were not able to compete with the Center party for the Catholic working-class vote until 1907. Catholic workers who were fully integrated into the Catholic social and cultural milieu of their hometowns did not shift their allegiance from religion to class. Protestant workers in the Social Democratic party ranks seldom expressed outward opposition to the church or demanded the removal of religious instruction from the schools. Until 1905 very few people availed themselves of the opportunity of disaffiliating themselves from the church.[205] Practice and popular preference had made the confessional school the norm in Prussia before the party politicians legally fixed it as the rule.

Conclusion

In the imperial era schoolteachers and left-wing liberals in Prussia viewed the confessional school under the supervision of school inspectors who were clergymen as an anachronism in a modern society. Its survival defied their expectation that demographic mobility and urbanization would increase the confessional mixture of the school enrollments and disproved their contention that the imperatives of national and social integration should make interconfessional schooling the goal of every modern state. Disheartened and demoralized after years of striving in vain to achieve their pedagogic ideal, the leaders of the Prussian Teachers' Association could not easily admit or accept the reasons for their failure. After the enactment of the school law of 1906, they contrived an explanation—"they wanted to fight Social Democracy through the law"—that obscured their inability to influence public opinion and the programs of the major parties and obviated a more probing investigation of why the political conflicts over the school question stretching over half a century ended with a law that made confessional schooling the rule.

The alarm of the governing class over the growth of the Social Democratic party affected the fate of school reform in Prussia far less than the experience of introducing the changes at the height of a religiopolitical conflict that deepened the divisions within the nation. The circumstances in which the interconfessional schools were opened in the 1870s gave them the reputation of being a "*Kulturkampf* institution," and this unfortunate association of school reform with *Kulturkampf* politics remained in the consciousness of both Catholics and Protestants for years to come.

Although the Ministry of Education under Adalbert Falk formulated a moderate and prudent policy for establishing interconfessional schools gradually with some consideration to the pedagogic benefits of the innovation, the liberals who agitated for the reform and the city officials who introduced it were more radical and were motivated by political objectives as well as by educational interests. The campaign for school reform became entangled in the political battle that zealous *Kulturkämpfer* waged against the Catholic church and the Center party. The introduction of interconfessional schooling did not have popular consent. Over the protests of the Catholic citizens, interconfessional schools were opened in Elbing, Krefeld, and other cities by a bourgeois Protestant elite who controlled municipal politics by virtue of an undemocratic franchise in city council elections.

Although the Center party mobilized a massive popular movement in opposition to Falk's school policies and fought the reform wherever the city councils voted to reorganize the schools, it would be an oversimplification to portray the school conflicts of the 1870s as a struggle between socially backward Catholics and enlightened and progressive liberals. Catholic outcries against the omnipotence of the state and the state's monopoly of education were not empty slogans. The school reformers in the National Liberal party did not always act in accord with traditional liberal principles. While they championed the emancipation of the school from the church, they defended the state's monopoly of education and attributed to the state a sovereign authority over the school that was limited in no way by the rights of the communes or the parents. Unchastened by the lack of popular support for their reform program, they relied on the coercive arm of the state bureaucracy to banish the clergy from the schools.

Moreover, the opposition to the liberals was not an exclusively Catholic movement in Prussia. The cause of school reform would not have suffered a defeat if the Catholics had been alone in fighting it. It was the opposition that emerged within the Protestant church that led to Falk's political decline and the repudiation of his school policies after he left office in July 1879.

The resistance of the Protestant clergymen to the opening of interconfessional schools in the Rhine Province was deeply affected by the experience of living amid a large Catholic majority. Extremely conscious of the historical hostility that divided the two confessions in Germany, Protestant churchmen did not share with the liberals the optimistic assumption that the integration of Catholic and Protestant children in the schools would foster tolerance and social cohesion. Fearful that Protestant culture would be engulfed by the Catholic environment of the Rhineland, they opposed the merging of confessional schools in cities with a small Protestant parish. Impressed by the vulnerability of their own church and the powerful resources available to the Catholic hierarchy, they thought that the dissolution of confessional schools would destroy an important agency of sustaining life for the Protestant parish and that the Protestant consciousness of the children would be repressed if they attended interconfessional schools with a predominantly Catholic enrollment.

The opposition of the Protestant clergymen in the Rhine Province found a hearing in the highest official circles in Berlin, and their arguments sealed the fate of interconfessional schooling in Prussia. They complained about the disadvantages of interconfessional schools for the Protestant church and contended that the reform would harm the religious and moral education of the youth because religion would become merely one subject in the curriculum and would no longer penetrate and inspire the entire instruction. Their arguments were reinforced by the school bureaucracy in the province whose reports to the Ministry of Education related the difficulties of teaching history and religion in the new schools and finding the proper form for religious devotion at the opening and closing of the school day. Falk knew how powerful this opposition was when he withstood the demands of the National Liberal and Progressive parties in the House of Deputies and decided in October 1877 not to introduce his school bill in the coming legislative session.

The debasement of school reform for political purposes begun during the *Kulturkampf* reached an extreme form in the Polish-speaking districts of Posen and West Prussia, where the government made an exception to the rule of confessional schooling after 1879 and placed Protestants in teaching offices in hitherto Catholic schools. Overriding the protests of the local school boards, the state authorities used their power of appointing teachers in the binational provinces under the exceptional law of 1886 to make interconfessional many Catholic schools in West Prussia in the interests of the Protestant minority living in communes heavily populated by German and Polish Catholics. Although the Catholic pupils outnumbered the Protestants, school officials ignored the relative size of the two confessions in the school enrollments when they appointed a disproportionately large number of Protestant teachers and selected Protestants for the school principals. They rationalized their inequitable treatment of the two confessions on the grounds of protecting the German nationality against acculturation from the predominant Polish population.

The pace of making the schools interconfessional in Posen was slow at first because the state government followed a policy of establishing separate schools for German children in order to strengthen and shield small German settlements against the Polish cultural environment of the province. German teachers in the provincial branch of the Prussian Teachers' Association as well as school officials in the province were critical of the state government's reluctance to pursue a resolute policy of interconfessional schooling. They regarded the interconfessional school as the most effective means of diminishing the cultural differences and political hostility that separated the two nationalities and assimilating the Polish youth into German society. When Catholic schools were made interconfessional in greater numbers from the turn of the century on, the reform was harnessed to a coercive policy of germanization. The state authorities distrusted the political loyalty of Polish teachers and, wherever possible, appointed German Protestant teachers whose presence would constrain the Polish teachers from nationalist propagandizing and who could be relied on to inculcate German patriotism in the Polish schoolchildren.

What the liberals in the teaching profession and the school reformers in the Progressive party intended was not what actually happened. In practice the interconfessional schools did not turn out to be a benevolent reform. In Frankfurt am Main, Krefeld, and other cities in the west where they were established, the results were political strife rather than social integration and mutual respect between the religious groups. In the binational provinces in the east, the interconfessional school was put in the service of a policy to suppress the Polish nationality.

In imperial Germany, nonconfessional public schools instructing Catholic and Protestant pupils together became the prevailing form of elementary education in Baden and Hesse–Darmstadt, where commanding National Liberal party majorities in the state parliaments succeeded in enacting school laws during the *Kulturkampf*. Thereafter the National Liberals in both states were sufficiently strong to deter the Center party from starting a fight to restore confessional schools. In Prussia, on the other hand, the National Liberals and the Progressives were thwarted by the powerful influence of the Conservatives and were unsuccessful in their efforts to press Falk to introduce legislation that would sever the ties between the school and the church and grant the communes the freedom to open interconfessional schools by a vote of the city councils. In the years after the *Kulturkampf* the National Liberals ceased to be a pressure group for school reform. As early as December 1879—soon after the party's disastrous setback in the *Landtag* elections that autumn—Heinrich von Sybel and other National Liberals began to moderate their defense of the interconfessional school. The Progressives now upheld the cause of school reform alone, and their declining popular support reduced them to a small *Fraktion* in the House of Deputies with a courageous but uninfluential voice in school politics.

The leaders of the Prussian Teachers' Association contended that fear of Social Democracy had dampened the enthusiasm of the National Liberals for innovations that would improve popular education. Though true, this observation offers no more than an oversimplified explanation. In the political conflicts over the schools in the 1870s, the National Liberals discovered the strength of public hostility to the interconfessional school and the vulnerability of their party in election campaigns in which the Center and the Conservative parties fought in defense of the confessional school. In the following decades what remained of their earlier commitment to school reform was an impulse, inspired partly by anti-Catholic feeling, to expand the state's sovereign power over the schools and to safeguard the state's monopoly of education. The National Liberals in the Wilhelminian period were more sensitive to the strength of confessional identity in Prussian society and no longer held, as in former times, optimistic expectations of the social benefits that interconfessional schooling would bring to a divided nation. Recognizing that popular sentiment as well as the school administration's policy had made the confessional school the rule in Prussia, the leadership of the party saw nothing to be gained from breaking a lance for the interconfessional school. Motivated by considerations of party interests and parliamentary strategy, they collaborated with the Conservatives to enact the school law of 1906.

The key to an understanding of school policy and the administration of the schools in Prussia in the imperial era are the maintenance of the state's monopoly of education and supreme supervision over the schools in the context of a positive relationship between the school authorities and the Catholic and Protestant churches, the awesome respect for and fear of the Catholic church as a power in society, and the priority given to the interests of the Protestant confession.

Officials in the Ministry of Education routinely identified Protestant interests with the interests of the state and the German nationality. Government decisions determined by considerations of Protestant church interests or influenced by partiality for the Protestant community led to inconsistencies and inequities in the treatment of the Catholics in the school system. State appropriations for school subsidies distributed for the benefit of the German nationality produced gross disparities in the school facilities for German Protestants and Polish Catholics in the eastern provinces. The inconsistent and discriminatory behavior of the school administration, with personnel almost exclusively Protestant from the minister down to the provincial school bureaucracy, kept the Catholics conscious of and preoccupied with the confessional issue in school politics long after the *Kulturkampf* ended.

The notion of extending the state's authority over the *Volksschule* by breaking its bonds with the church never took hold in the Prussian school administration. Since 1848, officials in the Ministry of Education were unwavering in their belief that the removal of religion from the school curriculum and the secularization of the schools would have detrimental consequences for the state. They feared that such a radical reform would impel the Catholics to open a system of church schools independent of the state and did not see how the government could logically deny the Catholics the freedom to teach guaranteed in Article 22 of the constitution as a basic right. They doubted that religiously neutral communal schools would compete successfully with Catholic private schools and thought that a large part of popular education would soon be removed from the control of the state. The surest way to preserve the state's monopoly of education was to have the public schools serve the purposes of the church as well as the state.

Government measures in the 1870s strained but did not break irrevocably the traditional partnership of the state and the church in the field of elementary education. The Catholic bishops were restrained and cautious in their reaction to the School Supervision Law of 1872 and did not issue a defiant order instructing the clergy to resign their school inspection offices en masse. In their opposition to Falk's decree of 1876 on the state's supervision of religious instruction, Catholic political leaders threatened the government with the possibility that the church would not recognize the instruction of religion in the public schools as authentic Catholic teaching and would open private schools. The bishops never carried their opposition to such an extreme point and instead waited prudently for Falk's dismissal.

In the "reaction" of the 1880s, Falk's conservative successors repealed neither the School Supervision Law nor his decree of 1876. Robert von Puttkamer and Gustav von Gossler declined to engage in discussions with the Catholic episcopacy on the church's claims to formal rights in the administration of the schools on the basis of Article 24 of the constitution. They thought that the extent of the church's participation in school life should be regulated from the sole point of view of state interests. Despite the lingering dissatisfaction on the Catholic side, much of the church's earlier influence was, in practice, restored except in the Polish-speaking areas. The collaboration of the state and the church in the *Volksschule* ensured the preservation of the state's monopoly of education. In 1901 fewer than 1 percent of all Catholic schoolchildren attended private elementary schools. The total number of pupils of all religious faiths enrolled in private elementary schools was about 13,000 in comparison with more than 5.5 million in public schools.

The bitter conflicts over the use of German or Polish as the language of religious instruction for Polish schoolchildren in Posen and West Prussia could have been settled easily by removing religion from the public school curriculum or by allowing the Catholics in both provinces to open private schools. State officials could accept neither one of these solutions because of their apprehensions about turning Catholic religious instruction over to the church completely and because of their conviction that the state had to possess control over the education of the people. Their fears that private Catholic schools would work contrary to the goals pursued by the state in public education were all the greater in the Polish-speaking areas.

The supporters of the National Liberal and Progressive parties were also apprehensive about the power of the Catholic church and did not uphold freedom of teaching or advocate publicly the secularization of the public schools. Apart from the sporadic agitation of the Social Democrats, there was in Prussia no movement to abolish the instruction of religion in the schools and to leave religious education up to the churches alone. The liberals thought that the school monopoly of the state should extend to the instruction of religion. Teaching religion as a required subject in the public schools guaranteed that the instruction remained under the state's oversight and served the state's interest. The intention of the liberals to have religion taught in a *Staatsschule* without conceding to the church the prerogatives of directing the instruction and certifying the qualifications of the teachers was never realized.

Notes

ABBREVIATIONS

GSA   *Geheimes Staatsarchiv*, Berlin–Dahlem
HAD   *Hauptstaatsarchiv Düsseldorf*
HAM   *Hessisches Staatsarchiv*, Marburg
LAK   *Landeshauptarchiv Koblenz*
ZSA   *Zentrales Staatsarchiv*, Abteilung Merseburg
Centralblatt   *Centralblatt für die gesamte Unterrichtsverwaltung
in Preussen*
Sten. Berichte   *Stenographische Berichte über die Verhandlungen
des Preussischen Hauses der Abgeordneten*

INTRODUCTION

1. Rainer Bölling, *Volksschullehrer und Politik. Der Deutsche Lehrerverein 1918–1933* (Göttingen, 1978), p. 131ff; Christoph Führ, *Zur Schulpolitik der Weimarer Republik* (Weinheim, 1970), pp. 31ff, 345; Günther Grünthal, *Reichsschulgesetz und Zentrumspartei in der Weimarer Republik* (Düsseldorf, 1968), pp. 53ff, 294–95.

2. Apart from discussing the School Supervision Law of 1872, the following accounts of the *Kulturkampf* in Prussia do not examine the fight that the state waged against the Catholic church in the elementary school system: Günther Dettmer, *Die ost- und westpreussischen Behörden im Kulturkampf* (Heidelberg, 1958); Erich Schmidt-Volkmar, *Der Kulturkampf in Deutschland, 1871–1890* (Göttingen, 1962); Adalbert Wahl, *Deutsche Geschichte 1871–1914* (Stuttgart, 1926); and Zygmunt Zielinski, "Der Kulturkampf in der Provinz Posen," *Historisches Jahrbuch* 101 (1981): 447–61. Heinrich Schiffers takes note of the extensive conflict in the school domain without analyzing its full importance in *Der Kulturkampf in Stadt und Regierungsbezirk Aachen* (Aachen, 1929).

3. Erich Foerster, *Adalbert Falk: Sein Leben und Wirken als preussischer Kultusminister* (Gotha, 1927).

4. J. Alden Nichols, *Germany after Bismarck. The Caprivi Era, 1890–1894* (Cambridge, Mass., 1958), p. 157ff; J. C. G. Röhl, *Germany without Bismarck. The Crisis of Government in the Second Reich, 1890–1900* (Berkeley and London, 1967), p. 77ff.

5. Folkert Meyer, *Schule der Untertanen. Lehrer und Politik in Preussen 1848–1900* (Hamburg, 1976), pp. 166, 172–78; Hartmut Titze, *Die Politisierung der Erziehung. Untersuchungen über die soziale und politische Funktion der Erziehung von der Aufklärung bis zum Hochkapitalismus* (Frankfurt am Main, 1973), pp. 226–33.

6. Assumptions about the antisocialist purpose of the school law heavily influenced the judgments made by Eugene Anderson and Geoffrey Field. Anderson concluded that "Protestant teachers and the left liberal parties lost the battle for secularization to those who maintained that the confessional school best served the purpose of developing religious character and combatting unbelief, that is democracy, and especially Social Democracy" in "The Prussian Volksschule in the Nineteenth Century," in Gerhard A. Ritter (ed.), *Entstehung und Wandel der modernen Gesellschaft: Festschrift für Hans Rosenberg* (Berlin, 1970), p. 276. Field contended that "it was the challenge of Social Democracy above all that shaped Prussian school legislation after 1890; the legislative tightening of confessional controls over the next two decades was guided by the belief that the *Volksschule* was a crucial locus of the class struggle and that to implant Christian principles was the best deterrent against revolutionary politics" in "Religion in the German Volksschule, 1890–1928," *Leo Baeck Institute Year Book* 25 (1980): 45. Field added that the school law of 1906 was passed by "the conservative-clerical alliance" (p. 52).

7. For a critical evaluation of recent radical reinterpretations of Prussian elementary schooling, see Kenneth Barkin, "Social Control and the Volksschule in Vormärz Prussia," *Central European History* 26 (1983): 31–52; Konrad Jarausch, "The Old 'New History of Education': A German Reconsideration," *History of Education Quarterly* 26 (1986): 231–32.

8. Christa Berg, *Die Okkupation der Schule. Eine Studie zur Aufhellung gegenwärtiger Schulprobleme an der Volksschule Preussen 1872–1900* (Heidelberg, 1973), pp. 7–8; Anita Mächler, "Aspekte der Volksschulpolitik in Preussen im 19. Jahrhundert," in Peter Baumgart (ed.), *Bildungspolitik in Preussen zur Zeit des Kaiserreichs* (Stuttgart, 1980), p. 227.

9. In addition to the works by Christa Berg, Folkert Meyer, and Hartmut Titze, see Friedhelm Nyssen, "Das Sozialisationskonzept der Stiehlschen Regulative und sein historischer Hintergrund. Zur historisch-materialistischen Analyse der Schulpolitik in den 50er und 60er Jahren des 19. Jahrhunderts," and Franz Wenzel, "Sicherung von Massenloyalität und Qualifikation der Arbeitskraft als Aufgabe der Volksschule," in Klaus Hartmann, Friedhelm Nyssen, and Hans Waldeyer (eds.), *Schule und Staat im 18. und 19. Jahrhundert. Zur Sozialgeschichte der Schule in Deutschland* (Frankfurt am Main, 1974); Ingeborg Schumann, Hans-Jürgen Korff, and Michael Schumann, *Sozialisation in Schule und*

Fabrik. Entstehungsbedingungen proletarischer Kindheit und Jugend (West Berlin, 1976).

10. Meyer, *Schule der Untertanen*, pp. 168–75, 193–94. See also Titze, *Die Politisierung der Erziehung*, p. 227ff.

11. Geoff Eley, "State Formation, Nationalism and Political Culture in Nineteenth-Century Germany," in *From Unification to Nazism: Reinterpreting the German Past* (Boston, 1986), p. 68.

12. Wolfgang Kopitzsch, "Zur 'Politisierung' des Geschichtsunterrichts in Scheswig–Holstein nach dem 1. Mai 1889," in Franklin Kopitzsch (ed.), *Erziehungs- und Bildungsgeschichte Schleswig–Holsteins von der Aufklärung bis zum Kaiserreich* (Neumünster, 1981), pp. 149–92.

13. HAM, Reg. Kassel, no. 6129, minister of education to the district governments and provincial school boards, October 13, 1890.

14. Ibid., see the doubtful comments on the effectiveness of the new history lesson plan, given the limited time devoted to the subject, in the report of County School Inspector Kley, December 7, 1890.

15. Albert Grimpen, *Welche Aufgaben erwachsen der Schule aus der stetigen Zunahme der Sozialdemokratie?* (Hamburg, 1901), pp. 23, 33–35.

16. See Geoff Eley's criticism of the unidimensional view of the *Kulturkampf* based on Bismarck's politics in "German Politics and Polish Nationality: the Dialectic of Nation Forming in the East of Prussia," in *From Unification to Nazism*, p. 206.

17. Norbert Schlossmacher, *Düsseldorf im Bismarckreich. Politik und Wahlen, Parteien und Vereine* (Düsseldorf, 1985), pp. 252–53.

18. Winfried Becker, "Liberale Kulturkampf-Positionen und politischer Katholizismus," in Otto Pflanze (ed.), *Innenpolitische Probleme des Bismarck-Reiches* (München, 1983), pp. 53, 56; Adolf Birke, "Zur Entwicklung und politischen Funktion des bürgerlichen Kulturkampfverständnisses in Preussen-Deutschland" in Dietrich Kurze (ed.), *Aus Theorie und Praxis der Geschichtswissenschaft* (Berlin, 1970), pp. 260–63, 273–79; Heinrich Bornkamm, "Die Staatsidee in Kulturkampf," *Historische Zeitschrift* 170 (1950): 50–52.

19. Josef Becker, *Liberaler Staat und Kirche in der Ära von Reichsgründung und Kulturkampf. Geschichte und Strukturen ihres Verhältnisses in Baden 1860–1876* (Mainz, 1973), pp. 194–95; David Blackbourn, "Progress and Piety: Liberals, Catholics and the State in Bismarck's Germany," in *Populists and Patricians: Essays in Modern German History* (London, 1987), pp. 143, 148–50; Lothar Gall, *Der Liberalismus als regierende Partei. Das Grossherzogtum Baden zwischen Restauration und Reichsgründung* (Wiesbaden, 1968), pp. 192–94.

20. Eley, "State Formation, Nationalism and Political Culture," pp. 69–73.

21. Gall, *Der Liberalismus als regierende Partei*, pp. 194, 294, 301–2; idem, "Die partei- und sozialgeschichtliche Problematik des badischen Kulturkampfes," *Zeitschrift für die Geschichte des Oberrheins* 113 (1965): 168–71, 194; Werner Trapp, "Volksschulreform und liberales Bürgertum in Konstanz," in Gerd Zang (ed.), *Provinzialisierung einer Region. Regionale Unentwicklung und liberale*

Politik in der Stadt und im Kreis Konstanz im 19. Jahrhundert (Frankfurt am Main, 1978), pp. 408–9.

22. Becker, *Liberaler Staat und Kirche*, pp. 136–37, 196–97, 373–74.

23. Schlossmacher, *Düsseldorf im Bismarckreich*, pp. 66–67, 248–53.

24. David Blackbourn, "The Problem of Democratization: German Catholics and the Role of the Centre Party," in Richard J. Evans (ed.), *Society and Politics in Wilhelmine Germany* (New York and London, 1978), pp. 162–65, 170–77.

25. Wilfried Loth, *Katholiken im Kaiserreich. Der politische Katholizismus in der Krise des wilhelminischen Deutschlands* (Düsseldorf, 1984), pp. 24, 150–51, 218–19.

26. Stanley Suval, *Electoral Politics in Wilhelmine Germany* (Chapel Hill, N.C., 1985), pp. 72–73.

CHAPTER 1

1. Wilhelm von Ketteler, "Deutschland nach dem Kriege von 1866," in Erwin Iserloh (ed.), *Sämtliche Werke und Briefe* (Mainz, 1977), vol. 2, pp. 67–72.

2. For the text of the school regulations in the General Civil Code of 1794, see Ludwig von Rönne (ed.), *Das Unterrichtswesen des preussischen Staates* (Berlin, 1855), p. 221.

3. *Preussische Statistik* 209 (1908), pt. I, pp. 137–38.

4. Anthony J. La Vopa, *Prussian Schoolteachers. Profession and Office, 1763–1848* (Chapel Hill, N.C., 1980), p. 124; Thomas Nipperdey, "Volksschule und Revolution im Vormärz," in Kurt Kluxen and Wolfgang Mommsen (eds.), *Politische Ideologien und nationalstaatliche Ordnung: Festschrift für Theodor Schieder* (München, 1968), pp. 127–28; idem, *Deutsche Geschichte 1800–1866: Bürgerwelt und starker Staat* (München, 1983), pp. 453, 463–67.

5. Rönne (ed.), *Das Unterrichtswesen*, pp. 158, 362–63.

6. Ibid., p. 363.

7. Ibid., pp. 344–51, 365–67.

8. Bernard Krueger, *Stiehl und seine Regulative. Ein Beitrag zur preussischen Schulgeschichte* (Weinheim, 1970), pp. 116–17.

9. Rönne (ed.), *Das Unterrichtswesen*, p. 360.

10. Ibid., p. 659.

11. Karl Schneider, "Geschichtliche Darstellung des Verfahrens der preussischen Unterrichtsverwaltung bei Einrichtung der Volksschulen in Gegenden mit konfessionell gemischter Bevölkerung," *Centralblatt* (1878), pp. 328–30.

12. Ibid., pp. 332–33.

13. Rönne (ed.), *Das Unterrichtswesen*, pp. 789–801.

14. La Vopa, *Prussian Schoolteachers*, p. 109.

15. *Statistisches Handbuch für den Preussischen Staat* 1 (1888): 423.

16. F. W. C. Dieterici, "Statistische Übersicht des öffentlichen Unterrichts im preussischen Staate im Jahre 1816 und im Jahre 1846," *Mitteilungen des Statist-*

ischen Bureaus in Berlin 1 (1849): 35–37; *Tabellen und amtliche Nachrichten über den preussischen Staat für das Jahr 1849* (1851), pp. 557–58.

17. *Tabellen und amtliche Nachrichten über den preussischen Staat für das Jahr 1849*, p. 549; "Statistische Nachrichten über das Elementarschulwesen in Preussen für die Jahre 1859 bis 1861," *Centralblatt* (1864), p. 2ff; "Statistische Nachrichten über das Elementarschulwesen in Preussen für die Jahre 1862–1864," *Centralblatt* (1868), p. 61; Goldschmidt, "Schulpflicht und Schulbesuch in Berlin," *Zeitschrift des königlich preussischen Statistischen Bureau* 7 (1867): 250.

18. Leopold Clausnitzer, *Geschichte des preussischen Unterrichtsgesetzes mit besonderer Berücksichtigung der Volksschule* (Berlin, 1891), pp. 246–47, 262–65.

19. *Centralblatt* (1874), pp. 210–11.

20. "Statistische Nachrichten über das Elementarschulwesen in Preussen für die Jahre 1859 bis 1861," pp. vii–viii; *Preussische Statistik* 176 (1905), pt. I, p. 58.

21. "Statistische Nachrichten über das Elementarschulwesen in Preussen für die Jahre 1859 bis 1861," p. 2ff.

22. *Tabellen und amtliche Nachrichten über den preussischen Staat für das Jahr 1849*, p. 554.

23. Titze, *Die Politisierung der Erziehung*, p. 141.

24. Rönne (ed.), *Das Unterrichtswesen*, pp. 642–43.

25. From Stiehl's draft of a school law printed in the appendix of Krueger, *Stiehl und seine Regulative*, pp. 190–91.

26. Karl-Ernst Jeismann, "Die 'Stiehlschen Regulative': Ein Beitrag zum Verhältnis von Politik und Pädagogik während der Reaktionszeit in Preussen," in Rudolf Vierhaus and Manfred Botzenhart (eds.), *Dauer und Wandel der Geschichte. Aspekte europäischer Vergangenheit: Festgabe für Kurt von Raumer* (Münster, 1966), p. 428ff.

27. From the *Regulativ* of October 3, 1854, printed in the appendix of Krueger, *Stiehl und seine Regulative*, pp. 321, 328.

28. Rönne (ed.), *Das Unterrichtswesen*, pp. 560–61, 586–88, 594–97.

29. Ibid., pp. 603–6.

30. *Tabellen und amtliche Nachrichten über den preussischen Staat für das Jahr 1849*, pp. 557, 560–61; Karl-Heinz Ludwig, "Die Fabrikarbeit von Kindern im 19. Jahrhundert," *Vierteljahrschrift für Sozial- und Wirtschaftsgeschichte* 52 (1965): 72–73. Jürgen Kuczynski, on the other hand, claims that the figures on child labor gathered by the government's statistical bureau are too low and that throughout the nineteenth century manufacturers concealed the practice of employing youths under the age of fourteen. See Kuczynski's *Studien zur Geschichte der Lage des arbeitenden Kindes in Deutschland von 1700 bis zur Gegenwart* (Berlin Hauptstadt der D.D.R., 1968), pp. 72, 101–4.

31. Ludwig, "Die Fabrikarbeit von Kindern im 19. Jahrhundert," pp. 80–83.

32. Kuczynski, Studien zur Geschichte der Lage des arbeitenden Kindes, pp. 152ff, 161ff. See also Christa Berg, "Volksschule im Abseits von 'Industrialisierung' und 'Fortschritt.' Über den Zusammenhang von Bildung und Indus-

trieentwicklung," in Ulrich Herrmann (ed.), *Schule und Gesellschaft im 19. Jahrhundert* (Weinheim, 1977), pp. 246–49; Margarete Flecken, *Arbeiterkinder im 19. Jahrhundert: eine sozialgeschichtliche Untersuchung ihrer Lebenswelt* (Weinheim, 1981), pp. 121–25.

33. *Centralblatt* (1868), pp. 369–70, 505.

34. Goldschmidt, "Schulpflicht und Schulbesuch," p. 251.

35. Rudolf Vandré, *Schule, Lehrer und Unterricht im 19. Jahrhundert* (Göttingen, 1973), p. 171.

36. Konrad Jarausch writes, "On the primary school level a youth-centered approach could hardly be successful due to lack of evidence; it rather became subsumed in the history of family and childhood." See Jarausch's "The Old 'New History of Education': A German Reconsideration," p. 233.

37. Berg, "Volksschule im Abseits von 'Industrialisierung' und 'Fortschritt,'" pp. 243, 252–55; Peter Lundgreen, "Schulbildung und Frühindustrialisierung in Berlin/Preussen. Eine Einführung in den historischen und systematischen Zusammenhang von Schule und Wirtschaft," in Ulrich Herrmann (ed.), *Schule und Gesellschaft im. 19. Jahrhundert* (Weinheim, 1977), pp. 71, 102–9; Titze, *Die Politisierung der Erziehung*, pp. 129–30, 196. For a broader discussion of the shifts in the historiography of European education since the 1960s, see Mary Jo Maynes, *Schooling in Western Europe. A Social History* (New York, 1985).

38. Nipperdey, *Deutsche Geschichte 1800–1866*, pp. 463, 465–69. See also Kenneth Barkin, "Social Control and the Volksschule in Vormärz Prussia," pp. 31–51.

39. H. Gräfe, *Die deutsche Volksschule oder die Bürger- und Landschule*, 2nd ed. (Leipzig, 1850), pp. 600–601, 673–78; Vandré, *Schule, Lehrer und Unterricht im 19. Jahrhundert*, pp. 199–227.

40. "Religionsbekenntnis und Schulbildung der Bevölkerung des preussischen Staates," *Zeitschrift des königlich preussischen Statistischen Bureaus* 14 (1874): 148–49. See also Rolf Engelsing, *Analphabetentum und Lektüre. Zur Sozialgeschichte des Lesens in Deutschland zwischen feudaler und industrieller Gesellschaft* (Stuttgart, 1973), p. 101ff.

41. Theodore Hamerow, *The Social Foundations of German Unification, 1858–1871: Ideas and Institutions* (Princeton, N.J., 1969), vol. 1, pp. 286–88.

42. Ludwig Wiese, *Lebenserinnerungen und Amtserfahrungen* (Berlin, 1886), vol. 1, p. 177.

43. La Vopa, *Prussian Schoolteachers*, pp. 53–60.

44. Ibid., pp. 82–98.

45. Carl Louis Albert Pretzel, *Geschichte des Deutschen Lehrervereins in den ersten fünfzig Jahren seines Bestehens* (Leipzig, 1921), pp. 31–33.

46. Rönne (ed.), *Das Unterrichtswesen*, pp. 475–80.

47. Gottlieb Lüttgert, *Preussens Unterrichtskämpfe in der Bewegung von 1848* (Berlin, 1924), pp. 180–81; Helmut Albrecht, *Die Stellung des politischen Katholizismus in Deutschland zu den Fragen des Unterrichts und der Erziehung in den Jahren 1848–1850* (Leipzig, 1929), pp. 126–27.

48. LAK, Oberpräsidium, no. 10393, school program of the democrats in the National Assembly, July 21, 1848.

49. Ibid., petitions of Catholic priests in the Rhine Province and, in particular, the petition of Fathers Reismann and Stuker from Kaldenkirchen, July 28, 1848. See also Lüttgert, *Preussens Unterrichtskämpfe*, pp. 186–89.

50. Albrecht, *Die Stellung des politischen Katholizismus*, pp. 124–26.

51. Ibid., pp. 141–43.

52. Krueger, *Stiehl und seine Regulative*, pp. 87–91; Walter Reichle, *Zwischen Staat und Kirche. Das Leben und Wirken des preussischen Kultusministers Heinrich von Mühler* (Berlin, 1938), pp. 81–84.

53. See Ladenberg's "Erläuterungen, die Bestimmungen der Verfassungsurkunde vom 6. Dezember 1848 über Religion, Religionsgesellschaft und Unterrichtswesen betreffend," in Rönne (ed.), *Das Unterrichtswesen*, pp. 142–43.

54. Ernst Rudolf Huber (ed.), *Dokumente zur deutschen Verfassungsgeschichte* (Stuttgart, 1961), vol. 1, p. 403.

55. See Ladenberg's letter to the bishops in Ferdinand Stiehl (ed.), *Die Gesetzgebung auf dem Gebiete des Unterrichtswesens in Preussen vom Jahre 1817 bis 1868* (Berlin, 1869), pp. 188–93.

56. See the draft of the school law in ibid., p. 162ff.

57. Stiehl (ed.), *Die Gesetzgebung*, p. 189.

58. Lüttgert, *Preussens Unterrichtskämpfe*, pp. 311–14.

59. Stiehl (ed.), *Die Gesetzgebung*, pp. 190–92.

60. Rönne (ed.), *Das Unterrichtswesen*, p. 234.

61. *Stenographische Berichte über die Verhandlungen der Zweiten Kammer* (1852), vol. 1, p. 493.

62. Wiese, *Lebenserinnerungen*, vol. 1, pp. 191–92. See also John R. Gillis, *The Prussian Bureaucracy in Crisis, 1840–1860* (Stanford, Calif., 1971), p. 170ff.

63. Wiese, *Lebenserinnerungen*, vol. 1, p. 207; vol. 2, pp. 53–54, 133.

64. The reports of the education committee, August 20, 1862, and March 11, 1863, in *Anlagen zu den Sten. Berichten* (1863), vol. 3, p. 288ff; *Sten. Berichte* (March 23, 1863), pp. 650–51, 665–66; idem (March 24, 1863), p. 707.

65. James J. Sheehan, *German Liberalism in the Nineteenth Century* (Chicago, 1978), pp. 16–17, 32–33, 40–41, 160–69.

66. Rudolf Gneist, *Die konfessionelle Schule. Ihre Unzuverlässigkeit nach preussischen Landesgesetzen* (Berlin, 1869), pp. 29–31.

67. Ibid., pp. 42–44.

68. Ibid., p. 85.

69. Stiehl (ed.), *Die Gesetzgebung*, pp. 195–96.

70. Ibid., p. 197.

71. See the *Motive* of the draft of the school law of 1862 in ibid., pp. 226–30.

72. Wiese, *Lebenserinnerungen*, vol. 1, pp. 236–40, 312.

73. *Motive* of the school bill of 1868 in *Anlagen zu den Sten. Berichten* (1868–69), vol. 1, pp. 204–6.

74. Ibid., p. 206.

75. School bill of 1868, in ibid., p. 199ff.

76. *Motive*, in ibid., p. 215.

77. *Sten. Berichte* (November 4, 1869), pp. 307–8.

78. J. Becker, *Liberaler Staat und Kirche*, p. 120ff; Gall, *Der Liberalismus als regierende Partei*, p. 282ff.

79. Stiehl (ed.), *Die Gesetzgebung*, pp. 198, 231–33.

CHAPTER 2

1. George C. Windell, *The Catholics and German Unity 1866–1871* (Minneapolis, 1954), pp. 75–81; Ellen Lovell Evans, *The German Center Party 1870–1933: A Study in Political Catholicism* (Carbondale, Ill., 1981), pp. 26–27.

2. Margaret L. Anderson, *Windthorst. A Political Biography* (Oxford, 1981), pp. 134–36, 141; Rudolf Lill, "Die deutschen Katholiken und Bismarcks Reichsgründung," in Theodor Schieder and Ernst Deuerlein (eds.), *Reichsgründung 1870–71* (Stuttgart, 1970), pp. 351–59; Erich Schmidt-Volkmar, *Der Kulturkampf*, pp. 25–31.

3. Schmidt-Volkmar, *Der Kulturkampf*, pp. 60–63.

4. Adelheid Constabel (ed.), *Die Vorgeschichte des Kulturkampfes. Quellenveröffentlichung aus dem deutschen Zentralarchiv* (Hauptstadt der D.D.R. Berlin, 1957), pp. 115–16, 119.

5. Ibid., pp. 126–27.

6. Adolf Birke, "Zur Entwicklung und politischen Funktion des bürgerlichen Kulturkampfverständnisses in Preussen-Deutschland," pp. 265, 268; Wolfgang Tilgner, "Volk, Nation und Vaterland im protestantischen Denken zwischen Kaiserreich und Nationalsozialismus," in Horst Zillessen (ed.), *Volk, Nation, Vaterland. Der deutsche Protestantismus und der Nationalismus* (Gütersloh, 1970), pp. 141–42.

7. Günther Dettmer, *Die ost- und westpreussischen Behörden im Kulturkampf*, appendix, p. 122.

8. Otto von Bismarck, *Die gesammelten Werke* (Berlin, 1931), vol. 6b, p. 291.

9. Constabel (ed.), *Die Vorgeschichte des Kulturkampfes*, pp. 127–28.

10. Ernst Rudolf Huber and Wolfgang Huber (eds.), *Staat und Kirche im 19. und 20. Jahrhundert. Dokumente zur Geschichte des deutschen Staatskirchenrechts* (Berlin, 1976), vol. 2, p. 530.

11. Constabel (ed.), *Die Vorgeschichte des Kulturkampfes*, pp. 136–41.

12. Ibid., pp. 138, 140.

13. Ibid., pp. 142–44.

14. Foerster, *Adalbert Falk*, pp. 74–75; Schmidt-Volkmar, *Der Kulturkampf*, pp. 78–79.

15. Foerster, *Adalbert Falk*, pp. 89–96; Karl Schneider, *Ein halbes Jahrhundert im Dienste von Kirche und Schule. Lebenserinnerungen* 2nd ed. (Stuttgart, 1901), p. 328; Ludwig Wiese, *Lebenserinnerungen*, vol. 2, pp. 31–32.

16. These figures were given by Malinckrodt in *Sten. Berichte* (February 10, 1872), p. 717.

17. Otto von Bismarck, *Werke in Auswahl*, ed. by Gustav Adolf Rein et al. (Stuttgart, 1973), vol. 5, p. 176.

18. *Sten. Berichte* (February 8, 1872), pp. 670–74; idem (February 10, 1872), pp. 718–21; idem (February 13, 1872), pp. 738–39.

19. Ibid. (February 8, 1872), pp. 659, 663–67.

20. Ibid. (February 9, 1872), pp. 703–4.

21. Ibid. (February 8, 1872), pp. 656–57, 677–78; idem (February 13, 1872), p. 740.

22. Wolfgang Rädisch, *Die evangelisch-lutherische Landeskirche Hannovers und der preussische Staat 1866–1885* (Hildesheim, 1972), pp. 111–12.

23. Ibid., pp. 111–13.

24. Erwin Gatz (ed.), *Akten der Fuldaer Bischofskonferenz 1871–1899* (Mainz, 1977), vol. 1, pp. 50–78.

25. Leopold Clausnitzer, *Geschichte des preussischen Unterrichtsgesetzes*, pp. 261, 275–81.

26. Friedrich Wilhelm Dörpfeld, *Ein Beitrag zur Leidensgeschichte der Volksschule*, in *Gesammelte Schriften* (Gütersloh, 1899), vol. 9, pp. 27–28, 116.

27. Winfried Jestaedt, *Der Kulturkampf im Fuldaer Land* (Fulda, 1960), pp. 128–31; Lech Trzeciakowski, "The Prussian State and the Catholic Church in Prussian Poland 1871–1914," *Slavic Review* 26 (1967): 620–21; Zygmunt Zielinski, "Der Kulturkampf in der Provinz Posen," pp. 452, 460.

28. Gatz (ed.), *Akten der Fuldaer Bischofskonferenz*, vol. 1, pp. 421–22.

29. HAD, Reg. Düsseldorf, Präsidialbüro, no. 1308, Falk to the provincial governor, March 25, 1873.

30. Ibid., District Governor August vom Ende to the district governors in Aachen, Cologne, Koblenz, and Trier, April 8, 1873; the replies from Cologne, April 21, 1873, and from Trier, April 12, 1873.

31. *Sten. Berichte* (January 31, 1874), p. 982.

32. Christa Berg, *Die Okkupation der Schule*, pp. 55–56; Karl Schneider (ed.), *Volksschulwesen und Lehrerbildung in Preussen* (Berlin, 1875), p. 301.

33. *Sten. Berichte* (January 31, 1874), pp. 976–77.

34. HAD, Reg. Düsseldorf, no. 2619, district governor's directive to the county councillors, April 6, 1872; reports of the *Landrat* of Moers county, June 8, 1872, and the *Landrat* of München-Gladbach county, May 6, 1872.

35. Ibid., county councillor's report to the district government, March 25, 1873; district government to the minister of education, May 4, 1873; Falk's reply, May 15, 1873.

36. Ibid., district government to the minister of education, July 14, 1873.

37. Schmidt-Volkmar, *Der Kulturkampf*, p. 168ff; Adalbert Wahl, *Deutsche Geschichte 1871–1914* (Stuttgart, 1926), vol. 1, pp. 186–89.

38. For the political activity of the Catholic clergy in the Rhineland, see

Jonathan Sperber, *Popular Catholicism in Nineteenth-Century Germany* (Princeton, N.J., 1984), p. 211ff; Hubert Thoma, *Georg Friedrich Dasbach. Priester, Publizist, Politiker* (Trier, 1975), p. 41ff.

39. HAD, Reg. Köln, no. 2722, reports of the county councillors; reports of the *Landrat* of Bonn county, October 23 and December 26, 1873; district government to the minister of education, November 28, 1873.

40. HAD, Reg. Düsseldorf, Präsidialbüro, no. 1308, district governor to the *Abteilung des Innern*, November 26, 1873.

41. HAD, Reg. Düsseldorf, no. 2619, district governor to the minister of education, December 5, 1873; idem, no. 2620, provincial governor to the five district governors, December 15, 1873.

42. LAK, Oberpräsidium, no. 10412, Cologne district government to the provincial governor, January 7, 1874.

43. Ibid., Aachen district government to the provincial governor, January 13, 1874.

44. LAK, Oberpräsidium, no. 10412, Koblenz district government to the provincial governor, January 10, 1874; Cologne district government to the provincial governor, January 7, 1874.

45. Ibid., provincial governor to the minister of education, January 28, 1874, and March 30, 1874; minister of education to the provincial governor, February 12, 1874.

46. Ibid., Düsseldorf district government to the provincial governor, February 7, 1874, and the provincial governor's reply of February 17, 1874. HAD, Reg. Düsseldorf, no. 2620, a copy of Falk's letter to the provincial governor, February 12, 1874.

47. LAK, Reg. Koblenz, no. 26204, district government to the minister of education, July 8 and August 31, 1875; Falk's replies of July 20 and September 14, 1875. HAD, Reg. Düsseldorf, Präsidialbüro, no. 1309, copy of Falk's letter to Emperor William, January 6, 1876, in which he gave an account of his meeting with officials of the Düsseldorf district and their proposal.

48. HAD, Reg. Düsseldorf, Präsidialbüro, no. 1309, copies of Emperor William's letter to Falk, January 5, 1876, and the minister's reply of January 6, 1876; minister of education to the district governor, January 7, 1876.

49. Ibid., letters of the *Landrat* of Moers county to the district governor, June 17 and August 29, 1876; see also Mayor Schless of Xanten to the district governor, June 19, 1876.

50. LAK, Reg. Koblenz, no. 26204, minister of education to the district government, April 4, 1876.

51. LAK, Oberpräsidium, no. 10412, minister of education to the Düsseldorf district government, April 3, 1876.

52. HAD, Reg. Düsseldorf, Präsidialbüro, no. 1309, *Landrat* of Moers county to the district governor, June 17, 1876; district governor to the minister of education, June 28, 1876; Falk's reply of August 19, 1876.

53. *Sten. Berichte* (March 15, 1876), pp. 655–56.

54. *Sten. Berichte* (February 22, 1877), p. 773.

55. The minister gave these statistics in the House of Deputies. *Sten. Berichte* (March 17, 1882), p. 947.

56. LAK, Oberpräsidium, no. 10524.

57. Ibid., Düsseldorf district government to *Landrat* Devens, August 28, 1874 [copy]; Düsseldorf district government to the provincial governor, November 14, 1874; provincial governor's reply of December 9, 1874.

58. Ibid., Düsseldorf district government's report to the provincial governor, September 27, 1875, explaining the reasons for issuing the order of February 11, 1875. Regarding the regulations on religious instruction in the schools, issued by the district governments, see the report in *Anlagen zu den Stenographischen Berichten über die Verhandlungen des Herrenhauses* (1876), vol. 2, pp. 184–87.

59. LAK, Oberpräsidium, no. 10524, minister of education to the provincial governor, January 12, 1874, and to the Koblenz district government, December 31, 1874. See also Falk's directive of January 9, 1873 in *Centralblatt* (1875), pp. 104–5.

60. *Centralblatt* (1875), pp. 12–19.

61. A spokesman for Falk gave this explanation in the *Herrenhaus. Stenographische Berichte über die Verhandlungen des Herrenhauses* (May 27, 1876), p. 257.

62. Falk alluded to this motive in his defense of the decree. See *Sten. Berichte* (March 14, 1876), p. 612.

63. *Centralblatt* (1876), pp. 120–23.

64. *Sten. Berichte* (March 14, 1876), pp. 609–10, 618–19; idem (January 24, 1877), pp. 73–77.

65. *Sten. Berichte* (March 14, 1876), pp. 617–19; idem (January 24, 1877), pp. 74–75; *Stenographische Berichte über die Verhandlungen des Herrenhauses* (May 24, 1876), p. 252.

66. *Sten. Berichte* (March 14, 1876), pp. 615–16.

67. *Sten. Berichte* (January 24, 1877), p. 86.

68. *Stenographische Berichte über die Verhandlungen des Herrenhauses* (June 17, 1876), pp. 297–98.

69. For the minutes of the conference meetings, see *Centralblatt* (1872), p. 385ff.

70. Schneider (ed.), *Volksschulwesen*, pp. 8, 19–21.

71. See his "Geschichtliche Darstellung des Verfahrens der preussischen Unterrichtsverwaltung bei Einrichtung der Volksschulen in Gegenden mit konfessionell gemischter Bevölkerung," in *Centralblatt* (1878), pp. 337–39.

72. *Centralblatt* (1874), p. 549; idem (1875), p. 52.

73. GSA, Rep. 90, no. 2398a, school law draft of 1877, pp. 67–68 of the *Motive* appended to it.

74. Ibid., see Articles 81–88.

75. Schneider, *Ein halbes Jahrhundert*, pp. 369–76; *Stenographische Berichte über die Verhandlungen des Herrenhauses* (June 17, 1876), pp. 297–99.

76. *Jahrbuch für die amtliche Statistik des preussischen Staates* 5 (1883): 559.

77. HAM, Reg. Kassel, no. 192, county councillors' replies to the ministry's inquiry concerning the interconfessional schools on June 22, 1876.

78. Ludwig Friedrich Seyffardt, *Erinnerungen* (Leipzig, 1900), pp. 132–37. Horst Dräger overlooks completely the interconfessional school movement—an important chapter in the organization's history—in *Die Gesellschaft für Verbreitung von Volksbildung. Eine historisch-problemgeschichtliche Darstellung von 1871–1914* (Stuttgart, 1975).

79. *Sten. Berichte* (March 12, 1875), p. 749.

80. Seyffardt, *Erinnerungen*, p. 139. See also *Sten. Berichte* (March 12, 1875), p. 705; *Anlagen zu den Sten. Berichten* (1876), vol. 3, p. 1543. German liberals were critical of the Belgian school law of July 1, 1879, which excluded religious instruction from the public elementary schools and left this task to the parents and the clergy. The Catholics in Belgium reacted to the secularization of the public schools by establishing private schools under their legal right to teach. The Belgian experience made a profound impression on the Germans. See Jürgen Bona Meyer, *Der Kampf um die Schule. Historisch-pädagogische Erörterungen über die Fragen: Staatsschule oder Kirchenschule? Religionsunterricht und Staatsschule?* (Bonn, 1882), pp. 39, 83.

81. Jürgen Bona Meyer, *Die Simultanschulfrage* (Berlin, 1879), p. 84ff; Ludwig Wilhelm Seyffarth, *Die paritätische Schule* (Liegnitz, 1880), p. 75ff.

82. Jürgen Bona Meyer, *Zum Bildungskampf unserer Zeit* (Bonn, 1875), pp. 153–60. See also David Blackbourn, "Progress and Piety: Liberals, Catholics and the State in Bismarck's Germany," pp. 144–49.

83. Ludwig Friedrich Seyffardt, *Die katholische Volksschule am Niederrhein unter geistlicher Leitung* (Krefeid, 1876), pp. 11–22.

84. HAD, Reg. Köln, no. 2885, Linnig's proposals for the reform of the school system in Cologne, June 25 and December 2, 1874.

85. Ibid., no. 2886, district government to Mayor Becker, October 13, 1875.

86. Ibid., no. 2885, Mayor Bachem to the district government, May 5, 1875.

87. Ibid., district government to the minister of education, May 15, 1875.

88. Ibid., presbytery of the Protestant congregation in Cologne to the minister of education, May 11, 1875.

89. Ibid., no. 2886, minister of education to the district government, August 16, 1875.

90. Ibid., Mayor Becker to the district governor, February 22, 1877, and to the district government, March 15, 1877.

91. Ibid., district government to the minister of education, June 4, 1877; presbytery of the Protestant congregation to the district government, May 11, 1877.

92. Ibid., minister of education to Mayor Becker, July 9, 1877 [copy].

93. *Sten. Berichte* (November 30, 1877), pp. 632–33.

94. HAD, Reg. Düsseldorf, Präsidialbüro, no. 1317, Mayor Roos to the district government, September 24, 1875. See also Ludwig Friedrich Seyffardt, *Die Entwicklung des Simultanschulwesens in der Stadt Krefeld* (Bonn, 1881).

95. Helmut Croon, "Die Stadtvertretungen in Krefeld und Bochum im 19. Jahrhundert. Ein Beitrag zur Geschichte der Selbstverwaltung der rheinischen und westfälischen Städte," in Richard Dietrich and Gerhard Oestreich (eds.), *Forschungen zu Staat und Verfassung: Festgabe für Fritz Hartung* (Berlin, 1958), pp. 292–95.

96. HAD, Reg. Düsseldorf, Präsidialbüro, no. 1317, district government to Mayor Roos, October 30, 1875.

97. Ibid., Mayor Roos to the district government, January 22, 1876.

98. Seyffardt, *Die katholische Volksschule*, p. 33.

99. Seyffardt, *Erinnerungen*, p. 349.

100. Seyffardt, *Die katholische Volksschule*, pp. 32–33.

101. *Sten. Berichte* (February 23, 1876), pp. 188–90.

102. Ibid., pp. 190–92.

103. HAD, Reg. Düsseldorf, Präsidialbüro, no. 1317, Mayor Roos to the minister of education, March 8, 1876 [copy].

104. Ibid., minister of education to the district governor, April 6, 1876.

105. Ibid., district governor's report to Falk, April 11, 1876.

106. Seyffardt, *Die Entwicklung des Simultanschulwesens*, pp. 45, 59.

107. The circumstances in which Bitter's decision was made are not clear. When his successor came to the office, he found the correspondence missing in the files. HAD, Reg. Düsseldorf, Präsidialbüro, no. 1317, report of District Governor von Hagemeister to Falk, February 16, 1878.

108. LAK, Reg. Koblenz, no. 26316, Mayor Rau to *Landrat* Otto Agricola of Kreuznach county, June 11, 1874; county councillor to the district government, August 30, 1874; district government's reply of October 2, 1874.

109. Ibid., Mayor Rau to the minister of education, November 9, 1874.

110. Ibid., district government to *Landrat* Agricola, December 17, 1874; protocol of the Catholic school board in Kirn.

111. Ibid., district government to the minister of education, March 30, 1875.

112. Ibid., minister of education to the district government, April 26, 1875.

113. *Stenographische Berichte über die Verhandlungen des Herrenhauses* (June 17, 1876), p. 299.

114. LAK, Reg. Koblenz, no. 26316, district government's two reports to the minister of education, September 27, 1876, and September 9, 1878.

115. Ibid., report of September 9, 1878.

116. Meyer, *Die Simultanschulfrage*, p. 66.

117. HAD, Reg. Köln, nos. 2722, 2723, and 2725, correspondence concerning the removal of Catholic priests from local school inspection offices.

118. Ibid., nos. 2722 and 2725.

119. Ibid., no. 2725, Pastor Berrisch to the provincial governor, June 12, 1875;

district government's two letters to the provincial governor, July 2 and October 25, 1875; *Landrat* Wolff to the district government, October 19, 1875.

120. Meyer, *Die Simultanschulfrage*, pp. 22–24; *Der Schulfreund. Eine Quartalschrift zur Förderung des Elementarschulwesens und der Jugenderziehung* (1876): 165–66, 301–2.

121. Norbert Schlossmacher, *Düsseldorf im Bismarckreich*, pp. 39–40, 64–68, 248–53.

122. *Die Schulfrage oder was muss and soll die Schule sein?* (Paderborn, 1876), pp. 28–33.

123. *Archiv für katholisches Kirchenrecht* 36 (1876): 440–43.

124. *Verhandlungen des 25. Generalversammlung der Katholiken Deutschlands am 10.–13. September 1877*, pp. 159–60.

125. Albert Rosenkranz, *Abriss einer Geschichte der Evangelischen Kirche im Rheinland* (Düsseldorf, 1960), pp. 88–94.

126. *Vierteljahrshefte zur Statistik des Deutschen Reiches* (1873): 145.

127. Hermann Johann Graeber, *Die konfessionelle Schule. Ein Vortrag gehalten auf der Synode in Duisburg am 11. Februar 1876* (Ruhrort, 1876), p. 15.

128. Ibid., p. 15.

129. HAD, Reg. Düsseldorf, Präsidialbüro, no. 1317, "Zur Abgeordnetenwahl," a campaign leaflet published in 1876 by the *Verein zur Erhaltung der evangelischen Volksschule*.

130. *Verhandlungen der fünfzehnten Rheinischen Provinzial-Synode vom 19. September bis zum 6. Oktober 1874* (Neuwied, 1875), pp. 175–76.

131. Graeber, *Die konfessionelle Schule*, pp. 13–14. See also Pastor Karl Thönes' criticism of the establishment of interconfessional schools "for the purpose of the *Kulturkampf*" in *Was ist gegen und für konfessionell gemischte Volksschulen zu sagen?* (Barmen, 1877), pp. 30–37.

132. HAD, Reg. Düsseldorf, Präsidialbüro, no. 1317, *Consistorialrat* Natorp to the district governor, March 17, 1876; article on the meeting from the *Rhein- und Ruhrzeitung* (March 20, 1876).

133. Ibid., resolutions adopted by the Düsseldorf assembly on March 15, 1876.

134. Ibid., district government's order of March 14, 1876; district governor's letters to Graeber, March 10, 1876, and to Engelbert, March 17, 1876; article entitled "Der Kampf der rheinischen evangelischen Orthodoxie gegen unsere Staatsregierung" from the *Düsseldorfer Zeitung* (March 14, 1876).

135. *Stenographische Berichte über die Verhandlungen des Herrenhauses* (June 17, 1876), pp. 293–96.

136. HAD, Reg. Düsseldorf, Präsidialbüro, no. 1317, Hermann von Rath reported on his conversation with Falk in March in his letter to District Governor von Bitter, April 13, 1876.

137. *Centralblatt* (1876), pp. 495–96.

138. *Verhandlungen der sechzehnten Rheinischen Provinzial-Synode vom 15. September bis zum 1. Oktober 1877* (Elberfeld, 1878), p. 104.

139. HAD, Reg. Düsseldorf, Präsidialbüro, no. 1317, announcement of the founding committee of the *Verein zur Erhaltung der evangelischen Volksschule.*

140. Ibid., leaflets with the heading "Zur Abgeordnetenwahl! Von Freunden der evangelischen Volksschule an ihre Glaubensgenossen" and "An die Freunde der evangelischen Volksschule."

141. HAD, Reg. Düsseldorf, Präsidialbüro, no. 1309, *Kurze Mitteilungen für die Freunde der evangelischen Volksschule,* no. 10 (February/March 1878).

142. HAD, Reg. Düsseldorf, Präsidialbüro, no. 1317, minister of education to District Governor von Hagemeister, February 2, 1878; the district governor's reply of February 16, 1878.

143. LAK, Reg. Koblenz, no. 26316, Consistory of the Rhine Province to the Protestant High Church Council, January 18, 1878.

144. HAD, Reg. Düsseldorf, Präsidialbüro, no. 1317, General Superintendent Nieden to the district governor, February 20, 1878; the district governor's reply of April 10, 1878.

145. Ibid., district governor to the minister of education, April 24, 1879.

146. *Verhandlungen der ersten ordentlichen General-Synode der evangelischen Landeskirche Preussens, eröffnet am 9. Oktober 1879, geschlossen am 3. November 1879* (Berlin, 1880), pp. 565–66.

147. Margaret L. Anderson, *Windthorst,* pp. 229–33.

148. GSA, Rep. 30, no. 2398a, minutes of the Ministry of State's meeting on October 6, 1877.

149. *Sten. Berichte* (November 30, 1877), pp. 643–44.

150. LAK, Oberpräsidium, no. 15193, Cologne district government to the provincial governor, March 4, 1882. On the problems of School Inspector Klein, an Old Catholic, see his letter to the Düsseldorf district government, February 26, 1882; district government to the provincial governor, March 1, 1882.

151. LAK, Oberpräsidium, nos. 15191 and 15194; idem, Reg. Koblenz, nos. 26205 and 26206; idem, Reg. Trier, no. 2203, correspondence concerning the recruitment and appointment of county school inspectors.

152. HAD, Reg. Aachen, no. 2122, reports of the clerical school inspectors.

153. HAD, Reg. Aachen, Präsidialbüro, no. 2123; idem, Reg. Köln, no. 2777; LAK, Reg. Trier, no. 1033, school inspectors' reports and the correspondence of school officials in the district governments concerning the deficiencies in the schools.

154. *Centralblatt* (1881), pp. 200–201; *Jahrbuch für die amtliche Statistik des preussischen Staates* 5 (1883): 552–57; 568–69; *Preussische Statistik* 101 (1889), pp. 36–37.

155. *Jahrbuch für die amtliche Statistik* 5 (1883): 561; *Statistisches Handbuch für den preussischen Staat* 4 (1903): 420.

156. HAD, Reg. Aachen, no. 735, district government's school administration report, January 31, 1881.

157. Christa Berg overlooks a large body of archival evidence when she contends that Falk was not swayed by political considerations and made decisions in

school cases in an objective and unbiased manner. See Berg, *Die Okkupation der Schule*, pp. 112–13.

158. Ibid., p. 56.

159. *Sten. Berichte* (March 12, 1875), pp. 719–21; idem (February 24, 1877), p. 872; idem (November 30, 1877), pp. 643–45.

CHAPTER 3

1. Puttkamer's reply to the petition was reprinted in *Centralblatt* (1879), pp. 501–4.

2. An account of the Elbing school case was given in a report of the committee on school affairs in the House of Deputies in *Anlagen zu den Sten. Berichten* (1879–80), vol. 2, p. 1226.

3. Ibid., p. 1228.

4. *Sten. Berichte* (December 17, 1879), p. 672.

5. *Centralblatt* (1879), p. 503.

6. *Sten. Berichte* (December 15, 1880), p. 751.

7. *Centralblatt* (1880), pp. 228–29.

8. ZSA, Rep. 76 VII neu, sec. 1B, pt. I, no. 2, vol. 16, Archbishop of Cologne to the minister of education, March 19, 1889; the minister to the Cologne district government, April 10, 1889.

9. *Sten. Berichte* (March 17, 1882), p. 946.

10. The minister of education gave this report in the House of Deputies. *Sten. Berichte* (March 17, 1882), p. 947.

11. *Preussische Statistik* 176 (1903), pt. II, p. 50.

12. *Centralblatt* (1884), pp. 128–39.

13. *Anlagen zu den Sten. Berichten* (1900), vol. 3, p. 1556; *Sten. Berichte* (March 15, 1899), p. 1499.

14. *Sten. Berichte* (February 28, 1883), pp. 1004–5.

15. HAM, Reg. Kassel, no. 332, minister of education to the district government, January 24, 1882.

16. HAD, Reg. Düsseldorf, Präsidialbüro, no. 1318, provincial governor to the district governor, September 18, 1889; district governor's reply of October 28, 1889.

17. *Sten. Berichte* (February 23, 1893), pp. 1080–81.

18. *Anlagen zu den Sten. Berichten* (1900), vol. 3, pp. 1554–55; *Sten. Berichte* (March 13, 1900), p. 2895.

19. *Sten. Berichte* (March 13, 1900), pp. 2899–2901; idem (March 11, 1901), p. 3118ff.

20. LAK, Oberpräsidium, no. 15192, list of the county school inspectors in the entire state in 1908; Johannes Tews, *Ein Jahrhundert preussischer Schulgeschichte* (Leipzig, 1914), p. 169.

21. *Sten. Berichte* (December 17, 1879), pp. 667–69, 672–73; idem (February 11, 1880), p. 1635.

22. *Sten. Berichte* (February 28, 1883), p. 1004.

23. See Gossler's report of his findings in *Anlagen zu den Sten. Berichten* (1879–80), vol. 2, pp. 1233–34; *Sten. Berichte* (December 18, 1879), p. 704.

24. HAD, Reg. Düsseldorf, Präsidialbüro, no. 1317, minister of education to the district governor, January 28, 1880; two letters of Mayor Roos to the district government, April 7 and 16, 1880; district government to the minister, April 20, 1880.

25. Ibid., articles from the *Niederrheinische Volkszeitung* (March 20, 1880) and (April 17, 1880).

26. Ibid., district governor to the minister of education, September 11, 1880; Mayor Roos to the district government, October 15, 1880.

27. Ibid., district governor to the minister of education, November 3, 1880; minister to the district governor, March 25, 1881.

28. HAD, Reg. Düsseldorf, Präsidialbüro, no. 1318, district governor to the minister of education, March 25, 1882. On the classroom enrollment, see the article from the *Niederrheinische Volkszeitung* (March 18, 1882).

29. Ibid., district governor to the minister of education, October 6, 1882; Hagemeister's instructions to von Schütz, the director of the *Abteilung für Schulwesen*, September 22, 1882; district government to Mayor Küper, September 26, 1882.

30. *Preussische Statistik* 101 (1889), p. 33; idem, 176 (1903), pt. II, pp. 32–33.

31. Karl Schneider and Alwin Petersilie (eds.), *Die Volks- und die Mittelschulen im preussischen Staate im Jahre 1891* (Berlin, 1893), Appendix V; *Preussische Statistik* 176 (1902), pt. III, p. 177

32. *Preussische Statistik* 176 (1902), pt. III, pp. 166–67.

33. *Theologisches Jahrbuch für die evangelische Kirche in Deutschland* 20 (1893): 156; idem, 27 (1900): 141. On the demographic growth, geographic distribution, and internal migration of the Catholics and Protestants in the provinces of the Prussian state, see the informative analyses in *Kirchliches Handbuch für das katholische Deutschland* 1 (1907–1908): 82–87; idem, 2 (1908–1909): 191–218.

34. *Preussische Statistik* 101 (1889), pp. 32–33; idem, 176 (1903), pt. II, pp. 44–49; idem, 176 (1905), pt. I, p. 128; idem, 209 (1908), pt. I, pp. 64–65.

35. Margaret L. Anderson, *Windthorst*, pp. 296–97; Rudolf Morsey, "Die deutschen Katholiken und der Nationalstaat zwischen Kulturkampf und Erstem Weltkrieg," in Gerhard Ritter (ed.), *Deutsche Parteien vor 1918* (Köln, 1973), p. 272.

36. *Sten. Berichte* (February 5, 1880), p. 1426; idem (December 15, 1880), pp. 755–57; idem (March 17, 1882), pp. 950–51; idem (March 1, 1883), p. 1038; idem (February 6, 1884), pp. 1214–16.

37. On Catholic perceptions of a Protestant bias in the school administration, see especially Windthorst's comments in *Sten. Berichte* (December 6, 1890), p. 322.

38. *Sten. Berichte* (February 5, 1880), p. 1426; idem (December 15, 1880),

pp. 748–50, 755–57; idem (March 17, 1882), pp. 945–46; idem (February 28, 1883), pp. 1014–15; idem (February 6, 1884), pp. 1246–49.

39. *Verhandlungen der 27. Generalversammlung der Katholiken Deutschlands am 13.–16. September 1880*, pp. 315–18, 362–77; *Verhandlungen der 29. Generalversammlung der Katholiken Deutschlands am 11.–14. September 1882*, pp. 201–8.

40. Anderson, *Windthorst*, p. 266.

41. *Verhandlungen der 32. Generalversammlung der Katholiken Deutschlands vom 30. August bis 3. September 1885*, pp. 49–50, 310, 313.

42. Rudolf Morsey, "Georg Kardinal Kopp 1837–1914," in Rudolf Morsey (ed.), *Zeitgeschichte in Lebensbildern. Aus dem deutschen Katholizismus des 20. Jahrhunderts* (Mainz, 1973), pp. 15–17; Ronald Ross, "Critic of the Bismarckian Constitution: Ludwig Windthorst and the Relationship between Church and State in Imperial Germany," *Journal of Church and State* 21 (1979): 494–96.

43. Erwin Gatz (ed.), *Akten der Fuldaer Bischofskonferenz*, vol. 1, p. 765.

44. *Sten. Berichte* (February 23, 1893), pp. 1077–80. See also idem (February 22, 1895), p. 821; idem (February 28, 1896), pp. 910–11; idem (April 28, 1897), p. 2195; idem (March 15, 1898), p. 1474; idem (March 15, 1899), p. 1491.

45. Ibid. (March 1, 1894), pp. 757–62, 767–73; idem (March 15, 1898), pp. 1472–73.

46. Ibid. (March 1, 1894), pp. 762, 773; idem (February 22, 1895), pp. 822–24; idem (February 28, 1896), pp. 913–17; idem (April 28, 1897), p. 2204; idem (March 15, 1899), p. 1499.

47. Schneider and Petersilie (eds.), *Die Volks- und die Mittelschulen*, p. 185.

48. Otto von Bismarck, *Werke in Auswahl*, ed. by Gustav Adolf Rein et al. (Stuttgart, 1973), vol. 5, p. 530.

49. *Sten. Berichte* (March 18, 1882), p. 979; idem (February 28, 1885), p. 759.

50. *Centralblatt* (1881), p. 472.

51. *Jahrbuch für die amtliche Statistik des preussischen Staates* 5 (1883), pp. 562–63, 572, 574; *Centralblatt* (1880), p. 410.

52. *Jahrbuch für die amtliche Statistik*, p. 561; *Statistisches Handbuch für den Preussischen Staat* 1 (1888): 423; Schneider and Petersilie (eds.), *Die Volks- und die Mittelschulen*, pp. 168–69, 201.

53. *Jahrbuch für die amtliche Statistik*, pp. 556–57, 568–69; *Statistisches Handbuch für den Preussischen Staat* 1 (1888): 419; Schneider and Petersilie (eds.), *Die Volks- und die Mittelschulen*, p. 177.

54. Schneider und Petersilie (eds.), *Die Volks- und die Mittelschulen*, p. 80; *Preussische Statistik* 101 (1889), pp. 36–37; *Statistisches Handbuch für den Preussischen Staat* 1 (1888): 418.

55. *Preussische Statistik* 101 (1889), pp. 44–47, 53; Schneider and Petersilie (eds.), *Die Volks- und die Mittelschulen*, pp. 121, 127.

56. *Centralblatt* (1881), pp. 637–38; idem (1883), pp. 668–69. See also Gossler's statements in *Sten. Berichte* (March 1, 1883), p. 1041; idem (February 28, 1885), p. 767.

57. GSA, Rep. 84a, no. 4687, Bismarck to the minister of education, February 15, 1884.

58. Ibid., minister of education to the minister of justice, February 26, 1886; protocol of the Ministry of State meeting on March 7, 1886. Both documents record Bismarck's role in the drafting of this law. For the text of the law, see *Centralblatt* (1887), pp. 436–37.

59. *Sten. Berichte* (April 23, 1887), pp. 861–62.

60. Ibid., pp. 849–51, 867–68, 873–74.

61. Ibid., pp. 855–58; idem (April 26, 1887), pp. 902–903.

62. GSA, Rep. 84a, no. 4687, memorandum of the finance minister and the minister of education on the draft law, December 24, 1887.

63. For the text of the law, see *Centralblatt* (1888), pp. 497–98.

64. *Sten. Berichte* (May 25, 1888), p. 1623.

65. *Preussische Statistik* 176 (1905), pt. 1, pp. 213, 216, 219, 221.

66. GSA, Rep. 92, Nachlass Bosse, no. 10, vol. 9, Bosse's diaries, entry for February 20, 1899.

67. *Sten. Berichte* (January 30, 1896), pp. 193–95; idem (November 27, 1896), pp. 109–11. On the financial effects of this law on the big cities and on rural and small-town school districts, see the *Begründung* appended to the bill in *Anlagen zu den Sten. Berichten* (1896–1897), vol. 1, pp. 683–87.

68. See, for example, James Russell Parsons, Jr., *Prussian Schools through American Eyes. A Report to the New York State Department of Public Instruction* (Syracuse, N.Y., 1891); Charles Copeland Perry, *Reports on German Elementary Schools and Training Colleges* (London, 1887). Parsons and Perry were impressed by the successful enforcement of compulsory school attendance, the uniform curriculum and length of school hours prescribed by the General Regulations of 1872, the professionalization of teacher training, and the system of examinations set up for the certification of teachers. They seem to have paid little attention to the many deficiencies in rural education, especially in the provinces of East Elbia.

69. *Preussische Statistik* 176 (1905), pt. I, pp. 70, 124, 218.

70. Ibid., pt. I, pp. 108–11; idem, 176 (1903), pt. II, pp. 14–22, 64–65.

71. Ibid., pt. I, pp. 82–83; see also idem, 209 (1908), pt. I, pp. 25–26, pt. II, pp. 2–3.

CHAPTER 4

1. Lawrence Schofer, *The Formation of a Modern Labor Force. Upper Silesia, 1865–1914* (Berkeley, 1975), p. 32; Lech Trzeciakowski, "The Prussian State and the Catholic Church in Prussian Poland 1871–1914," pp. 629–34.

2. *Preussische Statistik* 101 (1889), pp. 22–25, 42. This inquiry of the Ministry of Education in 1886 may well be the most reliable statistical record of the use of the Polish language in the eastern districts. After 1890 official statisticians showed a marked tendency to inflate the number of German-speaking inhabi-

tants. Inaccuracies in the figures on the two nationalities in many bilingual areas make the censuses of 1905 and 1910 of questionable value, if not worthless. See Volker Hentschel, "Wirtschaftliche Entwicklung, soziale Mobilität und nationale Bewegung in Oberschlesien 1871–1914," in Werner Conze, Gottfried Schramm, and Klaus Zernack (eds.), *Modernisierung und nationale Gesellschaft im ausgehenden 18. und im 19. Jahrhundert* (West Berlin, 1979), pp. 244, 255.

3. Rudolf Korth, *Die preussische Schulpolitik und die polnischen Schulstreiks* (Würzburg, 1963), pp. 37–38; John Jacob Kulczycki, *School Strikes in Prussian Poland, 1901–1907: The Struggle over Bilingual Education* (New York, 1981), pp. 3–4.

4. Korth, *Die preussische Schulpolitik*, p. 38.

5. *Sten. Berichte* (February 9, 1872), pp. 698–702; idem (February 10, 1872), pp. 729–31. On Bismarck's Polish policies, see Richard Blanke, *Prussian Poland in the German Empire 1871–1900* (New York, 1981), p. 17ff; William Hagen, *Germans, Poles, and Jews: The Nationality Conflict in the Prussian East, 1772–1914* (Chicago, 1980), p. 124ff.

6. ZSA, Rep. 76 VII neu, sec. 6B, pt. I, no. 1, vol. 9, Posen district government's triennial school administration reports in 1893 and 1896 comment on the extensive responsibilities entrusted to the county school inspectors.

7. Christa Berg, *Die Okkupation der Schule*, p. 56.

8. *Sten. Berichte* (February 24, 1877), pp. 858–60; idem (December 18, 1879), p. 697.

9. *Jahrbuch für die amtliche Statistik des preussischen Staates* 5 (1883): 559–60.

10. *Sten. Berichte* (December 18, 1879), pp. 696–97; idem (February 5, 1880), p. 1450.

11. Gustav Lange, *Die Simultanschule in der Ostmark, ihre historische Entwicklung und ihr gegenwärtiger Stand* (Lissa, 1905), pp. 32–38; idem, "Das Volksschulwesen in der Provinz Posen," *Pädagogische Abhandlungen* (Bielefeld, 1901), vol. 6, no. 8, pp. 144, 163–65.

12. GSA, Rep. 30, Abt. II, no. 2522, vol. 1, Bromberg district government's report to the provincial governor, May 29, 1900.

13. On the observations of the ministry's councillors on the tour, see Gustav Wätzoldt's remarks in the *Sten. Berichte* (January 31, 1874), p. 982.

14. Karl Schneider (ed.), *Volksschulwesen*, pp. 55–59. In comparison, the school language regulation issued in 1878 for the instruction of Danish schoolchildren in North Schleswig was moderate because of the strong stand that the provincial governor took against any measure suppressing the Danish language in the schools completely. See Oswald Hauser, "Polen und Dänen im Deutschen Reich," in Theodor Schieder and Ernst Deuerlein (eds.), *Reichsgründung 1870–71. Tatsachen—Kontroversen—Interpretationen* (Stuttgart, 1970), pp. 310–12. In the Alsace-Lorraine, the German administration extended the use of German in the elementary schools in the French-speaking areas with great reserve over a long transition period and allowed many exceptions to the German language

requirements. See Dan S. Silverman, *Reluctant Union. Alsace–Lorraine and Imperial Germany 1871–1918* (University Park, Pa., 1972), p. 76ff.

15. Schneider (ed.), *Volksschulwesen*, pp. 60–62.

16. Erich Schmidt-Volkmar, *Der Kulturkampf*, p. 168ff; Zygmunt Zielinski, "Der Kulturkampf in der Provinz Posen," p. 453ff.

17. ZSA, Rep. 76 VII neu, sec. 6B, pt. I, no. 1, vol. 8, Karl Schneider's school inspection reports, November 9, 10, and 24, 1887.

18. *Sten. Berichte* (November 30, 1877), p. 623.

19. ZSA, Rep. 76 VII neu, sec. 6B, pt. I, no. 1, vol. 8, Posen district government to the minister of education, February 16, 1887.

20. *Centralblatt* (1880), pp. 354–56.

21. *Centralblatt* (1882), pp. 134–38.

22. *Jahrbuch für die amtliche Statistik des preussischen Staates* 5 (1883): 550–51; Schneider and Petersilie, *Die Volks- und die Mittelschulen*, Appendix II.

23. ZSA, Rep. 76 VII neu, sec. 6B, pt. I, no. 7, vol. 1, minister of education to the provincial governor of Posen, February 28, 1888.

24. GSA, Rep. 30, Abt. II, no. 2858, vol. 1, the archbishop's directive to the archdeacons in his diocese, October 27, 1887; provincial governor of Posen to Archbishop Dinder, December 27, 1887.

25. ZSA, Rep. 76 VII neu, sec. 6B, pt. I, no. 7, vol. 1, minister of education to the provincial governor of Posen, February 28, 1888. On Gossler's relationship with Archbishop Dinder, see Erwin Gatz (ed.), *Akten zur preussischen Kirchenpolitik in den Bistümern Gnesen–Posen, Kulm und Ermland 1885–1914* (Mainz, 1977), pp. xxvii–xxxiii, 44–45, 55, 63.

26. ZSA, Rep. 76 VII neu, sec. 6B, pt. I, no. 7, vol. 1, Posen district government to the minister of education, August 14, 1888; GSA, Rep. 30, Abt. II, no. 2858, vol. 2, provincial governor to the Bromberg district government, March 11, 1889.

27. ZSA, Rep. 76 VII neu, sec. 6B, pt. 1, no. 7, vol. 1, two lists of Catholic clergymen who were denied permission to direct religious instruction in the schools, enclosed in the provincial governor's report to the minister on February 2, 1889; see also the Bromberg district government's report, September 18, 1888.

28. Ibid., provincial governor to the minister of education, November 24, 1890; article from the *Germania* (June 22, 1888), no. 141, reporting on the reaction of the clergy in Posen. See also Jażdżewski's criticism of the conditions set by the government in *Sten. Berichte* (May 6, 1891), p. 2200.

29. ZSA, Rep. 76 VII neu, sec. 6B, pt. I, no. 7, vol. 2, Archbishop Stablewski to the minister of education, February 24, 1896; provincial governor to the archbishop, July 12, 1896.

30. ZSA, Rep. 76 I, sec. 31, lett. "K," no. 71, article on Kuegler's professional career from the *Berliner Tageblatt* (December 18, 1889), no. 642; articles criticizing his anti-Polish school policy from the *Germania* (October 22, 1898), and the *Kölnische Volkszeitung* (October 21, 1898).

31. Ibid., Gossler to King William I, December 5, 1889, recommending Kuegler's promotion to the rank of ministerial director.

32. ZSA, Rep. 76 VII neu, sec. 7B, pt. I, no. 1, vol. 6, minister of education to the Bromberg district government, May 2, 1885; *Sten. Berichte* (February 24, 1886), pp. 766–67.

33. *Sten. Berichte* (February 6, 1884), pp. 1230–31; idem (February 24, 1886), pp. 768–69.

34. For an account of the two cabinet meetings on January 10 and 24, 1886, see Blanke, *Prussian Poland*, p. 51ff; Joachim Mai, *Der preussisch-deutsche Polenpolitik 1885/87* (Hauptstadt der D.D.R. Berlin, 1962), p. 103ff.

35. *Sten. Berichte* (February 24, 1886), pp. 747–53.

36. ZSA, Rep. 76 VII neu, sec. 6B, pt. I, no. 1, vol. 8, the minister's letter to the Posen district government, July 26, 1886, summarized the discussion at the conference of June 23.

37. Ibid.

38. Ibid.

39. Ibid., provincial governor to the minister of education, February 27, 1889.

40. ZSA, Rep. 76 VII neu, sec. 6B, pt. I, no. 1, vol. 8, translated article from the *Dziennik Poznański* (December 14, 1888), no. 287.

41. *Sten. Berichte* (February 23, 1887), pp. 429–30.

42. ZSA, Rep. 76 VII neu, sec. 1B, pt. I, no. 3, vol. 14, article from the *Germania* (June 17, 1900); idem, Rep. 76 VII neu, sec. 4B, pt. I, no. 1, vol. 8, two reports of the Danzig district government to the minister of education, August 23, and September 1, 1900.

43. ZSA, Rep. VII neu, sec. 4B, pt. I, no. 1, vol. 8, three reports of the Danzig district government to the minister of education, June 17, 1890, April 15, 1892, and November 4, 1894.

44. Ibid., articles on the issue of *Imparität* in the school system of West Prussia from the *Germania* on August 21, 1890, and October 18, 1893, the *Schlesische Volkszeitung* on December 25 and 28, 1889, and October 16, 1893, and the *Westpreussisches Volksblatt* on January 16, 1892. *Sten. Berichte* (February 27, 1885), pp. 739–41; idem (March 12, 1890), pp. 657–59; idem (February 26, 1895), pp. 927–31, 945, 950–51.

45. Karl Schneider and Alwin Petersilie (eds.), *Die Volks- und die Mittelschulen*, Appendix V.

46. ZSA, Rep. 76 VII neu, sec. 1B, pt. I, no. 3, vol. 12, article from the *Germania* (June 19, 1892).

47. ZSA, Rep. 76 VII neu, sec. 4B, pt. I, no. 1, vol. 8, minister of education to the Danzig district government, March 15, 1890; the district government's reply of June 17.

48. Ibid., minister of education to the district governments in Danzig and Marienwerder, October 30, 1890.

49. ZSA, Rep. 76 VII neu, sec. 6B, pt. I, no. 1, vol. 8, minister of education to the Posen district government, July 20, 1886.

50. Ibid., Posen district government to the provincial governor, August 17, 1887.

51. *Centralblatt* (1887), p. 664.

52. *Sten. Berichte* (February 24, 1877), pp. 859–60; see also *Anlagen zu den Sten. Berichten* (1876), vol. 3, p. 1547ff, for the House committee's report on the protests of Polish Catholics in Upper Silesia against the introduction of German as the language of religious instruction in the schools.

53. *Sten. Berichte* (January 25, 1888), pp. 141–42.

54. *Sten. Berichte* (March 20, 1889), pp. 1195–98, 1202–3, 1206.

55. ZSA, Rep. 76 VII neu, sec. 7B, pt. I, no. 1, vol. 7, Bromberg district government to the minister of education, April 15, 1890; idem, Rep. 76 VII neu, sec. 6B, pt. I, no. 1, vol. 9, Posen district government to the minister, March 24, 1890.

56. ZSA, Rep. 76 VII neu, sec. 6B, pt. I, no. 1, vol. 9, two reports of the Posen district government to the minister of education, March 9, 1891.

57. ZSA, Rep. 76 VII neu, sec. 6B, pt. I, no. 2, vol. 2, Posen district government's report to the minister of education, January 4, 1897, citing the provincial governor's directive.

58. *Sten. Berichte* (February 13, 1893), p. 804.

59. ZSA, Rep. 76 VII neu, sec. 6B, pt. I, no. 1, vol. 9, Posen district government to the minister of education, September 13, 1889.

60. Ibid. The district government forwarded to Berlin a report from School Inspector Lux of the city of Posen, August 9, 1889, advising the school authorities not to permit the establishment of private schools for Polish children.

61. Blanke, *Prussian Poland*, p. 126.

62. Ibid., p. 130; Korth, *Die preussische Schulpolitik*, p. 49.

63. Gatz (ed.), *Akten zur preussischen Kirchenpolitik*, pp. 154–57.

64. Ibid., pp. 157–58; GSA, Rep. 92, Nachlass Bosse, no. 8, vol. 7, Bosse's diaries, entries for May 24, July 9, 14, and 15, 1893.

65. Korth, *Die preussische Schulpolitik*, pp. 50–51; Kulczycki, *School Strikes*, p. 33.

66. *Sten. Berichte* (February 13, 1893), p. 803; idem (February 23, 1895), pp. 851–52; idem (February 27, 1896), p. 875.

67. *Sten. Berichte* (February 27, 1896), pp. 875–76; idem (February 28, 1896), p. 900.

68. *Sten. Berichte* (February 23, 1895), p. 852; idem (February 27, 1896), p. 876; idem (February 28, 1896), p. 900.

69. *Sten. Berichte* (February 27, 1896), p. 872; idem (February 28, 1896), p. 894ff; idem (April 28, 1897), pp. 2211–12.

70. ZSA, Rep. 76 VII neu, sec. 6B, pt. I, no. 1, vol. 9, Posen district government's triennial school administration reports in 1893 and 1896; vol. 10, the report in 1902.

71. *Statistisches Handbuch für den preussischen Staat* 4 (1903): 419–20.

72. Quoted in Blanke, *Prussian Poland*, p. 75.

73. GSA, Rep. 84a, no. 4088, finance minister's memorandum of February 18, 1896, on the draft law concerning the maintenance of continuation schools in Posen and West Prussia.

74. ZSA, Rep. 76 VII neu, sec. 7B, pt. I, no. 1, vol. 6, minister of education to the Bromberg district governor, March 7, 1886.

75. ZSA, Rep. 76 VII neu, sec. 7B, pt. I, no. 1, vol. 7, Bromberg district government's triennial school administration report in 1893; idem, Rep. 76 VII neu, sec. 6B, pt. I, no. 1, vol. 9, Posen district government's triennial school administration report in 1896.

76. *Preussische Statistik* 176 (1905), pt. I, pp. 116, 124.

77. ZSA, Rep. 76 VII neu, sec. 6B, pt. I, no. 1, vol. 9, Ferdinand von Hansemann to the minister of education, June 8, 1892.

78. ZSA, Rep. 76 VII neu, sec. 7B, pt. I, no. 1, vol. 7, provincial governor's postscript, February 9, 1894, appended to the Bromberg district government's triennial school administration report in 1893.

79. Blanke, *Prussian Poland*, pp. 193–94.

80. ZSA, Rep. 76 VII neu, sec. 7B, pt. I, no. 1, vol. 6, Dr. Peters' report to the Bromberg district government, June 17, 1888.

81. GSA, Rep. 30, Abt. II, no. 2522, vol. 1, Bromberg district government to the county councillors, March 15, 1889; idem, Rep. 30, Abt. II, no. 2523, reports of the county councillors to the Bromberg district government; Bromberg district government to the minister of education, February 20, 1890.

82. ZSA, Rep. 76 VII neu, sec. 7B, pt. I, no. 1, vol. 7, Bromberg district government's triennial school administration report in 1893.

83. Ibid., triennial school administration reports in 1896 and 1899.

84. Ibid.

85. ZSA, Rep. 76 VII neu, sec. 6B, pt. I, no. 2, vol. 2, two reports of the Posen district government to the minister of education, July 25, 1896, and June 23, 1897.

86. Ibid., Posen district government to the minister of education, July 25, 1896.

87. Ibid., three reports of the Posen district government to the minister of education, January 4, 1897, September 28, 1898, and October 19, 1898.

88. Ibid., Posen district government to the minister of education, April 20, 1899.

89. *Sten. Berichte* (March 7, 1900), pp. 2471–73.

90. GSA, Rep. 30, Abt. II, no. 2522, vol. 1, Minister of Commerce Brefeld to the minister of education, November 13, 1899 [copy].

91. ZSA, Rep. 76 VII neu, sec. 7B, pt. I, no. 1, vol. 7, Preische's report on his school inspection tour in the Bromberg district, December 20, 1898; idem, Rep. 76 VII neu, sec. 6B, pt. I, no. 1, vol. 9, Preische's memorandum to the minister of education, January 6, 1900.

92. GSA, Rep. 30, Abt. II, no. 2522, vol. 1, minister of education to the provincial governor, November 30, 1899.

93. ZSA, Rep. 76 VII neu, sec. 6B, pt. I, no. 1, vol. 9, minister of education to the district governments in Bromberg and Posen, January 30, 1900.

94. GSA, Rep. 30, Abt. II, no. 2522, vol. 1, Provincial Governor Bitter to the Posen district government, January 12, 1900.

95. ZSA, Rep. 76 VII neu, sec. 6B, pt. I, no. 1, vol. 10, "Denkschrift über die Lage des Volksschulwesens in der Provinz Posen."

96. GSA, Rep. 30, Abt. II, no. 2964, county councillors' reports on the voting of schoolteachers in the elections of the House of Deputies and the Reichstag.

97. Adam Galos, "Der deutsche Ostmarkenverein von 1894 bis 1900," in Felix-Heinrich Gentzen (ed.), *Die Hakatisten. Der deutsche Ostmarkenverein 1894–1934* (Berlin, 1966), pp. 85–86; Hagen, *Germans, Poles, and Jews*, pp. 178–79, 188–89.

98. *Sten. Berichte* (March 20, 1903), pp. 3554–57.

99. GSA, Rep. 6B, no. 89, Posen district government to the county councillors, July 11, 1904; idem, Rep. 30, Abt. II, no. 2964, *Landrat* of Gnesen county to the Bromberg district government, December 8, 1903; provincial governor to the Bromberg district government, March 1, 1906; idem, Rep. 30, Abt. II, no. 2972, minister of education to the Bromberg district government, July 29, 1904.

100. *Sten. Berichte* (March 15, 1899), p. 1463ff; idem (March 5, 1902), pp. 2799–2800; idem (March 14, 1903), pp. 3040–41, 3046.

101. *Sten. Berichte* (March 12, 1900), p. 2834ff; idem (March 1, 1901), p. 2540; United States Bureau of Education, *Annual Report of the Commissioner of Education for 1910* (1911), vol. 2, pp. 684, 1336–37. School expenditures per pupil were $12.67 in Prussia in 1905, $17.63 in England and Wales in 1908, and $26.27 in the United States in 1905–1906. The outlays per capita were $2.94, $3.02, and $3.66, respectively.

102. *Sten. Berichte* (March 15, 1899), p. 1465.

103. *Sten. Berichte* (March 14, 1903), p. 3046.

104. Hagen, *Germans, Poles, and Jews*, pp. 192–93.

105. ZSA, Rep. 92, Nachlass Schmidt–Ott A LXXX, no. 1, vol. 4, District Governor Guenther of Bromberg to the provincial governor, August 7, 1905; District Governor Krahmer of Posen to the provincial governor, August 7, 1905.

106. Ibid., Provincial Governor Waldow to the minister of education, September 17, 1905.

107. ZSA, Rep. 76 VII neu, sec. 6B, pt. I, no. 1, vol. 10, Posen district government's triennial school administration reports in 1905 and 1908.

108. *Preussische Statistik* 209 (1908), pt. II, pp. 233–34.

109. Ibid., pp. 2, 14; GSA, Rep. 30, Abt. II, no. 2522, vol. 2, Bromberg district government to the minister of education, June 15, 1905; ZSA, Rep. 92, Nachlass Schmidt–Ott A LXXX, no. 14, vol. 2, surveys on the number of overcrowded schools.

110. GSA, Rep. 30, Abt. II, no. 2570, county school inspectors' reports to the Bromberg district government in 1910.

111. *Preussische Statistik* 176 (1905), pt. I, pp. 141–59. See also ZSA, Rep. 76 VII neu, sec. 6B, pt. I, no. 1, vol. 10, Posen district government's triennial school administration report in 1908; Gustav Lange, "Das Volksschulwesen der Provinz Posen im Spiegel der Statistik," *Posener Lehrerzeitung* (October 15, 1908), no. 42.

112. GSA, Rep. 30, Abt. II, no. 2522, vol. 1, Bromberg district government's report to the provincial governor, May 29, 1900.

113. ZSA, Rep. 76 VII neu, sec. 6B, pt. I, no. 7, vol. 2, Bromberg district government to the provincial governor, April 29, 1898; provincial governor to the minister of education, June 29, 1898. See also the district government's triennial school administration reports in 1899 and 1902 in Rep. 76 VII neu, sec. 7B, pt. I, no. 1, vol. 7.

114. Stating that the government's school policy in Posen took a sharply anti-Polish course after Studt entered office, Rudolf Korth speculates that the final ascendancy of a nationalistic school policy was occasioned by his appointment. He writes (*Die preussische Schulpolitik*, p. 63) that the archival records give no information on the circumstances of the *Kursverschärfung*. I believe, to the contrary, that there is sufficient archival evidence that demonstrates that the pressure for changing the school language policy for religious instruction came from the school administrators in the province, whose arguments were heavily based on political considerations.

115. ZSA, Rep. 76 VII neu, sec. 6B, pt. I, no. 2, vol. 2, Posen district government to the minister of education, June 24, 1900; see also its letter to him on May 18, 1900.

116. Ibid., minister of education to the Posen district government, July 16, 1900; the district government to the minister, July 24, 1900.

117. Korth, *Die preussische Schulpolitik*, p. 64.

118. ZSA, Rep. 76 VII neu, sec. 6B, pt. I, no. 2, vol. 3, Studt's handwritten marginal note on the Posen district government's report of July 21, 1901, discloses these facts. The documents are not in the file.

119. ZSA, Rep. 76 VII neu, sec. 6B, pt. I, no. 1, vol. 10, Posen district government's triennial school administration report in 1902.

120. GSA, Rep. 30, Abt. II, no. 2886, Bromberg district government to the county councillors of *Kreise* (counties) Filehne and Czarnikau, June 16, 1901.

121. ZSA, Rep. 76 VII neu, sec. 6B, pt. I, no. 1, vol. 7, Bromberg district government's triennial school administration report in 1902.

122. Ibid.; GSA, Rep. 30, Abt. II, no. 2886, Bromberg district government to the minister of education, October 7, 1902.

123. On the Wreschen affair, see Korth, *Die preussische Schulpolitik*, p. 82ff; Kulczycki, *School Strikes*, p. 49ff.

124. Korth, *Die preussische Schulpolitik*, pp. 95–101.

125. ZSA, Rep. 92, Nachlass Studt, no. 17, Kuegler's memorandum on the events in Wreschen, December 8, 1901.

126. *Sten. Berichte* (January 13, 1902), pp. 88–90; idem (March 5, 1902), pp. 2780–83.

127. Witold Jakóbczyk, "Der deutsche Ostmarkenverein von 1900 bis 1914," in Gentzen (ed.), *Die Hakatisten*, pp. 239–41.

128. *Sten. Berichte* (January 13, 1902), p. 53.

129. *Sten. Berichte* (January 15, 1902), pp. 179–82.

130. *Sten. Berichte* (January 13, 1902), pp. 94–101.

131. Ibid., pp. 86–88; *Sten. Berichte* (January 15, 1902), pp. 219–21; see also idem (March 8, 1902), p. 2932.

132. Korth, *Die preussische Schulpolitik*, pp. 120–21.

133. Kulczycki, *School Strikes*, pp. 91–95.

134. Korth, *Die preussische Schulpolitik*, pp. 133–34.

135. In the House of Deputies, Jażdżewsky expressed the bitterness of the Catholic clergy in Posen. See *Sten. Berichte* (March 5, 1902), pp. 2771–72.

136. *Stenographische Berichte über die Verhandlungen des Reichstags* (December 5, 1906), p. 4163.

137. ZSA, Rep. 77, tit. 863B, no. 1, vol. 1, protocol of the Ministry of State's meeting on November 27, 1906.

138. Ibid., minister of education to the king of Prussia, October 13, 1906; memorandum of the minister of education to the Ministry of State, October 23, 1906.

139. Ibid., provincial governor to the ministers of education and the interior, October 20, 1906.

140. Ibid., memorandum of the minister of education to the Ministry of State, October 23, 1906.

141. Ibid., provincial governor to the minister of the interior, October 16, 1906.

142. Ibid., guidelines for countermeasures against the strikes sent by the provincial governor to the two district governments on October 13, 1906.

143. ZSA, Rep. 76 VII neu, sec. 6B, pt. I, no. 1, vol. 10, Posen district government's triennial school administration report in 1908 gave a summary of the countermeasures that were used to break the school strikes.

144. ZSA, Rep. 76 VII neu, sec. 6B, pt. I, no. 1, vol. 9, article from the *Preussische Lehrerzeitung* (July 10, 1898), no. 159.

145. Jakóbczyk, "Der deutsche Ostmarkenverein von 1900 bis 1914," p. 148.

146. ZSA, Rep. 77, tit. 863B, no. 1, vol. 3, translated articles from the *Gazeta Grudziadska* on July 30 and August 15, 1907, criticizing the conduct of the schoolteachers during the strike.

147. Ibid., vol. 2, reports of the Bromberg district governor to the minister of the interior, November 29, December 15, and December 20, 1906, and January 16 and March 15, 1907.

148. Ibid., provincial governor to the minister of the interior, February 16, 1907; idem, vol. 3, provincial governor to the minister of the interior, December 3, 1907.

149. Ibid., vol. 2, Posen district governor to the minister of education, March 27, 1907 [copy].

150. GSA, Rep. 6B, no. 84, Posen district government to the county school inspectors, April 24, 1907; district government to the county councillors, April 30, 1907.

151. ZSA, Rep. 77, tit. 863B, no. 1, vol. 2, translated article from the *Kurjer*

Poznański on December 8, 1906. On the rift between the Center party and the Polish *Fraktion* during the school strike, see Kulczycki, *School Strikes*, p. 172ff.

152. ZSA, Rep. 77, tit. 863B, no. 1, vol. 2, translated articles from the *Postemp* (May 18, 1907); idem, vol. 3, from the *Kurjer Poznański* (June 2, 1907), and the *Gazeta Polska* (June 4, 1907).

153. This decision was made at the meeting of the provincial governor with the district governors on October 10, 1906, and was listed in the guidelines of countermeasures. See footnote 142.

154. ZSA, Rep. 92, Nachlass Studt, no. 22, Studt to Hermann von Lucanus, the chief of the civil cabinet, September 7, 1907. This passage in the first draft of Studt's letter was subsequently deleted.

155. ZSA, Rep. 77, tit. 863B, no. 1, vol. 3, Schiemann's memorandum under the heading "Zur Polenfrage," January 19, 1908.

156. Ibid., minister of education to Chancellor Bernhard von Bülow, January 17, 1908; minister of the interior to minister of education, January 30, 1908; provincial governor of Posen to minister of education, March 7, 1908; provincial governor of West Prussia to the minister of education, March 10, 1908.

157. Ibid., two letters of the minister of the interior to the minister of education, January 30 and April 16, 1908.

158. Ibid., Undersecretary of State Loebell to the minister of education, May 20, 1908, writing that the chancellor agreed that Schiemann's proposal could not be considered for the reasons given by Holle.

159. Ibid., two letters of the minister of education to Chancellor Bernhard von Bülow, January 17 and April 30, 1908.

CHAPTER 5

1. Anderson, "The Prussian Volksschule in the Nineteenth Century," p. 276; Field, "Religion in the German Volksschule, 1890–1928," pp. 45, 52.

2. *Centralblatt* (1883), pp. 586–87.

3. ZSA, Rep. 92, Nachlass Studt, no. 11, Bosse's memorandum to the Ministry of State, December 24, 1898, on the problems of school maintenance in Silesia; *Sten. Berichte* (March 1, 1883), pp. 1023–25; idem (April 23, 1888), pp. 1253–54.

4. *Anlagen zu den Sten. Berichten* (1887), vol. 3, pp. 2086–87.

5. *Sten. Berichte* (May 14, 1887), pp. 1286–87.

6. *Sten. Berichte* (April 23, 1888), pp. 1253–57.

7. *Sten. Berichte* (March 8, 1889), pp. 916, 918; idem (March 11, 1889), p. 944.

8. Folkert Meyer examines the school bills of Gossler and Zedlitz in the context of the state government's fight against Social Democracy in *Schule der Untertanen*, pp. 166, 172–78. See also Titze, *Die Politisierung der Erziehung*, pp. 226–33. To depict Zedlitz's school bill as "a kind of *Kampfgesetz* against Social Democracy" is to confuse the tactics of Chancellor von Caprivi in a parliamentary counteroffensive against his National Liberal critics with the actual purpose of the bill.

9. "Begründung des Entwurfs eines Gesetzes, betreffend die öffentliche Volksschule," in *Anlagen zu den Sten. Berichten* (1890–1891), vol. 1, pp. 454, 465; HAM, Reg. Kassel, no. 6129, Cabinet Order of May 1, 1889; the directive of the Ministry of Education to the district governments and the provincial school boards on the implementation of the emperor's decree, dated October 13, 1890. The minister's guidelines aimed at strengthening the instruction of history in the *Lehrerseminare* and emphasizing the history of Germany in modern times in the new editions of schoolbooks.

10. *Sten. Berichte* (December 5, 1890), pp. 288, 303.

11. *Sten. Berichte* (December 6, 1890), p. 322.

12. *Kölnische Volkszeitung* (December 6, 7, and 9, 1890).

13. *Sten. Berichte* (December 6, 1890), pp. 313–14.

14. *Sten. Berichte* (March 11, 1889), p. 941; idem (December 6, 1890), pp. 316, 336.

15. John C. G. Röhl (ed.), *Philipp Eulenburgs politische Korrespondenz* (Boppard, 1976), vol. 1, p. 628.

16. Erwin Gatz (ed.), *Akten der Fuldaer Bischofskonferenz*, vol. 2, p. 130ff.

17. Ibid., p. 135ff; ZSA, Rep. 77, tit. 123, no. 10, vol. 8, protocol of the Ministry of State's meeting on December 7, 1890.

18. Victor Rintelen, *Der Volksschulgesetz-Entwurf des Ministers Dr. von Gossler und die Verhandlungen der Volksschulgesetz-Kommission des Preussischen Abgeordnetenhauses* (Mainz, 1891), p. 73ff.

19. Erwin Gatz (ed.), *Akten der Fuldaer Bischofskonferenz*, vol. 2, pp. 144, 147, 153–55.

20. *Kölnische Volkszeitung* (March 12 and 14, 1891).

21. J. Alden Nichols, *Germany after Bismarck*, pp. 19, 100; John C. G. Röhl, *Germany without Bismarck*, pp. 50, 79.

22. *Neue Preussische Zeitung* (December 4, 1890), no. 567; idem (December 8, 1890), no. 574.

23. *Neue Preussische Zietung* (April 3, 1891), no. 154; idem (April 4, 1891), no. 155; Friedrich Zillessen, *Der von Gossler'sche Volksschul-Gesetzentwurf, von evangelisch-kirchlichem Standpunkte aus beurteilt* (Berlin, 1891), pp. 5–28. Protestant laymen and clergymen attending the general synod in 1891 were critical of the school bill. See *Verhandlungen der dritten ordentlichen General-Synode der evangelischen Landeskirche Preussens* (Berlin, 1892), p. 708ff.

24. ZSA, Rep. 77, tit. 123, no. 10, vol. 9, protocol of the Ministry of State's meeting on April 12, 1891.

25. "Begründung des Entwurfs eines Volksschulgesetzes," in *Anlagen zu den Sten. Berichten* (1892), vol. 2, pp. 919–20; see Zedlitz's speech in *Sten. Berichte* (May 4, 1891), p. 2143.

26. ZSA, Rep. 77, tit. 123, no. 10, vol. 9, Zedlitz to the minister of the interior, October 16, 1891.

27. "Entwurf eines Volksschulgesetzes," in *Anlagen zu den Sten. Berichten* (1892), vol. 2, pp. 880–916.

28. "Begründung des Entwurfs," pp. 923–24.

29. ZSA, Rep. 77, tit. 123, no. 10, vol. 9, finance minister's memorandum, November 26, 1891.

30. Ibid., protocol of the meeting of the Ministry of State on December 23, 1891.

31. Nichols, *Germany after Bismarck*, pp. 162–63.

32. *Kölnische Volkszeitung* (January 12, 1892).

33. Gatz (ed.), *Akten der Fuldaer Bischofskonferenz*, vol. 2, pp. 216–17.

34. *Sten. Berichte* (January 22, 1892), pp. 40, 65ff.

35. *Sten. Berichte* (January 25, 1892), pp. 89–93, 104; idem (January 26, 1892), pp. 147–48; idem (January 28, 1892), pp. 168–75; idem (January 29, 1892), pp. 200–201. See also Jürgen Bona Meyer, *Gegen den Entwurf eines Volksschulgesetzes. Ein Mahnruf an Preussens deutsches Gewissen* (Bonn, 1892), pp. 28–29, 44–46; Heinrich von Treitschke, *Der Entwurf des preussischen Volksschulgesetzes* (Stuttgart, 1892), reprinted in his *Deutsche Kämpfe. Schriften zur Tagespolitik* (Leipzig, 1896), p. 410ff.

36. *Sten. Berichte* (January 29, 1892), pp. 212–13.

37. *Sten. Berichte* (January 26, 1892), p. 148.

38. *Sten. Berichte* (January 25, 1892), pp. 95–97; idem (January 28, 1892), pp. 152–53.

39. *Sten. Berichte* (January 29, 1892), p. 201.

40. Röhl (ed.), *Eulenburgs politische Korrespondenz*, vol. 2, p. 748. On the finance minister's attempt to resign, see Nichols, *Germany after Bismarck*, p. 167; Kurt Richter, *Der Kampf um den Schulgesetzentwurf des Grafen Zedlitz-Trützschler vom Jahre 1892* (Halle, 1934), pp. 65–66.

41. The accounts of the political conflict over the school bill of 1892 in the works by Nichols and Richter, cited above, surprisingly do not discuss this aspect of the liberal opposition. The evidence of anti-Catholicism in the controversy is abundant.

42. ZSA, Rep. 77, tit. 123, no. 10, vol. 9, protocol of the meeting of the *Städtetag* in Westphalia on February 24, 1892.

43. *Kirchliche Korrespondenz. Organ des Evangelischen Bundes zur Wahrung der deutsch-protestantischen Interessen* 4 (1890): 288; A. Wächter, *Der Evangelische Bund nach zwanzig Jahren* (Leipzig, 1906), p. 2ff. See also Klaus Erich Pollmann, *Landesherrliches Kirchenregiment und soziale Frage. Der evangelische Oberkirchenrat der altpreussischen Landeskirche und die sozialpolitische Bewegung der Geistlichen nach 1890* (Berlin, 1973), pp. 65–70.

44. LAK, Oberpräsidium, no. 10394, the declaration of the Evangelical Union published in the *Sonntagsblatt für innere Mission* (March 6, 1892), no. 10.

45. Willibald Beyschlag, *Gegen die neue Volksschulgesetz-Vorlage*, 2nd ed. (Berlin, 1892), pp. 6–7.

46. LAK, Oberpräsidium, no. 10394, report of the assembly of the *Freunde der evangelischen Volksschule* in Düsseldorf on February 17, 1892, in *Sonntagsblatt für innere Mission* (March 6, 1892), no. 10, Beilage.

47. *Neue Preussische Zeitung* (March 18, 1892), no. 132.

48. Norman Rich and M. H. Fisher (eds), *The Holstein Papers* (Cambridge, 1961), vol. 3, pp. 400–401, 406; Röhl (ed.), *Eulenburgs politische Korrespondenz*, vol. 2, pp. 750, 771–72.

49. Röhl (ed.), *Eulenburgs politische Korrespondenz*, vol. 2, pp. 788–91.

50. Ibid., pp. 796–98.

51. Ibid., pp. 824–27.

52. Nichols, *Germany after Bismarck*, pp. 180–81.

53. GSA, Rep. 92, Nachlass Bosse, no. 8, vol. 7, Bosse's diaries, entry for March 24, 1892. Zedlitz discussed the reasons for his resignation with his successor on this day.

54. Nichols, *Germany after Bismarck*, pp. 182–83.

55. GSA, Rep. 92, Nachlass Bosse, no. 8, vol. 7, Bosse's diaries, entry for March 22, 1892; Röhl (ed.), *Eulenburgs politische Korrespondenz*, vol. 2, pp. 822–23.

56. *Sten. Berichte* (April 28, 1892), p. 1383.

57. *Neue Preussische Zeitung* (March 21, 1892), no. 136; idem (March 23, 1892), no. 140.

58. *Sten. Berichte* (April 28, 1892), pp. 1381–82; idem (April 29, 1892), pp. 1416, 1435.

59. *Kölnische Volkszeitung* (January 14, 1892), no. 26; idem (January 24, 1892), no. 47; idem (February 2, 1892), no. 64; *Sten. Berichte* (April 29, 1892), pp. 1433–34.

60. *Sten. Berichte* (April 28, 1892), p. 1381.

61. *Sten. Berichte* (May 4, 1893), pp. 2230, 2234.

62. *Sten. Berichte* (January 30, 1896), pp. 179–80.

63. Ibid., pp. 191–93.

64. *Sten. Berichte* (April 22, 1896), p. 1289.

65. GSA, Rep. 92, Nachlass Bosse, no. 8, vol. 7, Bosse's diaries, entry for March 7, 1896.

66. Ibid., entries for April 19 and 25, 1897.

67. *Sten. Berichte* (March 9, 1899), pp. 1267, 1271.

68. GSA, Rep. 92, Nachlass Bosse, no. 8, vol. 9, Bosse's diaries, entries for March 11, 18, and 19, 1899.

69. *Sten. Berichte* (April 19, 1899), p. 1923.

70. GSA, Rep. 92, Nachlass Bosse, no. 8, vol. 9, Bosse's diaries, entries for August 27 and 31 and September 23, 1899.

71. *Sten. Berichte* (April 19, 1899), p. 1907.

72. Georg F. Dasbach, *Imparität im Volksschulwesen* (Trier, 1899).

73. *Sten. Berichte* (February 26, 1895), pp. 927–29; idem (April 28, 1897), p. 2193; idem (April 29, 1897), pp. 2232–33.

74. See the statement of Chapuis, an official in the ministry, in *Sten. Berichte* (April 7, 1897), p. 2118.

75. *Sten. Berichte* (February 26, 1895), p. 931; idem (May 15, 1898), p. 1495.

See also *Verhandlungen der 39. Generalversammlung der Katholiken Deutschlands vom 28. August bis 1. September 1892*, p. 334.

76. *Sten. Berichte* (March 29, 1900), p. 3701ff.

77. Ibid., p. 3716.

78. Ibid., p. 3721.

79. ZSA, Rep. 77, tit. 1124, no. 10, vol. 11, Studt to the Ministry of State, January 22, 1901.

80. Ibid., finance minister to the Ministry of State, January 30, 1901.

81. ZSA, Rep. 92, Nachlass Studt, no. 11, Kuegler's memorandum to Studt, February 4, 1901.

82. *Sten. Berichte* (February 14, 1893), pp. 836, 841; idem (March 1, 1895), pp. 1057–58; idem (March 4, 1901), pp. 2670–72.

83. *Sten. Berichte* (March 4, 1901), p. 2679. On the new perspective of the Center party leadership in the 1890s, see Blackbourn, "The Problem of Democratization: German Catholics and the Role of the Centre Party," p. 164ff; Loth, *Katholiken im Kaiserreich*, pp. 74–80; Rudolf Morsey, "Die deutschen Katholiken und der Nationalstaat zwischen Kulturkampf und Erstem Weltkrieg," in Gerhard Ritter (ed.), *Deutsche Parteien vor 1918* (Köln, 1973), p. 279ff.

84. *Sten. Berichte* (March 4, 1901), p. 2711; idem (March 11, 1901), p. 3130.

85. ZSA, Rep. 77, tit. 1124, no. 10, vol. 11, Grundzüge eines Gesetzes, betreffend die Unterhaltung der öffentlichen Volksschulen.

86. Ibid., minister of education to the minister of the interior, June 26, 1900.

87. Ibid., minister of the interior to the minister of education, August 2, 1900.

88. Ibid., minister of education to the minister of the interior, December 19, 1900.

89. Ibid., finance minister to the minister of the interior, June 22, 1901.

90. HAM, Oberpräsidium, no. 1127, minister of education to the provincial governor of Hesse–Nassau, October 10, 1901. This stenciled directive was sent to all provincial governors.

91. ZSA, Rep. 77, tit. 1124, no. 10, vol. 11, Studt's letter to the finance and interior ministers on March 5, 1902, summarized the conclusions of the provincial governors' reports.

92. HAM, Oberpräsidium, no. 1127, provincial governor of Hesse–Nassau to the minister of education, December 12, 1901.

93. ZSA, Rep. 76 I, sec. 31, lett. "K," no. 71, article on Kuegler from the *Germania* (October 22, 1898).

94. ZSA, Rep. 76 I, sec. 31, lett. "S," no. 134, Otto Pautsch's articles on Schwartzkopff from the *Berliner Abendpost* (September 21, 1911) and *Der Tag* (June 5, 1914). On the reasons for Studt's choice of Schwartzkopff, see idem, Rep. 92, Nachlass Studt, no. 18, Studt to Chancellor von Bülow, March 16, 1902; idem, no. 17, Undersecretary of State Wever to Studt, July 15, 1906.

95. ZSA, Rep. 76 I, sec. 31, lett. "S," no. 134, articles on Schwartzkopff from the *Magdeburgische Zeitung* (September 20, 1911) and the *Weser Zeitung* (September 26, 1907).

96. ZSA, Rep. 77, tit. 1124, no. 10, vol. 12, minister of education to the minister of the interior, May 31, 1903; protocol of the discussions of the councillors representing the education, finance, and interior ministers on December 14, 1903, and January 5, 1904.

97. Ibid., Grundzüge eines Gesetzes, betreffend die Unterhaltung und örtliche Verwaltung der öffentlichen Volksschulen [1903].

98. Ibid., minister of education to the minister of the interior, May 31, 1903.

99. Ibid., protocols of the interdepartmental discussions on October 17 and December 10, 1903.

100. Ibid., memorandum of the minister of the interior on the draft of the school law, August 6, 1903; protocols of the interdepartmental discussions on October 17 and December 10, 1903.

101. Ibid., protocols of the interdepartmental discussions on July 21 and October 17, 1903.

102. Ibid., protocols of the interdepartmental discussions on October 17, 1903, and July 5, 1904.

103. Ibid., protocols of the interdepartmental discussion on December 10, 1903.

104. Ibid.

105. ZSA, Rep. 2.2.1, no. 22493, vol. 3, Studt's letter to Emperor William on May 21, 1904, gave an account of the negotiations.

106. *Kölnische Volkszeitung* (May 14, 1904), no. 398.

107. *Sten. Berichte* (May 13, 1904), p. 5331.

108. Ibid., pp. 5337–38.

109. Ibid., p. 5348ff.

110. In the House of Deputies, Hackenberg baited the Center party with his attacks on "ultramontanism" and his defense of the Evangelical Union. See *Sten. Berichte* (March 7, 1900), pp. 2485–86; idem (March 5, 1901), pp. 2759–61.

111. *Kölnische Volkszeitung* (May 15, 1904), no. 402, reprinted an article from the National Liberal organ, the *Kölnische Zeitung*, explaining the reasons for the decision of the *Fraktion*; *Neue Preussische Zeitung* (May 19, 1904), no. 231.

112. *Kölnische Volkszeitung* printed excerpts of articles from the National Liberal press in no. 402 (May 15, 1904) and no. 405 (May 16, 1904).

113. *Freisinnige Zeitung* (May 18, 1904), no. 115.

114. *Freisinnige Zeitung* (May 28, 1904), no. 123; idem (June 5, 1904), no. 130; idem (June 10, 1904), no. 134; *Kölnische Volkszeitung* (May 27, 1904), no. 435; idem (June 6, 1904), no. 464.

115. *Kölnische Volkszeitung* (May 27, 1904), no. 436; idem (May 31, 1904), no. 447; idem (June 1, 1904), no. 450; idem (June 2, 1904), no. 452; idem (June 10, 1904), no. 476.

116. *Kölnische Volkszeitung* (May 18, 1904), no. 410; *Freisinnige Zeitung* (June 14, 1904), no. 137, quoted the National Liberals' official organ.

117. *Berliner Tageblatt* (June 13, 1904), no. 295; *Kölnische Volkszeitung* (June 14, 1904), no. 488.

118. *Freisinnige Zeitung* (May 15, 1904), no. 113; idem (June 14, 1904), no. 137; idem (June 15, 1904), no. 138.

119. *Neue Preussische Zeitung* (May 18, 1904), no. 229.

120. *Kölnische Volkszeitung* (May 27, 1904), no. 435; idem (June 1, 1904), no. 450.

121. ZSA, Rep. 77, tit. 1124, no. 10, vol. 13, minister of education to the finance and interior ministers, August 30, 1904; the letter of the interior minister to Studt on April 28, 1905, referred to the December conference.

122. ZSA, Rep. 92, Nachlass Schmidt–Ott A LXXX, no. 1, vol. 4, minister of education to the provincial governors, June 30, 1905; GSA, Rep. 30, Abt. II, no. 2754, minister of education to the provincial governors of Posen and West Prussia, July 15, 1905.

123. *Preussische Statistik* 209 (1908), pt. I, pp. 21, 25–26; pt. II, pp. 2–3.

124. Ibid., pt. I, p. 64; pt. II, pp. 44–45.

125. ZSA, Rep. 92, Nachlass Schmidt–Ott A LXXX, no. 1, vol. 4, the replies of the district and provincial governors to the minister's inquiry of June 30, 1905 [copies].

126. Ibid., replies of the district governors of Merseburg and Münster, July 28 and July 31, 1905, respectively.

127. Ibid., replies of the district governors of Frankfurt an der Oder and Potsdam, August 6 and August 28, 1905, respectively.

128. On the diverse rights of the communes in the appointment of the schoolteachers, see the statistical data in the "Begründung des Entwurfs eines Gesetzes, betreffend die öffentlichen Schulen" in *Anlagen zu den Sten. Berichten* (1890–91), vol. 1, pp. 482–83.

129. "Begründung des Entwurfs eines Gesetzes, betreffend die Unterhaltung der öffentlichen Volksschulen" in *Sammlung der Drucksachen des Preussischen Hauses der Abgeordneten* (1905–1906), vol. 1, p. 221.

130. ZSA, Rep. 92, Nachlass Schmidt–Ott A LXXX, no. 1, vol. 4, replies of the district governor of Breslau and the provincial governor of Saxony, August 14 and August 17, 1905, respectively.

131. Ibid., reply of the provincial governor of Posen, September 17, 1905.

132. Ibid., replies of the district governors of Bromberg and Posen on the same date, August 7, 1905.

133. Ibid., replies of the district governors of Danzig and Marienwerder, August 12 and August 18, 1905, respectively; reply of the provincial governor of West Prussia, August 26, 1905.

134. Ibid., replies of the district governor of Oppeln and the provincial governor of Silesia, August 12 and August 28, 1905, respectively.

135. ZSA, Rep. 77, tit. 1124, no. 10, vol. 13, two letters of the minister of the interior to the minister of education, October 5 and 13, 1905.

136. ZSA, Rep. 92, Nachlass Schmidt–Ott A LXXX, no. 1, vol. 4, minister of education to the Ministry of State, October 27, 1905.

137. Ibid.

138. ZSA, Rep. 92, Nachlass Studt, no. 11, Schwartzkopff to the minister of education, November 27, 1905; no. 12, Schwartzkopff's memorandum on the National Liberals and the interconfessional school question, n.d., Bl. 27–39.

139. ZSA, Rep. 2.2.1, no. 22493, vol. 3, minister of education to Emperor William, November 28, 1905.

140. Ibid., minister of education to Hermann von Lucanus, the chief of the Civil Cabinet, November 29, 1905.

141. ZSA, Rep. 92, Nachlass Studt, no. 11, Studt's memorandum, November 1, 1905. Studt had good reason to expect Cardinal Kopp's cooperation. During the preparation of the school bill in 1905, the Catholic bishops in Prussia were moderate in their demands and no longer insisted that the school law regulate matters that had proved so controversial in the debate over the school bill of 1892. Writing at the behest of the episcopacy, Kopp demanded provisions safeguarding the confessional character of the schools and the position of the parish priests as local school inspectors and members of the local school boards. See idem, Rep. 77, tit. 1124, no. 10, vol. 13, Kopp to the minister of education, July 3, 1905 [copy].

142. ZSA, Rep. 92, Nachlass Studt, no. 11, Schwartzkopff to the minister of education, November 23, 1905.

143. ZSA, Rep. 2.2.1, no. 22493, vol. 3, minister of education to Emperor William, November 28, 1905.

144. For the government's draft of the school law and the amendments made by the House Committee, see *Sammlung der Drucksachen des Preussischen Hauses der Abgeordneten* (1905–1906), vol. 7, p. 4017ff.

145. ZSA, Rep. 92, Nachlass Studt, no. 12, Schwartzkopff's memorandum, n.d., Bl. 27–39; "Begründung des Entwurfs eines Gesetzes," in *Sammlung der Drucksachen* (1905–1906), vol. 1, p. 205.

146. "Begründung des Entwurfs eines Gesetzes," p. 205; "Bericht der 12. Kommission über den Gesetzentwurf, betreffend die Unterhaltung der öffentlichen Volksschulen," in *Sammlung der Drucksachen* (1905–1906), vol. 7, p. 3823.

147. *Centralblatt* (1898), p. 725.

148. "Bericht der 12. Kommission über den Gesetzentwurf," p. 3867.

149. "Begründung des Entwurfs eines Gesetzes," p. 217.

150. Albert Ernst, a school principal and a Progressive deputy, expressed this complaint in the first reading of the school bill. *Sten. Berichte* (December 12, 1905), p. 250. See also Johannes Tews' criticism of Studt's lack of contact with the teaching profession in *Ein Jahrhundert preussischer Schulgeschichte*, p. 230.

151. *Pädagogisches Jahrbuch* 3 (1906): 72–73; ZSA, Rep. 92, Nachlass Studt, no. 12, Studt's note on the teachers' associations, n.d., Bl. 69.

152. See Heydebrand's criticism of the teachers' associations in *Sten. Berichte* (December 11, 1905), p. 180.

153. *Berliner Tageblatt* (December 19, 1905), no. 645; idem (December 21, 1905), no. 649; idem (December 23, 1905), no. 653; idem (December 29, 1905), no. 660; *Pädagogisches Jahrbuch* 3 (1906): 185ff.

154. Johannes Tews, *Schulkämpfe der Gegenwart. Vorträge zum Kampf um die Volksschule in Preussen* (Leipzig, 1906), p. 24. At the national convention of the German Teachers' Association on June 5 and 6, 1906, Carl Pretzel led the Prussian delegation in opposition to a resolution in favor of secular schools introduced by radicals in the teaching profession in Bremen and Hamburg. See *Berliner Tageblatt* (June 8, 1906), no. 285; *Pädagogische Zeitung* (August 16, 1906), no. 33, pp. 686–87; Friedrich Köhne and Carl L. A. Pretzel, *Die Simultanschule in Nassau, Hessen und Baden* (Berlin, 1906), pp. 47–49.

155. Johannes Tews, *Die preussische Schulvorlage* (Berlin, 1906), pp. 17–18.

156. Ibid., p. 42, see also Julius Kopsch's speech in *Sten. Berichte* (May 25, 1906), pp. 5263–64.

157. *Berliner Tageblatt* (December 18, 1905), no. 643; idem (December 21, 1905), no. 649; idem (January 2, 1906), no. 2; idem (January 6, 1906), no. 10.

158. "Verzeichnis der bei dem Hause der Abgeordneten zu dem Entwurfe eines Gesetzes, betreffend die Unterhaltung der öffentlichen Volksschulen, eingegangenen Petitionen" in *Sammlung der Drucksachen* (1905-1906), vol. 7, pp. 4048-57.

159. *Berliner Tageblatt* (January 15, 1906), no. 26.

160. *Berliner Tageblatt* (March 10, 1906), no. 127.

161. *Berliner Tageblatt* (February 5, 1906), no. 64; Max Quarck, "Volksbildung und Sozialdemokratie," *Sozialistische Monatshefte* (1906), no. 9, pp. 756–57.

162. Tews, *Schulkämpfe der Gegenwart*, p. 47.

163. Karl Kautsky, *Das Erfurter Programm in seinem grundsätzlichen Teil*, 3rd ed. (Stuttgart, 1899), p. 204. When the Social Democrats' official press discussed the elimination of religious instruction in the public schools, it avoided anticlerical polemics and argued from the principle that "religion is a private matter." ZSA, Rep. 76 VII neu, sec. 1B, pt. I, no. 2, vol. 19, articles from the *Vorwärts* (August 17, 1900) and (August 30, 1900).

164. Norbert Schwarte, *Schulpolitik und Pädagogik der deutschen Sozialdemokratie an der Wende vom 19. und 20. Jahrhundert* (Köln, 1980), pp. 134–37, 145, 338.

165. Ibid., pp. 365-67. Following the vote on the school bill compromise of May 13, 1904, in the House of Deputies, Heinrich Schulz and Klara Zedkin tried without success to put the school question on the agenda of the party's congress in Bremen that year. After the congress Hugo Lindemann criticized his party for not taking a stand in the current school conflicts in Prussia and complained that the Social Democratic leadership did not have a full understanding of the importance of the school question.

166. Vernon L. Lidtke, *The Alternative Culture. Socialist Labor in Imperial Germany* (New York, 1985), p. 159ff.

167. Karl Christ, *Sozialdemokratie und Volkserziehung. Die Bedeutung des Mannheimer Parteitages der SPD im Jahre 1906 für die Entwicklung der Bildungspolitik und Pädagogik der deutschen Arbeiterbewegung vor dem Ersten Weltkrieg* (Frankfurt am Main, 1975), pp. 87–89; Schwarte, *Schulpolitik und Pädagogik*, pp. 369–70.

168. Christ, *Sozialdemokratie und Volkserziehung*, pp. 90–91.

169. Leo Arons, "Die Volksschulvorlage im Preussischen Landtag," *Sozialistische Monatshefte* (1906), no. 1, pp. 10–11; Schwarte, *Schulpolitik und Pädagogik*, pp. 368–71.

170. *Kölnische Zeitung* (January 2, 1906), no. 1.

171. *Berliner Tageblatt* (January 9, 1906), no. 14.

172. *Sten. Berichte* (May 23, 1906), pp. 5107–12; see also *Freisinnige Zeitung* (May 23, 1906), no. 238.

173. *Sten. Berichte* (May 23, 1906), pp. 5115–19.

174. *Berliner Tageblatt* (March 24, 1906), no. 152; idem (April 27, 1906), no. 212; *Pädagogisches Jahrbuch* 4 (1907): 60.

175. *Freisinnige Zeitung* (April 14, 1906), no. 175.

176. "Bericht der 12. Kommission über den Gesetzentwurf," p. 3876.

177. Ibid., p. 3969.

178. ZSA, Rep. 2.2.1, no. 22493, vol. 3, Studt to the chief of the emperor's Civil Cabinet, May 7, 1906.

179. Ibid., Studt to the chief of the emperor's Civil Cabinet, May 6, 1906.

180. ZSA, Rep. 92, Nachlass Studt, no. 13, Studt's memorandum, May 14, 1906.

181. Ibid., typewritten memorandum prepared from Studt's notes, May 12, 1906.

182. *Neue Preussische Zeitung* (July 7, 1906), no. 312. For the text of the School Law of July 28, 1906, and the final wording of Articles 59–61 on the appointment of teachers and principals, see *Centralblatt* (1906), pp. 651–52.

183. Excerpts of the articles in the Free Conservative and National Liberal newspapers were printed in the *Kölnische Volkszeitung* (April 11, 1906), no. 306 and (April 18, 1906), no. 325.

184. *Sten. Berichte* (May 25, 1906), pp. 5233–34.

185. *Neue Preussische Zeitung* (March 28, 1906), no. 146; idem (May 6, 1906), no. 210.

186. ZSA, Rep. 92, Nachlass Studt, no. 13, Studt's memorandums, May 12 and 14, 1906; idem, Rep. 2.2.1, no. 22493, vol. 3, Studt to the chief of the emperor's Civil Cabinet, May 27, 1906.

187. See Articles 8 and 9 in the school law in *Centralblatt* (1906), pp. 625–26.

188. *Sten. Berichte* (May 22, 1906), p. 5058.

189. ZSA, Rep. 2.2.1, no. 22493, vol. 3, Studt to the chief of the emperor's Civil Cabinet, May 6, 1906.

190. *Sten. Berichte* (May 23, 1906), p. 5121. At the *Katholikentag* Porsch spoke about the "mixed feelings" of the Center party toward the new school law. While he declared that no other major European state safeguarded confessional schooling as much as Prussia, he pointed out that the school law fell far short of what the Center party wanted. *Verhandlungen der 53. Generalversammlung der Katholiken Deutschlands vom 19. bis 23. August 1906*, pp. 213–19.

191. *Sten. Berichte* (May 23, 1906), p. 5125.

192. "Verzeichnis der bei dem Hause der Abgeordneten zu dem Entwurfe eines Gesetzes, betreffend die Unterhaltung der öffentlichen Volksschulen, eingegangenen Petitionen," p. 4066.

193. ZSA, Rep. 92, Nachlass Studt, no. 12, "Bemerkungen zu der Eingabe des Kirchenvorstands der Katholischen Gemeinde zu Frankfurt am Main von 10. April 1906," written by Lezius, the ministry's legal councillor, on May 29, 1905.

194. *Kölnische Volkszeitung* (May 26, 1906), no. 451.

195. G. Noth, *Die Simultanschulfrage* (Jena, 1906), pp. 7–8. On Jewish opposition to the school bill and the efforts of the *Verband der deutschen Juden* to amend it, see Marjorie Lamberti, *Jewish Activism in Imperial Germany. The Struggle for Civil Equality* (New Haven, Conn., 1978), p. 139ff.

196. On the differences between the Catholic Teachers' Association and the liberal leadership of the German Teachers' Association, see Josef Tymister, *Die Entstehung der Berufsvereine der katholischen Lehrerschaft in Deutschland. Beiträge zur Schul- und Standespolitik der katholischen Lehrerschaft im 19. Jahrhundert* (Köln, 1965), pp. 177–80, 252–54.

197. Tews, *Die preussische Schulvorlage*, p. 7.

198. Tews, *Schulkämpfe der Gegenwart*, pp. 43–44, 65.

199. For the text of the petitions, see Ernst Rudolf Huber and Wolfgang Huber (eds.), *Staat und Kirche im 19. und. 20. Jahrhundert*, pp. 145–48.

200. *Pädagogische Zeitung* (July 12, 1906), no. 28, pp. 590–91.

201. Noth, *Die Simultanschulfrage*, pp. 35–37; ZSA, Rep. 76 VII neu, sec. 1B, pt. I, no. 2, vol. 19, article from the *Deutsch-evangelische Korrespondenz* (December 29, 1903), entitled "Zur Konfessionalität der Volksschule," discussed how the National Liberals had changed their views.

202. Theodor Kaftan, *Die Schule im Dienste der Familie, des Staates und der Kirche* (Hamburg, 1906), pp. 23–25.

203. *Monats-Korrespondenz für die Mitglieder des Evangelischen Bundes* 19 (1905): 259.

204. Tews, *Schulkämpfe der Gegenwart*, p. 70.

205. Wolfgang Köllmann, *Sozialgeschichte der Stadt Barmen im 19. Jahrhundert* (Tübingen, 1960), pp. 206–7; Antje Kraus, "Gemeindeleben und Industrialisierung. Das Beispiel des evangelischen Kirchenkreises Bochum," in Jürgen Reulecke and Wolfhard Weber (eds.), *Fabrik, Familie, Feierabend. Beiträge zur Sozialgeschichte des Alltags im Industriezeitalter* (Wuppertal, 1978), pp. 273–95; Vernon L. Lidtke, "Social Class and Secularization in Imperial Germany. The Working Classes," *Leo Baeck Institute Year Book* 25 (1980): 22ff; Rainer Marbach, *Säkularisierung und sozialer Wandel im 19. Jahrhundert* (Göttingen, 1978b), p. 37ff; Karl Rohe, "Konfession, Klasse und lokale Gesellschaft als Bestimmungsfaktoren des Wahlverhaltens," in Lothar Albertin and Werner Link (eds.), *Politische Parteien auf dem Weg zur parlamentarischen Demokratie in Deutschland* (Düsseldorf, 1981), pp. 112–20; Stanley Suval, *Electoral Politics in Wilhelmine Germany*, pp. 59–78.

Sources

ARCHIVES

Zentrales Staatsarchiv, Abteilung Merseburg
Rep. 2.2.1, Zivilkabinett
Rep. 76, Kultusministerium
Rep. 77, Ministerium des Innern
Rep. 92, Nachlass Friedrich Schmidt-Ott
Rep. 92, Nachlass Konrad von Studt
Rep. 151, Finanzministerium

Geheimes Staatsarchiv, Berlin-Dahlem
Rep. 6B, Landratsamt Meseritz
Rep. 30, Regierungsbezirk Bromberg—Abteilung für Kirchen- und Schulwesen
Rep. 84a, Preussisches Justizministerium
Rep. 90, Staatsministerium—Abteilung Q, Unterrichtssachen
Rep. 92, Nachlass Robert von Bosse

Hauptstaatsarchiv Düsseldorf, Zweigstelle Schloss Kalkum
Regierung Aachen—Präsidialbüro; Abteilung für Kirchen- und Schulwesen
Regierung Düsseldorf—Präsidialbüro; Abteilung für Kirchen- und Schulwesen
Regierung Köln—Abteilung für Kirchen- und Schulwesen

Hessisches Staatsarchiv, Marburg
Bestand 150, Oberpräsidium der Provinz Hessen-Nassau
Bestand 166, Regierung Kassel—Abteilung für Kirchen- und Schulwesen

Landeshauptarchiv Koblenz
Bestand 403, Oberpräsidium der Rheinprovinz
Bestand 441, Regierungsbezirk Koblenz
Bestand 442, Regierungsbezirk Trier

NEWSPAPERS AND PERIODICALS

Archiv für katholisches Kirchenrecht (Mainz) 1876–1880
Berliner Tageblatt (Berlin) 1904–1906

Centralblatt für die gesamte Unterrichtsverwaltung in Preussen (Berlin) 1860–1914

Freisinnige Zeitung (Berlin) 1904–1906

Kirchliches Handbuch für das katholische Deutschland (Freiburg) 1907–1914

Kirchliche Korrespondenz. Organ des Evangelischen Bundes zur Wahrung der deutsch-protestantischen Interessen (Leipzig) 1887–1914

Kölnische Volkszeitung (Köln) 1890–1892, 1904–1906

Neue Preussische Zeitung (Berlin) 1890–1892, 1904–1906

Pädagogische Zeitung. Hauptorgan des Deutschen Lehrervereins (Berlin) 1906

Pädagogisches Jahrbuch. Rundschau auf dem Gebiete des Volksschulwesens (Berlin) 1904–1906

Der Schulfreund. Eine Quartalschrift zur Förderung des Elementarschulwesens und der Jugenderziehung (Trier) 1872–1879

Sozialistische Monatshefte (Berlin) 1904–1906

Theologisches Jahrbuch für die evangelische Kirche in Deutschland (Gütersloh) 1893–1914

Newspaper clippings in the archive files

STATISTICS

Jahrbuch für die amtliche Statistik des preussischen Staates

Mitteilungen des Statistischen Bureaus in Berlin

Preussische Statistik. Vol. 101: *Das gesamte Volksschulwesen im preussischen Staate im Jahre 1886.* Berlin, 1889.

———. Vol. 176: *Das gesamte niedere Schulwesen im preussischen Staate im Jahre 1901,* pts. I–III. Berlin, 1902–1905.

———. Vol. 209: *Das gesamte niedere Schulwesen im Jahre 1906,* pts. I–III. Berlin, 1908.

———. Vol. 231: Das niedere Schulwesen in Preussen im Jahre 1911, pts. I–II. Berlin, 1913.

Schneider, Karl, and Petersilie, Alwin, eds. *Die Volks- und die Mittelschulen im preussischen Staate im Jahre 1891.* Berlin, 1893.

Statistik des Deutschen Reiches

Statistisches Handbuch für den preussischen Staat

Tabellen und amtliche Nachrichten über den preussischen Staat für das Jahr 1849. Vol. 2. Berlin, 1851.

United States Bureau of Education. *Annual Report of the Commissioner of Education,* 1893–1894, 1907–1911.

Zeitschrift des königlich preussischen Statistischen Bureaus

OTHER PRIMARY SOURCES

Adler, Salo. *Das Schulunterhaltungsgesetz und die preussischen Bürger jüdischen Glaubens.* Frankfurt am Main, 1906.

Anlagen zu den Stenographischen Berichten über die Verhandlungen des Hauses der Abgeordneten. Berlin, 1860–1904.

Auler, H. *Die Volksschule (confessionell oder konfessionslos) und die Schulinspektion.* Bonn, 1882.

Aus der Duisburger II. Generalversammlung des Evangelischen Bundes. Halle, 1888.

Beyschlag, Willibald. *Gegen die neue Volksschulgesetz-Vorlage.* 2nd ed. Berlin, 1892.

Bismarck, Otto von. *Werke in Auswahl.* Ed. by Gustav Adolf Rein et al. 8 vols. Stuttgart, 1962–1983.

Constabel, Adelheid, ed. *Die Vorgeschichte des Kulturkampfes. Quellenveröffentlichung aus dem deutschen Zentralarchiv.* Hauptstadt der D.D.R. Berlin, 1957.

Dasbach, Georg Friedrich. *Imparität im Volksschulwesen.* Trier, 1899.

Dörpfeld, Friedrich Wilhelm. *Gesammelte Schriften.* Vol. 9: *Ein Beitrag zur Leidensgeschichte der Volksschule.* Gütersloh, 1899.

Foerster, *Das Schulunterhaltungsgesetz und die Zukunft der evangelischen Schulen in Frankfurt am Main.* Frankfurt am Main, 1906.

Gatz, Erwin, ed. *Akten der Fuldaer Bischofskonferenz 1871–1899.* 2 vols. Mainz, 1977–1979.

————. *Akten zur preussischen Kirchenpolitik in den Bistümern Gnesen–Posen, Kulm und Ermland 1885–1914.* Mainz, 1977.

Gneist, Rudolf. *Die konfessionelle Schule. Ihre Unzuverlässigkeit nach preussischen Landesgesetzen.* Berlin, 1869.

————. *Die Selbstverwaltung der Volksschule.* Berlin, 1869.

————. *Die Simultanschule.* Berlin, 1880.

————. *Die staatsrechtliche Fragen des preussischen Volksschulgesetzes.* Berlin, 1892.

Graeber, Hermann Johann. *Die konfessionelle Schule. Ein Vortrag gehalten auf der Synode in Duisburg am 11. Februar 1876.* Ruhrort, 1876.

Gräfe, H. *Die deutsche Volksschule oder die Bürger- und Landschule.* 2nd ed. Leipzig, 1850.

Grimpen, Albert. *Welche Aufgaben erwachsen der Schule aus der stetigen Zunahme der Sozialdemokratie?* Hamburg, 1901.

Grünewald. *Der Kampf gegen die sozialistischen Ideen, beleuchtet vom Standpunkte der Volksschule.* Berlin, 1889.

Grünweller, August. *Die Konfessionsschule.* Berlin, 1906.

Harkort, Friedrich. *Bemerkungen über die preussische Volksschule und ihre Lehrer.* Hagen, 1842.

Hubatsch, Walther, ed. *Die Evangelischen General-Kirchen- und Schulvisitationen in Ost- und Westpreussen 1853 bis 1944.* Göttingen, 1970.

Huber, Ernst Rudolf, ed. *Dokumente zur deutschen Verfassungsgeschichte.* 2 vols. Stuttgart, 1961.

Huber, Ernst Rudolf, and Huber, Wolfgang, eds. *Staat und Kirche im 19. und 20.*

Jahrhundert. Dokumente zur Geschichte des deutschen Staatskirchenrechts. 3 vols. Berlin, 1973–1983.

Kaftan, Theodor. *Die Schule im Dienste der Familie, des Staates und der Kirche.* Hamburg, 1906.

Ketteler, Wilhelm Emmanuel von. *Sämtliche Werke und Briefe.* Ed. by Erwin Iserloh. Vols. 1–2. Mainz, 1977.

Köhne, Friedrich, and Pretzel, Carl Louis Albert. *Die Simultanschule in Nassau, Hessen und Baden.* Berlin, 1906.

Lange, Gustav. *Die Simultanschule in der Ostmark, ihre historische Entwicklung und ihr gegenwärtiger Stand.* Lissa, 1905.

————. "Das Volksschulwesen in der Provinz Posen, wie es war, ist und sein soll." *Pädagogische Abhandlungen.* Vol. 6, no. 8, Bielefeld, 1901.

————. "Volksschule und Deutschtum in der Ostmark." *Pädagogische Abhandlungen.* Vol. 9, no. 3. Bielefeld, 1903.

Langermann, Johannes. *Schulleitung und Schulaufsicht. Entwurf einer Denkschrift welche Staatsminister Dr. Studt überreicht werden sollte von dem Rheinischen Provinziallehrerverein.* Minden, 1905.

Linde, Ernst. *Wer hat ein Recht auf die Volksschule? Grundlagen einer Schulpolitik vom freiheitlich-protestantischen, deutschnationalen und wissenschaftlich-pädagogischen Standpunkt.* Leipzig, 1906.

Meyer, Jürgen Bona. *Gegen den Entwurf eines Volksschulgesetzes. Ein Mahnruf an Preussens deutsches Gewissen.* Bonn, 1892.

————. *Der Kampf um die Schule. Historisch-pädagogische Erörterungen über die Fragen: Staatsschule oder Kirchenschule? Religionsunterricht oder Staatschule?* Bonn, 1882.

————. *Die Simultanschulfrage.* Berlin, 1879.

————. *Zum Bildungskampf unserer Zeit.* Bonn, 1875.

Münz, Paul. *Fragmente zur Schulaufsichtsfrage. Rückblicke und Ausblicke mit besonderer Berücksichtigung der preussischen Verhältnisse.* Wiesbaden, 1905.

Noth, G. *Die Simultanschulfrage, beleuchtet vom Standpunkte der theoretischen Pädagogik aus.* Jena, 1906.

Parsons, James R., Jr. *Prussian Schools through American Eyes. A Report to the New York State Department of Public Instruction.* Syracuse, N.Y., 1891.

Perry, Charles Copeland. *Reports on German Elementary Schools and Training Colleges.* London, 1887.

Pretzel, Carl Louis Albert. *Schulaufsicht und Schulleitung in den deutschen Staaten.* Leipzig, 1909.

Quarck, Max. *Kommunale Schulpolitik. Ein Führer durch die Gemeindetätigkeit auf dem Gebiete der Volksschule.* Berlin, 1906.

Rich, Norman, and Fisher, M. H., eds. *The Holstein Papers.* Vol. 3. Cambridge, 1961.

Richter, Karl. *Die Emanzipation der Schule von der Kirche und die Reform des Religionsunterrichts in der Schule.* Leipzig, 1870.

Rintelen, Victor. *Das Verhältnis der Volksschule Preussens zu Staat und Kirche.* Paderborn, 1888.

————. *Der Volksschulgesetz-Entwurf des Ministers Dr. von Gossler und die Verhandlungen der Volksschulgesetz-Kommission des Preussischen Abgeordnetenhauses.* Mainz, 1891.

————. *Der Volksschulgesetz-Entwurf des Ministers Grafen von Zedlitz-Trützschler und die Verhandlungen über denselben im Plenum und in der Volksschulgesetz-Kommission des Preussischen Abgeordnetenhauses.* Frankfurt am Main, 1893.

Röhl, John C. G., ed. *Philipp Eulenburgs politische Korrespondenz.* 2 vols. Boppard, 1976–1979.

Rönne, Ludwig von, ed. *Das Unterrichtswesen des preussischen Staates.* 2 vols. Berlin, 1855.

Ruete, Hermann. *Welche Anforderungen stellt der kaiserliche Erlass von 1. Mai 1889 über die Bekämpfung sozialistischer und kommunistischer Ideen an uns?* Leipzig, 1893.

Sammlung der Drucksachen des Preussischen Hauses der Abgeordneten. Berlin, 1905–1906.

Schneider, Karl. *Ein halbes Jahrhundert im Dienste von Kirche und Schule. Lebenserinnerungen.* 2nd ed. Stuttgart, 1901.

————, ed. *Volksschulwesen und Lehrerbildung in Preussen.* Berlin, 1875.

Die Schulfrage oder was muss und soll die Schule sein? Paderborn, 1876.

Seyffardt, Ludwig Friedrich. *Die Entwicklung des Simultanschulwesens in der Stadt Krefeld.* Bonn, 1881.

————. *Erinnerungen.* Leipzig, 1900.

————. *Die katholische Volksschule am Niederrhein unter geistlicher Leitung.* Krefeld, 1876.

Seyffarth, Ludwig Wilhelm. *Die paritätische Schule. Ein Wort zur Verständigung über das Verhältnis der Volksschule zu den Konfessionen.* Liegnitz, 1880.

Stenographische Berichte über die Verhandlungen der durch das allerhöchste Patent vom 5. Dezember 1848 einberufenen Kammern. Berlin, 1849.

Stenographische Berichte über die Verhandlungen der Zweiten Kammer. Berlin, 1849, 1851–1852.

Stenographische Berichte über die Verhandlungen der zur Vereinbarung der preussischen Staatsverfassung berufenen Versammlung. Berlin, 1848.

Stenographische Berichte über die Verhandlungen des Herrenhauses. Berlin, 1876.

Stenographische Berichte über die Verhandlungen des Preussischen Hauses der Abgeordneten. Berlin, 1860–1906.

Stiehl, Ferdinand, ed. *Die Gesetzgebung auf dem Gebiete des Unterrichtswesens in Preussen vom Jahre 1817 bis 1868. Aktenstücke mit Erläuterungen aus dem Ministerium der geistlichen, Unterrichts- und Medicinal-Angelegenheiten.* Berlin, 1869.

————. *Meine Stellung zu den drei Preussischen Regulativen vom 1., 2., und 3. Oktober 1854.* Berlin, 1872.

Tews, Johannes. *Der preussische Schulgesetzentwurf im Lichte der deutschen Unterrichtsgesetzgebung.* Leipzig, 1892.

————. *Die preussische Schulvorlage. Eine Abwehr.* Berlin, 1906.

————. "Die preussische Volksschule, ihr gegenwärtiger Stand und ihre jüngste Entwicklung." *Sammlung pädagogischer Vorträge.* Vol. 2, no. 9. Bielefeld, 1889.

————. *Schulkämpfe der Gegenwart. Vorträge zum Kampf um die Volksschule in Preussen.* Leipzig, 1906.

Thönes, Karl. *Was ist gegen und für konfessionell gemischte Volksschulen zu sagen?* Barmen, [1877].

Treitschke, Heinrich von. *Deutsche Kämpfe. Schriften zur Tagespolitik.* Leipzig, 1896.

Verhandlungen der General-Synode der evangelischen Landeskirche Preussens. Berlin, 1879–1894.

Verhandlungen der Generalversammlung der Katholiken Deutschlands. 1877–1906.

Verhandlungen der Rheinischen Provinzial-Synoden. 1874–1887.

Wächter, A. *Der Evangelische Bund nach zwanzig Jahren* (Flugschrift des Evangelischen Bundes). Leipzig, 1906.

Wiese, Ludwig. *Lebenserinnerungen und Amtserfahrungen.* 2 vols. Berlin, 1886.

Zillessen, Friedrich. *Die Bedeutung der Konfessionsschule für das Volksleben.* Stuttgart, 1877.

————. *Der von Gossler'sche Volksschul-Gesetzentwurf, von evangelisch-kirchlichem Standpunkte aus beurteilt.* Berlin, 1891.

————. *Zur Schulaufsichtsfrage. Vortrag gehalten auf dem zweiten Deutschen Evangelischen Schulkongress zu Kassel.* Frankfurt am Main, 1884.

SELECTED ARTICLES AND MONOGRAPHS

Albisetti, James. *Secondary School Reform in Imperial Germany.* Princeton, N.J., 1983.

Albrecht, Hellmuth. *Die Stellung des politischen Katholizismus in Deutschland zu den Fragen des Unterrichts und der Erziehung in den Jahren 1848–1850.* Leipzig, 1929.

Anderson, Eugene. "The Prussian Volksschule in the Nineteenth Century." *Entstehung und Wandel der modernen Gesellschaft: Festschrift für Hans Rosenberg.* Ed. by Gerhard A. Ritter. Berlin, 1970.

Anderson, Margaret L. *Windthorst. A Political Biography.* Oxford, 1981.

Anderson, Margaret L., and Barkin, Kenneth. "The Myth of the Puttkamer Purge and the Reality of the *Kulturkampf*: Some Reflections on the Historiography of Imperial Germany." *Journal of Modern History* 54 (1982): 647–86.

Barkin, Kenneth. "Social Control and the Volksschule in Vormärz Prussia." *Central European History* 26 (1983); 31–52.

Baske, Siegfried. "Praxis und Prinzipien der preussischen Polenpolitik von Beginn der Reaktionszeit bis zur Gründung des Deutschen Reiches." *Forschungen zur osteuropäischen Geschichte* 9 (1963): 7–268.

Becker, Josef. *Liberaler Staat und Kirche in der Ära von Reichsgründung und Kulturkampf. Geschichte und Strukturen ihres Verhältnisses in Baden 1860–1876.* Mainz, 1973.

Becker, Winfried. "Liberale Kulturkampf-Positionen und politischer Katholizismus." *Innenpolitische Probleme des Bismarck-Reiches.* Ed. by Otto Pflanze. München, 1983.

Berg, Christa. *Die Okkupation der Schule. Eine Studie zur Aufhellung gegenwärtiger Schulprobleme an der Volksschule Preussens, 1872–1900.* Heidelberg, 1973.

———. "Volksschule im Abseits von 'Industrialisierung' und 'Fortschritt.' Über den Zusammenhang von Bildung und Industrieentwicklung." *Schule und Gesellschaft im 19. Jahrhundert.* Ed. by Ulrich Herrmann. Weinheim, 1977.

Beyer, Hermann. *Die Geschichte des Gustav Adolf Vereins in ihren kirchen- und geistesgeschichtlichen Zusammenhängen.* Göttingen, 1932.

Birke, Adolf. "Zur Entwicklung und politischen Funktion des bürgerlichen Kulturkampfverständnisses in Preussen-Deutschland." *Aus Theorie und Praxis der Geschichtswissenschaft.* Ed. by Dietrich Kurze. Berlin, 1970.

Blackbourn, David. *Class, Religion and Local Politics in Wilhelmine Germany.* New Haven, 1980.

———. *Populists and Patricians: Essays in Modern German History.* London, 1987.

———. "The Problem of Democratization: German Catholics and the Role of the Centre Party." *Society and Politics in Wilhelmine Germany.* Ed. by Richard J. Evans. New York and London, 1978.

———. "Die Zentrumspartei und die deutschen Katholiken während des Kulturkampfes und danach." *Innenpolitische Probleme des Bismarck-Reiches.* Ed. by Otto Pflanze. München, 1983.

Blackbourn, David, and Eley, Geoff. *The Peculiarities of German History.* Oxford, 1984.

Blanke, Richard. *Prussian Poland in the German Empire 1871–1900.* New York, 1981.

Blankertz, Herwig. *Bildung im Zeitalter der grossen Industrie. Pädagogik, Schule und Berufsbildung im 19. Jahrhundert.* Berlin, 1969.

Bloth, Peter C. *Religion in den Schulen Preussens. Der Gegenstand des evangelischen Religionsunterrichts von der Reaktionszeit bis zum Nationalsozialismus.* Heidelberg, 1968.

Böhning, Peter. *Die Nationalpolnische Bewegung in West Preussen 1815–1871.* Marburg, 1973.

Bölling, Rainer. *Sozialgeschichte der deutschen Lehrer. Ein Überblick von 1800 bis zur Gegenwart.* Göttingen, 1983.

———. *Volksschullehrer und Politik. Der Deutsche Lehrerverein 1918–1933.* Göttingen, 1978.

Bornkamm, Heinrich. "Die Staatsidee im Kulturkampf." *Historische Zeitschrift* 170 (1950): 41–72, 273–306.

Bressler, Hannes. *Das Volksschulwesen in Südhessen zwischen 1803 und 1874.* Frankfurt am Main, 1969.

Brunkhorst, Heinz Ernst. *Die Einbeziehung der preussischen Schule in die Politik des Staates 1808–1918.* Düsseldorf, 1956.

Buchheim, Karl. *Ultramontanismus und Demokratie: Der Weg der deutschen Katholiken im 19. Jahrhundert.* München, 1963.

Bungardt, Karl. *Die Odyssee der Lehrerschaft. Sozialgeschichte eines Standes.* Hannover, 1965.

Christ, Karl. *Sozialdemokratie und Volkserziehung. Die Bedeutung des Mannheimer Parteitages der SPD im Jahre 1906 für die Entwieklung der Bildungspolitik und Pädagogik der deutschen Arbeiterbewegung vor dem Ersten Weltkrieg.* Frankfurt am Main, 1975.

Clausnitzer, Leopold. *Geschichte des preussischen Unterrichtsgesetzes mit besonderer Berücksichtigung der Volksschule.* Berlin, 1891.

Cloer, Ernst. *Sozialgeschichte, Schulpolitik und Lehrerfortbildung der Katholischen Lehrerverbände im Kaiserreich und in der Weimarer Republik.* Ratingen, 1975.

Croon, Helmut. "Die Stadtvertretungen in Krefeld und Bochum im 19. Jahrhundert. Ein Beitrag zur Geschichte der Selbstverwaltung der rheinischen und westfälischen Städte." *Forschungen zu Staat und Verfassung: Festgabe für Fritz Hartung.* Berlin, 1958.

Dettmer, Günther. *Die ost- und westpreussischen Verwaltungsbehörden im Kulturkampf.* Heidelberg, 1958.

Eley, Geoff. *From Unification to Nazism: Reinterpreting the German Past.* Boston, 1986.

Engelsing, Rolf. *Analphabetentum und Lektüre. Zur Sozialgeschichte des Lesens in Deutschland zwischen feudaler und industrieller Gesellschaft.* Stuttgart, 1973.

Erlinghagen, Karl. *Die Säkularisierung der deutschen Schule.* Hannover, 1972.

Evans, Ellen Lovell. *The German Center Party 1870–1933: A Study in Political Catholicism.* Carbondale, Ill., 1981.

Evans, Richard. *Rethinking German History. Nineteenth-Century Germany and the Origins of the Third Reich.* London, 1987.

Field, Geoffrey. "Religion in the German Volksschule, 1890–1928." *Leo Baeck Institute Year Book* 25 (1980): 41–71.

Flecken, Margarete. *Arbeiterkinder im 19. Jahrhundert: Eine sozialgeschichtliche Untersuchung.* Weinheim, 1981.

Flitner, Andreas. *Die politische Erziehung in Deutschland. Geschichte und Probleme, 1750–1880.* Tübingen, 1957.

Foerster, Erich. *Adalbert Falk: Sein Leben und Wirken als preussischer Kultusminister.* Gotha, 1927.

Franz, Georg. *Kulturkampf, Staat und katholische Kirche in Mitteleuropa von der Säkularisierung bis zum Abschluss des preussischen Kulturkampfes.* München, 1954.

Friedrich, Gerd. *Die Volksschule in Württemberg im 19. Jahrhundert.* Weinheim, 1978.

Führ, Christoph. *Zur Schulpolitik der Weimarer Republik.* Weinheim, 1970.

Gall, Lothar. *Der Liberalismus als regierende Partei. Das Grossherzogtum Baden zwischen Restauration und Reichsgründung.* Wiesbaden, 1968.

Galos, Adam. "Der deutsche Ostmarkenverein von 1894 bis 1900." *Die Hakatisten. Der deutsche Ostmarkenverein 1894–1934.* Ed. by Felix-Heinrich Gentzen. Berlin Hauptstadt der D.D.R., 1966.

Hagen, William. *Germans, Poles, and Jews: The Nationality Conflict in the Prussian East, 1772–1914.* Chicago, 1980.

Hall, Alex. "The War of Words: Anti-socialist Offensives and Counterpropaganda in Wilhelmine Germany 1890–1914." *Journal of Contemporary History* 11 (1976): 11–42.

Hamerow, Theodore. *The Social Foundations of German Unification.* 2 vols. Princeton, N.J., 1969–1972.

Hanssler, Bernhard, ed. *Die Kirche in der Gesellschaft. Der deutsche Katholizismus und seine Organisationen im. 19. und 20. Jahrhundert.* Paderborn, 1961.

Hartmann, Klaus, Nyssen, Friedhelm, and Waldeyer, Hans, eds. *Schule und Staat im 18. und 19. Jahrhundert: Zur Sozialgeschichte der Schule in Deutschland.* Frankfurt am Main, 1974.

Hauser, Oswald. "Poles und Dänen im Deutschen Reich." *Reichsgründung 1870–71. Tatsachen—Kontroversen—Interpretationen.* Ed. by Theodor Schieder and Ernst Deuerlein. Stuttgart, 1970.

———. "Zum Problem der Nationalisierung Preussens." *Historische Zeitschrift* 202 (1966): 529–41.

Heinel, Jürgen. *Die deutsche Sozialpolitik des 19. Jahrhunderts im Spiegel der Schulgeschichtsbücher.* Braunschweig, 1962.

Heinemann, Manfred. "'Bildung' in Staatshand: Zur Zielsetzung und Legitimationsproblematik der 'niederen' Schulen in Preussen unter besonderer Berücksichtigung des Unterrichtsgesetzentwurfs des Ministeriums Falk (1877)." *Bildungspolitik in Preussen zur Zeit des Kaiserreichs.* Ed. by Peter Baumgart, Stuttgart, 1980.

Helmreich, Ernst Christian. *Religious Education in German Schools: An Historical Approach.* Cambridge, 1959.

Jakóbczyk, Witold, "Der deutsche Ostmarkenverein von 1900 bis 1914." *Die Hakatisten. Der deutsche Ostmarkenverein 1894–1934.* Ed. by Felix-Heinrich Gentzen. Berlin, 1966.

Jarausch, Konrad. *Students, Society, and Politics in Imperial Germany.* Princeton, N.J., 1982.

Jeismann, Karl-Ernst. "Die 'Stiehlschen Regulative': Ein Beitrag zum Verhältnis von Politik und Pädagogik während der Reaktionszeit in Preussen." *Dauer und Wandel der Geschichte. Aspekte europäischer Vergangenheit: Festgabe für Kurt von Raumer.* Ed. by Rudolf Vierhaus and Manfred Botzenhart. Münster, 1966.

Jestaedt, Winfried. *Der Kulturkampf in Fuldaer Land.* Fulda, 1960.

Knopp, Gisbert. *Die preussische Verwaltung des Regierungsbezirks Düsseldorf in den Jahren 1899–1919.* Köln, 1974.

Kopitzsch, Wolfgang. "Zur 'Politisierung' des Geschichtsunterrichts in Schleswig–Holstein nach dem 1. Mai 1889." *Erziehungs- und Bildungsgeschichte Schleswig-Holsteins von der Aufklärung bis zum Kaiserreich.* Ed. by Franklin Kopitzsch. Neumünster, 1981.

Korth, Rudolf. *Die preussische Schulpolitik und die polnischen Schulstreiks. Ein Beitrag zur preussischen Polenpolitik der Ära Bülow.* Würzburg, 1963.

Krueger, Bernhard. *Stiehl und seine Regulative. Ein Beitrag zur preussischen Schulgeschichte.* Weinheim, 1970.

Kulczycki, John Jacob. *School Strikes in Prussian Poland, 1901–1907: The Struggle over Bilingual Education.* New York, 1981.

Kupisch, Karl. *Die deutschen Landeskirchen im 19. und 20. Jahrhundert.* Göttingen, 1966.

Lamberti, Marjorie. *Jewish Activism in Imperial Germany. The Struggle for Civil Equality.* New Haven, 1978.

————. "State, Church, and the Politics of School Reform during the Kulturkampf." *Central European History* 29 (1986): 63–81.

La Vopa, Anthony J. *Prussian Schoolteachers. Profession and Office 1763–1848.* Chapel Hill, N.C., 1980.

Lidtke, Vernon. *The Alternative Culture. Socialist Labor in Imperial Germany.* New York, 1985.

————. "August Bebel and German Social Democracy's Relation to the Christian Churches." *Journal of the History of Ideas* 27 (1966): 245–64.

————. "Social Class and Secularization in Imperial Germany. The Working Classes." *Leo Baeck Institute Year Book* 25 (1980): 21–40.

Lill, Rudolf. "Die deutschen Katholiken und Bismarcks Reichsgründung." *Reichsgründung 1870–71.* Ed. by Theodor Schieder and Ernst Deuerlein. Stuttgart, 1970.

Loth, Wilfried. *Katholiken im Kaiserreich. Der politische Katholizismus in der Krise des wilhelminischen Deutschlands.* Düsseldorf, 1984.

Lüdicke, Reinhard. *Die preussischen Kultusminister und ihre Beamten im ersten Jahrhundert des Ministeriums 1817–1917.* Stuttgart, 1918.

Ludwig, Karl-Heinz. "Die Fabrikarbeit von Kindern im 19. Jahrhundert." *Vierteljahrschrift für Sozial- und Wirtschaftsgeschichte* 52 (1965): 63–85.

Lundgreen, Peter. "Schulbildung und Frühindustrialisierung in Berlin/Preussen.

Eine Einführung in den historischen und systematischen Zusammenhang von Schule und Wirtschaft." *Schule und Gesellschaft im 19. Jahrhundert.* Ed. by Ulrich Hermann. Weinheim, 1977.

―――. *Sozialgeschichte der deutschen Schule im Überblick.* Vol. 1: *1770–1918.* Göttingen, 1980.

Lüttgert, Gottlieb. *Preussens Unterrichtskämpfe in der Bewegung von 1848.* Berlin, 1924.

Mai, Joachim. *Die preussisch-deutsche Polenpolitik 1885/87.* Berlin Hauptstadt der D.D.R., 1962.

Maynes, Mary Jo. *Schooling for the People. Comparative Local Studies of Schooling History in France and Germany, 1750-1850.* New York, 1985.

―――. *Schooling in Western Europe. A Social History.* Albany, N.Y., 1985.

McClelland, Charles. *State, Society, and University in Germany, 1700-1914.* Cambridge, 1980.

Meyer, Folkert. *Schule der Untertanen. Lehrer und Politik in Preussen 1848-1900.* Hamburg, 1976.

Meyer, Helmut. *Das Selbstverständnis des Volksschullehrers in der zweiten Hälfte des 19. Jahrhunderts 1850–1880.* Münster, 1965.

Mies, Horst. *Die preussische Verwaltung des Regierungsbezirks Marienwerder 1830 bis 1870.* Köln, 1972.

Milberg, Hildegard. *Schulpolitik in der pluralistischen Gesellschaft. Die politischen und sozialen Aspekte der Schulreform in Hamburg 1890-1933.* Hamburg, 1970.

Morsey, Rudolf. "Die deutschen Katholiken und der Nationalstaat zwischen Kulturkampf und Erstem Weltkrieg." *Deutsche Parteien vor 1918.* Ed. by Gerhard Ritter. Köln, 1973.

―――, ed. *Zeitgeschichte in Lebensbildern. Aus dem deutschen Katholizismus des 20. Jahrhunderts.* Mainz, 1973.

Nichols, J. Alden. *Germany after Bismarck: The Caprivi Era, 1890-1894.* Cambridge, Mass., 1958.

Nipperdey, Thomas. *Deutsche Geschichte 1800-1866; Bürgerwelt und starker Staat.* München, 1983.

―――. "Volksschule und Revolution im Vormärz." *Politische Ideologie und nationalstaatliche Ordnung: Festschrift für Theodor Schieder.* Ed. by Kurt Kluxen and Wolfgang Mommsen. München, 1968.

Olson, James M. "Nationalistic Values in Prussian Schoolbooks prior to World War I." *Canadian Review of Studies in Nationalism* 1 (1973): 47-59.

―――. "Radical Social Democracy and School Reform in Wilhelminian Germany." *History of Education Quarterly* 17 (1977); 4-13.

―――. "Social Views of Prussian Primary School Teachers." *Paedagogica Historica* 15 (1975): 73-89.

Petrat, Gerhardt. *Schulunterricht: Seine Sozialgeschichte in Deutschland, 1750 bis 1850.* München, 1979.

Pretzel, Carl Louis Albert. *Geschichte des deutschen Lehrervereins in den ersten fünfzig Jahren seines Bestehens.* Leipzig, 1921.

Rädisch, Wolfgang. *Die Evangelisch-Lutherische Landeskirche Hannovers und der Preussische Staat 1866–1885.* Hildesheim, 1972.

Reichle, Walter. *Zwischen Staat und Kirche. Das Leben und Wirken des preussischen Kultusministers Heinrich von Mühler.* Berlin, 1938.

Richter, Kurt. *Der Kampf um den Schulgesetzentwurf des Grafen Zedlitz-Trützschler vom Jahre 1892.* Halle, 1934.

Roessler, Wilhelm. *Die Entstehung des modernen Erziehungswesens in Deutschland.* Stuttgart, 1961.

Röhl, John C. G. *Germany without Bismarck. The Crisis of Government in the Second Reich, 1890–1900.* Berkeley and London, 1967.

Rosenkranz, Albert. *Abriss einer Geschichte der Evangelischen Kirche im Rheinland.* Düsseldorf, 1960.

Ross, Ronald. *Beleaguered Tower: The Dilemma of Political Catholicism in Wilhelmine Germany.* Notre Dame, Ind., 1976.

————. "Critic of the Bismarckian Constitution: Ludwig Windthorst and the Relationship between Church and State in Imperial Germany." *Journal of Church and State* 21 (1979): 483–506.

————. "Enforcing the Kulturkampf in the Bismarckian State and the Limits of Coercion in Imperial Germany." *Journal of Modern History* 56 (1984): 456–82.

Saul, Klaus. "Der Kampf um die Jugend zwischen Volksschule und Kaserne: Ein Beitrag zur 'Jugendpflege' im Wilhelminischen Reich, 1890–1914." *Militärgeschichtliche Mitteilungen* 9 (1971): 97–143.

Scheibe, Wolfgang. *Die reformpädagogische Bewegung 1900–1932.* Weinheim, 1969.

Schiffers, Heinrich. *Der Kulturkampf in Stadt und Regierungsbezirk Aachen.* Aachen, 1929.

Schlander, Otto. *Der Aufbau des Schulwesens im Grossherzogtum Hessen-Darmstadt nach 1815.* Frankfurt am Main, 1978.

Schleunes, Karl A. "Enlightenment, Reform, Reaction: The Schooling Revolution in Prussia." *Central European History* 12 (1979): 315–42.

Schmid, Eugen. *Geschichte des württembergischen evangelischen Volksschulwesens von 1806 bis 1910.* Stuttgart, 1933.

Schmidt-Volkmar, Erich. *Der Kulturkampf in Deutschland, 1871–1890.* Göttingen, 1962.

Schumann, Ingeborg, Korf, Hans-Jürgen, and Schumann, Michael. *Sozialisation in Schule und Fabrik. Entstehungsbedingungen proletarischer Kindheit und Jugend.* West Berlin, 1976.

Schwarte, Norbert. *Schulpolitik und Pädagogik der deutschen Sozialdemokratie an der Wende vom 19. und 20. Jahrhundert.* Köln, 1980.

Sheehan, James J. *German Liberalism in the Nineteenth Century.* Chicago, 1978.

Sperber, Jonathan. *Popular Catholicism in Nineteenth-Century Germany.* Princeton, N.J., 1984.

Spranger, Eduard. "Zur Geschichte der deutschen Volksschule." *Gesammelte Schriften.* Ed. by Hans Walter Bahr et al. Vol. 3. Heidelberg, 1970.

Stadelhofer, Manfred. *Der Abbau der Kulturkampfgesetzgebung im Grossherzogtum Baden, 1878-1918.* Mainz, 1969.

Tews, Johannes. *Ein Jahrhundert preussischer Schulgeschichte. Volksschule und Volksschullehrerstand im Preussen im 19. und 20. Jahrhundert.* Leipzig, 1914.

Thoma, Hubert. *Georg Friedrich Dasbach. Priester, Publizist, Politiker.* Trier, 1975.

Tilger, Wolfgang. "Volk, Nation und Vaterland im protestantischen Denken zwischen Kaiserreich und Nationalsozialismus." *Volk, Nation, Vaterland. Der deutsche Protestantismus und der Nationalismus.* Ed. by Horst Zillessen. Gütersloh, 1970.

Titze, Hartmut. *Die Politisierung der Erziehung. Untersuchungen über die soziale und politische Funktion der Erziehung von der Aufklärung bis zum Hochkapitalismus.* Frankfurt am Main, 1973.

Trzeciakowski, Lech. "The Prussian State and the Catholic Church in Prussian Poland 1871-1914." *Slavic Review* 26 (1967): 618-37.

Tymister, Josef. *Die Entstehung der Berufsvereine der katholischen Lehrerschaft in Deutschland. Beiträge zur Schul- und Standespolitik der katholischen Lehrerschaft im 19. Jahrhundert.* Köln, 1965.

Vandré, Rudolf. *Schule, Lehrer und Unterricht im 19. Jahrhundert.* Göttingen, 1973.

Vorländer, Herwart. *Evangelische Kirche und soziale Frage in der werdenden Industriegrossstadt Elberfeld.* Düsseldorf, 1963.

Wegmann, Dietrich. *Die leitenden staatlichen Verwaltungsbeamten der Provinz Westfalen 1815-1918.* Münster, 1969.

Wien, Albrecht. *Die preussische Verwaltung des Regierungsbezirks Danzig, 1870-1920.* Köln, 1974.

Windell, George C. *The Catholics and German Unity 1866-1871.* Minneapolis, 1954.

Zeender, John. *The German Center Party 1890-1906.* Philadelphia, 1976.

Zielinski, Zygmunt. "Der Kulturkampf in der Provinz Posen." *Historisches Jahrbuch* 101 (1981): 447-61.

Index